L. (Luise) Mühlbach

Henry the Eighth and his Court

L. (Luise) Mühlbach

Henry the Eighth and his Court

ISBN/EAN: 9783743310032

Manufactured in Europe, USA, Canada, Australia, Japa

Cover: Foto ©Thomas Meinert / pixelio.de

Manufactured and distributed by brebook publishing software
(www.brebook.com)

L. (Luise) Mühlbach

Henry the Eighth and his Court

"WHO DARES TO DISTURB US?" P. 26.

HENRY THE EIGHTH
AND HIS COURT.

AN HISTORICAL ROMANCE.

BY

L. MÜHLBACH.

AUTHOR OF "THE EMPRESS JOSEPHINE," "MARIE ANTOINETTE," "JOSEPH II. AND HIS COURT," "FREDERICK THE GREAT AND HIS FAMILY," "BERLIN AND SANS-SOUCI," ETC., ETC., ETC.

COMPLETE IN ONE VOLUME.

With Illustrations.

NEW YORK:
D. APPLETON AND COMPANY,
443 & 445 BROADWAY.
1868.

PREFACE.

In the opinion of the authoress of this volume, the province of the Historical Romance is to show you the heart of history, and to bring near to you what else would stand so far off. Although some of its objects may be to throw light on the dark places of history, to group historical characters according to their internal natures, and to discover and expose the motives which impelled individual personages to the performance of great acts, yet others more important remain. One of these is the presentation of history in a dramatic form and with animated descriptions. It is of less consequence whether the personages actually spoke the words or performed the acts attributed to them; but it is necessary that those words and deeds should be in accordance with the spirit and character of such historical personages, and nothing be attributed to them which they could not have spoken or done. The circumstances and events presented must be in accordance with historical tradition. Subsequent investigations, since these pages were given to the press, may have modified the historical aspect of the character of Henry VIII., but it is sufficient to say that these were unknown at the time when the work was written, and the aim of the authoress has been to delineate that character as represented by the standard English historians.

CONTENTS.

BOOK I.

THE WEDDING-DAY.

BOOK II.

THE CHASE.

BOOK III.

THE QUEEN'S ROSETTE.

BOOK IV.

THE WOMEN'S WAR.

HENRY VIII. AND HIS COURT.

BOOK I.

THE WEDDING-DAY.

CHAPTER I.

THE CHOICE OF A FATHER-CONFESSOR.

It was in the year 1543. King Henry the Eighth of England thought himself again the happiest and most enviable man of his realm, for he had this day once more celebrated his nuptials; and Katharine Parr, the youthful widow of Lord Latimer, had the perilous fortune of being chosen as the sixth wife of the king.

The bells pealed forth from all the towers of London, announcing to the people that the sacred ceremony was about to commence which should consecrate Katharine Parr as the sixth queen of Henry the Eighth.

The ever-curious and sight-loving multitude thronged the streets, and eagerly pressed forward toward the royal palace, hoping to see Katharine, when she should appear on the balcony by the side of her royal husband, to present herself to the English people as their queen, and to receive their homage.

Undoubtedly it was a high and exalted destiny for the widow of an humble baron to become the wife of the King of England, and to wear a royal diadem upon her brow. But Katharine Parr's heart was filled, nevertheless, with anxious foreboding; her cheeks were pale and cold, and her firmly-compressed lips had scarcely the power of uttering the decisive "I WILL" before the altar.

At length the sacred ceremony was over. Whereupon the two spiritual dignitaries—Gardiner, Bishop of Winchester, and Cranmer, Archbishop of Canterbury—led the young spouse, conformably with court etiquette, to her apartments, in order to consecrate them, and to pray with her once more, ere the temporal festivities should begin.

Anxious and pale though she was, Katharine sustained with true royal bearing and dignity the various ceremonies of the day; and as she now, with proudly-raised head and firm step, proceeded through the sumptuous apartments between the two episcopal dignitaries, nobody suspected what a heavy burden oppressed her heart, or what portentous voices were whispering in her bosom.

Accompanied by her attendants, and followed by the train of her new courtiers, she had passed through the state apartments, and now stood within the private chambers of the palace. She here dismissed her courtiers according to the etiquette of the time, and only the two bishops and the ladies of her suite were permitted to enter the drawing-room. Even the bishops were not suffered to attend her beyond this apartment. The king himself had laid down the rules of proceeding for this day, and he would have declared as a traitor any person who might have had the temerity to violate these rules in the slightest degree,—nay, perhaps have sent the offender to the scaffold.

Katharine accordingly turned, with a faint smile, to the two spiritual functionaries, and requested them to await her commands. She then beckoned to her ladies in waiting to follow her into her boudoir.

Meanwhile the two bishops remained alone in the drawing-room, and this peculiar juxtaposition seemed to produce upon each of them an equally unfavorable impression; for with scowling and averted looks, and as if by mutual accord, they each withdrew to opposite sides of the spacious apartment.

A long pause ensued Nothing was heard but the monotonous strokes of the pendulum of a large and costly clock, which stood over the fireplace, and the noisy acclamations of the multitude in the streets, who pressed forward toward the palace like a troubled sea.

Gardiner at length advanced to the window, and glanced with a peculiar and gloomy smile at the clouds, which were swept by the hurricane along the sky.

Cranmer still held aloof at the other side of the room, and, plunged in deep thought, stood contemplating the large portrait of Henry the Eighth — the work of Holbein's master-hand. As he scanned this countenance, which betrayed at once so much dignity and so much ferocity—as he gazed into those eyes which looked forth with such sullen and stern severity—as he observed those lips which smiled so wantonly and withal so implacably—the prelate felt a deep sympathy for the young wife, whom he had this day devoted to such splendid wretchedness.

He reflected that he had already, on former occasions, conducted two of the king's wives to the altar, and had blessed their nuptials; and he reflected too, that he had attended both those queens, at a later period, when they were about to mount the scaffold.

How easily might the unenviable young wife of the king fall a victim to the same gloomy fate;—how speedily might Katharine Parr, like Anna Bullen and Katharine Howard, have to pay for a few short days of splendor by an ignominious death! A single thoughtless word—a look—a smile—might be her ruin; for the anger and the jealousy of the king were incalculable, and no punishment seemed to him, in his ferocious moods, too great for those who had offended him.

It was thoughts of this kind that occupied the mind of Archbishop Cranmer. They called forth within him feelings of pity and tenderness, and caused the dark clouds to vanish from his brow.

He even smiled now at the ill-humor he had so recently evinced, and reproached himself for having been so forgetful of his sacred calling—for having, in short, shown so little readiness to meet his enemy in a conciliating spirit.

For Gardiner was his enemy, as Cranmer well knew. Gardiner had often enough proved this to him by deeds,—however much he had endeavored, by words, to assure him of his friendship.

But even if Gardiner hated him, it did not follow that Cranmer must return his enmity—that he must regard as his foe the man whom, by virtue of their elevated calling on both sides, he was bound to reverence and love as his brother.

The high-minded Cranmer therefore experienced a feeling of self-reproach for his momentary ill-humor. A gentle smile played upon his calm features; and with a courteous and dignified bearing, but with a subdued cordiality, he crossed the room, and approached the Bishop of Winchester.

The latter looked at him with a sullen scowl, and, without moving from the recess in which he stood, near the window, awaited Cranmer's approach. As Gardiner beheld the noble and ingenuous countenance before him, he felt as though he would raise his hand, and smite the face of the man who had thus dared to enter the lists, and contest with him the palm of fame and honor. But he seasonably reflected that Cranmer was still the king's favorite, and that he must therefore be dealt with judiciously. He accordingly drove his fierce impulses back into his heart, and suffered his features to resume their wonted stern and impenetrable expression.

Cranmer now stood before him, and his clear and animated glance rested upon the sullen features of Gardiner.

"I have come to your lordship," said Cranmer, in his mild, well-modulated voice, "to tell you that I heartily wish the queen may choose you for her director and father-confessor, and to assure you that if she do so, I shall not feel the slightest envy or animosity on that account—indeed I shall perfectly understand and appreciate the circumstance, if her majesty should select the eminent and distinguished Bishop of Winchester for her spiritual adviser; and the esteem and admiration which I now entertain for you will only become enhanced. Let me therefore confirm this assurance to your lordship, by offering my hand."

He presented to Gardiner his hand, which the latter accepted with some hesitation, and barely touched.

"Your grace is very generous," said Gardiner, "and I must compliment you on being an excellent diplomatist; for you would give me to understand, in a very ingenious manner, what my duty will be, in case the queen should select you for her spiritual guide. That she will do so, indeed, you know full well as I do myself. This is therefore but a humiliation imposed upon me by etiquette, which obliges me to stand waiting here, to know if I shall be chosen or disdainfully set aside."

"Why do you view the matter in such an unfriendly manner?" said Cranmer, mildly—"why regard it as a mark of contempt, if you should not be selected for an office to which indeed neither worth nor merit can summon you—but only the personal feeling and confidence of a young woman?"

"Ah! then you admit that I shall not be chosen!" exclaimed Gardiner, with a sinister smile.

"I have already told you, my lord, that I am wholly unacquainted with the queen's wishes, and I believe it is known that the Archbishop of Canterbury is in the habit of speaking the truth."

"Certainly; but it is equally well known that Katharine Parr has heretofore been a zealous admirer of the Archbishop of Canterbury; and that now, when she has attained her object, and has become queen, it will be her duty to testify her gratitude to him."

"Do you wish to insinuate by that," said Cranmer, "that I have been the instrument of her elevation?—If so, I assure your lordship, that in this, as well as in many other matters which concern me, you are misinformed."

"Possibly so," replied Gardiner, coldly. "At all events, it is certain that the young queen is an enthusiastic protector of the infamous new doctrines hatched in Germany, which are spreading like a pestilence over Europe, and bearing mischief and ruin to all Christendom. Yes, Katharine Parr, the present queen, is favorably disposed toward the arch-heretic, against whom the Holy Father of Rome has hurled his crushing anathema: she is an adherent of the Reformation."

"You forget," said Cranmer, with a quiet smile, "that this anathema has also been hurled at the head of our own king, and that it has proved as ineffective against Henry the Eighth as against Martin Luther. I might remind you, at the same time, that we no longer call the Pope of Rome, 'Holy Father,' and that you have yourself acknowledged the king to be the supreme head of the Church of England."

Gardiner turned aside his face, in order to conceal the ill-humor and rancor depicted on his countenance. He felt that he had gone too far—that he had too far betrayed the secret thoughts of his soul.

But he was not at all times able to curb the passionate impulses of his nature; and albeit a man of the world, and a diplomatist, there still were moments when the fanatical priest bore sway over the courtier, and the wily diplomatist gave way to the ecclesiastic.

Cranmer felt compassion for Gardiner's embarrassment, and, yielding to the natural kindness of his disposition, he said, in a friendly tone:

"Let us not here dispute about dogmas, or attempt to decide which is most at fault, Luther or the pope. We are here in the apartment of the young queen, and let us therefore consider for a moment what may be the probable fate of this lady, whom God has appointed to so brilliant a destiny."

"Brilliant!" said Gardiner, with an ironical smile. "Let us first await the end of her career, before we decide if it was brilliant or not. Many queens already have believed that they should find a bed of roses here, who speedily became convinced that their couch was a glowing furnace, which consumed their very bones."

"True," murmured Cranmer, with a slight shudder, "it is a perilous fate to be the wife of a king. But, even for this reason, let us not enhance the danger of her position by adding to it our hostility and ill-will. For this reason I beg of you (and for my own part I pledge my word upon the matter), whatever may be the queen's choice, not to feel annoyed thereat, nor to seek revenge. For we all know that women are strange, unaccountable creatures in their wishes and inclinations."

"Ah! it seems you understand women tolerably well," said Gardiner, with a malicious smile. "Really, if you were not the Archbishop of Canterbury, and had the king not forbidden the marriage of ecclesiastics under a severe penalty, one might suppose you had a wife yourself, and that you had learned from your own experience the fundamental points of the female character."

Cranmer turned away, and, with a certain embarrassment, seemed to avoid the keen and sarcastic glance of Gardiner.

"It is not of me that we were speaking," said the archbishop, at length, "but of the young queen, and I would earnestly entreat your good-will on her behalf. I have seen her to-day for the first time, and have never spoken to her; but her countenance made a strong impression upon me, and her looks seemed as if they besought us both to continue steadfast friends by her side, along the thorny path which lies before her, and which five women have already trodden—only to find wretchedness and tears—ignominy and blood!"

"Katharine, too, must beware, and not abandon the right paths, as her predecessors did," exclaimed Gardiner. "Let us hope, for her own sake, that she will be prudent and watchful, and that she may be enlightened by God with a knowledge of the true faith, and not suffer herself to be led astray by the errors of ungodly heretics, but remain faithful and constant with the true believers."

"Who can say who the true believers are?" murmured Cranmer. "There are so many ways that lead to Heaven, who can tell which is the right one?"

"That which we travel!" exclaimed Gardiner, with the haughty pride of the genuine ecclesiastic. "Woe betide the queen if she should swerve into strange paths! Woe betide her if she lend an ear to the errors which are wafted hither from Germany and from Switzerland, and if she fancy, in the worldly wisdom of her heart, that she will be able to rest securely! For my part, I shall be her most zealous and devoted servant, if she is for me—but her most implacable enemy, if against me!"

"And shall you consider it as against you, if the queen should not choose you for her father-confessor?"

"Do you wish to understand that I should consider it as for me?"

"Well, then, God grant that her choice may fall upon you!" exclaimed Cranmer, fervently, while he clasped his hands, and looked up toward heaven. "Poor, hapless queen! The first proof of thy husband's love may become the prime source of thy misfortune! Why, then, did he leave thee the liberty of choosing thy own director—why not himself have made the choice for thee?"

And with a deep sigh, Cranmer bent his head upon his breast.

At this moment, the door of the royal closet opened, and Lady Jane, the daughter of Lord Douglas, and first lady-in-waiting to the queen, appeared on the threshold.

The two prelates looked toward her in breathless silence. It was an anxious and a solemn moment—the deep significance of which they all three understood.

"Her majesty the queen"—said Lady Jane, in a faltering voice—"her majesty the queen commands the attendance of his grace the Archbishop of Canterbury in her closet, that he may join with her in prayer."

"Unhappy queen!" murmured Cranmer, as he crossed the apartment toward the royal closet—"unhappy queen! she has just made for herself an implacable enemy for life."

Lady Jane waited until Cranmer had disappeared through the door, and then approaching the Bishop of Winchester with rapid steps, and bending her knee before him, said, with an accent of deep humility:

"Pardon, my lord, pardon! My words were vain—they were powerless to shake her resolution."

Gardiner assisted the fair postulant to rise, and said, with a forced smile:

"It is well, Lady Jane, it is well. I doubt not your zeal. You are a faithful daughter of the Church, and for this she will love and reward you as a mother. Then the matter is decided—the queen is—"

"A heretic!" whispered Lady Jane. "Woe betide her!"

"And will you be faithful and constant to me?"

"Faithful in deed and in thought, to the last drop of my blood!"

"Then we shall conquer Katharine Parr as we have conquered Katharine Howard. To the scaffold with the heretic! We have found the means of sending Katharine Howard to the block, and now, Lady Jane, you must find a way for us to lead Katharine Parr to the same destiny."

"I will undertake to do so," said Lady Jane, placidly. "She loves me, and confides in me. I will betray her friendship, that I may remain true to my faith."

"Then Katharine Parr is lost!" said Gardiner, aloud.

"Yes, she is lost," repeated Lord Douglas, who had just entered, and had overheard the last words of the bishop,—"yes, she is lost, for we shall ever be her watchful and inexorable enemies. But I fear it is not prudent to utter these sentiments in the queen's anteroom. Let us therefore abide a more seasonable opportunity. But now, my lord, you must betake yourself to the grand audience-chamber, where the whole court is already assembled, and only awaits the king's pleasure to conduct the young queen in solemn procession to the balcony."

Gardiner nodded a silent assent, and forthwith proceeded to the audience-chamber.

Lord Douglas followed him with his daughter. "Katharine Parr is lost," he whispered in Lady Jane's ear, "and you will be the seventh wife of the king."

During this conversation in the antechamber the young queen was on her knees before Cranmer, and with him was addressing a prayer to Heaven for prosperity and peace. Tears filled her eyes, and she felt her heart tremble within her, as if anticipating some approaching misfortune.

CHAPTER II.

THE QUEEN AND HER BOSOM FRIEND.

This long day of ceremonials and solemnities was at length drawing to a close, and Katharine hoped soon to be relieved from the simulated homage and the artificial smiles of her courtiers.

She had shown herself on the balcony beside her husband, in order to receive the greetings of the people, and to bow her acknowledgments. After this, the newly-appointed members of her court moved in solemn procession before her in the throne-room; and to each of these noble lords and ladies in turn she addressed a few affable observations as they passed along. And this being over, she assisted her royal husband in giving audience to the deputation from the metropolis and from the Parliament. Yet it was with an inward shudder that she heard from their lips the stereotyped congratulations and the fulsome addresses with which those deputies had on similar occasions greeted five of the king's former wives.

Nevertheless she succeeded in her efforts to smile and to look happy, for she knew that the gaze of the king was continually fixed upon her, and that all the noble lords and ladies who now approached her with such demonstrations of apparent humility and homage, were all of them at heart her most bitter enemies—for, by her marriage with the king, she had foiled the schemes and destroyed the hopes of so many, who thought themselves better entitled to occupy the high position of a queen. She knew that those disappointed ones would never forgive her—that she, who had only yesterday been their equal, was to-day lifted above their heads, as their queen and mistress; and she knew that all of them watched like spies her every word and gesture, that they might perchance be able to fabricate an accusation against her which would seal her doom.

But still she smiled! She smiled, although she felt that the king's jealous anger—so easily excited and so fiercely violent—hung evermore above her head like the sword of Damocles.

She smiled lest this sword should one day descend upon herself.

At length, however, all these state ceremonies and pageantries and all these outward marks of homage and rejoicing were over; and now the more agreeable and satisfactory part of the festivity was about to commence.

The guests had assembled at table. This was the first moment of quiet and repose which Katharine had enjoyed throughout the day. For when Henry sat down to table he ceased to be a dignified monarch or a jealous husband—he was only the skilful epicure, the sensual gourmand; and whether the pasties were well seasoned, or the pheasants savory, were for him far more important questions than what concerned the welfare of his people or the good of his kingdom.

After dinner, however, a novel recreation was introduced, a new species of entertainment, which at least for a time banished from Katharine's heart all gloomy apprehensions and sinister forebodings, and which imparted to her countenance a glow of cheerful and serene enjoyment. The king had prepared a surprise for his young wife, which was at that time of a novel character. He had caused a theatre to be erected within the palace of Whitehall, on the stage of which was represented one of the comedies of Plautus, by the gentlemen of the court.

Dramatic representations had hitherto been confined to those pieces called "Moralities" and "Mystery Plays," which were acted by the people on the occasion of certain church festivals. Henry the Eighth was accordingly the first monarch who had a theatre established in England for secular entertainments, and who introduced what perhaps may be called "the legitimate drama," as distinguished from mere dramatized episodes of ecclesiastical history. As he had liberated the Church from the spiritual dominion of the pope, so he wished to render the stage free from the control of the Church, and to see comedies performed of a less serious character than those which depicted the broiling of saints or the massacre of pious women.

Moreover, what need of such scenic butchery on the stage, when the king had a real performance daily exhibited? The burning of Christian martyrs and of godly-minded maidens was a matter of such everyday occurrence under the reign of Henry the Eighth, that it no longer furnished himself or his court with an amusing entertainment.

But the representation of a Roman comedy promised a new and piquant pleasure, and would at least be a surprise for the young queen. Henry therefore caused the "CURCULIO" to be acted before his wife; and whenever Katharine blushed at the obscene and scurrilous jests of the Roman poet, the king felt highly amused, and accompanied the most indecent allusions and the most licentious passages with boisterous laughter and loud applause.

This entertainment too was at length over. And now Katharine was at liberty to retire with her ladies to her private apartments.

With a gracious smile she dismissed the gentlemen of her suite, and requested her ladies, among whom was Anne Askew, the second lady of her bedchamber, to await her commands in her dressing-room. She then gave her arm to her friend, Lady Jane Douglas, and they both entered the queen's closet.

At length she was alone—at length unwatched. The smile vanished from her lips, and an expression of deep sadness marked her features.

"Jane," she said, "shut the doors and draw the window-curtains, that no one may see or hear me—no one but yourself, my friend, the companion of other and happier days. Alas! alas! why was I ever so ill-advised as to leave my father's quiet mansion, and go abroad into the world—so full of snares and terrors?"

She sighed and groaned deeply; and covering her face with her hands, she sank back in her chair, weeping and trembling.

Lady Jane contemplated her mistress with a peculiar and sinister smile.

"She is a queen, and yet she weeps," said the maid of honor, to herself. "Ah, well! how can one be a queen nowadays, and not feel unhappy?"

She approached Katharine, and sitting on a stool at her feet, seized her hand, which she kissed.

"Your majesty weeps," she said, with an insinuating tone. "Alas, I fear you are unhappy, while I, who heard, with an outburst of delight, the news of this wonderful good fortune of my friend, thought I should find her radiant with joy, as an exalted and happy queen; and my only anxiety—my only fear, was, lest the queen should have ceased to be my friend any longer. For this reason, I urged my father to come away at once, according to your commands, and, leaving Dublin, to hasten hither without delay."

Katharine removed her hand from her face, and looked at her friend with a smile of sadness.

"Well, Jane," she said, "are you not satisfied with what you have seen? Have I not shown you, all this day, a queen smiling in the guise of happiness—did I not wear costly robes embroidered with gold—did not my neck sparkle with brilliants, and did not a royal diadem adorn my brow, while a king sat by my side? Let this suffice for the present. You have all this day seen the queen. Allow me now, therefore, for a few brief and happy moments, to become the woman, with lively and sensitive feelings, who can disclose to her friend all her troubles and sorrows. Ah, Jane, if you only knew how I have longed for this hour, how I yearned for your sympathy as the only relief to this poor stricken and wounded heart;—how earnestly I besought Heaven to grant me this favor, that I might once more have my Jane back with me, that she might condole with my sorrows, and that I might always have near me one friend, at least, who could understand me, and who does not suffer herself to be dazzled by all this wretched parade and outward splendor!"

"Unhappy Katharine!" murmured Lady Jane. "Unhappy queen!"

Katharine started, and placed her hand, which glistened with diamonds, upon the lips of her friend.

"Pray do not address me so," said the queen. "Alas, that one word recalls all the terrors of the past. Queen! Does not that mean to be condemned like a criminal to the block? A death-shudder passes through my veins at the bare thought! I am the sixth queen of Henry the Eighth. I shall therefore be sent to the scaffold; or else be covered with disgrace, and turned adrift."

Once more she buried her face in her hands, and her whole frame trembled with violent emotion. She did not therefore perceive the malignant smile with which Lady Jane again contemplated her; nor did she suspect with what secret delight her "friend" perceived her tears and her anguish.

"Well, I'm revenged, at least!" thought Lady Jane, while she smoothed down the queen's hair caressingly—"yes, I'm revenged. She has robbed me of a crown; but in the golden cup which she raises to her lips she shall find nothing but wormwood and gall. If this sixth queen does not mount the scaffold, we shall at least be able to hasten her death by a broken heart."

She then continued aloud: "But why these fears, Katharine? The king loves you; the whole court observed with what earnest and affectionate looks the king gazed upon you to-day, and with what delight he hung upon every word you uttered. Certainly the king loves you."

Katharine grasped her hand ardently. "The king loves me," she whispered, "but still I tremble before him; nay, more, I have a horror of his love. His hands are steeped in blood, and as I saw him to-day in his purple robes, I shuddered, and thought how soon my blood too would encrimson that purple."

Lady Jane smiled. "You are unwell, Katharine," said she. "This sudden good fortune has overcome you, and your excited nerves cause all sorts of horrors to spring up in your imagination—nothing more."

"No, no, Jane, these thoughts are always present to my mind, and they have never left me since the moment the king made choice of me for his wife."

"And why did you not refuse him, accordingly?" asked Lady Jane. "Why not have declined the king's suit?"

"Ah, Jane, are you such a stranger to this court as not to know that one must either yield to the king's wishes or die? Alas, I am envied! People call me the greatest and mightiest woman in England. But they know not that I am poorer and more powerless than the mendicant in the streets, who has at least the right of refusing her hand at her own option. For me, I dared not refuse; I had no alternative but to accept the king's proffered hand—or die. I was unwilling to die so soon; I have still so many claims upon life, and as yet so few of them have been vouchsafed me. Alas for my poor cheerless existence! for what has it been, but a continued series of denials and privations—of sad reminiscences and blighted hopes? It is true, I have never experienced what is called misfortune; but what greater misfortune can there be than to be unhappy—than to sigh through life without a wish or a hope, and to suffer the perpetual tedium of an insipid and joyless existence in the midst of luxury and splendor?"

"You say that formerly you were not unhappy, and yet you were left an orphan?"

"I lost my mother so early that I scarcely knew her, and when my father died, I regarded it almost as a blessing, for he never acted toward me as a parent, but only as a harsh and tyrannical master."

'But then you were married?"

"Married!" said Katharine, with a sad smile. "Yes, that is to say, my father sold me to an old, gouty invalid, in whose sick-chamber I spent a cheerless and fearfully tedious year, until Lord Latimer made me a rich widow. People regarded that, too, as another piece of good fortune, for now I was a widow, young, rich, and independent. But what advantage was such independence to me?—it only fettered me with fresh bonds. Formerly I had been the slave of my father and of my husband, and I now became a slave to my riches: I ceased to be a sick-nurse, only to become the manager of my estates. That was certainly the most wearisome part of my life, and yet I am indebted to it for my only real happiness—for it was then that I made your acquaintance, Jane: and my heart, which had never experienced any more tender emotions, expanded toward you with all the warmth and eagerness of a first affection. And up to the moment that my long-absent nephew reappeared—after he had been supposed dead—and deprived me of the inheritance which properly belonged to him, my only thought had been to make your father and yourself the heirs to my property. The world condoled with me upon the loss of my wealth. But I thank God that He has relieved me of the burden, and has brought me to London in order to see life at last—to think and feel like others, and at length to know real happiness or real misfortune."

"And which did you find?"

"Unhappiness, Jane!—for am I not a queen?"

"But is that your only unhappiness?"

"Yes, but surely that is great enough. It condemns me to perpetual anxiety—perpetual dissimulation. It condemns me to breathe a love which I do not feel, and to suffer caresses which make me shudder, for they are but the heritage derived from five unhappy women.

Oh, Jane, do you know what it is to be obliged to embrace a man who has murdered three wives and put away two others—to kiss perforce the blood-stained lips which utter vows of love with the same readiness that they pronounce a decree of death? The very thought makes the blood run cold in my veins! I shall be called a queen, and yet I shall be doomed to tremble for my life every hour in the day, while I must conceal my anxiety and terror under the guise of happiness. I am barely five-and-twenty years old, and my heart is still the heart of a child—for it scarcely knows its own wishes. And now it is fated never to know them, for I am Henry's wife, and to love another would be to mount the scaffold. The scaffold! Look, Jane!—When the king approached me and confessed his love, and offered his hand, there suddenly rose up before me a terrible picture. It was no longer the king that I saw standing there, but the headsman! And it seemed to me as if I saw three corpses lying at his feet, and with a loud shriek I sank unconscious on the floor. On recovering myself, the king held me in his arms. He believed it was the suddenness of this unexpected honor which had overpowered me. He kissed me, and called me his bride; he did not think for a moment that I could refuse him. And I, Jane—despise me—I was such a coward that I could not find courage for a refusal—I yielded, for I did not wish to die. It seemed to me at this moment as if life beckoned to me with a thousand joys—a thousand delights yet in store, which I had never tasted, and for which my soul thirsted as for manna in the desert. I wished to live—yes, to live, at any cost—in order one day perhaps to enjoy the sweets of love and happiness. But only think, Jane, people call me ambitious; they say I have given my hand to Henry only because he is a king. Ah! little do they know how I shuddered inwardly at this crown. They little know that in the anguish of my heart I besought the king not to raise me to this dignity—so that I might avoid making enemies of all the ladies of his realm. They know not that I confessed my love to him, only that I might be able to add, that, for love of him, I was ready to forego his suit,—that for love of him I was willing to sacrifice my own happiness for his, and that I conjured him to choose for himself a worthy wife among the hereditary princesses of Europe. But Henry rejected the proposal. He wished to create a queen, and to possess a wife who should be his property, and whose blood he might shed as her supreme and sovereign lord. His queen I am accordingly. I have accepted my fate, and henceforth my life will be a perpetual struggle, an unceasing warfare with death; but I will at least sell my life as dearly as possible, and the maxim which Cranmer has suggested shall always be my rule of conduct on the thorny path which lies before me."

"And what may that maxim be?" asked Lady Jane.

"'Be wise as the serpent, and innocent as the dove,'" replied Katharine, with a faint smile, as she dropped her head upon her bosom, and abandoned herself to painful and ominous reflections.

Lady Jane now stood opposite her, and contemplated with unmoved and stern composure the convulsed and agonized features, and the trembling frame of the young queen, for whom all England had this day kept high festival, and who sat now so sad and woe-begone before her simulated friend.

Suddenly Katharine raised her head. Her countenance had now assumed quite a different expression,—it was calm, firm, and resolute. Bending slightly forward, she extended to Lady Jane her hand, and drew her friend closer to her side.

"I have to thank you, Jane," she said, while she kissed her brow, "I have to thank you, for your presence has done me good: it has relieved me of the oppressive burden of my secret sorrow. To express one's cares freely to a friend is the best cure for them. Henceforward you will find me more cheerful and composed. The woman has laid her griefs before you, but the queen knows she has a task to fulfil, as difficult as it is important, and I pledge my word to perform it. The new light which has gone forth to the world shall no longer be obscured by blood and tears, and no longer shall the wise and the just be condemned like malefactors and traitors in this unhappy land. This is the task which God has assigned me, and I swear in His presence that I will accomplish it! Will you help me to do so, Jane?"

Lady Jane replied by a few equivocal words, which Katharine did not catch, and as the latter looked at her, she perceived with astonishment the deadly pallor which of a sudden overspread the countenance of her maid of honor.

Katharine started, and looked at her with an earnest and steadfast gaze, as if to penetrate her thoughts.

Lady Jane shrank from the inquiring and animated glance of the queen, and cast her eyes toward the ground. Her religious zeal had for a moment overpowered her; and however much she was accustomed to conceal her thoughts and feelings, yet on this occasion she was for the moment thrown off her guard, so as to betray her sentiments to the keen eye of her mistress.

"It is a long time since we saw each other," said Katharine, sadly. "Three years! That is a long period in the history of a young girl's heart. And all this time you were with your father in Dublin—at that stanchly Catholic court—I had forgotten that. But, however your views may have altered, your heart I know is still the same, and you will always be the noble, high-minded Jane of former years—who would never stoop to a falsehood—even though it were to bring her fortune and splendor. I therefore ask you, Jane, what religion you now profess? Do you believe in the Pope of Rome, as the sole head of the Church, or do you adhere to the new teaching of Luther and Calvin?"

Lady Jane smiled. "Think you," she said, "I would have ventured to appear in your presence if I still belonged to the

Catholic party? Katharine Parr is hailed by the Protestants of England as the new protectress of their imperilled doctrines; and already the priests of the Roman Church launch their anathemas against you, and execrate you as their most dangerous enemy. And yet you ask me if I am an adherent of that Church which calumniates and condemns you! You ask me if I believe in the pope, who has excommunicated the king—the king who is not only my sovereign and supreme ruler, but also the husband of my noble and generous Katharine! I fear your majesty can scarcely love me, in asking such a question."

And, as if overcome by her emotion, Lady Jane sank down at Katharine's feet, and hid her face in the ample folds of the queen's robe.

Katharine stooped to raise her up and embrace her. Suddenly, however, she started, and a deadly paleness overspread her countenance.

"The king!" she whispered. "The king comes this way!"

CHAPTER III.

KING HENRY THE EIGHTH.

KATHARINE was not mistaken. The doors opened, and the earl-marshal appeared upon the threshold with his gold staff of office.

"His majesty the king!" said the marshal, in his grave and solemn tone, which filled Katharine with secret horror, as if sentence of death had just been pronounced against her.

But she constrained herself to smile, and approached the door in order to receive the king.

A heavy rolling was now heard, and along over the well-polished floor of the anteroom came the king's in-door equipage.

This in-door carriage consisted of a large arm-chair mounted upon wheels, which, instead of horses, was drawn by men, and to which, from a kind of delicate flattery, was given the form and shape of a triumphal chariot—such as that of the Roman victorious emperors of old—in order, whenever the king was drawn about the apartments in this manner, to maintain the agreeable illusion that he was making a triumphal march, and that it was in nowise the weight of his unwieldy limbs which compelled him to mount this quasi-imperial chariot. Henry willingly yielded to the flatteries of his courtiers, and whenever he rode about in this guise through the gilded saloons, adorned with Venetian mirrors, which multiplied and reflected his likeness from every side, he readily lulled himself in the illusion that he was a triumphal conqueror, and wholly forgot that it was not his achievements but his corpulency which had raised him to the victor's car.

For this huge mass which filled the colossal arm-chair—this mountain of purple-robed flesh—this lumbering and shapeless form, was Henry the Eighth,—the king of happy England.

But this unwieldy mass had a head!—a head full of dark and sinister thoughts,—a heart full of bloodthirsty and ferocious instincts. The colossal body was indeed bound to the arm-chair by its own ponderous bulk; yet the mind of its owner never rested, but hovered—as though with the eye and talons of an unclean bird of prey—over his people,—always ready to pounce upon some poor innocent dove, to drink its blood, and tear out its heart—that he might present it, still quivering, upon the altar of his sanguinary god.

The domestic chariot of the king now stopped, and Katharine hastened forward to assist her royal spouse in alighting.

Henry greeted her with a gracious nod, and ordered the pages in attendance to stand back.

"Go away!" he exclaimed, "get ye gone! My Katharine alone shall give me her hand here, and welcome me to her bridal chamber. Away! We feel ourself this day as young and vigorous as in our best and happiest years; and the young queen shall find that it is no feeble, tottering graybeard who weds her, but a hale and vigorous man, whose youth has been renewed by love.—Do not think, Kate, that it is from any bodily ailment that I use this carriage. No—it was only my wish to see thee, which made me eager to come the more speedily."

He kissed her brow with a self-satisfied smile, and, leaning lightly on her arm, descended from his chariot.

"Away with this carriage, and with you all!" he exclaimed. "It is our will to be left alone with this young and beautiful woman, whom my lords the bishops have this day made our own."

And with a wave of his hand he dismissed the whole train of his courtiers, and Katharine was now alone with the king.

Her heart beat so violently that it made her lips tremble and her bosom heave with emotion.

Henry perceived it, and smiled; but it was a cold and grim smile, which made Katharine turn pale.

"He has always the smile of a tyrant upon his lips," she whispered to herself. "With this same smile with which he now expresses his love for me, perhaps he yesterday signed a death-warrant, or to-morrow perhaps will witness an execution."

"Do you love me, Kate?" suddenly exclaimed the king, who had for a moment been contemplating her in silent thought. "Tell me, Kate, do you love me?"

Saying which, he looked with a fixed and scrutinizing gaze into her eyes, as if he would scan the secret thoughts of her heart.

Katharine met his glance with firmness, and without shrinking. She felt that the present moment was all-decisive, and would determine her whole future; and this conviction restored to her all her energy and presence of mind.

She was now no longer the timid or trembling girl, but the resolute and determined woman, who was prepared to wrestle with Fate for the greatness and splendor of her existence.

"Do you love me, Kate?" repeated the king, while a cloud seemed gathering on his brow.

"I don't know," replied Katharine, with a smile which enchanted the king; for her charming features betrayed no less graceful coyness than modest and winning reserve.

"You don't know?" repeated Henry, with surprise. "Now, by God's mother, this is the first time in my life that a woman has ventured to tell me as much! You are a brave woman, Kate, to give me such an answer, and I commend you for it. I like bravery, for it is a thing I so rarely meet with. All of them tremble before me here, Kate—all! They know that I don't shrink from blood, and that, secure in the strength of my kingdom, I can sign a death-warrant or a billet-doux with equal composure."

"Oh, you are a great king!" murmured Katharine.

Henry did not notice this observation. He was plunged in one of those fits of self-contemplation, in the indulgence of which he found so much pleasure, and which generally had for their object his own greatness and glory.

"Yes," he continued, and his eyes (which, despite his corpulence, and his brawny countenance, remained wide open) became fiercely animated—"yes, they all tremble before me, for they know that I am a just and severe king, who does not spare his own blood when the punishment and expiation of crime require it; and who scourges the offender with an inexorable hand—even if he should be the nearest to his throne. Take care, accordingly, Kate—take care. You see in me the avenger of God, and the judge of men! Kings wear purple—not because it is splendid or becoming, but because it is red, like blood, and because it is the highest prerogative of kings to be free to shed the blood of their rebellious subjects, and thereby expiate the crimes of the human race. It is thus alone that I understand a monarch's duties, and thus alone will I execute them to the end of my days. It is not the right of pardon, but that of punishment, by which the sovereign is distinguished from the base herd of mankind. The thunder of heaven should be upon his lips, and the king's wrath should descend like lightning upon the heads of the guilty."

"But God is not only the angry, but also the merciful and the pardoning," said Katharine, as she leaned her head timidly upon the king's shoulder.

"That is just the privilege which God enjoys above us kings," said Henry; "that He can exercise mercy, whereas we can only punish and condemn. There must be some point in which God is superior to kings.—But how now, Kate!—you tremble, and that sweet smile has left your lips. Don't be afraid of me, Kate. If you are true and faithful to me, I shall always love you. And now, Katty, explain to me what you meant by saying you don't know if you love me."

"No, your majesty—I really don't know. How should I understand or designate a feeling which I have never yet experienced?"

"What! Never loved, Kate?" exclaimed the king, with a look of joyful astonishment.

"Never, Sire! My father treated me harshly, and never excited any sentiments in me but those of anxiety and terror."

"And your husband, child—the man who was my predecessor in your affections. Did you not love your husband, either, Kate?"

"My husband?" she asked, musingly. "It is true my father sold me to Lord Latimer, and when the priest joined our hands together, people said he was my husband. But he knew very well that I didn't love him, and he didn't even desire that I should. He gave me his name, as a father gives his name to his daughter, and I was his daughter—an obedient and dutiful daughter, who fulfilled her duties faithfully, and tended him to his death."

"And after his death? Why, years have passed since that, Kate. Tell me, I entreat you—tell me the truth—the simple truth—have you never loved any one since your husband's death?"

The king looked at her with visible anxiety, eager to learn her reply, and Katharine did not shrink from his inquiring gaze.

"Sire," she replied, with a charming smile, "until within the last few weeks, I have often lamented my own fate, and I felt as though, in despair at my cheerless and solitary life, I ought to look into my bosom to see if it contained a heart, which, cold and unmoved, had never betrayed any symptoms of its existence. Oh, sire, I was full of anxiety; and in my rash folly I even blamed Heaven for having withheld from me the noblest feelings and the happiest privilege of a woman—the faculty of loving."

"You say it was so until within the last few weeks, Kate?" continued the king, with breathless eagerness.

"Yes, sire, until the day when first you did me the high honor of addressing me."

"And since then, Kate, tell me has your heart beat, you dear, amiable little dove?"

"Oh, yes, sire; it beats very often indeed, as if it would burst. When I hear your voice, when I see your face, I feel as if a cold thrill ran through my whole frame, and drove all the blood to my heart. Indeed, my heart tells me of your approach before I have seen you; for I then feel a peculiar nervous and choking sensation, and by that I know that you are drawing near, and that your presence will relieve me of this painful strain upon my emotions. When you are not beside me I think of you, and when I sleep I dream of you; and now sire, you, who understand all things, can tell me if you think I love you."

"Oh, yes, yes. You love me indeed!" exclaimed Henry, to whom this sudden and joyous surprise had imparted a glow of youthful animation. "Yes, Kate, I am sure you love me, and if I may believe your graceful avowal, I am also your first love. Repeat it once more, Kate! You were nothing more than a daughter to Lord Neville?"

"Nothing more, sire!"

"And after him you had no other lover?"

"None, sire."

"Then I am about to see realized a singular miracle. Can it be true that I have not taken a widow, but a youthful maiden, for my queen?"

As he now looked at her with a glance of glowing and passionate affection, Katharine modestly cast down her eyes, and a deep blush suffused her beautiful countenance.

"Oh, what a precious sight is a woman who blushes from modesty and reserve!" exclaimed the king, while he pressed Katharine violently to his breast; "what foolish, short-sighted beings we all are—even we kings! In order not to be obliged perchance to hand over my sixth wife to the scaffold, I chose, in anxious misgiving of the flagrant inconstancy of your sex, a widow for my queen; and now this widow mocks the new decree of Parliament with a blissful avowal, and realizes for me what she did not promise. Come, Kate, a kiss for all this! You have to-day opened before me a happy future, and prepared a joyful surprise, which I did not anticipate. I thank thee, Kate, and I swear, by God's mother, that I will never forget thee for this!"

And, taking from his finger a costly ring, which he placed upon the finger of Katharine, he continued: "Let this ring be a memento of the present hour, and if ever you should present it to me with a request, I will grant it, Katy!"

He kissed her affectionately, and was about to draw her more closely to his side, when suddenly there was heard without the roll of drums and the ringing of bells.

The king started for a moment, and relaxed his hold of Katharine. He listened. The sound of the drums continued; and from time to time there arose in the distance the peculiar hoarse murmur which resembles the surging of a troubled sea, and which can only be produced by a vast concourse of people.

With a fierce oath the king pushed open the glass door leading to the balcony, and stepped forward.

Katharine looked after him with a half-timid, half-angry glance. "I have not told him at least that I love him," she murmured. "He has interpreted my words as it pleased his vanity. Well and good. I *won't* die upon the scaffold!"

With a firm step, and with a resolute and energetic bearing, she followed the king to the balcony.

Still the roll of the drums continued, and the bells rang out from all the towers.

The night was gloomy and dull, and the dim outlines of the houses rose like so many tombs amidst the murky darkness around.

Suddenly the horizon became illumined—the sky was streaked with a dull, reddish glare, which rose higher and higher, until it seemed to inflame the whole firmament with its fiery glow, which was again reflected in purple gleams upon the balcony where the royal couple stood.

Still the bells continued to peal forth,

and at intervals was heard in the distance a wild, piercing yell, mingling with the uproar as of ten thousand voices.

Suddenly the king turned round to Katharine, and his face, which was lit up by the fiery reflection; as if covered by a blood-red veil, now assumed an expression of demoniac joy.

"Ah!" he exclaimed, "I now perceive what it is. You had quite confused me, you little enchantress, and I had forgotten for the moment that I was a king, from my wish to be nothing but your lover. But now I am reminded once more of my right of punishing, as a ruler. Those are the fagots of the stake which blaze up so lustily yonder; and that shouting and uproar signifies that my merry subjects are enjoying the comedy which I have caused to be played before them to-day—to the honor of God and of my unassailable dignity as king."

"The stake!" exclaimed Katharine, trembling with horror. "Does your majesty mean that human beings are about to die a fearful and revolting death; that at the moment when you express yourself a happy and contented king, there are some of your subjects about to be condemned to a horrible martyrdom? Oh, no, your majesty will not obscure your queen's wedding-day by such a gloomy death-cloud. You will not be so cruel as thus to dim my happiness."

The king laughed. "No, I will not dim it, but on the contrary I will light it up with a good blaze," he replied; and pointing to the glowing sky, he continued: "Those are our wedding-torches, Kate, and they are the best and brightest I could think of, for they burn in honor of God and of the king. And yonder flame, which shoots up to the skies and bears away the souls of the heretics, will give the Almighty joyful tidings of His most faithful and devoted son, who, even on the day of his happiness, does not forget his kingly duties, but always continues to be the scourging and scathing servant of the God of hosts."

At this moment his look was terrible His face, which glowed with the fiery glare, wore a threatening and ferocious expression; his eyes shot forth flames, and a cold, cruel smile played round his thin, compressed lips.

"Oh, he knows no pity," murmured Katharine to herself, while she stared with a shudder of astonishment at the king, who was looking with fanatical fervor toward the flames, into which, perhaps at that moment, a wretched creature was being flung at his command. "No, he knows no pity, and no mercy!"

Henry now turned round to her, and laying his hand gently on her shoulder, he spanned her slender neck with his fingers, whispering at the same time tender words and promises in her ear.

Katharine trembled. These caresses of the king, however harmless they might be, had in them something dismal and repulsive. It was the involuntary and instinctive touch of the executioner, who examines the neck of his victim, to fix upon the spot where he shall strike.

Thus had Anne Bullen, the king's second wife, once put her delicate fingers round her own fair neck, and said to the headsman, brought from Calais for the occasion, "I pray you strike a sure blow. You see I have but a very slender neck."

Thus had Henry clutched the neck of Katharine Howard, his fifth wife, when satisfied of her infidelity, and when clinging to him entreatingly, he flung her from him with wild imprecations. The marks of his talons were still visible on her neck when she laid it upon the block.

And now Katharine Parr must regard this ominous act as a caress, at which she is obliged to smile, and which she must needs receive with all the appearance of joy.

While thus spanning her neck, he bent his face close to her cheek, and whispered words of affection in her ear.

But Katharine paid no heed to his ardent whisperings. She saw nothing but the blood-red, fiery decree in the skies. She heard nothing but the doleful cries of the unhappy victims.

"Pardon! pardon!" she stammered. "Oh, let this day be a day of rejoicing for all your subjects. Be merciful, and if I am to believe that you really love me, grant me the first request which I shall ask you. Grant me the lives of these unhappy victims. Mercy, sire, mercy!"

And as if the prayer of the queen had found an echo, there was suddenly heard from the adjoining room, a woe-stricken and despairing cry of, "Pardon, sire, pardon!"

The king turned round angrily, and his brow assumed a severe and lowering expression. He looked inquiringly at Katharine, as though he would discover, from her features, if she knew who dared to disturb their conversation. But Katharine's face betrayed undissembled surprise. "Pardon, pardon!" repeated the voice from the adjoining apartment.

The king uttered an exclamation of anger, and retired hastily from the balcony.

CHAPTER IV.

KING BY THE WRATH OF GOD.

"Who dares to disturb us?" exclaimed the king, returning with impetuous steps to the room. "Who dares to speak of mercy?"

"I dare it, sire!" said a young lady, who, with pale and haggard features, now advanced in a state of fearful agitation toward the king, and flung herself at his feet.

"Maria Askew!" exclaimed Katharine, with astonishment. "What brings you here, Maria?"

"I want pardon—pardon for those unhappy beings who are suffering yonder!" cried the young maiden, with a terror-stricken look, while she pointed toward the lurid conflagration without. "I want mercy for the king himself, who so cruelly sends the noblest and the best of his subjects, like so many sheep, to the slaughter."

"Oh, sire, have pity on this poor child!" exclaimed Katharine, turning toward the king—"pity for her enthusiasm and youthful ardor. She is unaccustomed to these terrible scenes; she does not yet know that it is the sad duty of the king to be obliged to punish, where she would probably have mercy."

Henry smiled, but the look which he cast at the young kneeling maiden made Katharine tremble—for this look revealed a death-warrant.

"Maria Askew, if I mistake not, is your second maid of honor?" asked the king, "and it was at your express wish that she took this position?"

"Yes, sire."

"You knew her, therefore?"

"No, sire. I saw her a few days since for the first time. But her appearance and manner quite won my good opinion, and I feel that I shall love her as a friend; be therefore indulgent, sire."

But the king still continued in moody thought, and Katharine's answer by no means satisfied him.

"Then why did you interest yourself for this young lady if you did not know her?"

"She had been so strongly recommended to me."

"Who did so?"

Katharine hesitated for a moment; she felt that in her zeal she had perhaps gone too far, and that, probably, it was incautious on her part to have told him the whole truth. But the king's firm and penetrating glance rested upon her, and she remembered that he had, only this evening, strictly and solemnly enjoined her always to tell him the truth. Besides, it was no secret at court who the protector of this young maiden was, and who had been the means of her receiving the place of one of the queen's maids of honor—a position which so many noble families had sought in vain to procure for their own daughters.

"Who recommended this lady to you?" repeated the king, while his growing ire already began to flush his face and make his voice tremble.

"It was Archbishop Cranmer that did so, sire," replied Katharine, raising her eyes toward the king with a most captivating smile.

At this moment was heard, from without, the roll of drums, which, however, was drowned by fearful shrieks of agony and cries of anguish. The flames now rose higher and higher, and in their fierce and murderous fury illuminated the skies all around.

Maria Askew, who during the colloquy of the royal pair, had stood aloof in respectful silence, now felt herself overpowered by this fearful sight, and deprived of her remaining presence of mind.

"Merciful God!" she exclaimed, trembling as if with an inward shudder, while her hands were extended beseechingly toward the king, "Do you not hear the cries of those unhappy victims? I conjure you, sire, as you shall remember the hour of your death, and the day of judgment, to have mercy upon those wretched beings. As least do not suffer them to be flung alive into the flames.

Oh, spare them, sire, from this fearful martyrdom!"

Henry cast an angry glance at the prostrate girl, and strode past her, toward the door communicating with the anteroom, where the King's attendants awaited his commands.

He beckoned to the two bishops, Cranmer and Gardiner, to approach, and commanded the servants to throw the doors of the apartment wide open.

The scene now presented a strange and animated spectacle; and the queen's chamber, previously so still, became of a sudden the theatre of a great drama, which would probably end in blood. The principal personages of this drama were now assembled in the small but luxuriously decorated sleeping-apartment of the queen.

The king stood in the centre of the room, attired in his gold-embroidered robes, and covered with precious stones, which blazed resplendent with the light from the chandelier. Beside him was the young queen, whose beautiful and amiable countenance was turned toward the king with a look of the deepest anxiety, and who strove to read in the stern and glowering features of her royal husband the issue of this scene.

At a short distance from the queen still knelt the youthful Maria Askew, with her face bathed in tears, which she concealed with her hands;—whilst in the background were the bishops, who contemplated the spectacle before them with grave and unmoved composure. Through the open doors of the adjoining apartment were seen the eagerly-strained features of a host of courtiers crowded together at the door-way, whilst on the opposite side, through the open window of the balcony, might be seen the glowing skies—while the sound of bells and drums, mingling with the yells of the populace and the shrieks of woe and despair, resounded along the air.

A deep silence ensued, and when the king spoke, the tones of his voice were so harsh and chilling, that an involuntary shudder ran through all those around him.

"My lords of Canterbury and Winchester," said the king, "we have summoned you, in order that by the force of your prayers, and the wisdom of your speech, ye may rescue this young maiden from the devil, who, without doubt, has power over her, for she dares to accuse her king of cruelty and injustice."

The bishops approached the prostrate girl; they each of them stooped down and laid their hands upon her shoulder—but each with a very different expression of countenance.

That of Cranmer was mild, but resolute, and a compassionate and encouraging smile played around his lips.

Gardiner's features, on the contrary, betrayed an expression of cruel and cold-blooded irony, and the smile which sat upon his large, gaping mouth, was that of the exultant and pitiless priest, who is ready to present a victim to his deities.

"Courage, daughter—courage and discretion!" whispered Cranmer.

"The God who blesses the righteous,

and who punishes and crushes the wicked, be with thee, and with us all!" said Gardiner.

But Maria Askew shrank back from his touch, and pushed his hand violently from her shoulder.

"Touch me not! You are the executioner of those poor creatures yonder!" she exclaimed, with scornful accents; and turning once more to the king, she besought him, with outstretched hands, to have mercy upon the suffering victims.

"Mercy?" repeated the king. "Mercy? And for whom? Who are those that are yonder undergoing the penalty of their own crimes? Pray, my lord bishop, who are the persons who have this day been sent to the stake? What are those malefactors?"

"They are heretics, who hold the views lately brought over from Germany, and who have the hardihood to deny the supremacy of our lord the king," said Gardiner.

"They are Catholics, who regard the Pope of Rome as the head of the Christian Church, and who recognize none other but him," said Cranmer.

"You see, my lords!" exclaimed the king, "this girl accuses us of injustice, and yet ye say it is not heretics only who are expiating their crimes yonder, but also Catholics. It appears to me, therefore, that we have acted with our usual justice and impartiality by handing over the malefactors on both sides to the hands of the executioner."

"Oh, had you seen what I have seen," cried Maria Askew, with a shudder, "you would strain your whole energy to pronounce the single word, Mercy. And this word you would make heard from this spot to that terrible place of agony and horror."

"What, then, did you see?" said the king, with a grim smile.

Meanwhile, Maria Askew had stood erect, and her tall and slender figure presented a striking contrast to the dark forms of the bishops on either side. Her eyes were wide open and fixed, and her noble and gentle features wore an expression of horror and dismay.

"I saw a woman being led to the scaffold," she said, "not a malefactress, but a noble lady, into whose lofty and dignified mind a thought of treason or crime had never entered, but who, true to her faith and her convictions, will not forswear the God whom she serves. As she walked through the crowd, it seemed as if a glory shone around her head, and her white hair glistened like silver. All the people bowed before her, and even the most hardened men wept at the fate of this unhappy woman, who had outlived seventy years, and who was not suffered at length to die upon her bed, but was offered as a victim to the honor of God, and of the king. But she only smiled, and gently greeted the weeping and sobbing multitude. She mounted the scaffold, as if she were going to ascend a throne, to receive the homage of her subjects. Two years' confinement in a dungeon had made her cheeks pale, but it had not succeeded in dimming the fire of her eyes, or destroying the strength of her spirit; seventy years had not bowed her neck, or broken her courage. She mounted the scaffold with a firm step, and greeting the people once more, said she would pray to God for them in a better world. But when the executioner approached her, and sought to bind her hands, and make her kneel down in order to lay her head upon the block, she would not suffer it, and angrily pushed him aside. 'It is only traitors and criminals that lay their heads upon the block!' she exclaimed, with a loud voice. 'It is not for me to do so, and as long as I have breath in my body I will not submit myself to your bloodthirsty laws. Take my life, therefore, if you can.' And now began a scene which filled the heart of every spectator with horror and consternation. The countess ran about the scaffold like a poor hunted deer worried by the hounds; her white hair fluttered in the wind, and her dark robes of death swept around her figure like a murky cloud; while the headsman in his blood-red garments pursued her with uplifted axe—endeavoring to aim his deadly blow—which she sought to evade. But at length her resistance grew feebler. The strokes of the axe had reached her body, until she became bathed in her own blood, and grew faint from exhaustion. With a heart-rending shriek she swooned away. But by her side, likewise overcome, sank the headsman covered with perspiration. The terrible chase had lamed his arm and exhausted his strength. Panting and breathless, he was now unable to drag this poor bleeding and insensible woman to the block, or to lift the axe to cut off her venerable head. The crowd yelled with horror and disgust, while some wept and prayed aloud for mercy, and the high-sheriff himself could scarcely refrain from tears. He ordered that the fearful work should be delayed until the countess and the executioner had recovered themselves; for it was not a dying, but a living woman, that was to suffer according to the sentence of the law. The countess lay at full length upon the scaffold, while cordials were applied to restore her. The headsman swallowed large draughts of brandy, in order to revive his strength for the work of death, while the crowd turned round to the stakes, which were piled up on either side of the scaffold, and at which four other victims were about to be burned. But I fled hither to implore your majesty for mercy. And now, sire, behold me at your feet. There is still time. Mercy, sire. Mercy for the Countess of Salisbury, the last of the Plantagenets!"

"Mercy, sire, mercy!" repeated Katharine Parr, as weeping and trembling she clung to her husband's side.

"Mercy!" repeated Archbishop Cranmer, while the prayer was timidly and cautiously murmured by a few of the courtiers.

The king's large and flashing eyes glared with a hasty and penetrating look at the entire assemblage.

"Well, and you, my Lord Bishop Gardiner," said he, in a cold, ironical tone, "will you not beg for mercy, too

—like all these faint-hearted petitioners?"

"The Almighty is a God of vengeance," said Gardiner, solemnly, "and it is written 'that they who have sinned, them will God punish, even to the third and fourth generations.'"

"And what is written shall be verified!" exclaimed the king, with a voice of thunder. "No pardon for the evil-doer—no mercy for the guilty. The axe shall fall upon the necks of traitors, and the flames shall consume the bodies of heretics and malefactors!"

"Bethink you, sire, of your exalted destiny," exclaimed Maria Askew, with fervent enthusiasm. "Consider what a lofty title you have given yourself in your kingdom. You proclaim yourself as the head of the Church, and in that character you desire to rule and govern upon earth. Be gracious, then, sire, as you call yourself king, by the grace of God."

"No. I do not call myself king, by the grace of God. I call myself king, by the wrath of God!" exclaimed Henry, raising his arm in a threatening attitude. "My office is to dispatch sinners to God, and let Him have mercy upon them above, if He will. I am the punishing judge, and I judge inexorably and without mercy. Let the condemned appeal to God, and may He pardon them! I cannot do so, nor will I. Kings rule but to chastise, and it is not in pity or in love, but in vengeful wrath, that they resemble God."

"Then woe, woe to you and to us all!" exclaimed Maria Askew. "Woe to yourself, King Henry, if what you say be true! For then are those men bound to the stake yonder, right in denouncing you as a tyrant—then is the Bishop of Rome right in pronouncing you a disloyal and degenerate son, and in hurling his anathemas against you. Then you know not God, who is mercy and love—then are you no disciple of the Redeemer, who says: 'Love your enemies, bless them that curse you.' Woe to you I say, King Henry, if this be your unhappy state of mind, if—"

"Silence, unhappy girl!" cried Katharine Parr, and, drawing the young maiden violently away, she took the king's hand and pressed it to her lips.

"Sire," she murmured, with earnest fervor, "you told me just now that you loved me. Prove to me that you do so by pardoning this poor young girl, and exercising forbearance toward her frenzied excitement. Prove it to me, and allow me at the same time to lead Maria Askew to her room and command her to be silent."

But the king was at this moment wholly inaccessible to any other feelings than those of anger and bloodthirsty exultation.

He repulsed Katharine with apparent ill-humor, and with his penetrating glance still fixed upon the young girl, he said with a hasty but leaden tone, "Let her alone! She shall speak herself. Let no one dare to interrupt her."

Katharine, trembling with anxiety, and her feelings wounded by the harsh manner of the king, retired with a deep sigh to one of the recesses near the window.

Maria Askew had, meanwhile, been wholly unobservant of what was passing around her. She was in that state of passionate enthusiasm which excludes reflection and shrinks from no danger. At this moment she could have walked to the stake with joyful exultation, and she almost longed for this holy martyrdom.

"Speak, Maria Askew, speak!" said the king. "Tell me if you know what the countess has done, for whom you beg for mercy—if you know why those four men have been sent to the stake?"

"Yes. I know what it is, King Henry, by the wrath of God," said the young maiden, with impassioned earnestness, "I know well why you have condemned the noble countess to the scaffold, and why you will show her no mercy. She is of noble and royal blood, and Cardinal Pole is her son. You wish to punish the son through the mother, and as you cannot butcher the cardinal, you murder his noble mother."

"Oh, you are a very learned young lady," cried the king, with a sneering and ironical laugh. "You seem to know my most secret thoughts and purposes. Doubtless then you are a good Catholic since the death of the Catholic countess gives you such unspeakable grief. In that case, you must at least acknowledge that the other four heretics have been justly committed to the flames."

"Heretics!" said Maria, with animation. "Do you call those devoted men heretics who for their conscience and their faith have confronted an ignominious death? Oh, King Henry, woe to you if you condemn such men as heretics! They alone are the true believers—the real servants of God. They have emancipated themselves from human power, and as they have disowned the pope on the one hand, so on the other they will not recognize you as the head of the Church. God alone, they maintain, is the Head of His Church, and the master of their conscience, and who can, therefore, presume to call them malefactors?"

"I!" exclaimed Henry, with a voice of thunder, "I presume to do so. I say that they are heretics, that I will root them out, and will trample under foot all those who think as they do. I say that I will pour out the blood of those criminals, and will prepare punishments for them, which shall make humanity shudder and tremble. God will reveal Himself through me in fire and blood. He has put the sword of vengeance into my hand, and I shall wield it to His honor, and, like St. George, I will crush the dragon of heresy under my feet!"

And lifting up his inflamed and haughty countenance, and rolling his fierce and bloodshot eyes, he continued: "Hear it all ye who are here present—no mercy for heretics, no pardon for Catholics! I am he alone whom our Lord God has chosen and consecrated as His sovereign executioner. I am the high-priest of the Church, and who denies me denies God. Whoever has the temerity to bow to any other head of the Church, is a worshipper of Baal, and kneels to an idol. Kneel ye all down, therefore, and do homage in my person to that God whose vicar on earth I am, and who reveals Himself through me, in His supreme and terrible majesty. Kneel down, I say, for I am the sole head of the Church, and the high-priest of the Most High!"

And suddenly, as if touched by an electric shock, all those proud nobles—all those ladies sparkling with diamonds, and even the two bishops and the queen, fell upon their knees on the floor.

The king feasted his eyes for a moment upon this spectacle of abasement, and with beaming looks, and with a triumphant smile, he glanced around at this assembly of the noblest of the land, thus humbled in his presence.

Suddenly his eye rested upon Maria Askew. She alone had not bent her knee, but stood proudly erect, like the king himself, in the midst of the prostrate courtiers.

A dark cloud gathered on the king's brow.

"You do not obey my command?" he asked.

She shook her head, and looked at him with a firm and penetrating glance. "No," she replied, "like those victims yonder, whose last death-shriek has reached us—like them, I say to God alone belongs honor and worship—He alone is the head of His Church. If you ask me to kneel before you as my king I will do so, but I will not bow before you as the head of the Holy Church."

A murmur of amazement ran through the assembly, and every eye was turned with consternation and astonishment toward the daring young damsel, who with a wrapt and beaming countenance stood confronting the king.

At a signal from Henry, the kneeling courtiers arose, and in breathless silence awaited the terrible scene that was approaching.

A pause ensued. The king himself was panting for breath, and required a moment to revive himself and collect his faculties.

Not, indeed, that anger and passion had deprived him of speech. He was neither angry nor passionate, and it was only a sentiment of inward exultation that obstructed his breathing; exultation at having found another victim with which he could allay his thirst for blood—over whose torments he could gloat, and whose death-sighs he could greedily inhale.

The king never looked more serene or cheerful than when he had signed a death-warrant. For then he felt himself in the full enjoyment of sovereign power—as the arbiter of life and death over millions of his fellow-beings, and this feeling afforded him a grateful and lofty consciousness of his own dignity.

Accordingly, when he now turned to Maria Askew his countenance was calm and serene, and his voice cordial—almost affectionate.

"Maria Askew," he said, "do you know that the words you have just uttered make you guilty of high-treason?"

"I know it, sire."

"And you know the punishment that awaits traitors?"

"Death—I am aware."

"Death by fire!" said the king, with quiet composure.

A subdued murmur spread through the assembly. Only one voice ventured to utter the word mercy.

It was Katharine—the king's wife, who pronounced this single word. She stepped forward. She wished to hasten to the king, and once more implore him for mercy and pardon. But she felt herself gently held back. Archbishop Cranmer stood beside her, and looked at her with an expression of earnest entreaty.

"Calmness and discretion," he murmured. "You will not be able to save her—she is lost. Think of yourself, and of the pure and holy religion whose protectress you are. Preserve yourself to the Church and for the sake of your fellow-believers."

"And must she die?" asked Katharine, her eyes filled with tears, as she looked across toward this poor, tender girl, who with a smile of resignation stood before the king.

"We may yet, perhaps, be able to save her, but now is not the time. Any opposition would only tend to aggravate the king, and might perhaps, impel him to throw the unhappy damsel into the flames forthwith. Let us therefore be silent."

"Yes, we must be silent," murmured Katharine, with a shudder, as she withdrew once more to the recess near the window.

"The stake awaits you, Maria Askew," repeated the king. "No mercy for the traitress who dares to calumniate and contemn her king!"

CHAPTER V.

THE RIVALS.

At the moment that the king, with a voice of triumph, had pronounced the doom of Maria Askew, one of the king's gentlemen appeared at the door of the royal apartment and approached Henry.

This was a young man of noble and imposing mien, whose proud bearing contrasted strongly with the submissive and shrinking attitude of the other courtiers. His tall and slender figure was encased in a gold-embroidered coat-of-mail; from his shoulders hung a velvet mantle, bearing a prince's coronet —while his head, adorned with dark, flowing locks, was surmounted by a close-fitting gold-lace cap, from which a long white plume descended to his shoulders. His fine profile marked at once the type of aristocratic beauty; his cheeks were of a pure, transparent paleness; and around his slightly-parted lips played a smile, half listless and half supercilious. The high-arched brow, and the finely-chiselled aquiline nose, gave to his countenance an expression at once daring and thoughtful. The eyes alone did not correspond with the other features;—they were neither listless like the mouth, nor thoughtful like the brow. All the fire—all the uncurbed and haughty passion of youth, shone forth from those dark, lustrous orbs. Had those eyes been closed, one might have taken him for a *blasé* aristocrat, who despised the world at large; but when his keen and ever-ardent glance was revealed, it bespoke at once the young man, full of daring courage and ambitious thoughts—full of passionate enthusiasm and unbounded pride.

He approached the king, as above stated, and bending on one knee before him, said, with a full and well-toned voice, "Pardon, sire, pardon!"

The king retreated a few steps in astonishment, and looked with amazement at the daring speaker.

"Thomas Seymour!" he said—"Thomas, thou art, then, come back, and thy first act is again one of indiscretion and foolhardy enterprise."

The young man smiled.

"Yes, I am come back," he replied. "That is, I have had a good sea-fight with the Scots, and have taken from them four ships-of-war. With these I hastened hither in order to offer them as a wedding-present to my lord the king; and just as I entered the anteroom I heard your voice, which was pronouncing a sentence of death. And was it not natural that I, who brought your majesty news of a victory, should have the courage to utter a petition for mercy, for which, as it would seem, none of the noble gentlemen present could summon resolution."

"Ah!" said the king, breathing with greater freedom, "then you didn't even know for whom, or for what, you were suing for mercy?"

"Pardon me, sire," said the young man, while his glance was directed with an expression of contempt at the whole assembly. "Pardon me. I saw at once who the condemned person must be, for I saw this young maiden standing alone and abandoned by all, as if plague-stricken, in the midst of this brave and noble company; and you are aware, sire, that it is by this sign we recognize those who are condemned, or who have fallen into disgrace at court—that everybody shuns them. No one has the courage to touch such lepers—even with the ends of his fingers."

The king smiled.

"Thomas Seymour, Lord Sudley, you are now, as ever, thoughtless and hasty. You sue for mercy without even inquiring if the object of your suit be worthy of pardon or not."

"But I see she is a woman," said the undaunted young man. "A woman is always worthy of pardon, and it becomes every true knight to protect her, if it were only for the sake of offering his homage to a sex so beautiful and so helpless, and withal so noble and all-subduing. Let me therefore entreat your majesty for pardon for this young creature."

Katharine had listened to the young Sudley with a beating heart and with glowing cheeks. It was the first time she had seen him, and yet she already felt toward him a lively interest and an almost affectionate solicitude.

"He will ruin himself," she murmured, "he will not save Maria Askew, but will only bring mischief upon himself. O God, take pity upon my sad and suffering heart!"

She now fixed her anxious looks upon the king, firmly resolved to exercise her influence in favor of the earl who had so nobly come to the rescue of an innocent woman—in case he too should be threatened by the anger of her husband. But to her surprise, Henry's features were perfectly calm and serene.

Like the wild bird of prey, which, following its instinct, seeks for its bloody spoil only so long as it is hungry; like this bird Henry felt his appetite appeased for one day. Yonder still blazed the fires in which four heretics had just been burnt, and beside it stood the scaffold on which the Countess of Salisbury had just been butchered; and now at the present moment he had already found another victim. Besides, Thomas Seymour had always been his favorite. His temerity, his cheerfulness, and his energy, had always imposed upon the king, and, moreover, he strongly resembled his sister, the beautiful Jane Seymour, Henry's third wife.

"I cannot grant you this request," said the king. "Justice must not be checked in its course, and when justice has condemned, mercy must not belie the decree. Besides, it was the judgment of your king which pronounced the sentence. You have therefore done wrong in a double sense; for not only did you pray for mercy, but you even accuse the noble gentlemen here present. If the case of this girl were a just one, think you she would not have found a knight to take her part?"

"Yes, that I verily believe," said the young earl, with a laugh. "The sun of your favor has already turned aside from this poor maiden, and therefore the cavaliers of your court no longer see the form that is shrouded in darkness."

"You are in error, my lord—I have seen her," suddenly exclaimed a voice, and a second cavalier advanced from the antechamber into the royal apartment. He approached the king, and bending on his knee before him, said in a low, but firm tone:

"I too, sire, beg for mercy for Maria Askew."

At this moment was heard a faint scream from the side on which the ladies stood, and the pale and terrified countenance of Lady Jane Douglas was raised for an instant above the heads of the other ladies around her.

But this exclamation passed unobserved. All eyes were directed toward the group in the centre of the room—all looked with strained eagerness at the king, and at the two young men who dared to intercede for one whom the king had condemned.

"Henry Howard, Earl of Surrey!" exclaimed the king, and now an expression of anger was depicted in his countenance. "How is this—do you, too, venture to intercede for this girl—will you not allow Thomas Seymour to be the most indiscreet and rash man at my court?"

"I will not allow him, sire, to think that he is the most courageous," replied the young nobleman, darting at Seymour a look of haughty defiance, which the latter returned with a smile of cold contempt.

"Oh," said he with a sneer, "I allow you freely, my dear Lord Surrey, to follow my footsteps, on the path which I have already explored at the risk of my life. You saw that I did not lose my head in this rash enterprise—and this has doubtless emboldened you. However, it affords a new proof of your discreet bravery, my worthy Lord Surrey, and you deserve my praise on that account."

The blood of the noble earl mounted to his cheek; his eyes darted fire, and, trembling with rage, he laid his hand upon his sword.

"Praise from Thomas Seymour is—"

"Peace!" cried the king in a tone of authority. "It shall not be said that two of the noblest cavaliers of my court convert a day, which for you all should be one of rejoicing, into a day of discord. I therefore command you both to be reconciled with each other. Pledge your hands, my lords, and let your reconciliation be sincere. I, the king, command you."

The young courtiers exchanged looks of hatred and suppressed passion, and their eyes gave expression to the words of scorn and defiance which their lips dared not utter.

The king had commanded—and however great and powerful cavaliers they might be, the king must be obeyed.

They each, therefore, held out their hands, and muttered a few words of little meaning, which were perhaps intended as an apology, but which they did not so understand.

"And now, sire," said the Earl of Surrey, "I venture to repeat my request. Pardon, sire, pardon for Maria Askew!"

"Well, Thomas Seymour, and do you too renew your entreaties?"

"No: I give way. The Earl of Surrey protects her. I retire, for beyond doubt she is guilty; your majesty says it, and therefore it must be so. It would ill become a Seymour to defend a person who had offended against her sovereign."

This new and indirect attack upon the Earl of Surrey appeared to make a deep but varied impression upon those present. The faces of some were seen to grow pale, while those of others were lit up by a malicious smile. On the one side, words of menace were murmured; and on the other, expressions of concurrent approbation were uttered half aloud.

The king's brow became gloomy. The arrow which had been shot by the skilful hand of Lord Sudley had reached the mark. The king, ever suspicious and distrustful, felt his mind so much the more disturbed, at seeing that the greater part of his courtiers adhered openly to the side of Howard, and that Seymour's friends were much fewer.

"The Howards are dangerous, and I shall watch them," said the king to himself; and for the first time his eye rested, with a sinister and hostile expression, upon the noble countenance of Henry Howard.

But Thomas Seymour, who only wished to aim a blow against his old enemy of long standing, had at the same time decided the fate of Maria Askew.

It was now almost impossible to speak in her behalf—and to speak of mercy would be to share in her guilt.

Thomas Seymour had done with her, for she had made herself unworthy of his protection, as a traitress to her sovereign.

Who would now have the hardihood to intercede for her?

Henry Howard was the man. He repeated his prayer for mercy, for Maria Askew. But the king's brow became darker and more sullen, and the courtiers saw, with terror, the moment approaching when his rage would crush the poor Earl of Surrey.

Among the ranks of the ladies, too, might be seen, here and there faces growing pale, and many a beautiful and beaming eye was dimmed with tears, at sight of this brave and generous cavalier, who was putting his life in jeopardy for a woman.

"He is lost!" murmured Lady Jane Douglas, and quite overpowered by her emotions, she leaned against the wall for support. But she speedily recovered herself, and stood erect, while her eye flashed with resolution.

"I will endeavor to save him," she said to herself, and with a firm step she quitted the ranks of the ladies, and approached the king.

A murmur of applause ran through the assembly, and all eyes were turned, with an expression of lively satisfaction, toward Lady Jane.

They knew that she was a friend of the queen, although not an adherent of the new doctrine; and it would therefore be very significant and very important if she should support the Earl of Surrey in his magnanimous efforts.

Lady Jane bent her proud and beautiful head before the king, and said in her clear, silvery tones:

"Sire, in the name of all women, I pray for mercy for Maria Askew—for she too is a woman. Lord Surrey has done so, because a true cavalier can never disown himself, but must ever find consolation in the noble and sacred duty of being the protector of the helpless, and those that are in danger. A true gentleman does not ask if a woman deserves his protection—it is enough that she is a woman, and needs his help. If, therefore, in the name of all women, I thank the Earl of Surrey for the assistance which he wished to give a woman, I venture at the same time to unite my prayer with his—that it may not be said that we women are without courage, and that we dare not come to the succor of one who is in danger. I therefore beg, sire, for pardon for Maria Askew."

"And I too, sire," said the queen, approaching the king once more—"I too would add my prayer. This day is the votive day of love—my festive day, sire. Let love and mercy prevail therefore to-day, for my sake." She looked at the king while she spoke, with such a love-provoking smile—her eyes had such a beaming and bliss-beguiling expression—that the king could not resist her.

In his heart, therefore, he was ready

for this time to let the kingly mercy prevail; but for this purpose he required a pretext—a mediative influence.

He had solemnly sworn to pardon no heretic at the queen's request alone—so that he dared not break his word.

"Well, then," said he, after a pause, "I will grant your prayer; I will pardon Maria Askew, if she will only recall and solemnly abjure all that she has said. Are you satisfied with that, Kate?"

"Yes, I am satisfied," she replied, sadly.

"And you, Lady Jane Douglas; and you, Henry Howard, Earl of Surrey?"

"We are satisfied."

All eyes were now once more turned toward Maria Askew, who, although the assembly had been occupied concerning her, had been left unnoticed and overlooked.

She, too, had taken no part in what was passing around her, and scarcely observed it.

She stood leaning against the open window of the balcony, and gazed at the fire-glowing horizon. Her spirit was present with the suffering martyrs, for whom she offered fervent prayers to heaven, and whom, in her fevered enthusiasm, she envied for their agonizing death.

Wholly absorbed by her own thoughts, she had neither heard the entreaties of those who interceded for her, nor the answer of the king.

The touch of a hand upon her shoulder aroused her from her fanatical reverie.

It was Katharine, the young queen, who stood beside her.

"Maria Askew," she whispered, "if you value your life, obey the king's command. There is no other means of saving yourself."

She seized the hand of the young maiden, and led her to the king.

"Sire," she said, aloud, "pardon the warm and excited feelings of this poor damsel, who has witnessed an execution for the first time, and whose senses were so carried away by the scene, that she was scarcely conscious of the foolish and criminal words which she uttered in your presence. Pardon her therefore, sire, as she will gladly and willingly recall her words."

A cry of consternation burst from Maria's lips, and her eyes flashed wildly, while she flung the queen away from her.

"I recall my words?" she exclaimed, with a scornful smile. "Never, your majesty, never! No, as God shall be gracious to me in the hour of death, I will not recant. True, it was the pain and the horror I felt that spoke within me, but what I said was meanwhile the truth. Horror and dismay had urged me to speak, and had constrained me to reveal the inmost feelings of my soul. No, I will not recall my words! I tell you, those who have suffered yonder as martyrs, are blessed saints, who ascend to meet their God, and in His presence to accuse their kingly executioner. Yes, they are now sainted martyrs—for Eternal Truth had enlightened their souls, and beamed more brightly upon their faces than the flames of that fire upon which the murderous hand of an unjust judge had flung them. Ah! recall my words indeed! Shall I imitate the example of Shaxton, that wretched and faithless servant of his God, who, from fear of a temporal death, denied the everlasting truth, and, with blasphemous cowardice, forswore himself in the cause of his Redeemer?

"I tell you, then, King Henry, to beware of hypocrites and perjurers—beware of thy own proud and haughty mind. The blood of the martyrs will cry to heaven against thee, and God will one day be as merciless toward thee as thou hast been toward the noblest of thy subjects—who are His creatures. You give them over to the devouring flames, because they will not believe what the priests of Baal announce to them. You hand them over to the executioner, because they obey the truth, and are faithful disciples of their Lord and Master."

"And you share in the sentiments of those people whom you call martyrs?" said the king, as Maria Askew paused for a moment to take breath.

"I do."

"Then you deny the truth of the Six Articles?"

"I do."

"You do not recognize me as the head of the Church?"

"God alone is the Lord and Head of his Church."

A pause here ensued—a fearful and anxious pause. Every one felt that there was no hope and no pardon possible for this young maiden—that her fate was irrevocably sealed.

The king smiled.

The courtiers knew this smile, and feared it more than the foaming anger of the king.

When the king smiled in this manner he had formed a resolution, and then he no longer wavered or hesitated; the sentence of death was decreed, and his bloodthirsty spirit gloated over a new victim.

"My Lord Bishop of Winchester," said the king at length, "come hither."

Gardiner approached accordingly, and placed himself beside Maria Askew, who regarded him with a look of scornful disdain.

"I command you in the name of the law," continued the king, "to seize the heretic, and hand her over to the spiritual tribunals; she is damned and lost, and shall die the death she merits!"

Gardiner laid his hand upon the shoulder of Maria Askew. "In the name of God's law I seize you," he said, solemnly.

Not a word more was spoken. The lord chief justice silently obeyed the signal of Gardiner, and, touching Maria Askew with his staff, he commanded his soldi rs to take her away.

Maria Askew held out her hands with a smile, and, with a firm and dignified bearing, left the room, surrounded by the soldiers, and followed by the Bishop of Winchester and the lord chief justice. The courtiers had opened a passage for Maria Askew and her attendants. Their ranks now closed again, like the waves of the sea, when they have engulfed a dead body committed to the deep.

Maria Askew was for them all as a corpse—as one buried. The waves had closed above her, and all was again smiling and serene as before.

The king gave his hand to his young wife, and, bending close to her, whispered words in her ear which were not heard by the assembly, but which made her tremble, while the color mounted to her cheeks. The king, who perceived it, laughed, and imprinted a kiss upon her brow; and then turning to his courtiers he said, with a gracious bow:

"Now, my lords and gentlemen, we will dismiss you, and say good-night. The festivities are over, and we need rest."

"Forget not the Princess Elizabeth," whispered Cranmer, as he took his leave of Katharine, and pressed her hand to his lips.

"No, I will not forget her," murmured Katharine; and with a trembling heart and with feelings of inward anxiety she saw them all depart, and herself left alone with the king.

CHAPTER VI.

INTERCESSION.

"And now, Kate," said the king, when all the company had departed, and he was once more alone with her—"now, Kate, we will forget every thing but that we love each other."

He embraced her and pressed her passionately to his breast. She leaned her head gently upon his shoulder, and lay in that posture like a crushed flower, wholly overcome, and without the power of volition.

"How now, sweetheart—you don't kiss me, Kate?" said Henry, smiling. "I suppose you are angry with me still for not having granted your first request? But what would you have, child? How should I keep the purple of my robes ever fresh and brilliant, if I did not dye them anew, from time to time, in the blood of evil-doers? The king who punishes and destroys can alone claim the title—and trembling human nature will respect him the more for it. Mankind despise a faint-hearted and forgiving monarch, and laugh to scorn his merciful weakness. Bah! they are miserable and pitiful creatures; they esteem only those who make them quail with terror—who daily make them feel the lash, and occasionally scourge a few of them to death. Look at me, Kate. Is there a king in Europe who has reigned longer or more successfully than I have done—or whom his people love more, or more strictly obey? The reason of this is, that I have already signed more than two hundred death-warrants."

"Oh, you say you love me," murmured Katharine, "and yet when you are beside me you speak only of blood and of death."

The king laughed. "You are right, Kate," said he, "but believe me there are other thoughts that slumber in my bosom, and if you could only look into it, you would not accuse me of coldness or want of love. Yes, Kate, I love my own virgin bride truly and tenderly, and as a test thereof you may ask me for any favor you wish. Yes, Kate, ask me for some favor, and, whatever it may be, I give you my royal word, your favor shall be granted. Now, Kate, just think what can give you most happiness. Do you wish for jewels or a mansion by the sea-side? Would you like fine horses—or has any one perchance offended you, whose head you would have? If that be so, Kate, a nod from me, and it shall fall at your feet. I am absolute and all-mighty, and there is no one so spotless or innocent that my will cannot find a crime against him, which shall cost him his head. Speak, therefore, sweetheart, what is it would make your heart rejoice?"

Katharine smiled, despite her inward aversion and horror.

"Sire," she replied, "you have already given me so many jewels, that they glitter upon me like the stars of night. Were you to present me with a mansion by the sea-side, that would be to banish me from your presence at Whitehall; I will therefore have no private residence for myself. I only wish to dwell with you in your palaces, and the abode of my king shall also be mine."

"Well and wisely spoken, Kate," said the king. "I shall remember these words, if ever your enemies should attempt to conduct you to any other residence than the one which your king inhabits with you. The Tower you know is a residence too, Kate, but I give you my royal word that you shall never be its inmate. But you want no jewels—no palaces! Then it is the head of some individual you want me to give you?"

"Yes, sire; it is the head of an individual."

"Ah! I had guessed as much," said the king, with a laugh. "Well, then, speak, my little bloodthirsty queen. What head do you desire? Who is to lay it upon the block?"

"Sire, I certainly begged of you the head of an individual," said Katharine, with a soft, insinuating tone, "but not that such head should fall, but be exalted. I beg for the life of an individual—not indeed to destroy it, but to fill it with joy and happiness. I don't seek to cast any one into danger, but to restore a dear and beloved person to the freedom, the happiness, and splendor which are her due. You have allowed me, sire, to ask a favor for myself. Well, then, I entreat you to recall the Princess Elizabeth to your court. Let her live with us at Whitehall. Suffer her to be always near me, and to share with me my felicity and splendor. Only yesterday, sire, the Princess Elizabeth was raised far above me in rank, and if your all-ruling grace and power have elevated me above the other ladies of your realm, then I may venture to-day to love the Princess Elizabeth as my dearest friend and sister. Grant me this favor, sire. Allow the princess to live with us at Whitehall, and to share in the honors which are due to her."

The king seemed to hesitate for a moment. But his placid and smiling features indicated that the request of his young wife had not displeased him. A convulsive emotion was visible in his countenance, and for a moment his eyes were filled with tears.

A pale spectral image doubtless passed at this instant before his mind, and his retrospective glance presented to his imagination the beautiful and unhappy mother of Elizabeth, whom he had condemned to a hapless and cruel death, and yet whose last word was a blessing and a greeting of love for him.

He seized Katharine's hand with emotion, and pressed it to his lips.

"Thank you—you are unselfish and magnanimous; these are rare qualities, and I shall esteem you for them. But you are also brave and courageous; twice in one day you have besought me—for one who was condemned, and for another who had fallen into disgrace. Those who are fortunate, and who stand in my favor, have numerous friends; but I have never seen the unfortunate or banished find intercessors. But you are different from these pitiful, cringing courtiers—that fawning and trembling crowd—who fall down at my feet, and address me as if I were their Lord and Maker; different, I say, from those wretched and contemptible creatures, who call themselves my subjects, and who suffer themselves to be yoked by me, like so many beasts of burden, which are useful and subservient only because they are too brutish to know their own strength and power. Yes, Kate, believe me, I should be a more humane and benignant king, if the people whom I govern were not such abject and stupid dolts; like dogs, in fact, who only become caressing and affectionate the more we chastise them. But I am glad to find, Kate, that you are different. You knew that I had banished Elizabeth from my court, and from my heart forever, and yet you intercede for her; that is noble, and I shall love you for it, Kate, and will grant your request. And in order that you may see how much I love and trust you, I will now tell you a secret. I have already long wished to have Elizabeth near me, but I felt ashamed of this weakness of mine. I have long desired to look once more into the deep, intelligent eyes of my daughter, to be to her a kind and affectionate father, and in some measure to make amends to her for the severity which perhaps I showed her mother. For oftentimes, during sleepless nights, the beautiful face of Anne Bullen rises before me, and gazes at me with her mild, sad looks; and then my heart within me shudders at the sight. But I dare not confess this to any one, lest it should be said I have repented what I have done. A king must be infallible, like God himself, and must never acknowledge by any outward act that he is only a weak, erring mortal like other men. Wherefore I was compelled to check those feelings of paternal tenderness, which were suspected by nobody, and to appear a heartless parent, since no one would help me in this matter to become an affectionate father. Ah, those courtiers! they are so dull that they never can understand but the literal meaning of our word: of what our heart says they know nothing. But you know it, Kate; you are a woman of tact, and a generous woman to boot. Come, Kate; here is a kiss from the grateful father, and another from your husband, my charming and beautiful queen."

CHAPTER VII.

HENRY THE EIGHTH AND HIS WIVES.

THE stillness of night had now succeeded to the commotions of the day, and after so much excitement, festivity, and rejoicing, a deep repose reigned in the palace of Whitehall and throughout London. The happy subjects of King Henry might, for a few hours at least, remain undisturbed in their homes; and, under the protection of bolt and bar, might sleep and dream away the night, or else betake themselves to their devotional exercises, on account of which they had perhaps been denounced during the day. For a few hours they might yield to the sweet and blissful dream that they were free men, untrammelled in their faith and in their thoughts—for the king slept; and Gardiner, too, and the lord chancellor had closed their murder-stained, ever-watchful eyes, and rested a little from their office, as the king's myrmidons and Christian blood-hounds.

And as the king slept, so slept also the inmates of the court, and rested from the festivities of the royal wedding-day, which in pomp and splendor had far exceeded those of the five previous marriages.

Meanwhile, it seemed as though all the court officials had not followed the king's example in betaking themselves to repose. For, close to the chamber of the royal couple, one might perceive, though all the windows were shaded by rich damask curtains, that the lights were still burning, and, upon closer observation, it might be seen that a shadow fell upon the blinds from time to time.

The inmate of this chamber had not, therefore, yet gone to rest; and those must have been anxious thoughts which caused her to pace the room, to and fro, in such restless guise.

This apartment was occupied by Lady Jane Douglas, the first maid of honor to the queen. The powerful influence of Gardiner, Bishop of Winchester, had supported Katharine's wish of having once more near her the beloved friend of her earlier days; and, without suspecting it, the queen had assisted in bringing the schemes of the hypocritical bishop, directed against herself, nearer to their accomplishment.

For Katharine did not know what a change had taken place in her friend during the four years which the latter had been absent. She did not suspect how prejudicial a long residence at the strictly Catholic court of Dublin had been to the susceptible mind of her early companion, or how entirely it had changed her nature.

The once gay and lively Lady Jane had become a strict papist; who, in her fanatical zeal, thought she served God when she served the Church, and rendered unconditional obedience to her spiritual teachers.

Lady Jane had therefore—thanks to the bigotry of her instructors—become a complete dissembler.

She could smile, while in her heart she secretly brooded hatred and revenge. She could kiss the lips of the friend whose destruction she had perhaps just vowed; she could preserve an innocent and harmless mien while she observed all that was passing around her, and watched every breathing, every smile, and every motion of the eyelids.

It was accordingly a matter of great moment for Gardiner to have brought this "friend" of the queen to court, and to have made of the fair disciple of Loyola an ally and a friend.

Lady Jane Douglas was alone; and pacing the room up and down, she pondered over the incidents of the day just ended.

Now that no one observed her, she had laid aside that mild and demure mien, which she was wont to assume. Her countenance betrayed in rapid succession all the varied feelings—whether sad, serene, impetuous, or affectionate—by which she was alternately moved.

She, who had hitherto had before her eyes only the single object of serving the Church, and of consecrating her whole life to this purpose—she, whose heart had hitherto been open only to ambition and devotion, felt on this day entirely new and never-suspected feelings spring up within her.

A new sentiment had taken possession of her mind; the woman in her nature was aroused, and knocked impetuously at her heart, around which fanaticism had formed an indurated crust.

She had endeavored to collect herself by prayer, and to fill her mind so completely with thoughts of God and of the Church, that no earthly wish or desire might find a place in her heart. Yet, evermore, the noble countenance of Henry Howard would rise before her inward vision; evermore she thought she heard his earnest and melodious voice, whose magic tones made her heart beat and tremble.

At first she had struggled against this pleasing phantasy, which suggested to her such novel and singular thoughts; but at length the woman triumphed over the zealot and devotee, and sinking into a chair, she abandoned herself to her dreams and her fancy.

"Did he recognize me?" she thought to herself. "Does he still remember that, only a year since, we saw each other daily at the king's court at Dublin?"

"But no," she continued, musingly, "he has forgotten all about it. All his thoughts were then devoted to his young wife. Ah! and she was very beautiful too—as lovely as one of the Graces! But am I not beautiful also, and have not the noblest cavaliers paid me their homage, and sighed for me in vain? How comes it then that I am always overlooked when I fain would please? How comes it that the two men, of all others, whose attention I have alone coveted have never shown me the preference? I felt that I loved Henry Howard, but this love was sinful—for the Earl of Surrey was married; I therefore tore my heart away by violence and gave it to God—since the only man I could have loved did not desire me. But even heaven and devotion are insufficient to fill the heart of a woman. There was still in my bosom room for ambition, and as I could not be a happy wife, I was desirous, at least, of becoming a powerful queen. Oh! it was all so well calculated, so skilfully arranged! Gardiner had already spoken of me to the king, and inclined him to his project, and while I was hastening hither at his summons from Dublin, this creature, Katharine Parr, comes and snatches him away from me, and overthrows all our plans. But I will never forgive her for it. I shall compel her to relinquish a position which belongs to me; and if there be no other means of doing so, she shall mount the scaffold, as Katharine Howard did before her. I am resolved—I shall and will be Queen of England—I will—"

She suddenly broke off her monologue and listened. She thought she heard a gentle knock at her door.

She was not mistaken; the knock was now repeated, and in a peculiar manner, as if preconcerted.

"It is my father," said Lady Jane, and resuming once more her calm and composed mien, she proceeded to open the door.

"Ah! then you were waiting for me?" said Lord Archibald Douglas, kissing his daughter's brow.

"Yes, I was expecting you every moment," said Lady Jane, smiling. "I knew that you would come, in order to tell me the result of your experience and observation during the past day, and to give me some rules for my future conduct."

The earl reclined upon a sofa, and drew his daughter beside him.

"No one can hear us, I presume?"

"Not a soul. All my ladies sleep in the fourth room, and I have myself taken care to fasten the doors between us and them. And you know the anteroom through which you came is quite empty, so there is nothing to do but close the doors which lead to that and to the corridor, that we may be quite safe from any surprise."

And forthwith she hastened to close the doors of the anteroom.

"Now, my father, we are safe from every listener," said Lady Jane, as she returned and resumed her seat beside her father.

"But the walls, child—do you know if the walls too are safe? You look at me with doubt and surprise. Dear me, what an innocent, unsuspecting girl you are still! Have I not often given you the wise and prudent counsel to doubt every thing, and even to distrust what you see with your own eyes? Whoever would succeed at court must first of all distrust everybody, and regard him as his natural enemy—whom, however, for that very reason he must flatter, lest he might do injury; and whom he must embrace, until at length he can find a favorable opportunity of putting a dagger to his breast, or of holding poison to his lips. Believe neither men nor walls, Jane, for I tell you that both may seem ever so smooth outwardly, while there may be an ambush behind polished exteriors. But for the present I will presume that these walls are harmless and conceal no listeners. I do so because I know this room. Those were happy and delightful days when I first knew it. I was then young and handsome, and King Henry's sister was not yet married to the King of Scotland, and we loved each other so dearly! Ah, I could tell you wonderful stories of those happy days. I could—"

"But, my dear father," interrupted Lady Jane, secretly trembling at the prospect of listening once more to the oft-repeated stories of his youthful love; "surely you have not come here at this late hour to tell me what, you will pardon me for saying, I know already quite well. Rather, you were about to impart to me what your keen and experienced glance had discovered here."

"Very true," said Lord Douglas, pensively. "I know I am sometimes given to garrulity—a sure sign that I am growing old. Certainly I am not come to speak of the past, but of the present. Let us therefore talk about it. Ah, I have this day seen much and learned much, and the result of all my observations has been, that you will yet be King Henry's seventh wife."

"Impossible, my lord!" exclaimed Lady Jane, whose countenance, against her will, assumed an expression of pleasure.

Her father perceived it. "My child," said he, "let me remark to you that you have not always a perfect command of your features. At present, for instance, you are trying to play the reserved and innocent girl, and yet your face had an expression of exultant joy. But this is only *en passant*. The chief point is, that you will be King Henry's seventh wife. But in order to become so, you will have to be very watchful and observant. You must have a thorough knowledge of the present posture of affairs—you must study those around you incessantly—you must possess the art of impenetrable dissimulation; and finally, and above all, you must have an accurate and fundamental knowledge of the king's character and disposition, and of the history of his reign. Do you possess this knowledge? Do you know what it means to become Henry's seventh wife, and what should be done at the outset in order to attain that position? Have you ever studied the king's character?"

"A little, perhaps, but certainly not enough. For, as you know, my lord, worldly matters do not give me so much concern as those which relate to the Holy Church, to whose service I have devoted myself, and for which I would sacrifice my whole existence, with every faculty of my heart and soul, if the Church herself had not determined otherwise respecting me. Ah, my father, had it been permitted me to follow my own inclinations, I would have retired to a convent in Scotland, to devote myself to silent contemplation and pious penitential exercises, and so exclude every profane sound that might disturb my mind. But my wishes in this respect were not allowed; and by the mouth of His sacred and venerated priest, God has commanded me to remain in the world, and to take upon me the yoke of greatness and royal splendor. If, therefore, I use strenuous endeavors to become queen, it is not because vain pomp attracts me, but solely because the true Church would find support, through me, with the weak and vacillating king; and because I should be able to lead him back once more to the only true faith."

"Very well acted!" exclaimed her father, who, while she spoke, had been watching with a steady gaze every motion of her countenance. "Very well acted indeed! Every thing was in perfect keeping—the play of the features, the eyes, the voice, and the gestures. Daughter, I withdraw my former criticism. You have a perfect command of yourself. But let us speak of King Henry. We will now subject him to a thorough analysis, and not a fibre of his heart, nor an atom of his brain, shall we leave unscanned. We will contemplate him in his domestic, religious, and political aspects, and obtain an accurate idea of each of his peculiar characteristics, that we may be able to frame our course with him accordingly. In the first place, then, we will speak of his wives; their life and their death present excellent finger-posts for your guidance, for I won't deny that it is a difficult and a dangerous enterprise to become King Henry's wife. In order to succeed, one should have a good deal of personal courage, a cool, calculating head, and a disposition the reverse of romantic. Do you know which of all his wives possessed these qualities the most? It was his first wife, Katharine of Arragon. By Heaven! she was a prudent woman, and a born queen! Avaricious as King Henry is, he would willingly have given the brightest jewel of his crown, could he but have found in her the slightest shadow or trace of unfaithfulness. But there was absolutely no means of sending her to the scaffold, and to dispose of her by poison—why, for that, he was then too virtuous and too cowardly. He bore with her therefore until she was becoming an old woman, with her hair turning gray, and beginning to look unattractive in his eyes. Scruples of conscience suddenly changed the pious good king, and as he read in the Bible, 'Thou shalt not wed thy sister,' terrible qualms of conscience seized the noble and wily monarch. He fell upon his knees, smote his breast, and cried, 'I have committed a great sin; for I have married my brother's wife, who is my sister, but I will make atonement by undoing the criminal tie.' Do you know, child, why he wished to undo it?"

"Because he loved Anne Bullen," said Lady Jane, smiling.

"Exactly so. Katharine had become old, and the king was still a young man and his blood flowed like a fiery stream through his veins. But he was still somewhat virtuous, and the leading peculiarity of his whole character still undeveloped. As yet he was not bloodthirsty—that is to say, he had yet tasted no blood. But you will see how his thirst for blood increased with each succeeding queen, until it has now at length become a consuming disease. Had he known at that period the by-ways of falsehood and treachery, as he now does, he would have hired some slanderer who would have sworn that he had been the favored lover of Katharine. But he was still so seeming virtuous, that he wished to satisfy his amorous propensities by ostensibly lawful means. Anne Bullen must needs therefore become his wife, in order that he might be able to love her. And for the purpose of attaining this end, he threw down the gauntlet to the whole world, became the enemy of the pope, and rose in open rebellion against the sacred head of the Church. Because the Holy Father would not sanction his divorce, the king became a godless apostate. He made himself the chief of his church, and by virtue of this character, declared his marriage with Katharine of Arragon invalid. He alleged that he had not given his inward consent to such marriage, and that it was therefore incomplete. Katharine had indeed, in the Princess Mary, a living witness of the consummation of their nuptials. But what did that concern the amorous and self-willed monarch? The Princess Mary was declared illegitimate, and the queen was henceforward to be nothing more than the widow of the Prince of Wales. It was strictly forbidden to designate any longer by the title of QUEEN, the woman who for sixteen years had been Queen of England, and as such had been honored and recognized; or in any way to show her the respect due to the king's wife. No one dared call her any thing but the Princess of Wales; and in order that nothing should destroy this illusion on the part of the people, or of the noble queen herself, Katharine was banished from court, and exiled to the palace which she had once occupied as the wife of the Prince of Wales.

"I have always considered this as one of the finest and most skilful strokes of policy of our noble king, and yet, in the whole history of these divorces, he conducted himself with wonderful consistency and decision. But that shows he was incited by opposition to his will. Bear this well in mind, therefore, my dear child (and it is for this reason I have alluded so expressly to the subject): King Henry can in nowise endure a contradiction, or subject himself to any outward coercion. If you want to gain him over to any purpose, you must seek to withdraw the object: it must be surrounded with difficulties and obstacles. Show yourself accordingly prudish and indifferent; that will attract him: do not seek his glances, and he will seek yours. And when at length he declares his love, speak of your virtue and of your conscience, until eventually, to satisfy your scruples, he sends this troublesome Katharine Parr to the scaffold, or does as he did with Katharine of Arragon, and declares that he had not given his inward consent to this marriage, and that consequently Katharine is not a queen, but the widow of Lord Latimer. Ah, since he made himself the high-priest of his church there are no longer obstacles for him in such matters—for God alone is more powerful than the king.

"The beautiful Anne Bullen, Henry's second wife, is a proof of this. I have often seen her, and I tell you, Jane, she possessed wondrous beauty; whoever looked at her must love her, and those upon whom she smiled, felt as it were under an enchanted spell.

"When she presented the king with the Princess Elizabeth, I heard him say he then stood at the pinnacle of human happiness—at the goal of his wishes, for that the queen had borne him a legitimate heir to the throne. But this happiness was of brief duration.

"The king discovered one day that Anne Bullen was not the most beautiful woman in the world, but that there were still more attractive ladies at his court, and who therefore seemed to have a better claim to be Queen of England. He had seen Jane Seymour, and Jane was unquestionably more beautiful than Anne Bullen,—for she was not yet the king's wife, and an obstacle to possessing her intervened in the person of Anne Bullen.

"This obstacle must of course be set aside. Henry could now, by virtue of his omnipotence, have caused himself once more to be separated from his wife, but he was unwilling to repeat himself: he wished to be always original; and nobody should dare to say, that his divorces were only the cloak for his capricious and amatory impulses.

"It was on the ground of conscientious scruples that he got himself separated from Katharine of Arragon—but a different plan had to be invented for dealing with Anne Bullen.

"The shortest way of getting rid of her was the scaffold. Why should not Anne travel the same path that so many others had done before her? For a new era had commenced in the king's life. The tiger had licked blood; his instincts were aroused, and he no longer shrank back from the crimson rivulets which flowed through the veins of his subjects. He had bestowed a royal purple robe on Anne Bullen, and why should she not in return, yield him up her crimson life-blood? For this there was only a pretext wanting, and that was soon found. Lady Rochford was Jane Seymour's aunt; and she succeeded in finding some individuals who, she maintained, had been the lovers of the beautiful Anne Bullen. As first lady of the bed-chamber to the queen, Lady Rochford could certainly furnish the most plausible explanations upon such a subject, and the king believed her. He believed her, although the four pretended lovers of the queen, who were executed for the alleged crime, protested on the scaffold, with one exception, that Anne Bullen was innocent, and that they had never even approached her. The only one who accused the queen of an illicit correspondence with him, was a musician, named James Smeaton. But for this confession he had been promised his life. Meanwhile they did not deem it advisable to keep this promise, for they feared that if confronted with the queen, he might not have the hardihood to support his assertion. In order, however, not to appear wholly ungrateful for this useful confession, they extended to him the favor of not being executed by the axe, but he was granted the easier and more ignoble death of being hanged.

"The lovely and beautiful Anne Bullen had, therefore, to lay her head upon the block. On the day of her execution the king had commanded a large hunting-party, and in the morning we rode forth toward Epping Forest. The king was at first unusually cheerful and jocose, and he commanded me to ride beside him and relate the current gossip and court scandal. He laughed at my malicious anecdotes, and the more I defamed my fellow-courtiers the more was his mirth increased. At length we halted. The king had laughed and talked so much that he became hungry at last. He reclined under the shade of an oak, and, in the midst of his retinue and of his dogs, he partook of breakfast with wonderful zest and appetite—albeit he had now become somewhat more silent and reserved, and looked from time to time in the direction of London, with visible anxiety and uneasiness in his countenance. Suddenly, however, was heard the dull boom of a cannon. We all knew that this was the signal which was to announce to the king that Anne Bullen's head had fallen. We knew it, and a cold shudder ran through our veins. The king alone smiled; and standing up and taking his hunting accoutrements from my hands, he said, with a serene countenance: 'It is over! The work is done. Unleash the dogs, and let us follow the chase.'

"That," said Lord Douglas, with sadness, "was the funeral discourse which the king uttered concerning his lovely and innocent wife."

"Do you pity her, my lord?" asked Lady Jane, with surprise. "If I mistake not, Anne Bullen was an enemy of our Church, and an adherent of the detestable new doctrines."

Her father shrugged his shoulders with an air of contempt. "That did not prevent Queen Anne from belonging to the fairest and most charming women of England. And besides, however much she may have inclined to the new doctrines, she did us one essential service at least, for it was she who caused the death of Sir Thomas More. She hated him because he did not favor her marriage with the king, and so did the king likewise for his refusing to take the oath of supremacy. Nevertheless, Henry would have spared him—for at that time he still had some respect for learning and virtue, and Sir Thomas was so learned a man that he won the king's good graces. But Anne Bullen desired his death, and accordingly he had to mount the scaffold. Ah, believe me, Jane, it was a glorious, though a melancholy hour for all England, that hour when the head of Sir Thomas More was laid on the block. But we happy courtiers of Whitehall Palace—we alone were cheerful and merry on the occasion. We danced a new dance, the music of which the king himself had composed; for you know the king is not only an author, but also a musical amateur, and as he now writes pious books, so he then composed dance-music. Every evening when we had danced ourselves tired, we sat down to the card-table. And just as I had won a few guineas from the king, the governor of the Tower arrived with intelligence that the execution had taken place, and gave us an account of the last moments of the great scholar. The king threw down his cards, and, casting an angry glance at Anne Bullen, said with a tremulous voice, 'You are guilty of the death of this man.' He then rose up, and retired to his apartments, whither no one dared to follow him—not even the queen. You see, then, that Anne Bullen has a claim to our gratitude, for the death of Sir Thomas More delivered England from another great danger. Melancthon and Bucer, and with them some of the greatest pulpit orators of Germany, had set out on their journey to London, as delegates from the Protestant princes of Germany, to nominate the king as the chief of their league. But the fearful news of the execution ot their friend drove them back in terror, after they had accomplished half their journey.

"Peace, therefore, to the ashes of the unhappy Anne Bullen, who has meanwhile been avenged—avenged upon her rival and successor, on whose account she had to mount the scaffold—avenged on Jane Seymour!"

"But she was the king's favorite wife," said Lady Jane, "and when she died he mourned for her two whole years."

"Yes, he mourned," said Lord Douglas, with a sneer. "He mourned for all his wives. Even for Anne Bullen he put on a mourning suit, and in his white mourning robes he led Jane Seymour to the nuptial altar two days after the execution of Anne Bullen. What signifies outward mourning? Did not Anne Bullen mourn in like manner for Katharine of Arragon, whom she had driven from the throne. For eight weeks she wore weeds for Henry's first wife; but Anne was a prudent woman, and she knew that yellow robes became her admirably."

"But the king mourned for Jane Seymour not only outwardly, but in reality," said Lady Jane, "for it was only after the lapse of two years that he resolved upon a new marriage."

Lord Douglas laughed. "But during these two years of widowhood he was consoled in some measure, by having fallen in love with the beautiful Marguerite de Montreuil, a French lady, and he would have married her too, had her prudence not been as great as her beauty; and so she preferred returning to France, rather than accept the perilous distinction of becoming Henry's fourth queen."

"But yet, my father, the case of Jane Seymour was very natural, for she died in childbed."

"Ay, truly in childbed, and yet not a natural death, for she might have been saved. But Henry would not have it so. His love had already cooled down; and when the physicians asked if they should save the mother or the child, he replied, 'Save the child by all means; I can get wives enough.'

"Ah, my daughter, I hope you may not die such a natural death as poor Jane Seymour, for whom, as you say, the king mourned for two years. But, after this, the king met with quite a novel and extraordinary adventure. In short, he fell in love with a picture; and as, in his lofty self-complacency, he felt persuaded that the beautiful portrait of himself which Holbein had painted, did not at all flatter him, but was quite true to nature, he never suspected that Holbein's likeness of the Princess Anne of Cleves could have been flattered or incorrect. The king accordingly became enamoured of a portrait, and sent his envoys to Germany, in order to bring over the fair original of this picture to England for his wife. He even went forward himself to meet her at Rochester. Ah, Jane! I have seen many strange and ridiculous things in the course of my life, but that scene at Rochester must be reckoned as the most piquant of all my reminiscences. The king was glowing with more than poetic inspiration, and as madly in love as a boy of twenty, and thus began our romantic bridal excursion, in which Henry appeared incognito, as my cousin. To me was given the flattering commission, as master of the horse, to convey to the young queen the greetings of her ardent bridegroom, and to beg of her to receive the cavalier who should hand her a present from the king. She granted my request with a simpering smile, which disclosed to view a fearful set of yellow teeth. I opened the door, and allowed the king to enter. Ah, you should have witnessed that scene! It was the only bit of farce in the bloody tragedy of Henry's matrimonial career. You should have seen with what hasty impatience Henry rushed in, and then suddenly, on seeing her, staggered back, and stared at the princess; and then slowly retreating, put the costly gift which he had brought with him into my hand, without uttering a word, but casting a look of intense anger at Cromwell, who had brought him the portrait of the princess, and had led him into this marriage. The romantic and ardent lover vanished after this first glance at his fair bride. He approached the princess again, but on this occasion in his own character, and in a harsh and hasty manner said he himself was the king. He bade her welcome in a few words, and bestowed upon her a cold and formal greeting. Then, however, he suddenly took my hand and drew me away with him, while he made a signal to the others to follow; and when at length we got out of the atmosphere of this poor unprepossessing princess, and were some distance away, the king turned with an angry countenance to Cromwell, and said: 'Is that what you call beauty? I call her a Flemish mare, but not a princess.'

"Anne's plain face, I doubt not, was bestowed upon her by God, in order that the only true Church should be delivered from the danger which threatened it. For had Anne of Cleves—the sister, niece, aunt, and grand-daughter of all the German Protestant princes—had she, I say, been handsome, our church would have been threatened by dangers beyond conception. The king could not overcome his dislike, and once more his conscience, which always appeared most tender and scrupulous when it was most lax and irregular, must needs come to his aid.

"Accordingly, the king declared that he had only outwardly, and not in his inward conscience, consented to this marriage, from which he was now shrinking back; as it would, he alleged, be in reality nothing less than a breach of faith—a perjury and a bigamy. For had not Anne's father once already betrothed her to the son of the Duke of Lorraine? had he not pledged his solemn word that he would give him his daughter to wed when he should have attained his majority? Rings had already been exchanged, and the marriage contract already drawn up. Anne of Cleves therefore was really married already, and accordingly Henry, with his tender conscience, could not make the betrothed lady his wife. He therefore made her his sister, and gave her the palace at Richmond for a residence, if she wished to remain in England. She accepted it: her blood, which ran coldly and sluggishly through her veins, did not revolt at the thought of being rejected and contemned. She accepted the offer, and remained in England.

"Anne of Cleves was rejected because she was plain, and now the king chose Katharine Howard for his fifth wife because she was handsome. Of this marriage I can tell you but little, for at that time I had already been sent on a diplomatic mission to Dublin, whither you soon followed me. Katharine was very beautiful, and the king's heart, already feeling the effect of time, was once more inflamed with the fire of youthful love. He loved her more ardently than any of his former wives, and he was so happy in her society, that he publicly knelt down in church and thanked God for the felicity which he enjoyed with his beautiful young queen. But that did not last long; for at the very moment that the king was proclaiming his wedded bliss, he had already reached its culminating point, and the next day he was hurled from this pinnacle into the abyss. I speak without poetical exaggeration, my dear child; the previous day, he thanked God for his happiness, and on the morrow, Katharine Howard was already under confinement and accused of being a faithless wife and a shameless profligate. More than seven lovers had already preceded her spouse, and some of them had even accompanied her on the royal progress which she made in the north with her husband. On this occasion it was no pretext, for Henry had not yet had time to grow enamoured of any other woman, and Katharine had well understood how to attach him to her, and always to kindle fresh ardor in his breast. But for the very reason that he loved her, he could not pardon her for having deceived him. So much cruelty and hatred is there in love; and Henry, who only yesterday lay like a lamb at her feet, was to-day as excited with jealousy and rage as he had yesterday been with rapture and delight. Still in his anger he loved her, and when he held in his hands the unequivocal proofs of her guilt, he wept like a child. But as he could no longer be her lover, he resolved to be her executioner. As she had polluted the purple of his royal robes, he wished to dye them afresh in the crimson of her blood; and he did it. Katharine Howard was compelled to lay her beautiful head upon the block, as Anne Bullen had done before her, and the death of the latter was now once more avenged. Lady Rochford had been the accuser of Anne Bullen, and it was her testimony which brought that queen to the scaffold; but now she was herself convicted of having been privy and accessory to Katharine Howard's love-intrigues, and with Katharine's head fell also that of Lady Rochford, under the executioner's axe.

"Ah! it required a long time to recover the king from this blow; for the space of two years he sought for the pure and blameless virgin who could become his wife, without peril of the scaffold. But he found none, and so he took to himself Katharine Parr, the widow of Lord Latimer. But you know, my child, the name of Katharine is one of evil omen for Henry's wives. The first Katharine was put away—the second beheaded—what will be the fate of the third?"

Lady Jane smiled.

"Katharine does not love the king," she said, "and I believe she would willingly consent, like Anne of Cleves, to become the sister of Henry instead of his wife."

"What! Katharine not love the king?" asked Lord Douglas, with breathless eagerness. "Does she love another, then?"

"No, my lord. Her heart is still like a sheet of blank paper—for as yet no name is inscribed thereon."

"Then it will be our task to write a name upon it, and this name must send her to the block, or else cause her to be put aside," said Lord Douglas, with vehemence. "It will be your business, Jane, to write, with a pen of iron, some name or other so legibly on her heart that the king may be able to read it at some future day."

CHAPTER VIII.

FATHER AND DAUGHTER.

Both were now silent for some time. Lord Douglas had leaned back in his seat, and, breathing fast, seemed to recover himself a little from the effect of long speaking. But while he thus rested, his large, piercing eyes were unceasingly fixed upon Lady Jane, who had reclined on the ottoman, and looking with a meditative air of abstraction, seemed to have forgotten her father's presence.

An arch smile played for a moment upon the features of the earl, on perceiving the abstracted gaze of his daughter; but it speedily vanished, and then his brow became marked with lines of deep thought.

Seeing that his daughter was still wrapt in visionary dreams, he at length laid his hand upon her shoulder, and said, hastily, "What are you thinking of, Jane?"

She started violently, and looked at the earl with an air of confusion.

"I was thinking of all you had said to me, my father," she replied. "I was considering what advantage I could derive from it for our purpose."

Lord Douglas shook his head with an incredulous smile: "Take care, Jane," said he, at length, in a grave tone—"take care that your heart does not belie your head! If we are to attain our object in this matter, you must, above all things, keep your head and your heart cool. Do you think you possess both already?"

She cast down her eyes with visible embarrassment before the penetrating glance of Lord Douglas. He perceived it, and a hasty word rose to his lips, but he checked it. As a prudent diplomatist, he knew that it is sometimes more advisable to destroy a thing by ignoring it, than to enter into an open contest upon its merits.

The feelings are like the dragon's teeth of Theseus. When we overcome them they always grow afresh, and spring from the ground with increased vigor.

Lord Douglas was, therefore, careful not to remark his daughter's confusion. "Pardon me, Jane," he said, "if, in my zeal and my tender regard for you, I have gone too far. I know that your dear and beautiful head is cool enough to bear the crown; I know that in your heart dwell ambition and religion alone. Let us therefore consider what further we have to do in order to accomplish our purpose. We have already spoken of Henry as a husband and as a man, and I trust you have drawn some useful lessons from the fate of his wives. You have seen that a wife must possess all the good and all the bad qualities of a woman, in order to be able to rule this stiff-necked tyrant—this voluptuous—this vain, and sensual man. But, above all things, you must have a perfect knowledge of the art of coquetry. You must be a female Proteus. To-day, a Messalina—to-morrow, a devotee—the next day, a learned woman—and the day after, a toying girl; you must always seek to take the king by surprise—to keep his mind on the strain, and make him cheerful. You must never abandon yourself to the dangerous feeling of security, for, in fact, Henry's wife is never safe; the axe hangs continually above her head:—so that you must always regard your husband only as a capricious lover, whom you have each day to win anew."

"You speak, my father, as if I were already the wife of the king," said Lady Jane, smiling; "and yet it seems to me that there are still many difficulties to overcome before I reach that point;

difficulties which are perhaps insurmountable."

"Insurmountable?" said Lord Douglas, with a shrug. "With the aid of Holy Church there are no obstacles insurmountable; we have only to be quite sure beforehand of our object, and of the means to its attainment. Do not, therefore, disdain to probe the king's character again and again, and you may be certain you will always discover in it some new feature—some striking peculiarity. We have spoken of him as a husband and family man, but of his religious and political characteristics I have said nothing; and these it is which constitute the essence of his whole being.

"First of all then, Jane, I will tell you a secret. The king, who has made himself the chief priest of his church—whom the pope once called the champion and defender of the faith—the king, I say, has in his heart no religion whatever. He is merely a pliant reed, swayed to and fro by the wind. He does not himself know what he wishes; and dallying with both sides, he is to-day a heretic, in order to make it appear that he is a strong-minded, free-thinking man, of enlightened reason—to-morrow a Catholic, in order to exhibit himself as the obedient and humble servant of God, who only seeks for salvation through works of love and piety. But in his inmost soul, he has an equal indifference for both creeds; and had the pope formerly thrown no difficulties in his way—had he favored his divorce from Katharine, King Henry would still have continued a faithful and active member of the Catholic Church. But his holiness was so imprudent as to excite him by contradiction; Henry's pride and vanity were stung, until he revolted, and so he became a church reformer—not from conviction—but from a pure love of opposition. And this, my daughter, you must never forget, for by means of this lever you may once more convert him to be a strict, dutiful, and obedient son of the Holy Church. He has broken off with the pope, and has assumed the supremacy of the Church, but he could not find in himself the courage to carry out his work, and throw himself altogether into the arms of the Reformation. Though he opposed the papal authority, yet he has ever remained true to the Church—albeit perhaps he does not know it himself. He is a Catholic, and hears the mass; he has abolished the monasteries, and yet forbidden the priests to marry; he allows the Eucharist to be administered in one kind, and believes in transubstantiation. He abolishes monasteries, but still enjoins that the vows of celibacy, as well of monks as of nuns, shall be strictly maintained; and, finally, auricular confession is a very necessary part of his church. And that is what he calls his Six Articles, as the basis of his 'English Church.' Poor, vain, and short-sighted man! He knows not that he has done all this, only because he wished to make himself pope, while he is nothing more than the anti-pope of the Holy Father, whom he dares with scandalous effrontery to call the 'Bishop of Rome.'"

"But for this audacity," said Lady

Jane, with looks of vindictive triumph, "the anathema has smitten him and cursed his head, and has given him up to the scorn and contempt of his own subjects. For this the Holy Father justly denounces him as an apostate and abandoned son—the blasphemous usurper of the Holy Church. Therefore has the pope declared his crown forfeit, and has awarded it to any one that shall acquire it by force of arms. Therefore has the pope forbidden his subjects to obey him, or to honor and recognize him as their king."

"And yet he continues King of England, and his subjects obey him with slavish submission," exclaimed Lord Douglas, with a shrug. "It was rather unwise to carry threats so far; for one should never threaten unless he is prepared to carry his threats into execution. Unfortunately, the papal anathema has served the king more than it has injured him, for it has driven him to assume a more fierce opposition, and has proved to his subjects that he may be stricken by the ban of excommunication, and yet live happily in the full enjoyment of life.

"No; the anathemas of Rome have in nowise hurt the king, nor has his throne suffered the slightest shock; but the defection of the king has deprived the Holy See of a powerful support; and therefore we must lead the faithless monarch back once more to the Holy Church. And that is the task, my daughter, which God and the will of His sacred vicar commit to your hands—an excellent, a glorious, and a meritorious work, for it will make you a queen. But I repeat it, be cautious, and never rouse the king by opposition to his wishes. This vacillating man must be led unconsciously to that point which his salvation demands; for, as I have said, he is a vacillator, and in the haughty pride of his kingship he presumes to overrule all parties, and establish a new church for himself—a church which is neither Catholic nor Protestant, but his church—the laws of which are found in the Six Articles, or in the so-called 'Bloody Statute.'

"He will neither be a Catholic nor a Protestant, and in order to show his impartiality, he is an equally dreaded partisan of both sides. Thus it has come to pass that, in England, he hangs those who are Catholics, and burns those who are not. It affords the king pleasure to hold, with firm and relentless grasp, the balance between both parties, and on the same day on which he throws a papist into a dungeon for having questioned the royal supremacy, he puts a reformer on the rack for having denied transubstantiation—or for having perhaps rejected the doctrine of auricular confession. Even during the last session of Parliament five persons were hanged for having called the supremacy in question; and five others burned for having adhered to the principles of the reformers. And on this very evening, Jane—the evening of the king's wedding-day—both Catholics and Protestants, coupled two by two, like dogs, have been sent to the stake, at the special command of his majesty, who, as head of the Church, wished to show his impartiality—the Catholics being condemned as traitors, and the others as heretics."

"Oh," exclaimed Lady Jane, shuddering and turning pale, "I won't be Queen of England. I have a horror of such a cruel and ferocious king, whose heart knows neither pity nor mercy."

Her father laughed.

"Don't you know, then, child, how a hyena may be rendered harmless, and a tiger tamed? Why, we generally throw them some food that they can swallow, and as they love blood so much, we give them blood to drink, so that they may never have to thirst for it. The king's only constant and unchanging peculiarity is his cruelty and blood-craving—so that we must always have some food of this kind ready for him, and then he will always be a very gracious king and amiable husband.

"And there is no lack of objects to satisfy his appetite in this respect. There are so many men and women at his court; and when he is in his bloodthirsty humor, it makes no difference to Henry whose blood he swallows. He has shed the blood of his wives and relatives, he has sent to the scaffold those whom he called his most trusty friends, and he has sent the most worthy man in his realm to the block.

"Sir Thomas More knew him well, and in a single striking sentence he summed up the king's whole character. Ah, Jane, it seems to me as if I saw the mild, serene countenance of that sage, as I saw him standing in that embrasure of the window, and the king beside him with his arm on the shoulder of the Chancellor More, listening to his discourse with a kind of reverential devotion. And when the king had departed, I approached Sir Thomas, and wished him joy at the great favor, publicly recognized, which he possessed with the king. 'The king loves you most sincerely,' I observed. 'Yes,' he replied, with his sad, quiet smile, 'yes, the king loves me truly; but that would not for a moment prevent him from sacrificing my head for a costly jewel, a beautiful woman, or a square mile of territory in France.'

"He was right, and it was for a beautiful woman that the head of that great philosopher was made to fall—of whom the most Christian emperor, Charles the Fifth, said: 'Had I been the master of such a servant, of whose great powers and abilities I have myself had so much experience for many years—had I possessed so wise and firm a counsellor as Sir Thomas More, I would rather have lost the fairest city in my dominions than so worthy a statesman and servant.' Ay, Jane, that must be your first and holiest law, never to trust the king, and never to reckon upon the continuance of his affection or the marks of his favor. For, in the perfidy of his heart, it often pleases him to shower favors upon them whose ruin he has already resolved, and to deck with honors and orders to-day those whom to-morrow he has doomed to die. It flatters his self-love, like the tiger, to play for a while with the whelpling which he is about to rend. This he did with

Cromwell, the counsellor and friend of many years, who, moreover, had committed no other crime than that he had first shown the king the portrait of the unattractive Anne of Cleves, which Holbein had flattered to an uncommon extent. But the king was careful not to be angry with Cromwell thereat, nor to reproach him. On the contrary, he raised him, in recognition of his great merits, to the dignity of Earl of Essex; decorated him with the order of the Garter, and appointed him lord high chamberlain; and then only, when Cromwell felt himself quite safe, and basked in the sunshine of royal favor—then it was that the king had him seized and flung into the Tower on a charge of high-treason. And so Cromwell was executed because Anne of Cleves did not please the king, and because Hans Holbein's portrait had flattered her.

"But now we have said enough of the past, Jane; let us therefore speak of the present and of the future. Let us now bethink us of the means of overthrowing this woman who stands in our way. When once her downfall is accomplished, it will not be difficult for us to put you in her place; for now you are here in the king's vicinity. That was the great drawback to our previous endeavors, that we were not on the spot; and that we could only work through intermediators and confidants. The king had not seen you; and since the unhappy affair of Anne of Cleves, he distrusted portraits. I knew that very well, for I trust no one, Jane—not even my most faithful and dearest friend. I build upon no one but ourselves. Had we been here, you would already have been in the place of Katharine Parr,—you would have been Queen of England. But to our misfortune, I was still a favorite of the Regent of Scotland, and, a such, I durst not venture to come near Henry. It was necessary that I should fall into disgrace in the north, in order to become more certain of the king's favor here.

"Having, then, fallen into disgrace, I fled hither, and now that we are here let the contest begin. You have already this day taken a long stride toward the goal; you have drawn the king's attention upon you, and fixed yourself more firmly in Katharine's favor. I must confess, Jane, that I have been enchanted with your discreet behavior. You have to-day gained the good-will of all parties, and it was admirably prudent of you to come to the aid of the Earl of Surrey, while at the same time you won over the heretical court party, to which Maria Askew belongs. Yes, Jane, that was a clever stroke of policy; for the Howard family is the greatest and most powerful at court; and Henry, Earl of Surrey, is one of its most powerful representatives. We have, therefore, already a strong party at court—a party which has before its eyes only the high and sacred object of assisting Holy Church once more to regain the victory, and which works quietly and silently to reconcile the king with the pope. Henry Howard is like his father, the Duke of Norfolk,—a good Catholic, as in like manner was his niece,

Katharine Howard,—only that she, while devoted to God and the Church, was at the same time too earnest an admirer of the opposite sex to her own. That was what procured the victory for the other side, and which caused the Catholics once more to succumb to the heretical court party. Yes, for the moment, Cranmer has conquered us with Katharine Parr; but Gardiner, with the aid of Jane Douglas, will soon overcome the heretics, and send them to the scaffold. That is our plan, and with God's grace we shall bring it about."

"But it will be a difficult task," said Lady Jane, with a sigh. "The queen is a pure, unsullied woman, and she has besides a wise head and a keen perception. In her thoughts too she is innocence itself, and shrinks with virgin timidity from the very thought of sin."

"She must be weaned from this timidity, Jane, and that will be your task. You must expel all these strict notions of virtue from her mind; you must seek, by insinuating ways, to ensnare her heart, and seduce it from such rigid and scrupulous principles."

"Oh, that would be an infernal scheme!" exclaimed Lady Jane, turning pale. "That would be a crime, my father; for it would be not only to destroy her earthly happiness, but also to endanger her soul. That I should beguile her to sin and crime is surely not your odious request? If so, I will not obey you! It is true I hate her, for she stands in the way of my ambition; it is true I am willing to ruin her, for she wears the crown which I wish to possess: but I will never do any thing so infamous as to pour into her heart the poison by which she is to fall. Let her seek the deadly draught herself—I will not restrain her hand, I shall not warn her. Let her find the paths of sin if she will—I shall not tell her she is going astray; nay, I will watch all her movements, and listen to every word and every sigh that escapes her; and when she has committed herself by a false step, then I shall betray her, and give her up to her judges. That is what I can and will do. I shall be the evil genius, who in God's name will expel her from Paradise; but not the serpent who in the name of Satan would allure her to sin."

She ceased, and, panting for breath, leaned back in her chair; but now her father's hand was laid upon her shoulder with a convulsive grasp, and with eyes flashing with anger, and his face pale with rage, he looked at her with a fixed and stern gaze.

Lady Jane uttered a cry of terror. She, who had never seen her father but in a smiling and cordial mood, scarcely recognized the features now changed by anger. She could hardly convince herself that this man, with fire-flashing eyes and knitted brows, and lips quivering with passion, was really her father.

"You will not!" he exclaimed, in a deep, threatening tone. "Do you dare to resist the sacred behests of the Church? Or have you forgotten the promise you made to the holy fathers, whose disciple you are? Have you forgotten that the brethren and sisters of the holy league dare have no other will than that of their superior? Have you forgotten the solemn vow which you made to Ignatius Loyola, the chief of our order? Answer me, faithless and undutiful daughter of the Church! Repeat to me the oath which you took when he received you into the sacred order of the Society of Jesus! Repeat your oath, I say!"

As if impelled by an invisible power, Lady Jane had now risen from her seat, and with trembling humility, and with her hands folded across her breast, she stood before her father, whose tall, commanding, and angry form seemed to tower above her.

"I have sworn," she replied, "to subject my own mind and will, my life and all my actions, dutifully to the will of the holy fathers. I have sworn to be a blind instrument in the hands of my superiors, and to do only what they command or enjoin. I have promised to serve the holy and only saving Church, and to submit myself to its directions in every respect, and by every means; none of which I am to despise, or consider too trifling, provided it conduces to the end in view. For the end sanctifies the means, and nothing is a crime when done for the honor of God and of His Church."

"*Ad majorem Dei gloriam!*" said her father, devoutly folding his hands. "And do you know what awaits you if you break your vow?"

"Yes—disgrace here, and perdition hereafter—the execration of all my brethren and sisters—eternal reprobation and the pains of hell! The holy fathers will put me to death under numberless pains and tortures; and while they kill my body, and fling it for food to beasts of prey, they will curse my soul and deliver it to the flames!"

"And what awaits you if you remain true to your word, and obey the commands which you shall receive?"

"Honor and glory upon earth, and everlasting bliss in heaven!"

"Then you will be a queen on earth and a queen in heaven. Of course you know the laws of the society, and remember your oath?"

"I do."

"And you know that the blessed Loyola, before he left us, appointed a general superior for the Society of Jesus in England, which superior all the brethren and sisters must obey, and to whom they are bound to render blind and unconditional submission?"

"I know it."

"And you know also by what sign the members are enabled to recognize the general superior?"

"Yes, by the ring of Loyola, which he wears on the forefinger of his right hand."

"And here you behold the ring," said the earl, drawing forth his hand from his doublet.

Lady Jane uttered a loud cry, and fell almost unconscious at his feet.

Lord Douglas raised her up in his arms with a tender smile.

"You see, Jane, I am not only your father, but also your master. And you will obey me, will you not?"

"Yes, I shall obey you," she replied, in a faint voice, while she kissed the hand bearing the ominous ring.

"Then you will be for Katharine Parr, as you express it, the serpent that shall beguile her to sin?"

"I will."

"You will seduce her to sin, and allure her to a love which shall lead to her ruin?"

"Yes. I will do so, my father."

"I must now designate to you the person whom she shall love, and who shall be the instrument of her destruction. You are to lead her on to become enamoured of Henry Howard, Earl of Surrey."

Lady Jane uttered a loud cry, and seized the back of her chair to support her from falling.

Her father once more scanned her with an angry and penetrating glance.

"What means this cry? Why does the selection surprise you?" he asked.

Lady Jane had already recovered her self-possession. "It surprises me," she replied, "because the earl is already married."

A peculiar smile played around the lips of the earl. "It is not the first time," he said, "that a married man has become dangerous to a woman's heart, and it is just the impossibility of possession which has given fresh impulse to the flames of love. The hearts of women are full of caprice and contradiction."

Lady Jane looked away and did not reply; she felt that the keen and piercing glance of her father rested upon her features, and she knew that he was reading the thoughts of her heart, even though she did not return his gaze.

"Then you will no longer refuse?" he asked, at length. "You will inspire the young queen with love for the Earl of Surrey?"

"I will try to do so, my father."

"Then if you try with the proper intention, and with the will to succeed, you will gain your point. For, as you say, the queen's heart is still free; it is therefore like a fertile soil, which only requires the seed to be sown therein, that it may yield fruit and flowers. Katharine Parr does not love the king: you will therefore teach her to love the Earl of Surrey."

"But, my lord," said Lady Jane, with an ironical smile, "in order to attain this result with certainty, we should possess beforehand some magic spell, by virtue of which the earl should first be inspired with a passion for the queen. For the queen has a proud spirit, and she will never so far forget the dignity of her sex and station, as to love a man who has not already become deeply enamoured of her. But the earl possesses not only a wife, but also, it is said, a mistress."

"Ah, then you hold it as perfectly unworthy of a woman to love a man by whom she is not besought?" asked the earl, in a significant tone. "I am rejoiced to hear this from my daughter, and to be assured that *she*, at least, will not fall in love with the Earl of Surrey, who is everywhere known as the 'Lady-Killer.' And as you have taken the pains to become accurately informed of the private relationships of the earl, it was doubtless only because your acute and discerning mind had already anticipated the commission which I intended to give you respecting that nobleman. Moreover, daughter, you are in error; and if a certain high, but, nevertheless, unfortunate lady should haply fall in love with the Earl of Surrey, her fate will here be, as perhaps it is elsewhere, to exercise resignation."

While her father thus spoke, an expression of joyful surprise shone upon the features of Lady Jane; but it soon gave way to a ghastly paleness, as the earl added: "Henry Howard is destined for Katharine Parr, and you must help her to love this proud and handsome earl (who is a faithful servant of Holy Church) so ardently that she shall forget all the dangers and consequences of such a step."

Lady Jane did not venture an objection. She hung eagerly upon her father's words, in order once more to find means of escape.

"You say the earl is a true servant of our Church," she observed; "and yet you wish to implicate him in our dangerous plans. You have not, therefore, reflected that it is just as perilous to love the queen as to be loved by her. And if, peradventure, love for the Earl of Surrey should lead the queen to the scaffold, it will also cause the head of the earl to fall at the same time, whether he returns her love or not."

Lord Douglas shrugged his shoulders.

"If the good of the Church and our holy religion is concerned, we must not shrink from the danger which perchance one of our party may incur. To a holy cause, holy victims must frequently fall a sacrifice. Let therefore the earl's head be forfeit, provided the Church can but gain new life and energy from the martyr's blood. But see, Jane, the morning is already beginning to dawn, and I must hasten to leave you, lest these scandal-loving courtiers should regard the father as a lover, and throw suspicion on the pure virtue of my excellent daughter. Farewell, therefore, for the present. We both know our parts now, and we will endeavor to play them successfully. You are the confidential friend of the queen, while I am the harmless courtier who now and then attempts to win a smile from his king by some jocose pleasantry. That is all. Good-morning then, Jane, and good-night. For you must sleep, my child, lest your cheeks should lose their bloom, or your eyes their brightness. The king detests pale, languishing faces. Sleep, therefore, future Queen of England!"

He kissed her brow faintly, and left the room with a stealthy pace.

Lady Jane listened till the sound of his footsteps was lost; and then, exhausted and overcome, she sank upon her knees.

"Wretched one that I am!" she murmured, while streams of tears bathed her countenance. "I am to inspire the queen with love for the Earl of Surrey, at the same time that—I love him myself!"

CHAPTER IX.

THE NEXT DAY.

The grand drawing-room was over. Katharine, sitting on the throne beside the king, had received the congratulations of her court; and the smiling glances of the king, and the half-audible words of affection, which he now and then addressed to the queen, testified to the acute and quick-witted courtiers that the king was to-day as enamoured of his young wife as he had yesterday been of his bride. They accordingly vied with each other, to show their homage to her majesty, and to catch every look and smile which she bestowed on those around her, that they might thus perchance discover the future favorites of the queen, and already sue for their good graces.

But the eyes of the young queen were directed to no one in particular; she was cordial and smiling, but her courtiers felt that this cordiality was strained, and that her smile was tinged with sadness. The king alone did not observe it. He was cheerful and happy, and it therefore seemed to him that no one at his court could dare to sigh or feel weary—as the king himself was satisfied.

After the drawing-room was over—at which all the great and noble of the kingdom had passed in solemn procession before the royal pair, the king, conformably with the court etiquette of the time, gave his hand to his spouse, and assisting her to descend from the throne, led her into the midst of the saloon, in order to present to her the members of the court who were to form the staff on her service.

But this journey from the throne to the middle of the room had fatigued the king. This promenade of thirty paces was for him a very unusual and laborious task, and the king was anxious to exchange it for another and a more agreeable one. He therefore beckoned to the lord chamberlain, and commanded him to have the doors leading to the dining-room thrown open; he then ordered his "house chariot" to be brought forward, and sitting upright therein with all possible dignity, he caused it to stand beside the queen, waiting impatiently for the ceremony of presentation to be over, that Katharine might accompany him to dinner.

Already the presentation of the female portion and the maids of honor was ended, and now came the turn of the gentlemen.

The lord chamberlain read aloud from his list the names of those cavaliers who were for the future to attend upon the queen, and whom the king had designated in the list with his own hand. And as each new name was announced, an expression of smiling astonishment marked the faces of the courtly assemblage; for it was always one of the youngest and handsomest, and most agreeable of the lords, that was successively named by the chamberlain.

The king had perhaps contemplated a cruel game with his wife: in surrounding her with the young men of his court, he wished perhaps to throw her into the midst of danger, either that she might perish therein, or that, avoiding the snares around her, he might be able to place the unassailable virtue of his young wife in the clearest light.

The list had commenced with the subordinate offices, and, going upward, it had now reached the highest and most important posts of all.

As yet the master of the horse, and the queen's chamberlain, were not named, and these were doubtless the most weighty changes at the queen's court; for one or other of these officers was always bound to be in attendance upon the queen. When she was in the palace, the lord chamberlain must always wait in her anteroom; for it was only through him that any one could gain access to the queen; to him were committed her commands respecting the arrangements and pleasures of the day. He must therefore devise new modes of amusement and royal diversion; he had the privilege of joining the more private evening circles of the queen, and of standing behind the queen's chair, when the royal couple wished to sup together without ceremony.

This office of chamberlain was therefore a very important one; for as it confined him to the vicinity of the queen for the greater part of the day, it was almost inevitable that the chamberlain should become either the attentive and confidential friend, or the malevolent and prying enemy, of his royal mistress.

But the office of master of the horse was no less important; for whenever the queen left the palace, whether on foot or in her carriage, whether to take a ride in the forest, or to enjoy the air on the river in her gilded barge, the master of the horse had always to be at her side, had always to accompany her,—nay, this post was yet more exclusive, yet more important. For though the apartments of the queen were always open to the chamberlain, still he was never alone with her, as there was always some lady in waiting, who would hinder any private or confidential communication between the queen and her chamberlain.

It was otherwise, however, with the master of the horse. Many occasions were presented when he could approach the queen unobserved, or at least speak to her without listeners. It was his duty to assist her in entering and alighting from her carriage, outside of which he was permitted to ride; he accompanied her on her excursions by water, and on her rides on horseback; and these latter were so much the more important, as they offered him to a certain extent the opportunity of a *tête-à-tête* with the queen. For it was only the master of the horse that was permitted to ride by her side; he even had precedence of the ladies of her suite, in rendering assistance to the queen, in case of any accident—such as that of the horse stumbling or otherwise. On such occasions, therefore, none of her retinue could know what conversation might pass between the queen and her master of the horse.

We can thus understand how influential such a post must have been. Moreover, when the queen was at Whitehall the king was nearly always beside her; but, thanks to the daily increasing unwieldiness of his body, he was not in a condition to leave the palace, otherwise than in a carriage.

It was therefore very natural that the whole body of courtiers should look forward with strained attention and suspended breathing to the moment when the chamberlain should designate these two important personages, whose names had been kept so secret, that no one had yet been able to discover them. It was only this morning that the king had inscribed these names upon the list before handing it to the chamberlain.

But not only the court, but even the king himself, looked with anxiety to the mention of these two names. For Henry wished to see the effect which they might produce, and to discover by the varied expression of the countenances of his courtiers, who the friends were of the two nominees. The young queen alone evinced her usual unaffected cordiality—her heart alone beat with unmoved composure—she did not for a moment suspect the importance of the point of issue.

Even the voice of the lord chamberlain trembled a little as he now read: "To the office of chamberlain to the queen, his majesty appoints my Lord Henry Howard, Earl of Surrey."

A murmur of approbation was audible, and an agreeable surprise became evident in the faces of nearly all.

"He has a good many friends," muttered the king to himself. "He is therefore dangerous." An angry glance from his eye met the youthful earl, who was just approaching the young queen, to bend his knee before her, and to kiss the hand which was extended to him.

Behind the queen stood Lady Jane, and when she saw the young, handsome, long-sighed-for, and secretly-worshipped noble so near her, and when she thought of her vow, she felt an angry pang and a poignant jealousy against the young queen, who, without suspecting it, robbed her of the man she loved, and condemned her to the fearful agony of being herself the instrument of her own unhappiness.

The chamberlain now read with loud and solemn voice: "To the office of master of the horse to the queen, his majesty appoints my Lord Thomas Seymour, Earl of Sudley."

It was well that the king, at this moment, had directed his whole attention to his courtiers, and sought to read in their features the impression which the appointment produced.

Had he observed his young spouse, he would have perceived how an expression of joyful astonishment overspread the face of Katharine, and how a sweet smile played around her lips.

But the king, as we have said, thought only of his court; he only saw that the number of those who rejoiced at Seymour's appointment, did not nearly equal that of the others who had received the appointment of Surrey with such marked approbation.

Henry's brow became contracted, and

he muttered to himself: "These Howards are too powerful. I shall keep a watchful eye upon them."

In his turn, Thomas Seymour approached the queen, and, bending his knee, kissed her hand. Katharine received him with a kindly smile. "My lord," she said, "you are at once to enter upon your attendance with me, and in a way too which I trust will be agreeable to all the court. You will be pleased, my lord, to mount your swiftest courser, and hasten to the palace of Holt, where the Princess Elizabeth is staying. Give her this letter from her royal father, and she will follow you hither. Tell her that I long to embrace her as a friend and a sister, and that I trust she will forgive me, if I cannot resign to her the whole heart of her king and father, but would still keep therein a place for myself. Hasten to the palace of Holt, my lord, and bring with you the Princess Elizabeth."

BOOK II.

THE CHASE.

CHAPTER I.

THE KING'S JESTER.

Two years had elapsed since the king's marriage, and still Katharine Parr had maintained herself in favor with her husband. As yet her enemies had not been able to succeed in their efforts to overthrow her, and raise a seventh queen to the throne.

Katharine had always been cautious and circumspect. She had always kept her head and her heart cool; she had said to herself every morning, that this day might possibly be her last—that some thoughtless word or inconsiderate act might deprive her of her crown and of her life. For Henry's fierce and cruel disposition seemed, like his bodily ailments, to increase each day. It needed but a trifle to excite him to the highest fury—to a fury which smote with a fatal blow the individual who had roused his anger.

It was this consciousness and this knowledge which had made the queen circumspect. She did not yet wish to die. She loved life still—the more so, as it had hitherto afforded her so few pleasures: she still loved it because she hoped for so much happiness—for so many joys and delights, yet to come.

No. She did not wish to die; for she looked forward to life, of which she had already had but a dim foreshadowing in her dreams, and of which her trembling and anxious heart told her that life was at length ready to wake within her, and to rouse her with eyes of sunny brightness from the winter sleep of her existence.

It was a beautiful day in spring. Katharine wished to avail herself of it, in order to take an airing on horseback, and to forget for a few hours that she was a queen. She was anxious to enjoy a ride in the forest—to inhale the mild breezes of May—to hear the song of the wild birds—to gaze upon the verdant fields, and to breathe the balmy air of spring.

She wished to ride. No one suspected how much secret pleasure and hidden delight was contained in these words. No one suspected that for months she had looked forward to this excursion on horseback, albeit she had scarcely ventured to wish for it—just because it would be the fulfilment of her anxious desires.

She had already put on her riding-habit; and the little red velvet hat, with the long, white waving plume, already adorned her beautiful head. Pacing up and down her apartment, she only awaited the return of her chamberlain, whom she had sent to the king, to know if he wished to see her before going out for her excursion.

Suddenly the door opened, and a strange apparition stood upon the threshold. This was a little shrivelled old man, wrapped in a garment of reddish-purple silk, which was neatly adorned with puffs of many colors, and which, in its various hues and tints, contrasted strangely with the white hair and the dark, determined countenance of the old man.

"Ah! the king's jester," said Katharine, with a merry laugh. "Well, John Heywood, and what brings you here now? Have you any message from the king? or have you been playing some of your sly tricks again, and do you want me to take you under my protection?"

"No, your majesty," replied John Heywood, gravely, "I have not been playing any foolish tricks, and I don't bring you any message from the king. I only bring you myself. Ah, my lady queen, I see you are disposed to laugh, but I beg you will not forget for a moment that John Heywood is the king's jester, and that it does not become him to wear a serious look and have grave thoughts like other men."

"Oh, I am aware you are not only the king's jester, but also a poet," said Katharine, with a gracious smile.

"Yes," he returned, "I am a poet, and for that reason it is quite right that I should wear this fool's cap—for poets are all fools, and it would be better for them if they were taken and suspended from the next tree, rather than be allowed to run about in their mad ecstasy and prate of things in a way that must make them the scorn and derision of reasonable people. Yes, queen, I am a poet, and therefore I have donned the fool's livery that I wear, which puts me under the king's protection, and suffers me to tell him now and then strange truths which nobody else would have the hardihood to utter. But to-day, queen, I come to you neither as a fool nor as a poet, but I come to embrace your knees and lay my thanks at your feet. I come to tell you that you have made John Heywood forever your slave. Henceforth he will lie at your door like a faithful dog, and watch you against every enemy and every insidious attack that might threaten to reach you. Night and day he will be ready at your service, and will take neither rest nor repose, when a command or a wish of yours is to be fulfilled."

And while he thus spoke with faltering voice, and his eyes filled with tears, he knelt down and bent his head at Katharine's feet.

"But what have I done to inspire you with such a feeling of gratitude?" said Katharine, astonished. "How have I deserved that you, the powerful favorite of the king, and dreaded by all, should devote yourself to my service?"

"What have you done?" he asked. "My liege queen, you have saved my son from the scaffold. They had condemned him; yes, they had condemned this fine, noble young man for having spoken with reverence of Sir Thomas More—for having said that that great and good man had done right in preferring to die, rather than forswear his convictions. Ah, in our times it is such a mere trifle to be condemned to death—that even a thoughtless word is enough to do so. And this wretched, lick-spittle Parliament, in its cringing baseness, always judges and condemns, for it knows that King Henry is always athirst for blood, and hankers for the stake and the gibbet. They had consequently condemned my son; and were it not for your majesty's intercession, they would have taken his life. But you, whom God has placed as a conciliating angel upon a royal throne dripping with blood; you, who daily put your life and your crown in jeopardy for the safety and pardon of those unhappy beings who are condemned by fanaticism—you have also saved my son."

"What! Was the young man who was yesterday to be sent to the scaffold your son?"

"Yes; he was my son, my own son."

"And you did not tell the king so, nor intercede for him?"

"Had I done so, he would inevitably have been lost. For you know the king is so sensitive upon his impartiality and his virtue. Oh, had he known that Thomas was my son, he would have condemned him, in order to show his people that Henry the Eighth everywhere strikes down the guilty, and punishes the offender, whatever may be his name, and whoever may intercede for him. Nay, even your majesty's entreaties would not have saved him; for the high-priest of the English Church would never have been able to pardon the circumstance that this poor young man was not the legitimate son of his father, that he had no right to bear his name, but that his mother was the wife of another, whom Thomas must call his father."

"Poor Heywood! Yes, I now understand. Certainly the king would never have pardoned this, and if he knew it, your son would have been irretrievably lost."

"You have saved him, my queen. Do you now believe that I shall be eternally grateful to you?"

"I believe it," said the queen, with a sweet and gracious smile, while she presented her hand for him to kiss. "I believe you, and I accept your services."

"And your majesty will stand in need of them, for a storm is gathering over your head, and the thunder will soon roll, and the lightning flash."

"Oh, I am not afraid of that," said Katharine, smiling. "If a storm should come, it will serve to clear and purify the atmosphere, and we know that after a hurricane frequently comes sunshine."

"You have a stout heart," said John Heywood, pensively.

"That is to say, I am not conscious of any guilt."

"But your enemies will impute guilt to you. Ah, when the question is to calumniate a fellow-being and bring him to ruin, men, ay, and women too, have fertile imaginations—they are all poets."

"But you have just said that poets are mad, and that they should be hung from the next tree. We shall therefore treat these slanderers as poets—that is all."

"No, that is not all," said John Heywood, with energy; "for slanderers are like earthworms. You may cut them in pieces, but instead of killing them, you will only multiply each, and give it several heads."

"But what do they accuse me of?" exclaimed Katharine, impatiently. "Is not my life blameless and patent to all men? Do I ever take pains to have any secrets? Is not my heart, on the contrary, like a house of glass, into which you all may look, and perceive that it is an unfruitful soil, and that not even one solitary little flower grows therein?"

"Exactly so; but your enemies will sow weeds in it, and make the king believe that they are the growth of a consuming love which has sprung up in your heart."

"What! Accuse me of an unlawful passion?" asked Katharine, while her lips trembled visibly.

"As yet, I know not their plans, but I shall discover them. A conspiracy is brooding. Be, therefore, on your guard, my queen. Trust nobody, for enemies always conceal themselves under the mask of hypocrisy and flattering words."

"If you know my enemies, name them to me," said Katharine impatiently. "Name them to me, that I may guard against them."

"I am not here to accuse any one, but to bid you be watchful. I shall therefore be careful not to designate your enemies, but I will tell you who your friends are."

"Ah, then I have friends too?" said Katharine, with a quiet and gratified smile.

"Yes, you have friends, and those friends are ready to shed their hearts' blood for you if necessary."

"Oh, pray name them—name them!" cried Katharine, trembling with joyful eagerness.

"I name first of all Cranmer, the Archbishop of Canterbury. He is your true and faithful friend, upon whom you may safely rely. He loves you as his queen and esteems you as the colleague whom God has sent him, in order here at the court of our most Christian and most blood-thirsty sovereign, to bring the blessed work of the Reformation to a successful issue, and to cause the light of knowledge to illuminate this night of papal error and superstition. Build firmly upon Cranmer, for he is your surest and most steadfast support; and were he to fall, your own downfall would be the inevitable result."

"Yes, you are right," said the queen, thoughtfully. "Cranmer is a noble and constant friend, and very often already he has taken my part with the king against the petty darts of my enemies, which do not indeed kill, but make the whole body sore and ill at ease."

"Protect him—as you value your own safety."

"Well, and the other friends?"

"I have given precedence to Cranmer, but now, my queen, I name myself, as the second of your friends. As the archbishop is your stanch upholder, so will I be your watch-dog, and, believe me, while you have such a trusty supporter and such a faithful watch-dog, you are out of danger. Cranmer will warn you of every stumbling-block that may cross your path, and I shall bark and bite at the enemies that lurk in ambush behind the thicket, in order to attack you unawares."

"I thank you sincerely," said Katharine, with cordiality. "Now pray continue."

"Continue?" said Heywood, with a sad smile.

"Yes, name some of my other friends."

"Ah, my queen, it is much, very much, to have found two friends in life upon whom we can depend, and whose constancy is not determined by selfish motives. You are perhaps the only crowned head that can boast of such friends."

"I am a woman," said Katharine, pensively, "and many ladies surround me. and daily vow their unchanging fidelity and attachment. And am I to consider all these as unworthy the name of friends? Not even Lady Jane Douglas, whom I regard as one of my early friends, and in whom I confide as in a sister? Tell me, John Heywood, you who are said to know and discover whatever passes at this court—tell me, is not Lady Jane Douglas my friend?"

John Heywood suddenly became grave and silent, and seemed lost in thought. At length, he opened his large lustrous eyes and looked inquiringly around the room, as if to convince himself that there was really no listener concealed, and advancing close to the queen, he whispered:

"Trust her not—she is a papist, and Gardiner is her friend."

"Ah, I suspected it," murmured Katharine, sadly.

"But listen, my queen,—do not let this suspicion escape you by word or look, or by the slightest intimation of any kind. Lull this viper, in the belief that you think her harmless. Lull her to sleep, I say. She is a venomous and deadly serpent, that must not be provoked, lest she should bite you before you could suspect it. Only remember, queen, not to confide to Lady Jane what you would not tell Gardiner and Lord Douglas. Oh, believe me, she is like the lion in the doge's palace at Venice: the secrets which you confide to her will rise up in evidence against you at the bloody tribunal."

Katharine smiled and shook her head.

"You judge too severely, John Heywood. The religion to which she secretly adheres may possibly have estranged her heart from me, but she would never be so base as to betray me, or ally herself with my enemies. No, good John, you deceive yourself. It would be culpable in me to believe what you say. What a wicked and miserable world it would be if we dared not trust our most beloved and faithful friends!"

"Ay, indeed the world is wicked and miserable, and we must distrust it, or else regard it as a merry pastime with which the devil tickles our fancy. For me it is such a pastime, queen, and therefore I became the king's jester, which at least affords me the privilege of spreading all the venom of human contempt over the crawling brood of courtiers, and of telling the truth to those from whose tongues falsehood is always dripping like a honey-comb. Wise men and poets are the proper fools of our time; and as I did not feel within me the vocation to be a king or a philosopher—a hangman or a victim, I became the king's fool."

"Yes, that is to say, a dealer in epigrams whose caustic tongue makes all the court tremble."

"As I cannot send the culprits to the scaffold, like my royal master, I give them the sharp edge of my tongue; and I assure your majesty you will stand sorely in need of this ally. Be on your guard, queen. This very morning I heard the first growl of the thunder, and saw latent gleams of lightning in the eyes of Lady Jane. Trust her not: trust nobody here but your friends, Cranmer and John Heywood."

"And you say that amongst all the brilliant ladies, and all the noble and chivalrous cavaliers at this court, the poor queen has not a single friend, not a soul in whom she can confide? Oh, John Heywood, recollect yourself; have pity upon a helpless queen; pray recollect yourself. Only you both—no other friend, say you?"

And the eyes of the queen filled with tears which she strove in vain to check.

John Heywood perceived it, and sighed deeply. Better, perhaps, than the queen herself, he had read the thoughts of her heart, and knew its secret wounds. But he had compassion for her suffering, and wished to mitigate it as far as he could.

"Yes, I recollect," he murmured, in a low voice. "I now recollect you have a third friend at this court."

"Ah! a third friend!" exclaimed Katharine, in a tone which betokened secret joy. "Pray, who is it—who is he? I am quite impatient to know his name."

With a peculiar and inquiring glance, and with a pensive and expressive gaze, John Heywood looked into the glowing features of Katharine, and for a moment he dropped his head upon his breast and sighed.

"Well, John, name this third friend of mine."

"Do you not know who it is, my queen?" he asked, looking at her once more with a firm and fixed gaze. "Do you not know him? It is Thomas Seymour, Lord Sudley."

A gleam of sunshine seemed to pass over the countenance of Katharine, and she uttered a faint cry.

John Heywood resumed, in pensive tones:

"Queen, the sun shines directly upon your face, beware lest it dazzle your bright eyes. Repose in the shade, and—but, hark! here comes one who would be quite capable of affirming that the sunshine in your countenance was a conflagration."

At this moment the door opened, and Lady Jane Douglas appeared at the threshold. She cast a rapid, inquiring glance around the apartment, and a faint smile passed over her pale and beautiful features.

"Your majesty," she said, "all is ready, and only awaits your commands. The Princess Elizabeth is in the antechamber, and your master of the horse already holds your stirrup."

"And the chamberlain?" asked Katharine, slightly blushing; "has he no message for me from the king?"

"Yes," said the Earl of Surrey, entering. "His majesty bids me tell the queen that she may extend her ride as far as may be agreeable. This delightful weather deserves that the Queen of England should enjoy it, and enter into rivalry with the sun."

"Oh, the king is the most gallant of cavaliers," returned Katharine, with a smile of satisfaction. "Now, Jane, come, let us mount."

"Your majesty will pardon me," said Lady Jane, drawing back; "but I may not enjoy the favor of accompanying you to day, as Lady Anne Ettersville is at present in attendance."

"Very well, Jane; another time, then. And you, my Lord Douglas, do you not join in our excursion?"

"The king has commanded my attendance in his closet, your majesty."

"Now, only think! Here is a queen, abandoned by all her friends," said Katharine, in a tone of lively raillery; while, with a light, elastic step, she crossed the saloon, and proceeded to the court-yard.

"There is something going on here which I must find out," muttered John Heywood, who, with the others, had left the room. "A mouse-trap has been laid, for the cats are staying at home, and are hungry for their prey."

Lady Jane, however, remained behind in the saloon with her father. They both advanced to the window, and looked down in silence into the court-yard, where now the brilliant cavalcade of the queen, with all her attendants, were mingled together.

Katharine had just mounted her horse. The noble animal, who knew his mistress, neighed loudly, while he pranced and snorted under his royal burden.

The Princess Elizabeth, who kept beside the queen, uttered a cry of terror.

"Your majesty will fall," she exclaimed. "Your steed is such a high-spirited and wayward animal."

"Oh, not at all," said Katharine, smiling. "Hector is a quiet horse, only he is somewhat like myself to-day. The fresh May breeze has made us both rather lively and mettlesome. Let us away then, my lords and ladies; our horses must put on their best speed to-day: we ride to Epping Forest."

And through the open gates of the

court-yard rushed the goodly cavalcade. The queen led the procession; on her right was the Princess Elizabeth, on her left the master of the horse, Thomas Seymour.

When the queen and her retinue had vanished, the father and daughter withdrew from the window, and exchanged a glance of peculiar significance.

"Well, Jane," said Lord Douglas, at length, "she is still queen, and the king's health is daily growing more feeble and uncertain. It is quite time that we should present him with a seventh queen."

"Very soon, dear father; very soon."

"Does she love Henry Howard at last?"

"Yes, he loves her," said Lady Jane, while her features became deadly pale.

"I ask you if the queen loves *him?*"

"She will love him," murmured Lady Jane; and then, suddenly recovering herself, she continued: "But it is not enough to make the queen enamoured of the Earl of Surrey; it would doubtless be more effectual if the king could be inspired with a new passion. Did you observe, my father, with what ardent looks the king yesterday regarded the Duchess of Richmond and myself?"

"Did I observe it? Why, all the court noticed and spoke of it!"

"Well, then, make the king feel desperately *ennuyé* to-day, and then bring him to me. He will find the Duchess of Richmond and myself together."

"An excellent idea! Come, Jane, you will yet be Henry's seventh wife."

"I shall at least overthrow Katharine Parr, for she is my rival, and I hate her," said Lady Jane, with glowing cheeks and flashing eyes. She has already been queen long enough, and I have bowed before her. She shall now sink into the dust before me, and I will put my heel upon her neck!"

CHAPTER II.

THE EXCURSION.

The morning was delightful. The dew was still upon the grass on the meadows, over which they rode before entering the thick of the forest, in the trees of which gay song-birds piped their wild, melodious lays. They pressed forward along the course of a murmuring brook, and observed the herds of wild deer which flocked together in an open glade of the forest, as if, like the queen and her retinue, they would listen to the warbling of the birds and the murmur of the rivulet.

Katharine felt an indescribable sensation of happiness, which made her bosom swell with inward delight. To-day she was no longer the queen, surrounded by dangers and by enemies; not the wife of an unloved and tyrannical husband—not the queen, fettered by the trammels of etiquette. She was a free and happy woman, who, with hopeful yearning, looks forward smilingly to the future, and says to the fleeting hours: "Stay, stay, for ye are laden with delights!"

The happiness of the present hour was a visioned bliss, borrowed from the dreamland of the future. Ah, Katharine would joyfully have relinquished her crown if she could have rendered this hour enduring.

He was at her side. He of whom John Heywood had told her, that he was one of her most steadfast and faithful friends. He was there. And if she did not venture to look at him often, or often to address him, yet she felt his proximity, and felt, too, that the glowing beams from his eyes fell upon her features like a consuming fire. No one could observe them, for the members of the court rode at some distance in the rear, and before and around them was nothing but the love-breathing and smiling landscape, with the bright and beautiful sky above them.

Katharine had meanwhile forgotten that she was not quite alone, and that if Thomas Seymour rode at her left, the Princess Elizabeth rode at her right—this youthful girl of fourteen, who amidst fiery ordeals and the storms of ill-fortune, had suddenly sprung up to precocious womanhood, and whose heart had reached early maturity amidst the tears and bitter experience of her unhappy childhood. Elizabeth—the child in years, had nevertheless the strong and ardent feelings of a woman. Elizabeth—the rejected and disinherited princess, had still inherited from her father his pride and ambition; and when she looked at the queen, and perceived the small crown studded with diamonds, which she wore over her velvet riding-cap, she felt a keen inward pang, and thought to herself with bitter regret that this crown was destined never to adorn her own brow, as the king had excluded her from the succession by a solemn act of Parliament.

But the pain which she felt upon this subject had, for some weeks past, become somewhat mitigated. Another feeling had overpowered it. Elizabeth, who knew that she should not be a queen or a ruler, wished at least to enjoy the privileges of a woman. As she had been denied the chance of wearing a crown, she would at least enjoy the happiness of her sex; if not a crown of gold, at least a myrtle-wreath should deck her brow.

She had been early taught by experience to understand her own feelings, and she did not now shrink from examining with a firm and steady gaze the sentiments which were uppermost in her heart.

Yes—she knew that she loved, and that Thomas Seymour was the object of her affection.

But on the part of the earl—did he return her love? Did he understand the heart of the young girl? Had he recognized under her childish aspect the proud and passion-glowing woman? Had he discovered the secrets of this timid and maidenly, and yet withal this ardent and energetic spirit?

Thomas Seymour had never yet betrayed a secret; and what he had read, peradventure, in the eyes of the princess, and what, perchance, he had said to her in the quiet shady walks of Hampton Court, or in the long dark corridors of Whitehall—nobody knew but themselves; for Elizabeth had a strong masculine soul: she needed no confidant to impart her secrets to; and Thomas Seymour would have been apprehensive lest he should make for himself—like the immortal barber of Midas—a hole, and utter his secret therein; for he knew well that if the reed should grow up and repeat his words, he would have to lay his head upon the block.

Poor princess! She did not suspect that the secret of the earl and her own were not one and the same. She did not suspect that if Thomas Seymour discovered her secret, he would only use it, perhaps, for the purpose of making it a glittering foil to his own secret.

Like Elizabeth, he too had seen the jewelled crown upon the brow of the young queen, and he had observed how old and tottering the king was looking of late.

As he now rode beside the two princesses, he felt his heart swell with proud exultation, while his thoughts were occupied alone with bold and ambitious projects.

Of these thoughts, however, his companions knew nothing. They were both too much taken up with their own musings; and while Katharine's eye, beaming with lustre, wandered to the scenes around her, the brow of the princess became slightly clouded, and her keen glance was fixed upon Thomas Seymour with eager watchfulness.

She had observed those passionate glances which he sometimes directed toward the queen; and the slight and almost imperceptible tremor of his voice in addressing Katharine, had not escaped her.

The Princess Elizabeth was jealous. She felt the first painful emotions of this terrible malady, which she had inherited from her father, and in the feverish outbreaks of which the king had sent two of his wives to the scaffold.

She was jealous—but not of the queen; or rather she did not think for a moment that the queen could share or return Seymour's love. It never occurred to her to accuse Katharine of any complicity with the earl. She was only jealous of the glances which he bestowed upon the queen; and as she continued to observe those glances, she could not at the same time perceive in the eyes of her young step-mother the subdued fire which was kindled in them by Seymour's burning gaze, and which made her countenance to glow visibly.

But Thomas Seymour had perceived it, and had he now been alone with Katharine, he would have flung himself at her feet, and have confided to her all the deep and dangerous secrets which he had so long concealed in his bosom, and he would have left her the choice either of sending him to the scaffold, or of accepting the love which he cherished toward her.

But behind them were the watchful, all-observant courtiers—there was the Princess Elizabeth, who, had he ventured to speak to the queen, would have divined, from his countenance, the import of the words which she might not overhear—for love has keen eyes and jealousy quick ears.

Katharine suspected nothing of the thoughts of her companions. She alone was happy. She alone gave herself up to the perfect enjoyment of the moment. She inhaled with serene delight the pure air around her, which was rendered fragrant by the wild flowers of the forest. She listened with eager attention to the soft murmurs of song, which the wind breathed from amidst the trees. Her wishes did not extend beyond the present hour. She reposed in the consciousness and enjoyment of her lover's presence. Yes, HE was there! What more was needful to make her happy?

Beyond the hour her wishes did not extend. She was only conscious how delightful it was thus to be at the side of her lover—to breathe the same air that he breathed, to look upon the same bright sky, the same flowers upon which his eye rested, and in which, at least, their eyes might meet in the kisses which were denied their lips.

But as they thus proceeded in silence, each wrapt up in his own thoughts, the aid which Thomas Seymour had prayed for came, in the shape of a huge fly.

At first this fly played and buzzed around the nose of the proud and fiery charger which the queen rode, and being observed by no one, it remained undisturbed in Hector's mane, and crept quietly to the top of the noble steed's head, resting here and there, and sending its sting into the flesh of the restive animal, until he began to rear and neigh with pain.

But Katharine was a bold and skilful rider, and the uncurbed mettle of her steed only caused her pleasure, while it gave her master of the horse the opportunity of praising her coolness and dexterity.

Katharine received the compliments of her lover with a sweet smile. The fly, however, had crept along, until, instigated by a malicious pleasure, it fixed itself in the horse's ear.

The poor animal, thus tormented, made a dart forward, but this stride instead of freeing him from his enemy, only caused the latter to sink more deeply into his ear, until the sting of the horse-fly became fixed in the fleshy part of the ear.

Goaded to madness by the pain, the fiery animal became uncontrollable, and spurning bit and bridle, suddenly plunged forward, and with furious speed darted along through the glades of the forest, with the swiftness of an arrow.

"Help!—help for the queen!" shouted the master of the horse; and setting spurs to the flanks of his courser, he flew after her with impetuous speed.

"Help for the queen!" repeated the Princess Elizabeth, urging forward her horse, and accompanied by the whole retinue.

But what is the speed of ever so quick but sober a horse, compared with the frantic fleetness of an infuriated courser, who mocks the rein, and springs forward foaming with a sense of unchecked freedom, like an impetuous wave lashed into fury by the storm?

Already the glades lay far behind them—far behind them the avenue which led through the forest;—over brooks and ditches, over plains and sand-banks, dashed the enraged Hector with terrific speed.

Still the queen kept her saddle firmly; her cheeks were colorless, and her lips trembled, but her eye was lustrous and clear; she had not yet lost her self-possession, she was perfectly conscious of her danger. The shouts and cries which reached her at first, had died away for some time; an endless wilderness and a death-like stillness now surrounded her. She heard nothing but the panting and snorting of her horse, and the sounds of his hoofs as he darted onward.

But at length the sounds of a well-beloved voice fell upon her ear, and caused her to utter an exclamation of pleasure and delight.

This cry, however, terrified the furious animal afresh. Panting and exhausted, he had for a moment relaxed his furious speed, but he now pressed forward with renewed ardor and fleetness, as if urged upon the wings of the wind.

But nearer and nearer sounded the beloved voice;—ever nearer the foot-fall of his horse.

They soon found themselves upon a large plain, entirely surrounded by the forest; and while the queen's horse took a circuitous course, that of Seymour, obeying the rein of his rider, went straight across the plain, and was now close behind the queen.

"Only a moment longer! Hold your arms round the horse's neck, lest you should be thrown by the shock, while I seize him by the bridle!" cried Seymour; and setting spurs to his horse, the latter darted forward with a wild yell.

This yell roused Hector to fresh fury, and panting for breath, he now plunged ahead into the thick of the forest.

"I hear his voice no longer," murmured Katharine; and at length overcome by fear and by the dizzy course, and exhausted by her efforts, she closed her eyes, and her senses seemed to have left her.

But at this moment a strong and vigorous hand seized her horse's bridle, until the animal, trembling and as it were abashed, at discovering that he had found his master, dropped his head.

"Saved!—I am saved!" muttered Katharine, while breathless, and almost unconscious, she rested her head on Seymour's shoulder.

He lifted her from her saddle, and laid her upon the mossy turf, under an ancient oak. He then secured the horse to a branch of a tree, while Katharine, trembling and exhausted by her efforts, sank down to recover herself.

CHAPTER III.

THE DECLARATION.

Thomas Seymour speedily returned to Katharine. She still lay pale and motionless, and with her eyes closed.

He looked at her with a deep and ardent gaze, while he seemed to imbibe fresh draughts of love from the sight of this noble and beautiful woman—not suffering himself to reflect for a moment that she was his queen.

At length, then, he was alone with her. At length after two years of patience, of torment, and dissimulation, God had granted him this happy hour, for which he had so long sighed in vain—which he had so long imagined unattainable. She was now beside him. She was now his own.

And had the entire court—had even Henry himself approached at this moment, Thomas Seymour would not have heeded them—he would not have been terrified.

His blood had mounted to his brain, and had overcome his reason; his heart, which in consequence of this furious chase, and of his anxiety for Katharine, still bounded and panted violently, did not suffer him to hear any voice but the voice of his passion—of his love.

He knelt down beside the queen and gently seized her hand.

Perhaps it was this touch which roused her from her unconsciousness. She opened her eyes and looked vacantly around her.

"Where am I?" she asked, in a faint accent.

Thomas Seymour pressed her hand to his lips. "You are with the most faithful and devoted of your servants, my queen!"

Queen! This word woke her up from her lethargy, and she raised herself into a sitting posture.

"But where is my retinue? Where is the Princess Elizabeth? Where are all the eyes that are wont to guard and watch me? Where are all the spies and listeners that accompany the queen?"

"They are far away from here," replied Thomas Seymour, in a tone that betrayed his inward joy. "They are far behind us, and will not overtake us for at least another hour. And now, my queen, can you conceive what this hour is for me? An hour of freedom, after an imprisonment of two years—an hour of happiness, after two long years of daily pain and daily torment!"

Katharine, who had smiled at first, now became grave and thoughtful. Her eyes rested upon her hunting-cap, which had fallen from her head and lay beside her on the grass.

She pointed with trembling hand to the crown, and said, gently:

"Do you know what that means, my lord?"

"Yes, madam, I do; but at this moment I no longer shrink from it with terror. There are moments when life hangs upon a precipice, and when we do not heed the abyss that lies yawning at our feet. Such a moment is the present. I know that this hour makes me a traitor, and may lead me to the scaffold, but yet I will not be silent. The fire which rages in my breast consumes me, and I must at length give it an outlet. My heart, which has for years burned as in a fiery furnace, but which is withal so vigorous that in the midst of its torments it evermore felt a sensation of bliss, must at length be destroyed or be appeased. Your majesty must therefore deign to hear me."

"No! no!" she exclaimed, with almost painful emotion. "I will not—I dare not hear you. Remember that I am the wife of Henry the Eighth, and that it is dangerous even to speak to you. Be silent, therefore my lord,—pray be silent, and let us proceed on our ride."

She attempted to rise, but her own exhaustion, as well as Lord Seymour's gentle coercion, compelled her to resume her seat.

"No, I will not be silent," he replied. "I will not be silent until I have told you all that glows and rages within me. The Queen of England may either pardon or condemn me, but she shall at least know that she is not for me the wife of Henry the Eighth, but the most charming and attractive—the noblest and the loveliest woman in England. I will tell her I do not for a moment remember that she is my queen, or if I do so, it is only in order to execrate the king, who has been so presumptuous as to fix this dazzling and spendid jewel in his bloody crown."

Katharine, almost terrified, laid her hand upon Seymour's lips.

"Hold! unhappy man—hold!" she exclaimed. "Know you, that you are uttering words which would be your death-warrant were any one to overhear them?"

"But no one hears me—no one but the queen and God, who is perhaps even more compassionate and merciful than the queen herself. Accuse me therefore, madam—accuse me if you will. Go and tell your king that Thomas Seymour is a traitor—that he dares to love the queen; the king will send me to the scaffold, but I shall still esteem myself happy—for my death at least will be owing to and for you. O, queen—if I cannot live for you—surely it is a happy fate to meet death for your sake!"

Katharine listened to him with mute astonishment, while her senses seemed lost with intoxication. For her this language was wholly new, and it made her heart tremble with emotions of rapture; it filled her soul as if with melodies of magic spell, which lulled her into a blissful unconsciousness. She even forgot that she was the queen—the wife of Henry—the jealous and bloodthirsty. She only knew that the man whom she had so long loved, now knelt at her side, and that she listened with rapture to the music of his words—which were to her as nectar.

Thomas Seymour continued to urge his suit. He told her all that he had suffered, he told her that he had often resolved to die, in order at length to put an end to his torments; but that then a glance from her eyes, a word from her lips, had again given him the strength to live, and to endure still longer the tortures which were at once painful and full of delight.

"But now, madam, my powers are exhausted, and you must either endow me with life or consign me to death. I am ready to mount the scaffold to-morrow, unless you suffer me to live—to live for you alone."

Katharine looked at him with astonishment and tremulous emotion. She encountered his proud and commanding glance, which almost caused her fear—but it was the bliss-yielding fear of the loving and submissive woman before the strong and imperious man.

"Do you know," she said, with a charming smile, "that you almost look as if you wished to command me to love you?"

"No, madam," he replied, proudly. "I cannot command you to love me, but I must charge you to tell me the truth—this I must require of you, for I am a man who has the right of demanding this of a woman. I have already said that for me you are not the queen—for me you are only the loved and worshipped woman. This feeling has no connection with your kingdom, and in making this avowal of my love, I do not mean to convey that you would be lowering yourself in accepting it. For the true love of a man is always the most sacred gift which he can offer to a woman; and if even a beggar's love be offered to a queen, she must feel herself honored thereby. O queen, behold in me this beggar! I lie prostrate at your feet, and lift my hands beseechingly to you, but I do not ask for alms—nor would I crave your pity and compassion, which might perhaps tender me a gift in order to lessen my misery. No—I ask for yourself—I desire all or nothing. It will not suffice that you pardon my boldness, and throw the veil of silence over my rash enterprise. I desire that you pronounce the decree, whether of my doom or of my bliss. I know you are generous and merciful, and even though you should scorn and not return my love—yet perhaps you will not betray me: perhaps you will spare me and be silent. But I repeat to you, madam, I shall not accept this offering of your generosity. You shall either declare me to be a traitor, or exalt me to the heaven of bliss—for a traitor I am if you condemn my love, but a god among men if you return it."

"And now, my lord, do you know you are very cruel," returned Katharine, with gentle reproach. "You wish that I should become either an accuser or an accomplice. You only leave me the choice of being the instrument of your doom, or of becoming a perjured and faithless wife—a wife who forgets her sacred duties and her sworn vows, and who dishonors the crown which her husband has placed upon her head—which dishonor the king would assuredly wash away with your blood and with mine."

"Be it so!" exclaimed the earl, with exultation. "Let my head fall at once, if you but love me! I shall then indeed be immortal, for a moment in your arms is an eternity of bliss!"

"But I have just observed, that not only your life but also my own is at stake. You know the severe and vindictive character of the king. Even mere suspicion would suffice to condemn me. Ah, if he only knew what we have here been saying, he would send me to the block as he did Katharine Howard, though I am not guilty as she was. Oh, I shudder to think of the scaffold, and yet, Lord Seymour, you would condemn me to that wretched fate — and then you say you love me!"

With a deep sigh, Thomas Seymour dropped his head pensively on his breast.

"You have pronounced my sentence, gracious lady, and though you are too generous to tell me the truth, I have divined it. No, you do not love me, for you see with a quick eye the danger which threatens you, and you shrink from it. No, you do not love me, for otherwise you would think of nothing but of love itself; danger would only serve to inspire you, and the sword which threatens would be unseen, or else you would seize its naked edge and say, 'What care I for death, since I am happy? What matter the loss of life, since I have found undying felicity?' Ah, Katharine, you have a cool head and a cold heart. God give you a continuance of both, for then you will pass through life quietly and without harm; but you will still be a poor, cheerless, and deplorable being; and when you die a royal crown will be laid upon your coffin, but love will shed no tears over your grave. Farewell, Queen Katharine, and as you cannot love him, bestow at least your compassion upon the traitor, Thomas Seymour!"

Saying which, he bent down and embraced her feet. He then rose, and with a firm step advanced toward the tree to which the horses were bound.

But now Katharine sprang up, and rushing forward, seized his hand which held the bridle of his horse, and, breathless and trembling, said:

"What would you do? Whither are you going?"

"To the king, madam."

"And for what purpose?"

"To show him an arch-traitor, who has dared to love the queen. You have taken away the life from my soul, and the king will take the life of my body. The latter is the less painful, and I shall thank him for it."

Katharine uttered a cry of alarm, and drew him back with passionate violence to the spot where she had previously been resting.

"If you do what you threaten," she exclaimed, with trembling lips and faltering voice, "you will kill me! Hear me!—listen! At the very moment that you mount your horse to go to the king, I will mount mine too; not, however, to follow you—not to go back to London, but to rush headlong with my horse over yonder precipice. Oh, do not fear, you will not be accused as my murderer; it will be said that I have fallen over with my horse, and that the furious animal has caused my death!"

"I would advise your majesty to be cautious, and to consider well what you are saying," exclaimed Thomas Seymour, while his countenance brightened up, and his features became radiant with joy. "Consider that your words must either be a condemnation or an avowal. I will either die or secure your love. Not the love of a queen, who thinks to bestow a favor upon her subject, in perhaps lifting him one day to rank with herself, but the love of a woman who bows her head with yielding humility, the while she accepts her beloved as her lord and husband! Oh, Katharine, take good heed! If you come to me with the pride of a queen—if there be but one thought within you, which says that you favor your subject in taking him to your heart, then say no more, but let me go hence. I am proud and nobly born like yourself, and while love has vanquished me and flung me at your feet, still it shall not bow my head to the dust. But if you say, Katharine, that you love me, then will I consecrate to you my whole life. I will be at once your lord and your slave. I shall have no thought, no feeling, and no wish that will not be devoted to your service; and when I say that I will be your lord, I do not mean thereby that I shall not at the same time be constantly at your feet, and bow my head to the dust, and say to you, 'Trample upon me, for I am your slave!'"

And while he thus spoke, he fell upon his knees and bowed his head at Katharine's feet, while the noble and glowing expression of his countenance ravished her heart.

She stooped down, and raised him gently, looking meanwhile, with an indescribable expression of happiness, into the depths of his beaming eyes.

"Do you love me?" asked Seymour, while he gently placed his arm around her slender waist, and rose from his kneeling posture.

"Yes, I love you," she replied, with a firm voice, and with a smile of ineffable happiness. "Yes, I love you, not as a queen, but as a woman; and if this love should perchance bring us both to the scaffold, why then we shall at least die together, but only to meet again, and be reunited forever, in realms beyond the skies."

"Oh, no, Katharine; think not of dying at present; think only of living; of the delightful and rapturous future which awaits us, and which smiles for our approach. Think of the days which will speedily come, when our love will require no further secrecy, no further concealment, but when we shall be able to proclaim it to all the world, and to shout our joy aloud with happy and exulting hearts. Yes, my Katharine, let us look forward to the event which will at length loose the unnatural bonds which now bind you to this hoary tyrant; and then, when Henry is no more, you will be mine—mine with all your life and being; and then, instead of the proud royal diadem, your brow will be adorned with the bridal wreath. Swear this, Katharine. Vow solemnly that you will be mine as soon as you are set free by the king's death."

The queen shuddered and her cheek turned pale.

"Oh!" she sighed, "then death is

our hope, and the scaffold, perhaps, our goal."

"Not so, my Katharine. Love is our hope, and happiness our goal. Think of life and of our future! Fulfil my request. Swear to me here in the sight of heaven, with God as our witness, that from the day on which death shall have delivered you from the thraldom of your marriage with the king, you will be mine—my spouse, my wife. Swear to me that, disregarding etiquette, and in opposition to a tyrannical custom, you will become the wife of Lord Seymour, even before the funeral-knell shall have ceased for the king. We shall find a priest who will bless our love, and hallow the contract which we have made with each other this day and forever. Promise that you will keep your faith and love for me until the wished-for day, and that you will never forget that my honor is thine, and thy happiness mine!"

"This I swear!" said Katharine, solemnly. "You may depend upon me at all times, and under all circumstances. Never will I harbor a thought that does not belong to you. I shall love you as Thomas Seymour deserves to be loved; that is, with a devoted and confiding heart. It will be my pride to subject myself to you, and with a joyful heart I will serve and obey you, as your faithful, true, and dutiful wife."

"I accept your vow," said Seymour, in a like solemn tone. "And on my side I swear in return that I will honor and reverence you as my queen and mistress! I swear to you that you will never find a more disinterested counsellor, a more constant husband, or a more valiant protector than I shall be to you. 'My life for my queen, my heart for my mistress,' will henceforth be my motto, and may I be forsaken by Heaven and by you if I ever break this vow!"

"So be it!" said Katharine, with a bewitching smile.

Then they were both silent. It was that silence which is only known to love and happiness—that silence which is so rich in thoughts, and therefore so poor in words.

The wind whispered softly through the trees, in the dark foliage of which here and there might be heard the shrill or mellow notes of some wild song-bird. The sun flung its emerald and golden rays athwart the soft, velvet sward and mossy turf, along the ground, which, rising and falling in gentle undulations, formed miniature hills and valleys—while at intervals appeared the graceful form of a stag or a young fawn, which, looking around inquiringly, with its bright eyes, would suddenly disappear into the thicket on perceiving human beings in sight, with their horses encamped near them.

Suddenly the stillness was broken by the loud twang of the hunting-horn, and in the distance confused cries and shouts became audible, which resounded through the recesses of the forest, and found an echo which was repeated a thousand-fold.

The queen raised her head, with a sigh, from the shoulder of Lord Seymour. Her dream for the present was over; the angel with the fiery sword came to banish her from her paradise.

For she was no longer worthy of paradise; the fatal word was spoken, and while it had endowed her with love, it made her faithless to her vows.

The wife of Henry—his by the faith which she pledged at the altar—had just plighted her word to another, and had given him the love which she owed her husband.

"It is past!" she said, with a sad smile. "These sounds recall me to my slavery. We must both resume our several characters. I must once more take the part of queen."

"But swear to me again that you will never forget this hour—that you will always keep in memory the vows we have pledged to each other."

She looked at him with apparent surprise.

"What! can plighted faith and love be ever forgotten?"

"You will always remain true to me, Katharine?"

She smiled. "Now only imagine, my jealous lord—do I address such questions to you?"

"Ah, queen, you know that you possess the magic spell which binds me to you forever."

"Who knows?" she returned, musingly, while she directed her ardent gaze toward heaven, and appeared to follow the fleeting silvery clouds that glided slowly aloft through the blue firmament.

And then, her eye descending and resting on her lover, while her hand was laid on his shoulder, she said: "Love is like God Himself—eternal, everlasting, and omnipresent. But we must believe in it, in order to feel its presence. We must trust in it, that we may become worthy to receive its full blessings and rewards."

But the shouts and the clang of the horns were drawing nearer and nearer, and already the baying of the hounds and the sounds of the horses' hoofs were quite audible.

The earl had unfastened the horse, and led Hector, who was now as tame and quiet as a lamb, to his mistress.

"Queen," said Thomas Seymour, "here are two criminals who approach you. Hector is my fellow-culprit; and had it not been for the fly, which I now perceive, from the poor animal's swollen ear, made him furious, I should still have been the most wretched and unhappy man in your kingdom, whereas I am now the most fortunate and the most enviable."

The queen made no reply, but she put her arms round the neck of the noble animal and kissed it fervently.

"From this day forth," said she, "I will ride no other horse but Hector, and when he grows old, and unfit for service—"

"He shall be tended and nursed in the stables of Katharine, Countess of Sudley," interrupted Thomas Seymour, as he held the stirrup for the queen and assisted her into her saddle.

They both rode forward in silence toward the point whence came the sound of voices and the shrill twang of the horns—both too much occupied with their own thoughts to interrupt the current thereof by an indifferent word.

"He loves me!" thought Katharine. "I am a happy and an enviable woman—for I have secured the love of Thomas Seymour."

"The queen loves me!" said Thomas Seymour to himself with a proud, triumphant smile. "I shall therefore one day be Regent of England."

They had by this time reached the large open plain which they had previously crossed, and over which now advanced the whole of the royal cavalcade, in the strangest confusion, with the Princess Elizabeth at its head.

"One thing more," whispered Katharine: "whenever you want a messenger to send to me, apply to John Heywood; he is a friend in whom I can trust."

And then she dashed forward toward the Princess Elizabeth, in order to relate to her the whole account of this adventure, and the fortunate manner in which she had been saved by her master of the horse.

Elizabeth meanwhile heard her with a look of sullen distraction; and when the queen turned to the remainder of her retinue, and, surrounded by her ladies and gentlemen, received their congratulations, a slight nod from the princess brought Lord Seymour to her side.

She suffered her horse to canter forward a few paces, so that the earl and herself were a little apart from the others, and were sure of not being overheard.

"My lord," she said, in a hasty and almost threatening tone, "you have often besought me in vain to grant you an interview, which I refused. You urged that you had many things to say to me, which would make it necessary to be alone. Well, my lord, we are now alone, and I am at length prepared to hear you."

She ceased, and awaited his answer. But the earl was taken unawares, and was mute with surprise. He only made her a profound and respectful bow, until he almost touched his horse's neck.—"But no matter, I shall attend this rendezvous, even if it were only to dazzle Elizabeth's eyes, so that she may not see what she certainly never shall see—that's all."

The young princess cast upon him an angry look, and said, in a tone of sarcastic irony, "You understand well, my lord, the art of concealing your joy, and any one at seeing you might suppose—"

"That, at this dangerous court, Thomas Seymour is discreet enough not to suffer his delight to be visible in his countenance," interrupted the earl, in a subdued tone. "When, princess, may I venture to see you, and where?"

"Wait this evening for the message which John Heywood will bring you," whispered Elizabeth, as she turned round to rejoin the queen.

"John Heywood again!" murmured the earl—"the confidant of both, and therefore my executioner if he likes."

CHAPTER IV.

LE ROI S'ENNUIE.

King Henry was alone in his closet. He had spent a few hours in the composition of a Book of Homilies which he was writing for his subjects, and which, by virtue of his dignity as head of the Church, he wished to impose upon them as a substitute for the Bible.

He now laid down his pen, and glanced with infinite satisfaction over the pages he had written, which would afford his subjects a fresh proof of his paternal love and solicitude, and convince them that Henry the Eighth was not only the noblest and most virtuous of monarchs, but also the wisest and most learned.

This reflection, however, was unable to cheer the king on the present occasion; perhaps because he had contemplated the subject too often, until it had lost its novelty. He felt restless and dejected, as if oppressed by an uneasy sense of solitude—there were so many secret and hidden voices in his heart, the whispers whereof he feared, and which he therefore sought always to drown; there were so many reminiscences of blood ever present to his mind, however often he strode to efface them with fresh blood. These thoughts the king abhorred, although he wore the air of never repenting what he had done, and never feeling any remorse of conscience for his deeds.

He suddenly rang the gold bell which stood beside him, and his countenance brightened up when he saw the door open, and the Earl of Douglas appear on the threshold.

"Oh! at length," said Lord Douglas, who well understood the expression of Henry's features, "at length the king condescends to show favor to his people."

"What! I show favor?" asked the king, with astonishment. "And how is that, pray?"

"Because your majesty at length takes rest from your labors, and thinks a little of your health, which is so precious, and so needful to the public weal. Because you remember, sire, that the well-being of England consists alone in the welfare of her king; so that your majesty must preserve your health, sound and robust, in order that your people may be so."

The king smiled with satisfaction. It never occurred to him to doubt the earl's words. He thought it quite natural that the welfare of his subjects was centred in his own person, but still the assurance of this fact was ever a pleasing and grateful melody in his ears; for it appealed to his pride, and he loved to hear the flattering strains repeated again and again by his courtiers.

The king, as we have said, smiled, but in this smile there was something unusual, which did not escape Lord Douglas.

"He is in the condition of a hungry alligator," said Lord Douglas to himself. "He is on the watch for prey, and he will only recover his cheerfulness and good-humor, when he has tasted some human flesh and blood. Ah! well, fortunately, we have a large stock of that always on hand. It is the king's own, and we shall give him some. But we must be cautious, and go to work prudently."

He approached the king, and kissed his hand.

"I kiss this hand," said the wily lord, "which to-day has been the instrument whereby the wisdom of the head has been poured forth on this thrice-blessed paper. I kiss this paper which will reveal and proclaim to happy England the pure and unadulterated word of God; but still I would say, let it suffice for the present, sire, and take rest, in order to remember that you are not only a sage but also a man."

"Yea, verily, a feeble, tottering man!" sighed the king, while he attempted to rise with difficulty, and in doing so leaned upon the arm of the earl with such force, that the latter almost gave way under the huge burden.

"Tottering?" said Lord Douglas, reproachfully. "Your majesty moves with as much ease and freedom as a young man. And there was no need of my assistance to lift you up."

"Nevertheless we are growing old," said the king, who, being to-day affected with *ennui*, was unusually sensitive and melancholy.

"Old!" repeated the courtier, "with these fire-flashing eyes, this unfurrowed brow, and this noble and serene countenance? No, your majesty—kings, in common with the gods, enjoy the privilege of never growing old."

"And in that respect they resemble parrots to a hair," said John Heywood, who at this moment entered the room. "I have a parrot which my great-grandfather inherited from his great-grandfather, who was the barber of Henry the Fourth, and which at the present day chatters with as much glibness as he did a hundred years back, 'Long live the king—long live this noble pattern of virtue, grace, beauty, and goodness, long live the king!' That was the song my parrot sang a hundred years since, and he repeated it for Henry the Fifth, and Henry the Sixth, and for Henry the Seventh, and Henry the Eighth. And, wonderful!—the kings have changed—but this song of praise has endured, and has never been any thing but the pure and simple truth. Just like yours, my Lord Douglas. Your majesty will allow him to tell the truth, for he is nearly related to my parrot, who always calls him 'cousin,' and has taught him this immortal song of praise upon kings."

The king laughed at this merry speech, while Lord Douglas cast a scornful and withering glance at John Heywood.

"He is an insolent knave," said the king, "is he not, Douglas?"

"He is a fool!" said the earl, with a supercilious shrug.

"Exactly so, and consequently I have often told you the truth, for it is well known that fools and children tell the truth. And my object in becoming a fool was just in order that the king, whom you all belie with flattery, may have some creature, besides his looking glass, to tell him the truth."

"Well, and what truth are you going to dish up for me to-day, John?"

"It is already dished up, sire. Lay aside therefore your royal crown and your chief-priestship for a short time, and resolve to become a carnivorous animal for a brief space. There is no difficulty in being a king. A man has only to be born of a queen under a canopy, but it is a different thing to be a man with a good digestion. For this purpose one requires a sound stomach and a quiet conscience. Come, King Henry, come and let us see if you are not only a king, but also a man with a vigorous stomach."

And with a jocular grin, the jester took the king's arm and led him, with the earl on the other side, into the dining-room.

The king, who was an extraordinary feeder, nodded silently to his suite to take their places at the table, after he had himself sunk into his gilded arm-chair.

With a grave and solemn look, the king took from the hands of the chamberlain the ivory tablets on which were written the bill of fare for the day. The king's dinner was a serious and important matter. A large number of post-horses and messengers were continually engaged in fetching from the remotest parts of the kingdom and of Europe the most choice and dainty morsels for the king's table. The list accordingly exhibited on this day, as it always did, the rarest and most recherché edibles, and whenever the king found one of his favorite dishes set down, he nodded his head approvingly, which always made the face of the grand master of the ceremonies beam like rays of sunshine.

There were birds'-nests from the Indies, and capons from Calcutta, besides truffles from Languedoc, which the poetical King Francis the First had yesterday sent as a special mark of affection to his royal brother of England; the sparkling wine of Champagne, and the fiery wine of the Island of Cyprus, which the Republic of Venice had sent the king as a testimonial of high regard. There were, too, the hard Rhenish wines—lustrous as liquid gold, and yielding the fragance of an entire bouquet—with which the North German Princes hoped to intoxicate the king whom they wished to place at the head of their league. There were also huge pasties of partridges, which the Duke of Burgundy had sent, and the luscious fruits of the South and of the Spanish Main, with which the Emperor Charles the Fifth furnished the table of the King of England. For it was well known that in order to win the favor of the English monarch, his appetite must needs first be appeased, and his palate tickled, before his head or his heart could be won over.

All these delicacies, however, did not suffice on the present occasion to impart to the king that happy and cheerful humor, which he generally evinced when he sat down to table. He smiled pensively at John Heywood's jocular sallies and witty sarcasms, and a cloud hung upon his brow. The king needed specially the presence of the ladies to put him in a cheerful mood,—he needed them, as the hunter needs the stag in order to enjoy the pleasures of the chase,—pleasures which consist in this, that the defenceless are driven to death, and war declared against the peaceful and innocent.

The wily courtier, Lord Douglas, readily perceived the troubled temper of the King, and understood the secret cause of his sighs and gloomy looks. He had ardently hoped for this, and he resolved to take advantage of it in favor of his daughter, and to the prejudice of the queen.

"Sire," he said, "I am just on the point of becoming a traitor, and of accusing my king of injustice."

The king glanced at him with his flashing eyes, while he laid his hand, sparkling with brilliants, upon the golden goblet filled with Rhenish wine, that stood before him.

"Injustice! Me, your king?" he asked, with a thick utterance.

"Yes, of an injustice, inasmuch as you are for me the visible representative of God upon earth. I would accuse the Almighty if he were one day to deprive me of the sun's brightness and splendor, or of the fragrance of his flowers; for as we children of men are accustomed to enjoy these delights, we have acquired an undoubted claim to them in perpetuity. I therefore accuse you, sire, of having withdrawn from us the embodied essence of the flowers, and the incarnate light of the sun itself—for you have been so cruel as to send the queen to Epping Forest."

"Not so—the queen wished to ride," said Henry, pettishly. "The spring weather attracted her, and as unfortunately I do not possess that highest of God's attributes—omnipresence—I must needs dispense with her society for once. There is no longer a horse able to carry the King of England."

"Yet there is Pegasus, sire, and your majesty knows so well how to manage him. But how, sire—the queen wished to ride, though by doing so she would be deprived of your presence? Ah, how cold and selfish are the hearts of women! If I were a woman I would never leave your side; I would covet no greater happiness than to be near you, and listen to the lofty wisdom that flows from your heaven-inspired lips. Were I a woman—"

"My lord, I think your wish is already gratified," interrupted John Heywood, with assumed gravity. "At least your lordship gives me quite the idea of an old woman."

All the company laughed. But the king did not even smile: he remained serious and wore a sullen look of abstraction.

"It is true," he muttered to himself, "she seemed not only glad, but even elated at this excursion, and her eyes shone with a fire that I have rarely seen. There must be some peculiar circumstance connected with this ride to Epping Forest. Who accompanied the queen?"

"The Princess Elizabeth," said John Heywood, who had heard all, and who had clearly perceived the shaft which the earl had aimed at the queen. "The Princess Elizabeth, her faithful and devoted friend, who never leaves her side—and also her ladies, who, like the dragon in the fable, watch over the beautiful princess."

"Who is there besides in the queen's retinue?" asked Henry morosely.

"Her master of the horse, Lord Sudley," replied Douglas, "and—"

"That was quite a superfluous observation," interrupted John Heywood—"it is a matter of course, that the master of the horse should accompany the queen. It is as much his duty to do so as it is yours to sing the song of your cousin, my parrot."

"He is right. Thomas Seymour must accompany her," said the king, hastily—"that is my will and pleasure. Thomas Seymour is a faithful servant, and he has inherited that quality from his sister Jane, my much beloved queen, who rests with God. Thomas Seymour is devoted to his king with unwavering fidelity."

"The time is not yet ripe to assail the Seymour party," thought the earl. "The king is still favorable to them, and he will therefore be hostile to their enemies. Let us, accordingly, begin our attack against Henry Howard—that is to say, against the queen."

"Who accompanied the queen besides?" repeated Henry, draining the goblet at a draught, as if he wished thereby to cool the fire which was already kindling up within him. But the fiery Rhine wine, instead of cooling, only heated him still more; it fanned like a hurricane the flame which was burning in his jealous breast, until it rose to his head, and made his brain glow like his heart.

"Who else accompanied her?" said Lord Douglas, with an air of *nonchalance*. "Well, I think it was the queen's chamberlain—the Earl of Surrey."

The king knit his brows. The lion had scented his prey.

"The queen's chamberlain is *not* in the retinue!" said John Heywood with earnest vehemence.

"He is not?" cried Lord Douglas. "Poor Lord Surrey!—that will make him very sad."

"And why do you think it will make him sad?" demanded the king in a voice that resembled the rumbling of distant thunder.

"Because Lord Surrey is accustomed, sire, to live in the sunshine of royal favor—because he resembles that flower that always turns its face toward the sun, and receives from it life and color and splendor."

"Let him take care that the sun does not scorch him!" murmured the king.

"My lord," said John Heywood, "you should use a pair of spectacles to help you to see better. This time you have confounded the sun with one of its satellites. The Earl of Surrey is far too prudent a man to venture to bask in the sun, and so dazzle his eyes and affect his brain. He is content with worshipping one of the planets that surround the sun."

"What does the fool mean?" said Lord Douglas, with a scornful smile.

"The wise man means you to understand that you have this time confounded your daughter with the queen," replied John Heywood, laying a stress upon each word; "and that it has happened to you like many great astronomers, to mistake a—"

Lord Douglas cast an angry and scornful glance at John Heywood, which the latter returned with a look of stern defiance.

Their eyes became fixed upon each other, and they each read in the eyes of the other, the hatred and animosity which was fermenting in their hearts. They both knew that from this hour forth they had sworn an implacable and deadly animosity against each other.

Of this silent but most significant scene, the king had observed nothing. He hung his head, brooding gloomily upon the words of Lord Douglas, and the storm-clouds which gathered on his brow, were becoming more dense and murky each moment.

With a violent effort he raised himself from his seat, and this time he required no helping hand to stand upright. Anger was the powerful lever which lifted him up.

The courtiers rose silently from their seats, and nobody but John Heywood observed the glance of mutual understanding which Lord Douglas exchanged with Gardiner, Bishop of Winchester, and Wriothesley the chancellor.

"Ah! Why is Cranmer not here?" said John Heywood to himself. "I see the three tiger-cats prowling about, consequently there is prey somewhere to be swallowed. Well, at all events, I shall keep my ears wide open, so that I can hear their purring and miauling."

"Dinner is over, my lords," said the king, hastily, and the gentlemen of the court and the lords in waiting withdrew in silence to the antechamber.

Only Lord Douglas, Gardiner and Wriothesley remained behind, while John Heywood had glided, unperceived, into the king's closet, and there hid himself behind the gold-brocaded screen which covered the door leading from the king's study into the outer anteroom.

"My lords," said the king, "you will accompany me to my closet. As time hangs heavily on our hands, it will be most advisable to divert ourself by taking note of what concerns the welfare of our beloved subjects. Follow me therefore: we will hold a privy council."

"Lord Douglas, your arm." And while the king, leaning upon the arm of his courtier, proceeded slowly toward the cabinet, at the entrance of which the chancellor and the Bishop of Winchester awaited him, he asked quietly:

"You say that Henry Howard dares frequently to press into the society of the queen?"

"Sire; I did not say that. I only meant that he was continually to be seen in the vicinity of the queen."

"Oh! you meant, perhaps, that she encouraged him to do so," said the king, grinding his teeth.

"Sire: I hold the queen to be a noble and faithful wife."

"And if you thought otherwise, I should feel disposed to lay your head at your feet," returned the king, in whose countenance the first flash of the thunder-cloud seeking a vent began to burst forth.

"My head belongs to the king," said Lord Douglas, submissively. "Let his majesty do with it as he pleases."

"But Howard? Do you mean, then, that Henry Howard loves the queen?"

"Yes, sire, I venture to maintain that he does."

"Well then, by God's mother, I will crush the reptile under my feet. I will serve him as I did his sister?" exclaimed Henry, with passionate vehemence. "The Howards are a dangerous, an ambitious, and a hypocritical race."

"A race which never forgets that a daughter of their house has sat upon your throne."

"But they shall forget it!" exclaimed the king, "even if I were obliged to wash away the proud and arrogant thought with their heart's blood. It seems they have not already had proof enough in the example of their sister, how I can punish faithlessness and treason. This insolent race wants still another proof. If so, they shall have it. Only furnish me with the means, Douglas—give me the smallest hook that I can fix in the flesh of these Howards, and I tell you that with this little book I will land them on the scaffold. Only give me proofs of the audacious love of the earl, and I promise to grant you as a reward whatever you ask."

"Sire, I will undertake to furnish the proofs you require."

"When?"

"Within four days, sire,—at the grand tournament of poets, which you have commanded in honor of the queen's birthday."

"Thanks, Douglas, thanks," said the king, with a smile of satisfaction. "In four days you will have rid me of the troublesome race of the Howards."

"But, sire, if I cannot give the proofs you require, without accusing another person?"

The king who was about to enter the door of his closet, stood still and looked at the earl with a fixed gaze. Then he replied, with a grim and sinister smile: "You mean the queen? Well, if she is guilty I shall punish her! God has placed his sword in my hand—that I may wield it to his honor and to the terror of men. If the queen has sinned she shall suffer. Furnish me with the proofs of Howard's guilt, and be not concerned, if in procuring them we should discover the guilt of others. We will not shrink back faint-hearted, but let justice take its course!"

BOOK III.

THE QUEEN'S ROSETTE.

CHAPTER I.

THE QUEEN'S FRIEND.

Lord Douglas, Gardiner, and Wriothesley, had accompanied the king into his study.

The great blow was at length about to be struck, and the scene so long meditated by the three enemies of the queen was coming to a crisis.

Accordingly, as they followed the king, who strode along before them with unusual activity, they once more exchanged glances of intelligence with one another.

The look of Lord Douglas said: "The hour is come, hold yourselves ready!"

While the looks of his friends replied: "We are ready."

John Heywood, who was concealed behind a curtain, and who saw and noted all, could not forbear a slight shudder at the sight of these four men, whose hard and sinister features seemed inaccessible to every ray of pity and of mercy.

There was first of all the king, the man with the Protean countenance, in which storm and sunshine, heaven and hell, alternately marked fresh lines; who at one moment was an inspired enthusiast, and the next a sanguinary tyrant—at one time a sentimental connoisseur, and at another a sensual glutton—the king, upon whose constancy no one, not even himself, could build, who was always ready, when it suited his caprice or his interest, to betray his most devoted friends, and to send to the scaffold tomorrow those whom he yesterday embraced and had assured him of his unchanging attachment—the king, who thought himself justified in allowing his own private lusts, his revengeful impulses, and his sanguinary propensities to go unpunished; who was pious from vanity, because piety gave him the opportunity of always identifying his own cause with that of Heaven, and of regarding himself in a certain manner as the champion and patron of the Almighty.

There was Lord Douglas, the crafty

courtier with the ever-smiling countenance, who seemed to love every one, while he hated all; who assumed a look of perfect innocence, and appeared indifferent to every thing except pleasure, while he secretly held in his hands all the threads of the huge net with which the court and even the king himself was surrounded.

Lord Douglas, whom the king loved only because he called him the great and wise high-priest of the Church, and who was still the representative of Loyola, and the faithful and devoted adherent of the pope, who had condemned the king as a degenerate son, and handed him over to the wrath of God.

There were, in fine, the two men with truculent and sinister features, and with faces rigid and inflexible, never lighted up by a smile or a gleam of pleasure; who always punished, always condemned, and whose countenance only brightened when the death-cry of some unhappy being on the scaffold, or the shrieks of anguish of some wretch condemned to the rack, struck their ear; and who were the tormentors of human nature, while calling themselves the servants of God.

"Sire," said Gardiner, as the king sank back slowly on the ottoman, "let us first ask God's blessing upon our deliberations. May the Almighty, who is love, but who is also anger, enlighten and bless us!"

The king folded his hands devoutly, but it was only a prayer of anger that rose to his lips.

"Grant, O God! that I may be able to punish thine enemies, and everywhere to crush the guilty!" he murmured.

"Amen!" responded Gardiner, repeating the words of the king with solemn earnestness.

"Send us the lightning of thy wrath," prayed Wriothesley, "that we may be able to teach the world to recognize thy power and majesty."

Lord Douglas was careful not to pray aloud. The petitions which he had to send up were not for the king's ear to hear.

"Grant, O Lord!" he inwardly prayed, "grant that my scheme succeed, and that this dangerous queen may ascend the scaffold, in order to make way for my daughter, who is destined to bring back once more this criminal and faithless king to the arms of our holy mother Church."

"And now, my lords," said the king, "how do matters stand in our kingdom, and at our court?"

"Badly, sire!" returned Gardiner. "Heresy is daily lifting its head higher and higher. It is the dragon, which, when its head is cut off, only causes two others to spring up in its stead. These accursed sects of Reformers and Atheists are increasing day by day; our dungeons are no longer sufficient to hold them; and if we send them to the scaffold, their joyful and courageous conduct in meeting death only makes fresh proselytes and sectaries."

"Yes, very badly," pursued the Chancellor Wriothesley;—"in vain have we promised pardon and forgiveness to all who should come back penitent and contrite: they scorn our forgiveness, and prefer the death of a martyr to the royal pardon. What boots it that we have burnt Miles Coverdale, who has had the hardihood to translate the Bible? His death only appears to have been the alarum bell which has roused other fanatics, and though we cannot imagine where all these books come from, they inundate the whole country, and we have already more than four translations of the Bible. The people read them with eagerness, and the deadly seeds of enlightenment and free thinking wax daily stronger and more destructive."

"And now, my Lord Douglas, what have you to say?" asked the king, as the chancellor ceased. "These noble lords have told me what was passing in my kingdom, you will perhaps inform me how affairs are going on at my court."

"Sire," said Douglas, slowly and gravely—for he wished that every word should sink into the king's breast like a poisoned shaft—"Sire, the people only follow the example which the court gives them. How can your majesty expect that the people should believe, when they see how your own court itself mocks at faith, and when heretics and unbelievers find patrons and abettors within the court."

"You accuse, but you mention no names," said the king impatiently. "Who is there at my court that would dare to be the patron of heretics?"

"Cranmer, the Archbishop of Canterbury!" exclaimed the three noble lords in a breath.

The signal was given—the bloody standard was unfurled.

"Cranmer?" repeated the king, musingly. "And yet he has always been a faithful servant to me, and a careful friend. It was he who once delivered me from that unhallowed union with Katharine of Arragon: it was he who also warned me against Katharine Howard, and brought me the proofs of her guilt. Of what crime do you accuse him?"

"He denies the Six Articles," replied Gardiner, whose sullen countenance now became inflamed with an expression of sinister hate. "He condemns auricular confession, and does not believe that the vows of chastity, freely taken, are binding."

"If he does that, he is an arch-traitor!" exclaimed the king, who loved to inspire reverence for chastity and virtue, as a kind of sacred mantle to hide his own unchaste and profligate life, and whom nothing exasperated more than to meet another upon this path of crime—which he himself, by virtue of his royal dignity and his crown, by God's grace, could travel unscathed.

"If he does that, he is an arch-traitor, and my arm of vengeance will reach him," repeated the king once more. "It is I who have given to my subjects the Six Articles as holy dogmas of the faith, and I wont suffer any one to attack or obscure these only true and just doctrines. But you err, my lords! I know Cranmer, and I know that he is a faithful believer."

"And yet it is he," returned Gardiner,

"who confirms these heretics in their obstinacy and hardness of heart; he is the cause why these reprobates, if not from fear of the divine vengeance, do not return to you at least as their lord and high-priest. For he preaches to them that God is love and mercy,—he teaches them that Christ came into the world in order to bring to the world love and the forgiveness of sin, and that those alone are his disciples and servants who imitate his love. And do you not also perceive, sire, that there is a secret and covert attack upon yourself, and that while he praises the love that forgives, he at the same time attacks and condemns your just anger that inflicts punishment?"

The king made no reply for some time, but looked down gravely and thoughtfully. The fanatical priest had gone too far, and without knowing it, it was he himself who accused the king at this moment.

Lord Douglas felt this. He read upon the king's countenance that he found himself in one of those moments of contrition, which sometimes overtook him, when his mind cast an involuntary glance at its own workings.

It was necessary to rouse the sleeping tiger, and to show him his prey, in order to renew his thirst for blood.

"It would be all very well," he said, "if Cranmer only preached christian love. In doing so, he would only be a faithful servant of his master, and an imitator of his king. But he gives the world the abominable example of an undutiful and traitorous servant: he denies the truth of the Six Articles, not in words only but in deeds. You have commanded that the priests of the Church should be unmarried. Well, then, the Archbishop of Canterbury is married!"

"Married!" exclaimed the king, with anger-flaming countenance. "Ah, I'll punish him—this transgressor of my holy laws. A servant of the Church, a priest, whose whole life should be devoted to holy contemplation, to perpetual conversation with God, and whose high vocation it is to renounce all earthly desires and lusts of the flesh! He married! I shall make him feel the whole rigor of my royal anger; he shall now experience in his own person that the justice of the king is implacable, and never fails to reach the head of the guilty, whoever he be."

"Your majesty is the epitome of justice and wisdom," said Douglas, "and your faithful servants well know that if the royal justice sometimes delays to strike down the guilty, this occurs not with your will, but by means of your servants, who have the audacity to hold back the arm of justice."

"Where and when could this have taken place?" asked Henry, his features glowing with anger and excitement. "Who is the offender that I have not punished? Where lives there in my kingdom the being who has sinned against God or his king, and whom I have not crushed?"

"Sire," replied Gardiner, solemnly, "Maria Askew still lives."

"She lives in order to mock your

majesty's wisdom, and to contemn your holy doctrines!" exclaimed Wriothesley.

"She lives because Archbishop Cranmer is unwilling that she should die," said Douglas, with a shrug.

The king burst forth into a short, hard fit of laughter.

"Ah, indeed,—so Cranmer is not willing that Maria Askew should die," he said derisively. "He is unwilling that this young woman, who has so fearfully outraged her king and her God, should be punished?"

"Yes, she has committed a terrible outrage, and yet two years have elapsed since her deed of guilt," exclaimed Gardiner. "Two years, which she has spent in contemning her God, and despising her king."

"Ah," said the king, "we had always hoped to bring back this young misguided creature from the ways of sin and error to the paths of light and repentance. We wished at one time to give a striking example to our people, how willingly we pardon those who repent and renounce their heresy, and how we again make them partakers of our royal favor. Hence it was that we gave you, my Lord Bishop, the commission, by virtue of your impressive and convincing words, to recover this poor child from the clutches of Satan, who had led her astray."

"But she is inflexible," said Gardiner, and he gnashed his teeth. "In vain have I pictured to her the torments of hell which awaited her unless she returned to the faith; in vain have I subjected her to all sorts of pains and penances; in vain have I sent other converts into her prison cell, and caused them to pray continually with her night and day: she remains inflexible, as hard as a stone, and neither the fear of punishment nor the prospect of freedom and happiness can soften this heart of marble."

"There is one means which has not yet been tried," said Wriothesley. "A means, however, which is a more effectual preacher of penitence than the most inspired orators or the most eloquent prayers, and to which I am indebted for having brought back many of the most obstinate heretics to God and to the faith."

"And this means?"

"Torture, your majesty!"

"Ah, torture," repeated the king, with an involuntary shudder.

"All means are good which conduce to so holy an end!" said Gardiner, devoutly clasping his hands.

"The soul must be saved by wounding the body to the quick!" exclaimed Wriothesley.

"It must be proved to the people," said Douglas, "that the upright conscience of the king does not spare even those who are protected by powerful and influential persons. The people murmur that, in this case, justice is not suffered to prevail, because Archbishop Cranmer protects Maria Askew, and because the queen is her friend."

"The queen is never the friend of a malefactor," said Henry, sharply.

"Perhaps she does not consider Maria Askew to be a malefactor," returned

Lord Douglas, with a faint smile. "It is, indeed, well known that Queen Katharine is a great friend of the Reformation, and the people, who dare not call her a heretic, still call her 'The Protestant.'"

"Then people really think that it is the queen who protects Maria Askew and saves her from the scaffold?" asked the king, musingly.

"That is what they think, your majesty."

"Then they shall see that they have erred, and that Henry the Eighth well deserves to be called Defender of the Faith and Head of his Church," exclaimed the king, with rising anger. "For when have I shown myself so indulgent and so timid in punishing, that people should think me disposed to forgive or show leniency? Have I not caused Thomas More and Cromwell, two distinguished, and, in some respects, noble and highminded men, to mount the scaffold, because they dared to defy my power, and to revolt against the doctrines and ordinances in which I had commanded them to believe? Have I not sent two of my queens to the block for having roused my anger,—two young and beautiful women, in whom my soul found delight even while I punished them? Who, then, after such striking examples of our crushing justice, will dare to accuse us of being indulgent?"

"But at that time, sire," said Douglas, with his soft insinuating voice, "at that time, there was no queen at your side who called heretics orthodox believers, and esteemed traitors worthy of her friendship."

The king knit his brow, and his angry glance fell upon the dutiful and devoted countenance of the earl.

"You know," he exclaimed, "that I hate these covert attacks. If you can accuse the queen of any offence—well,—do it. But if not, pray be silent!"

"The queen is a noble and a virtuous lady," said the earl, "only that she suffers herself at times to be led astray by her generous disposition. Or perhaps it has been with your majesty's consent that my lady, the queen, holds a correspondence with Maria Askew?"

"What do you mean? The queen hold a correspondence with Maria Askew?" exclaimed the king, in a voice of thunder. "This is a lie—a scandalous lie, which has been invented in order to overthrow the queen; for it is well known that the unhappy king, who has been so often deceived and circumvented, believes, at length, that he has found in this woman a being whom he can trust and in whom he can believe. And people grudge him this—they wish to snatch even this last hope from him, in order that his heart may be wholly turned to stone, and that no emotion of mercy may any longer find an entrance to his bosom. Ah, Douglas, Douglas! beware of my anger, unless you can prove what you say!"

"I *can* prove it, sire! for it was only yesterday that Lady Jane had to convey a note from Maria Askew to the queen."

The king remained silent for some time, looking gloomily toward the floor. His three confidants regarded him with strained and breathless attention.

At length the king raised his head and directed his glance, which was now stern and fixed, toward the chancellor.

"My Lord Chancellor Wriothesley," he said, "I empower you to take Maria Askew to the rack, and to try whether the tortures prepared for the body may not, perchance, have power to bring back this erring soul to repentance. My Lord Bishop Gardiner, I give you my word, that I shall duly attend to your accusation against the Archbishop of Canterbury; and that if I find it justified, he shall not escape his punishment. My Lord Douglas, I shall prove to my people and to the whole world, that I am still the just and avenging Vicar of God upon earth, and that no regard can stem my anger,—no consideration check my arm, when once it is lifted to strike the head of the guilty.—And now, my lords, let us consider this sitting at an end. We will recruit ourselves a little after our efforts, and banish care for a brief season."

"You are dismissed, my lords Gardiner and Wriothesley. Douglas, you will accompany me into the small drawing-room. I wish to see merry and laughing faces around me. Call me, therefore, John Heywood, and if you meet any ladies in the palace, why, beg them to come and cheer us up with a ray of that sunshine, which you often say is peculiar to the women."

He leaned, laughing, upon the earl's arm, and once more quitted the closet.

Gardiner and Wriothesley stood in silence, and looked after the king, who slowly, and with unwieldy gait, strode through the adjoining chamber, and whose merry and laughing voice reached them, and resounded through the room.

"He is like a weather-cock, that turns each moment from side to side," said Gardiner, with a derisive shrug.

"He calls himself the avenging sword of God; and yet he is nothing more than a weak tool, that we can twist about and use at our pleasure," murmured Wriothesley, with a burst of hoarse laughter. "Poor, miserable fool, who thinks himself so great and powerful, and fancies he is a free, self-governing king, while in reality he is only our servant and slave. The great work is drawing to an end, and we shall one day triumph. Maria Askew's death will be the signal for a new league, which will save England, and tread down the heretics like dust under our feet. And when we have at length overthrown Cranmer, and led Katharine Parr to the scaffold, we shall give King Henry a queen who will reconcile him once more with God, and with the only sanctifying Church."

"Amen. So be it!" said Gardiner, and arm in arm they both left the closet.

A deep silence now reigned in this little room; and no one perceived how John Heywood stepped from behind the curtain, and, for a moment, wholly exhausted and weary, flung himself down into a seat.

"Well, now I know the plans, at least, of these bloodthirsty tiger-cats," he murmured. "They want to give Henry a Catholic queen, and for that reason Cranmer must be overthrown, in order that when they have robbed the queen of this powerful support, they may be able to destroy her and trample her in the dust. But so true as God lives this plot shall not succeed! God is just, and he will finally punish these malefactors. Ay, and even if there were no God, we would rouse the Devil to help us. No, they shall not ruin the noble Cranmer, and this beautiful and generous queen. I, John Heywood, the king's jester, won't have it. I'll see, hear, and observe all that passes. They shall find me everywhere in their path; and if they poison the ear of the king with their diabolical insinuations, I'll cure it all with my playful devilry. The king's fool will prove the queen's guardian angel."

CHAPTER II.

JOHN HEYWOOD.

After so many cares and anxieties, the king required some recreation and amusement. As the beautiful young queen was seeking enjoyment in the chase, and in the contemplation of nature, away from the king, Henry had to find entertainment for himself as best he could, without the help of the queen. His unwieldiness however, and the weight of his flesh prevented him from seeking the pleasures of life outside his palace. The lords and ladies of his court, therefore, must needs bring these pleasures home to him, and place the flattering goddess of joy, with folded wings, opposite the king's rolling chair.

The gout had completely overcome him to-day—this mighty king of men; and as he sat in his arm-chair, he looked a huge unshapen mass.

But his courtiers still called him a handsome and attractive man, and the ladies still smiled at him, and told him with their sighs and their glances, that they loved him,—that he was still to them the same handsome and seductive man he had been twenty years before, when he was still young, slender, and elegant. How they smiled and cast their sly glances at the monarch—those high-born and lovely women! How Lady Jane, formerly the proud and reserved maiden, tries to ensnare him with her glowing eyes, as with a net; how the Duchess of Richmond, lovely and voluptuous, laughs bewitchingly at the king's sensual witticisms, and equivocal puns!

Poor king! whose corpulence forbade him to dance, as he once used to do with so much grace and skill. Poor king! whose age forbade him to sing, as he once loved to do, to the delight of his court.

But still there are some delicious and exquisite moments full of enjoyment, when the man once more revives in the monarch—when youth once more opens the eyes of the king, and smiles upon him with some sweet and blissful joys.

The king has, at least, eyes still left to see beauty, and a heart to feel its effects.

"How beautiful Lady Jane is,—that

fair lily with the dark, star-glistening eyes,—how beautiful is her grace of Richmond, this full-blown purple rose, with the pearly-white teeth!"

And they both smile upon him, and when the king swears that he loves them, they blush and sigh with downcast looks.

"Do you sigh, Jane, because you love me?"

"Oh, sire, you mock me. It would be a crime in me to love you, for Queen Katharine is alive."

"Yes, she is alive!" murmured the king, and his brow grew dark, and the smile vanished for a moment from his lips.

Lady Jane had made a mistake. She had reminded the king of his wife, when it was yet too soon for her death.

John Heywood read this on the countenance of his royal master, and resolved to profit by it. He wished to divert the king's attention, and to lead his thoughts away from these beautiful and bewitching ladies who dazzled him with their charms.

"Yes, the queen lives!" he repeated, with animation. "And God be thanked she does! For how dreary and tedious would it be at this court, if we had not beside us our beautiful queen, who is as wise as Methusalem, and as innocent as a new-born child. You join with me, Lady Jane, do you not, in saying, God be thanked the queen lives?"

"I do!" said Lady Jane, with ill-dissembled chagrin.

"And you, King Henry, don't you say so too?"

"Certainly, fool!"

"Ah, would I were King Henry?" sighed John Heywood. "King, I envy you, not your crown and royal sceptre, not your courtiers and your wealth—I only envy you, that you can say, praised be God, my wife still lives!—while I never hear any other phrase, than would to God my wife were not alive! Ah very rarely, king, have I heard a husband speak otherwise. In this, as in all other matters, you are an exception, King Henry, and your people will never love you more ardently or sincerely than when you say, thank God that my wife lives! Trust me, you are, perhaps, the only man at your court who would imitate you in saying so, however ready they are to become your parrots, and to repeat what is said by their lord high-priest."

"The only man that loves his wife!" said the Duchess of Richmond. "Only listen to the chattering clown! Then you don't believe that we women desire to be loved?"

"I am convinced that you do not."

"And what do you take us for then?"

"For cats, which God has put into a smooth skin, not having any more catskins to spare."

"Take care, John, that we don't show you our claws," said the duchess, laughing.

"Please yourself, my lady duchess. I shall only make the sign of the cross and you'll vanish, for, you know, devils can't bear the sign of the cross, and ye women are devils."

John Heywood, who was an accomplished singer, seized the mandolin that lay beside him, and began to sing.

It was a song such as was only possible at that period, and at Henry's voluptuous and hypocritical court. A song full of the most licentious allusions, of the most offensive jests against monks and women—which made the king laugh and the ladies blush, and in which John Heywood had poured forth in glowing strains all his secret anger against Gardiner, the sneaking and hypocritical priest, and against Lady Jane, the false and dissembling friend of the queen.

But the ladies did not laugh. They directed looks full of anger at John Heywood, and Lady Richmond demanded gravely and urgently that the traitor should be punished, who had so dared to calumniate women.

The king laughed still more. The anger of the ladies was so infinitely diverting.

"Sire," said the beautiful Richmond, "he has offended not us alone but all our sex, and in the name of our sex I demand that this outrage be revenged."

"Yes, revenge!" cried Lady Jane, passionately.

"Only see what pious and gentle doves you are!" returned John Heywood.

"Very well, then, you shall have your will—you shall chastise him," said the king, laughing.

"Yes, yes, flog me with scourges, as the Messiah was once flogged for having told the Pharisees the truth. Just see. I am putting on the crown of thorns already."

And with a grave air he took the king's velvet cap and raised it to his head.

"Yes, flog him, flog him," cried the king laughing, as he pointed to the huge porcelain vases which contained immense rose bushes, from the long stems of which a prickly forest of thorns rose up.

"Turn those large bouquets round the other way,—take the roses in your hands, and flog him with the stems!" said the king, and his eyes glistened with grim delight, for the scene promised to be highly interesting. The stems of the rose bushes were long and hard, and the thorns upon them were pointed and sharp as daggers. How would they penetrate his flesh, and how he would cry out and make wry faces—the honest fool!

"Oh, yes, he must take off his coat, and we will flog him," cried the Duchess of Richmond, and the other ladies cried out after her in chorus, and like furies they rushed upon him, and forced him to doff his silken overcoat. Then hastening to the vases they tore out the rose bushes, and skilfully selected the longest and strongest stems, and screamed with delight when the thorns were very large and sharp, and so would pierce deep into the flesh of the offender.

The laughter and the shouts of applause of the king encouraged them more and more, and made them still more excited and furious.

Their cheeks glowed, their eyes glistened; they resembled the Bacchantes who, with their cry Evoe! Evoe! surround the god of mad festivity.

"Not yet! Don't strike yet," exclaimed the king. "You must first strengthen yourselves for the enterprise and give energy to your arm for a weighty stroke."

He took the large golden beaker that stood before him and handed it to Lady Jane.

"Drink, Lady Jane, drink, and give strength to your arm!"

And they all drank, and with animated smiles pressed their lips to the place which the king's mouth had touched; and now their eyes grew more inflamed and their cheeks glowed with fresh ardor.

It was a singular and piquant spectacle, to see all these beautiful women glowing with malicious joy, and thirst for revenge,—all of whom for the moment had laid aside their gentler attractions and their proud and haughty looks, in order to transform themselves into riotous Bacchantes, who wished to chastise the insolent transgressor, that had so often and so severely scourged them all with his tongue.

"How I wish we had a painter here!" said the king. "He should paint us a picture of the chaste Nymphs of Diana persecuting Actæon. You are Actæon, John."

"But they are not the chaste nymphs, king—certainly not," said John Heywood, laughing, "and between these beautiful ladies and Diana, I see no resemblance—but only a difference."

"And wherein consists the difference, John?"

"In this, sire, that whereas Diana carried her horn at her side, these beautiful ladies cause their husbands to wear it—on their foreheads."

A peal of laughter from the gentlemen, and a scream of rage from the ladies, was the answer to this new epigram of John Heywood.

They arranged themselves in two rows, and formed a lane through which John Heywood must pass.

"Come on, John Heywood! Come and receive your punishment!"

And they raised their thorny scourges, and swung them with angry gestures high above their heads.

The scene certainly began to be very *piquant* for John Heywood, for these scourges had very sharp thorns on them, and his back was defended by only a fine linen shirt.

Meanwhile, with unflinching step, he approached the fatal passage through which he must run the gauntlet. Already he saw the scourges waving behind him, and he felt as if the thorns were already pricking his back.

He remained standing, and with laughter in his eyes, turned round toward the king, "Sire, as you have condemned me to die by the hands of these nymphs, I must claim the right of every culprit about to suffer—a last favor."

"Which we grant you, John!"

"I claim the right of imposing a condition upon these fair ladies—the condition upon which they shall scourge me. Will your majesty grant it?"

"I will."

"And you will give me your royal

word, that this condition shall be faithfully observed and performed?"

"Yes, my royal word."

"Well then!" exclaimed John Heywood, as he entered the defile, "my condition is this: The lady among you all who has had the greatest number of lovers, and who has crowned her husband the oftenest, shall deliver the first blow upon my back."

A deep silence ensued. The uplifted arms of the beautiful ladies were suddenly relaxed, and the rose-trees fell from their hands to the ground. But a moment since, they were filled with spite and revenge, and now they have become the mildest and gentlest beings in the world.

But had their glances been able to kill, the latent fire thereof must have consumed the hapless John Heywood, who now looked round at them with derisive laughter.

"Now, my ladies, why don't you strike?" asked the king.

"We despise him too much, your majesty, even to wish to chastise him," said the Duchess of Richmond.

"Then, in that case, your enemy will have offended you unpunished?" inquired the king. "No, no, my ladies, it shall not be said that there is a man in my kingdom whom I would have suffered to escape a well-merited punishment! We will therefore impose another penalty upon him. He calls himself a poet, and has often boasted that he could cause his pen to move as nimbly as he wags his tongue. Well then, John, prove to us that thou art no vain boaster. I command thee to write an interlude for the great court festival, which will take place a few days hence;—such an interlude, hark ye, John, as shall afford mirth to the most serious, and which shall make these ladies laugh so heartily as to forget all their anger!"

"Oh!" replied John, plaintively, "what an equivocal and disorderly composition it must be, if intended to make these ladies laugh and be merry. In that case, my king, in order to please these dear ladies, we must forget a little of our modesty and bashfulness, and not stand upon ceremony or delicate reserve; and we must endeavor to speak as freely as possible—in the sense in which ladies understand license of speech."

"You are a wretch!" said Lady Jane. "A common hypocritical fool!"

"Lord Douglas, your daughter speaks with you," said John Heywood, calmly. "Your affectionate daughter flatters you very much."

"Well, John?" asked the king, "you have understood my command, and you will fulfil it? This festival was to have taken place within four days. I shall postpone it for two days longer. In six days, therefore, from this time, you will have prepared a new interlude for us. And if he fail, my ladies, then you shall scourge him unconditionally and without compunction, until the blood comes!"

A loud noise, and the clatter of horses' hoofs was now heard below in the court-yard.

"The queen has returned!" exclaimed John Heywood, and his face beamed with delight, while he directed a look of smiling, but malicious, satisfaction at Lady Jane. "There now remains for you nothing further to do than to go and meet your mistress on the grand staircase, and render your services,—for as you lately observed with so much wisdom,—'THE QUEEN STILL LIVES!'"

Without waiting for a reply, John Heywood sprang forward, and rushed along through the anterooms and down the steps to meet the queen. Lady Jane looked after him with a glance of anger and resentment, and as she slowly advanced toward the door in order to attend upon the queen, she murmured gently from between her compressed lips: "The fool must die, for he is the friend of the queen!"

CHAPTER III.

THE CONFIDANT.

THE queen was ascending the steps of the grand staircase, and she greeted John Heywood with a friendly smile.

"Your majesty," he said aloud, "I have a few private words to say to you in the name of the king!"

"*Private* words!" repeated Katharine, as she stood still on the landing. "Well then, ladies and gentlemen, will you retire a moment, while we receive the private message of his majesty."

The royal retinue withdrew silently and respectfully into the large anterooms of the palace, while the queen remained behind with John Heywood.

"Now, John, what is the message?"

"Attend, queen, to my words and engrave them upon your memory! A plot has been formed against you, and in a few days—at the great court festival—it will be ripe for execution. Be watchful, therefore, over every word you utter, and even keep a check upon your thoughts. Beware of every dangerous step, for you may be sure that you will always have a spy at your side. And if you should need a confidant for any purpose, trust to no one but to me. I tell you that great danger threatens you, and only by prudence and caution will you be able to escape it."

On this occasion the queen did not laugh at the warning voice of her friend. She looked grave—she even trembled.

She had lost her proud assurance and her cheerful confidence—she was no longer blameless—she had a dangerous secret to preserve,—she was, therefore, fearful of its discovery, and she trembled, not for herself alone, but for him she loved.

"And in what does this plot consist?" she asked with a shudder.

"As yet, I know not—I only know that it exists. But, I shall find it out, and if your enemies lurk like spies around you—why, in that case, I shall put on my spectacles to watch their movements."

"And am I the only person whom they threaten?"

"No. Your friend also is in danger, queen!"

Katharine trembled. "Which friend, John?"

"Archbishop Cranmer!"

"Ah! the archbishop!" she repeated, breathing more freely. "And is that all, John? Does their enmity pursue him and myself only?"

"Only you both!" said John Heywood, pensively, for he well understood the relieved breathing of the queen; and he knew that she had trembled for another. "But, remember, queen, that the overthrow of Cranmer would also be your own destruction; and that as you protect the archbishop, so also he protects you with the king—you and your *friends*, too, queen."

Katharine started slightly, and her color deepened.

"I shall always remember him, and shall never cease to be a true and stedfast friend both to him and to you, for you both are my only friends, are you not?"

"No, your majesty. I spoke to you of a third also—of Thomas Seymour."

"Oh, of him!" she cried, with a sweet smile. Then she added, suddenly, in a rapid undertone: "You said I should trust no one here but you. Well, then, I will give you a proof of my confidence. Wait for me to-night at twelve o'clock in the green garden saloon. You shall be my attendant on a dangerous excursion. Have you courage, John?"

"Yes; courage to die for you, queen."

"Then come; but bring arms with you."

"As you command. But are these your only orders to-day?"

"That is all, John. Only," she added, with hesitation, and blushing slightly, "only, if you should chance to meet Lord Sudley, tell him that I have commissioned you with greetings for him."

"Oh!" sighed John Heywood, sadly.

"He has to-day saved my life, John," she added, as if by way of excuse. "It is, therefore, right that I should be grateful to him."

And nodding to him in a friendly manner, she entered the palace.

"Now, who will say that accident is not the most malicious and spiteful of all devils," murmured John Heywood. "This devil throws in the queen's way just the very man whom she should avoid most of all; and makes it necessary that she should, at the same time, be most deeply bound in gratitude to the man she loves. Ho! ho! then he has saved her life. Who knows, however, but he may one day be the means of her losing it."

He bent his head pensively on his breast, when he suddenly heard a voice behind him, which gently called him by name; and, as he turned round, he saw the young princess Elizabeth, who, with rapid steps, was hastening after him.

She was very beautiful at this moment. Her eyes flashed with the fire of passion; her cheeks glowed, and round her thin, crimson lips played a gentle smile expressive of happiness. According to the fashion of the time, she wore a closely-fitting robe reaching to the throat, which set off the delicate outline of her slender and youthful figure, while the large high ruffle concealed the somewhat excessive length of her neck, and made her fresh and almost childlike face stand out as from a pedestal. On both sides of her high and thoughtful brow fell bright auburn locks in wanton lavishness; her head was adorned with a dark velvet cap, from which a white feather descended to her shoulder.

Altogether she presented a very lovely and attractive appearance, full of nobleness and grace, full of fire and energy; and, despite her youthfulness, not wanting in a certain lofty dignity. Elizabeth, though still almost a child, and although much humbled by misfortune, was yet the true daughter of her father; and although Henry had declared her illegitimate, and had excluded her from the succession, yet she bore the stamp of her royal lineage upon her proud and thoughtful brow, and in her keen, flashing glance.

As she now stood before John Heywood, she was no longer the haughty and imperious princess, but only the timid and blushing damsel, who trembles at confiding her first maiden secret to the ear of another, and who only ventures with trembling hand to draw aside the veil which hides her heart.

"John Heywood," she said, "you have often told me that you love me, and indeed I know that my poor unhappy mother trusted you, and called you as a witness of her innocence. At that time you were unable to save the mother; but will you now serve the daughter of Anne Bullen, and be a faithful friend to her?"

"I will," replied John Heywood, solemnly, "and as truly as there is a heaven above us, you shall never find in me a traitor."

"I believe you, John; I know that I may trust you. Listen, therefore. I will now tell you my secret—a secret which no one knows but God, and the betrayal of which might lead me to the scaffold. Will you, then, swear to me not to reveal to any one, under any pretext or motive whatsoever, a word of what I am about to tell you. Will you swear to me not to confide this secret to any one, even upon your dying bed, and not even to disclose it in the confessional?"

"Well, as to that matter, princess, you may feel perfectly secure. I never go to confession, for confession is a sort of priestly pabulum which my palate has rejected for many a long day; and as regards my death-bed, one cannot be quite sure, under the pious and blessed reign of Henry the Eighth, that he will really have such an accommodation, or that he may not make the journey to eternity in a much easier and speedier fashion, by the aid of the headsman."

"Oh! pray be serious, John, I entreat you! Let not the jester's mask, under which you conceal your more grave and your better countenance, now hide your true features from me. Be serious, John, and swear to me that you will keep my secret."

"Well, then, I will swear to do so,

princess. I swear to you, by the spirit of your mother, never to betray a word of what you shall tell me."

"I thank you, John. Now stoop forward, closer, that even the air may not catch one of my words and bear it away. John, I am in—love!"

She perceived the half-surprised, half-incredulous smile which played round John Heywood's lips.

"Ah," she continued, passionately, "you do not believe me. You think to yourself that as I am but fourteen years old, I am only a child, who can know nothing of the feelings of a woman. But remember, John, that young damsels who live under a warm sun, soon attain maturity from the influence of its glowing beams, and are already women and mothers, while they should still be children, living in dream-land. Believe me, John, I am deeply in love. An ardent and consuming fire rages within me—it is at once my torment and my delight—my happiness, and my future hope. As I shall never be a queen, I wish at least to be loved and to be happy as a wife. And if I am condemned to a life of lowliness and obscurity, it shall not at least be denied me to adorn this dark and inglorious existence with flowers, which do not thrive at the foot of the throne, and to illumine it, as if with stars, more brilliant than the splendors of the most dazzling royal diadem."

"Oh, you only mistake yourself and your own motives," said John Heywood, pensively. "You only choose the one because the other course is denied you; you only wish to love, because you can't govern; and as your heart which thirsts for glory and for fame, can find no other object of content, you wish to appease its thirst with some other potion, and so you offer it love as an opiate, with which to lull its burning pains to rest. Believe me, princess, you do not yet know yourself; you are not born merely to fulfil the part of an affectionate wife; your brow is far too lofty and too proud to wear only a crown of myrtle. Consider well, therefore, what you are doing, princess. Do not suffer yourself to be hurried away by the passionate blood of your father, which surges in your veins also. Reflect well before you act. Your foot still rests on one of the steps of the throne. Withdraw it not of your own accord! Maintain your place, and then the next step brings you one degree nearer. Renounce not willingly your just claims, but await patiently for the day of retribution and justice. Only do not, yourself, render it impossible that a complete and splendid satisfaction should then be offered you. The Princess Elizabeth may indeed some day become a queen, provided she have not exchanged her name for one of less glory and distinction."

"John Heywood," she replied, with a charming smile, "I told you truly when I said I loved him."

"Well, continue to love him still, by all means, but do so in secret, and do not let him know it, but teach your love the art of resignation."

"He knows it already, John."

"Alas! poor princess; you are indeed still like a child, which grasps at the fire with smiling hardihood and scorches its hands, because it knows not that fire burns."

"Let it burn, John, burn away, and let its flames meet above my head. Better far to be consumed by such a fire, than to die a wretched and lingering death from cold! I tell you I love him, and he knows it already."

"Well, love him if you will; but at least, do not marry him," cried John Heywood, peevishly.

"Marry!" she exclaimed with surprise. "Marry! Why I never dreamed of such a thing at present."

She bent her head upon her breast, and stood for some moments plunged in thought.

"I greatly fear I have been talking nonsense!" murmured John Heywood. "I have suggested a new train of thought to her. Ah, King Henry did right in appointing me his fool. Just when we think ourselves wisest, we are greater fools than ever."

"John," said Elizabeth, as she again raised her head, and looked smilingly, and with an ardent glance, at the court-jester, "John, you are quite right. When people love each other they should marry."

"But I said just the contrary, princess!"

"It is well," she exclaimed, with decision. "All this belongs to the future. We will now occupy ourselves with the present. I have promised my lover an interview."

"An interview!" cried John Heywood, astonished. "You will surely not be so foolhardy as to keep your promise."

"John Heywood," she replied, with an air of grave solemnity, "King Henry's daughter will never give a promise without keeping it. Whatever good or ill betide, I shall always be true to my word, once given—even though it should conduce to my grievous unhappiness and destruction."

John Heywood did not venture to oppose her further. There was at this moment something peculiarly noble and truly royal in her demeanor, which imposed upon him, and before which he bowed.

"I have promised him an interview, because he wished it," she continued, "and I will not conceal from you, John, that my own heart was disposed to grant his request. Do not therefore seek to shake my resolution; it is as firm as a rock. If, however, you are unwilling to assist me—say so, and then I shall look elsewhere for some friend who shall love me sufficiently well to impose silence on his doubts."

"But who will probably go and betray you, princess. No, no; as your resolution is unchangeable, no one but myself shall be your confidant. Tell me, therefore, what I am to do, and I shall obey you."

"You know, John, that my apartments are situated in that wing of the palace which faces the garden. Well, then, I have discovered behind a large picture on the wall of my toilet chamber, a secret door which opens into a dark and unfrequented corridor leading to that tower which you see beyond. This tower is never occupied. No one ever thinks of visiting that part of the palace. The rooms are as silent as the grave, but are nevertheless furnished with truly royal splendor. It is there that I intend to receive him!"

"But how is he to reach the spot?"

"Oh, don't be uneasy about that. I have thought over the matter for several days; and while I always denied my lover the interview for which he besought me, I was silently preparing every thing, in order that I might one day be able to grant his request. This day the goal is reached, and this day I fulfil his wish, wholly of my own free will, because I perceived that he had no longer the courage to renew his request. Listen, then; from the tower a winding staircase leads down to a small door by which the garden is reached. For that door I have a key. Here it is. With this key in his possession he has nothing more to do than in the evening, instead of leaving the palace, to remain behind in the park, and by means of this key he will be able to reach me; for I shall wait for him in the large tower saloon which lies exactly opposite the flight of steps. Here, take the key, and give it to him, and repeat to him all that I have told you."

"Very good, princess. There only remains that you should fix the hour at which you will receive him."

"The hour?" she repeated, turning aside to hide her blushes. "You will readily understand, John, that it is not possible to receive him there in the day time. I have not a single moment which I can call my own, unobserved."

"You will accordingly receive him at night," returned John Heywood, pensively. "At what hour?"

"At midnight! And now you know all, and I beg you, John, to make haste, and convey my message to him, for you see the sun is setting and it will soon be night."

She nodded to him with a smile and turned to go.

"Princess, you have as yet forgotten the most important point. You have not yet told me his name."

"What! did you not guess it yourself? John Heywood, who has such keen eyes, not to perceive that there is at this court but one person who deserves to be loved by the daughter of a king!"

"And the name of this one person?"

"Is Thomas Seymour—Lord Sudley," whispered Elizabeth, while she suddenly turned round and entered the palace.

"What! Thomas Seymour?" exclaimed John Heywood, with amazement. As if paralysed by terror, he continued standing and motionless, and looked up at the sky, repeating again and again: "Thomas Seymour!—Thomas Seymour! Why he is a kind of enchanter, who pours his love-potions into the hearts of all the sex, and befools them with that bold, handsome countenance of his. Thomas Seymour! The queen loves him; the princess loves him; and then there is the Duchess of Richmond, who wants to become his wife at all hazards!

This much, however, is certain, that he is a traitor who deceives them both, because he makes the same declarations of love to each alike. And then there is that wicked imp, chance, which has compelled me to become the confidant of both these women. But I shall take good care not to execute *both* the commissions which I have for this enchanter. Let him, if he pleases, become the husband of the princess. Perhaps this may be the surest means of weaning the queen from her unfortunate attachment."

He ceased, and for a moment seemed lost in deep thought. "Yes, it shall be so," he exclaimed at length. "I'll subdue the one love by means of the other. For the queen it would be dangerous to love him. I shall therefore bring the affair to such a pass that she must hate him. I shall still continue to be her confidant. I shall receive her letters and her commissions, only that I shall burn the letters and not execute the commissions. I dare not tell her that the faithless Thomas Seymour has betrayed her, for I have pledged my solemn word to the Princess Elizabeth to let no one suspect her secret, and I must and shall keep my word. Smile and love on then—dream the sweet dreams of thy love, O, queen; I am keeping watch for thee, and I shall cause this dark cloud to pass away from thee. It may perhaps touch thy heart, but at least it shall not crush thy noble and beautiful head, which—"

"Well, and what are you staring up at the sky for now, as if you were reading some new epigram there with which you want to make the king laugh and the priests angry?" inquired a voice beside him, and a hand was laid heavily on his shoulder.

John Heywood did not trouble himself to look round; he continued standing in his place, and stared on at the sky without changing or moving. He had easily recognized the voice of the person who addressed him; he knew quite well that the individual beside him was none other than the fool-hardy enchanter, whom he had just been execrating from the bottom of his heart—none other that Thomas Seymour, Earl of Sudley.

"Say, John, is it really an epigram?" asked Thomas Seymour, once more. "An epigram upon the knavish, greedy, and hypocritical rabble of priests, who with blasphemous flattery fawn round the king, and are always on the alert to see how they can lay a trap for one of us brave and honorable men? Is that what the sky has just been revealing to you?"

"No, my lord; I am only looking after a hawk, which I see yonder in the clouds. I saw him fly up there; and only imagine, he had in each of his claws a dove. Two doves for one hawk. Now is not that too much, and altogether opposed to nature and justice?"

The earl regarded him with a penetrating and distrustful glance. But John Heywood remained perfectly calm and composed, and still continued gazing at the clouds.

"What a stupid creature that is," he

continued, "not to perceive how injurious his avarice is to himself. For as he holds a dove in each of his claws, he will not be able to taste either of them,—for he will have no talons left free to tear his prey with. As soon as he attempts to devour the one, the other will slip away from him, and when he tries to catch the latter, the other will fly away,—and so at last he will have nothing because he was too greedy, and wished to have more than he could make use of."

"And are you really looking up into the clouds after this hawk? But perhaps you deceive yourself, and that what you are seeking is not up there, but down here, and perhaps even not very far away?" asked Thomas Seymour significantly.

John Heywood however would not understand him.

"Oh, no," he replied, "it is still flying, but it won't continue to do so much longer. For I have already seen the owner of the dove-cot, from which the hawk stole the two doves. He carried a fowling-piece in his hand, and you may be quite sure he will kill the hawk for having robbed him of both his pets."

"Enough, enough!" exclaimed the earl, impatiently. "You wish to give me a lesson, but you must know that I accept no counsel from a fool—even though he were the wisest of fools."

"In that you are right, my lord, for it is only fools who are so foolish as to listen to the voice of wisdom. Besides, every one must be the hammerman of his own fortune, and now, my wise master, I will give you a key which you have forged for yourself, and behind which your future stands. There, take this key, and if you will creep along stealthily through the garden to yonder tower, to-night, about twelve o'clock, this key will open the door for you, and then you can fly up the winding stairs without hesitation, and open the door opposite the landing. Behind that you will find the fortune which you have forged for yourself, Master Blacksmith, and which will bid you welcome with ardent lips and fair arms. And so commending you to God, my lord, I must now make haste and get home, in order to think over the comedy which the king has commanded me to write."

"But you do not even tell me from whom this message comes?" said Lord Dudley, holding him back. "You invite me to a rendezvous, and you give me a key, but I don't yet know who is expecting me in that tower."

"Oh! You don't know who it is? Then there is more than one who might be awaiting you there? Well then, it is the youngest and smallest of the two doves who sends you the key."

"The Princess Elizabeth?"

"You have named her—not I," replied John Heywood, as he disengaged himself from the hand of the earl, and hastened across the court-yard in order to betake himself to his dwelling.

"Then the princess is waiting for me?" he whispered softly. "Ah, who can read in the stars, or who can tell whither the crown will roll away, when it falls from the head of King Henry? I love Katharine; but I love ambition still more, and if ambition demand it,—why I must needs make a sacrifice of my heart!"

CHAPTER IV.

GAMMER GURTON'S NEEDLE.

SLOWLY, and plunged in gloomy thought, John Heywood reached his dwelling. This dwelling lay in the second, that is to say, the inner court of Whitehall Palace, in that wing of the building which contained all the residences of the superior servants of the royal household, and of course, that of the royal fool also; for at that time the king's fool was a very important personage, who occupied in a manner the rank of a royal chamberlain.

John Heywood was crossing this second court-yard, when suddenly the noise of loud voices scolding and jangling, and the sharp and peculiar sound of a box on the ear aroused him from his reverie.

He stood still and listened.

His countenance, previously so grave, now once more resumed its accustomed lively and sly expression—his large eyes were once more lighted up with humor, and with a species of malicious pleasure.

"Ah, this is my sweet and amiable housekeeper, Gammer Gurton, again," murmured John Heywood, laughing, "and she is once more quarrelling with that poor, long-legged, blear-eyed, but excellent creature, my servant, Hodge. Why, it was only yesterday that I surprised her bestowing a kiss upon him, at which the fellow made such a rueful countenance, that he looked as if a bee had stung him. To-day, however, she boxes his ears. Perhaps this makes him laugh, and he thinks it is a rose leaf to cool his cheeks. He is a singular being—this same Hodge. But we must just see what this farce is that they are playing to-day."

He glided softly up the steps and opened the door of his apartments, and then closed it noiselessly behind him as he entered.

Mistress Gammer Gurton, who was in the adjoining room, had neither heard nor seen any thing, and even had the sky fallen at this moment, she would scarcely have observed it; for she had eyes and ears for nothing else but for this lank, raw-boned fellow, who stood opposite her, trembling with pain, and who stared at her out of a pair of watery blue eyes. Her whole soul was centred in her tongue, and this tongue moved as fast as the clapper of a mill, and rattled and rolled like thunder.

How then could Mistress Gammer Gurton have had ears or time to hear her master, who had crept gently into his room, and had gently glided along to the door which stood ajar, and which separated his chamber from that of his housekeeper.

"What! you stupid blockhead?"

cried Mistress Gammer Gurton, "you want to make me believe it was the cat that took my needle away. As if my needle were a mouse, and smelt of bacon, you silly, blear-eyed fool!"

"Ah you call me a fool," cried Hodge, with a laugh, which produced a somewhat irregular slit across his face from ear to ear; "you call me a fool, which is a great honor for me, for then I am the worthy servant of my master. And as to the blear-eyed part of the business, why that comes, you see, of having nothing else before me to look at the whole day long, but yourself, Gammer Gurton—yourself, with your full-moon face—yourself sailing about the room like a great frigate, and with your hands for grappling hooks, smashing everything that comes in your way—except your own looking-glass."

"Now you shall pay ror that, you double-faced, shabby lout," cried Mistress Gammer Gurton, rushing at Hodge, with her clenched fist.

But the sly servant of John Heywood saw what was coming, and so he stooped down and took refuge under the large table which stood in the middle of the room. But when the housekeeper rushed forward to fetch him out from his stronghold, he pinched her leg with such hearty good will that she started back with a scream, and, smarting with intense pain, sank down into the huge leather-covered arm-chair which stood near the window alongside her work table.

"Oh, Hodge, you monster!" she groaned. "You horrid, heartless monster. Yes, and it was you that stole my needle from me, and nobody else. For you knew very well that it was my last, and that before I could get any more I must go a long way to the shop where they are sold. And that is just what you want, you weather-cock knave. You only want that I should go out, in order that you may have time to carry on your games with Tibby."

"Tibby? Why, who is Tibby?" asked Hodge, poking forward his long neck from under the table, and staring at Mistress Gammer Gurton with well-feigned astonishment.

"Just fancy this daddy-long-legs asking me who Tibby is!" cried the exasperated lady. "Then I'll tell you who she is. Tibby is the steward's cook over the way. She is a dark-eyed, deceitful, coquettish little minx, who is mean and wicked enough to try to steal away a lover from a respectable and virtuous woman like me;—a lover, God wot, who is such a pitiful little sneak, that one would suppose nobody else but myself could ever see him if they looked for him; and, indeed, I could never have done so, if my eyes hadn't been used to searching for things for the last forty years, and that, all that time, I've been looking for a man who would know my value, and lead me to the altar. And then at last my eyes rested upon this ghost of a man, and as nothing else turned up, I must needs drop upon you, you poor cobweb!"

"What, you call me a cobweb?" cried Hodge, creeping out from under the table, and with a threatening look, stretching himself at full length before Gammer Gurton's chair. "You call me a cobweb? Well, then, I vow and declare that you shall never be the spider that lives in this cobweb. For you are a garden-spider, a great, horrid, old garden-spider, for which such a cobweb as Hodge is much too fine and too delicate. Be quiet, therefore, Mistress Spider, and choose some clumsy cobweb to suit you elsewhere. You shan't live in my web, that's only for Tib. For I know Tib very well. She is a nice lively girl, and only sixteen; she is as nimble and as quick on her legs as a kid, with lips like the corals which you wear round your fat, puffy neck, with eyes that shine much brighter than your nose, and with a figure so slender and elegant that one could cut it out of one of your fingers. Oh, yes, I know Tib very well; she is a dear good girl, who would never be so hard-hearted as to abuse the man she loves, and call him all manner of names, and who would never be so mean or so low in herself, as to want to marry the man she doesn't love, merely because he is a man. Yes, I know Tib, and I'll just go across to her presently, and ask her if she will marry a good honest fellow, who is certainly rather lean, but who will doubtless get fatter when he has better keep than the horrid, hungry stuff that Mistress Gammer Gurton gives him; a fellow who, if he is blear-eyed just now, will soon get cured of that complaint when he loses sight of Gammer Gurton, who has the effect of rotten onions upon his eyes, and makes them look red, as if he was a crying all day. Good-by, old rotten onions; I'm off to Tib!"

But Mistress Gammer Gurton spun up like a top from her arm-chair, and rushed after Hodge, whom she held by the coat, and forced to remain.

"Only dare to go and see Tib—that's all! Just dare to cross this door, and you'll see that the mild, gentle, and patient Gammer Gurton will be changed into a tigress, if any one attempts to deprive her of her holiest and most precious property—I mean her husband. For you know you are my husband—in so far as you have given your word that you will marry me."

"But I haven't told you when and where I mean to do so, Gammer Gurton, and so you may wait for me to all eternity, for I won't marry you at least until we meet in Heaven."

"That's a horrid and a wicked lie, and you know it!" cried Gammer Gurton. "It's a mean, shocking lie, I say! For didn't you come begging and praying to me day after day, until I was obliged to promise you at last, that I would make my will, and that I would name my dear husband Hodge in it to be the heir of all my goods and chattels, and leave him every thing that I had scraped together during my virtuous and industrious life?"

"Yes; but you haven't made your will yet; you have broken your word, and so you cannot expect me to keep mine."

"But I have though,—you fickle man. I have made it, and this very day I intended to go with you to the lawyer's, and have it properly signed and witnessed, and then to-morrow we should go and get married."

"What, you have actually made your will, you charming little hemisphere?" said Hodge, affectionately, while he attempted to embrace the gigantic form his *fiancée* with his long bony arms. "You have made your will, and appointed me as your heir? Come along then, Gammer, come along and let us go to the lawyer's office at once."

"But don't you see," replied Gammer Gurton, with a tender, cat-like purr—"don't you see that you are crushing my collar in the way you hug me so. Let me go therefore, and help me at once to find the needle, for without this needle we can't go to the lawyer's."

"What, you can't go to the lawyer's without the needle?"

"No, for only look at this great hole which the cat lately tore in my best cap, just as I had taken it out of my box and laid it on the table. Surely I can't go to the lawyer's with such a hole as that in my cap! Look about then, Hodge, that I may be able to mend my cap and go with you to the lawyer's."

"Oh, lord, where is the unlucky needle! I must have it—I must find it—so that Gammer Gurton may be able to take her will to the lawyer's office."

And Hodge, with frantic desperation, looked about on the floor for the lost needle, and Gammer Gurton thrust her large spectacles upon her red shining nose, and looked once more all over the table. So zealous was she in her search, that she even allowed her tongue to rest for a little, and a deep silence reigned in the room.

This stillness was suddenly interrupted by a voice which proceeded from the court-yard. It was a sweet and a delicate voice which cried:

"Hodge, dear little Hodge, are you there? Just come out for a short time. I want to laugh, and I'm just in the humor to have some fun."

It seemed as if an electric shock had been suddenly produced by this voice, and had seized both Gammer Gurton and Hodge, at the same time.

They both shuddered, and stood still and immoveable, as if petrified; Hodge especially—poor Hodge—looked as if he had been struck by lightning. His great watery, blue eyes seemed as if they would start from their sockets; his long arms hung down dangling and wabbling at his sides like a flail; his knees tottered, and seemed as if they would give way under him, in expectation of the coming storm. This storm in fact burst forth without much delay.

"That's Tib!" cried mistress Gammer Gurton, rushing upon Hodge like a lioness, and grasping him round the shoulders with her arms. "That's Tib, you poor half-starved greyhound! Now, wasn't I right when I called you a faithless, good-for-nothing lout, who doesn't even spare innocence, and breaks the hearts of women like biscuits, which he swallows for his pleasure. Wasn't I right in saying that you were only watching for me to go out, that you might go across and flirt with Tib?"

"Hodge, my dear, dear little Hodge," cried a voice below, and this time louder and more affectionately. "Now, Hodge, ain't you coming down to me to-day, as you promised?—come and fetch the kiss you were begging so hard for this morning."

"Why, whatever is the girl thinking of! May I be hanged if I ever begged a kiss of her,—I don't understand a single word she says," cried Hodge, quite confused and trembling.

"Ah, don't you though, understand a word of what she says?" screamed Gammer Gurton. "Well then, I do. I understand that everything is now all over between you and me. I am quit of you—you Moloch you! I understand that I'm not going to the lawyer's to sign my will, in order to marry you and worry myself to death with a husband all skin and bone—to make you my heir and let you laugh at me. No, no; it's all over now! I shan't go to the lawyer's—I shall tear up my will!"

"Oh dear; she is going to tear up her will!" yelled Hodge. "And now I have had all this worry and trouble for nothing. I have put up with the awful misery of being made love to by this horrid old screech-owl. Oh dear, she won't make any will, and Hodge will still be the same poor fellow he always was."

Gammer Gurton laughed scornfully.

"Ah, now you see at last what a miserable creature you are, and how a fine, handsome woman, like me, lets herself down when she stoops to pick up a weed, like you, and choose it for a husband!"

"Yes, yes; I see it all!" said Hodge, snivelling. "And I only beg you to pick me up and take me, and above all to make your will!"

"No, I won't take you, and I won't make my will. I tell you it's all over now, and you can now get along and go to Tib, who has been calling you so affectionately. But first give me back my needle, you magpie, you. Give here my needle that you stole from me; it is no more use to you now, for there is no need for me to go out in order that you may be able to go and see Tib. We have nothing more to do with each other, and so you can go away wherever you like. My needle—I say—my needle—or I'll hang you as a scarecrow in some cornfield, to frighten away the sparrows. My needle, or—"

She raised her clenched fist threateningly at him, convinced that Hodge this time, as always, would take refuge under the bed or under the table from this formidable weapon of his jealous and sensitive inamorata.

But for once she had made a mistake. Hodge, who saw that all was lost, felt his patience at length exhausted, and his fear was now changed into the most desperate rage. The lamb was changed into a tiger, and with the rage of a tiger he flew at Gammer Gurton, flung her fist aside, and fetched her a sharp blow on the cheek.

The signal was given and the battle began, and was waged with equal strength and equal animosity on both

GAMMER GURTON'S NEEDLE. P. 121.

sides, only that Hodge's bony knuckles went home much more severely upon the mass of flesh with which Gammer Gurton was encumbered, and that he was much more sure of hitting this huge bulk; while Gammer Gurton's soft hand could rarely catch this lanky figure whose owner adroitly parried her blows.

"Hold! you blockhead," cried a stentorian voice, suddenly—"don't you see, fellow, that your master is present? Keep quiet there, ye imps of Satan, and don't strike, but love each other."

"It's the master!" cried Gammer Gurton, dropping her hands cautiously by her side.

"Oh, pray, master, don't turn me away?" whimpered Hodge; "don't turn me away for having at last beaten the old hag black and blue. She has deserved it this ever so long, and an angel himself must lose patience with her at last."

"I turn you away?" cried John Heywood, as he dried his eyes, which were moist with laughter. "No, Hodge; you are a real jewel—a very mine of drollery and fun, and you have both of you, without knowing it, given me the most valuable materials for a farce, which at the king's command I must write within six days. I owe both of you my thanks, and these thanks I will discharge forthwith. Listen to me, therefore, my pair of enamoured and affectionate turtle doves, and mark what I have to say to you. One cannot always know the wolf by his skin, for he sometimes appears in sheep's clothing, and in the same way one cannot always tell a man by his voice, for he borrows it for himself sometimes from his neighbor. For example, I know a certain gentleman called John Heywood, who can imitate quite correctly the voice of a certain little Tib, and can pipe his voice quite as sweetly as she does, and say,—'Hodge, my dear little Hodge!'"

And he repeated to them accurately, and with the same tone and expression, the words which the voice had previously uttered.

"Ah, then it was you, sir?" cried Hodge, with a grin. "The same Tib across the court yonder—the Tib about which we've been pummeling one another?"

"Yes, Hodge, I was that self-same Tib, and I was close at hand during the whole of your quarrel together, and I found it immensely amusing to throw in Tib's voice, like a shot from a cannon, in the midst of your lovers' quarrel. Ah, Hodge, that was a capital bombshell—was it not? And when I said, 'my dear little Hodge,' your head fell like an ear of corn that has been blown upon by a muck-worm. No, no, my worthy and virtuous mistress Gammer Gurton, it was not Tib that was calling your handsome Hodge—on the contrary I saw Tib going out the court-yard gate before your quarrel began."

"It was not Tib," cried Gammer Gurton, with a gust of tenderness. "It was not Tib, and she is not even in the court at all, and therefore Hodge could not have gone across to her while I was going to the shop for needles. Oh, Hodge, Hodge, will you forgive me for all this; will you excuse all the hard words that I spoke in the height of my temper and suffering; and will you try to love me again?"

"Well, I'll try," replied Hodge, somewhat gravely, "and I don't doubt but I shall succeed, provided beforehand that you go to the lawyer's this very day and make your will."

"Yes. I'll make my will, and to-morrow we'll get married, won't we, my love?"

"Yes, we'll get married to-morrow," growled Hodge, scratching his head, with a dismal grimace.

"And now, my pet, come and give me a kiss to show that we have made it up." She held out her arms, and as Hodge did not come to her, but remained stiff and motionless in his place, she went to Hodge and folded him affectionately to her heart.

Suddenly she gave a loud scream, and released Hodge from her embrace. She felt a terrible pain in her bosom, just as if a little dagger had penetrated her breast.

And there it was—the lost needle. And Hodge was therefore as innocent and as pure as the new-born day.

He had not wantonly purloined the needle, in order that Mistress Gammer Gurton should be obliged to leave the house and go to the shop to get some new needles; he had not intended to go to Tib, for Tib was not at home, but was gone out.

"Oh, Hodge, Hodge, —you good Hodge! you innocent dove, will you forgive me?"

"Come to the lawyer's, Gammer Gurton, and I'll forgive you."

They rushed affectionately into each other's arms, quite forgetting their master, who was standing beside them all the while, and who looked on, laughing and nodding approval.

"Thus then I have found the finest and richest materials for my comedy," said John Heywood, leaving the amorous couple, and retiring to his chamber. "Gammer Gurton has saved me, and King Henry will not have the pleasure of seeing me scourged by the highly virtuous and highly erotic ladies of his court. To work, then. To work at once!"

He sat down to his desk, and seized pen and paper.

"But how?" he asked, suddenly hesitating. "These are certainly valuable materials for a piece, but yet I shall never be able to convert them into an interlude. What then shall I do? Throw the matter overboard altogether, and once more rally the monks and turn the nuns into ridicule? That's old and used up long ago! I'll write something new—something quite new, and something that shall make the king so full of good humor, that for a whole day he won't sign a death-warrant. Yes, yes; it shall be a right merry play, and therefore I shall call it boldly and resolutely a pleasure play—or, in other words, a comedy."

And he seized his pen and wrote, "GAMMER GURTON'S NEEDLE: A RIGHT PRETTY, PLEASANT, AND MERRY COMEDY."

And thus originated the first English

comedy through John Heywood—King Henry's fool.

CHAPTER V.

LADY JANE.

ALL slept in the Palace of Whitehall. Even the king's servants, who kept watch in the ante-room of the king's bedchamber had already betaken themselves to slumber, for the king had been snoring for several hours, and the royal noise was the joyful signal to the inhabitants of the palace that they were relieved from their attendance for a happy night, and could once more be free men.

Even the queen had already long since retired to her apartments, and had dismissed her ladies at an unusually early hour. She said she felt herself fatigued from the chase, and required rest. No one must therefore attempt to disturb her unless by the king's command.

But the king, as before stated, slept, and the queen had therefore no cause to apprehend that her nightly slumbers would be disturbed.

Deep silence reigned in the palace. The corridors were empty and deserted; the apartments mute and forsaken.

Suddenly a figure tottered along softly and cautiously through the long, feebly-lighted corridor. She was wrapt in a dark mantle, and a thick veil concealed her features.

With her feet scarcely touching the ground, she flitted along, and descended a short flight of steps. Now she stops and listens. Nothing is to be heard. All is noiseless and silent.

Still onward. Now she quickens her step. For here she is sure of not being heard. This is the uninhabited wing of the Palace of Whitehall. Here no one can listen to her footsteps.

Onward, therefore—still onward—along that corridor, and up that flight of steps. And now she stops before the door which leads into the garden saloon. She applies her ear to the key-hole and listens. Then she claps her hands three times.

The sound finds an echo behind the door.

Oh, he is there—he is there! Forgotten are now all cares, all pains, all tears. He is there! She has him again!

She bursts the door open. The chamber indeed is dark, but yet she sees him, for the eye of love illumines the night, and if she does not see him, at least she feels his presence.

She rests upon his heart. He presses her closely to his breast. Leaning upon each other, they grope their way cautiously through the dark spacious saloon until they reach the ottoman yonder, and both, in rapturous embrace, sink down upon the luxurious cushions.

"At length I have thee once more! And my arms once more enfold this divine form, and again my lips press this rosy mouth! Oh, my beloved, what an eternity has been this separation from thee! Six whole days! Six long nights of torment! Hast thou not felt how my soul craved and yearned for thee? How I stretched forth my arms in the night time, and how I again withdrew them comfortless and chilled with pain, because I held nothing—nothing but the cold, cheerless night air. Didst thou not hear, beloved one, how I called thee with my sighs, my tears? how in glowing verses I poured out to thee my ardent longings, my love, my rapture? And yet, cruel one! thou didst remain the while unmoved and smiling. Thine eyes were lighted up with the pride, the majesty of a Juno; the roses on thy cheeks are not faded by a single breath. No, no! thou didst not yearn for me as I did for thee; thy heart has not felt that painful, that blissful torment; thou art above all things, and first of all the proud, the cold queen, and then,—and then the loving Katharine!"

"How unjust, and how severe thou art, my Henry!" she whispered softly. "Ah, I have indeed suffered, and perhaps my agonies have been more terrible and more bitter than thine own, for I was obliged to swallow my torments inwardly. Thou wast at liberty to give them vent; thou mightst stretch forth thine arms toward me; thou couldst cry out, couldst sigh in secret. Thou wast not like me—condemned to jest and smile, and, with an apparently attentive ear, to listen to all the oft-repeated, ever-renewed phrases of worship and adulation of those flatterers who surround me. Thou wast at least free to suffer! I was not! It is true I have smiled, but only with the pangs of death,—it is true my cheeks have not grown pale, but the tints of art were the veil which I used to hide the pallor of nature. And then, Henry, in the midst of my pains and my yearning, I had also a secret consolation,—thy letters, thy sonnets, which were as the dews of heaven to my ailing spirit, and restored it once more to new torments—new hopes! Oh! how I love those rapture-breathing melodies—in what noble and entrancing words they re-echo the story of our love and of our sufferings! How my whole soul flies forward to meet them, and how a thousand times I press my lips to the paper from which thy breath—thy sighs seem to emanate! How I love the kind, faithful Jane—the messenger of our love. When I see her enter my chamber with thy letter in her hand, she then seems to me like a dove bearing the olive branch which brings with it peace and happiness; and I rush toward her, and press her to my bosom, and give her the kisses which I fain would bestow on thee; and I feel how poor and helpless I am, in not being able to repay her for the happiness which she brings me. Ah, Henry, how much we are indebted to our poor Jane!"

"Why dost thou call her poor, when she is ever beside thee—can always see thee—always hear thee?"

"I call her poor, because she is not happy! For she loves, Henry; she loves to desperation—to madness, and she is not loved in return. She is wasting away with sorrow and pain, and wrings her hands in agony with immeasurable woe. Hast thou not perceived how pale she is, and how her eyes are daily growing more dim?"

"No, I have not perceived it, for I see nothing but thee, and Lady Jane is for me a mere inanimate picture, like all other women. But how now? Thou tremblest and thy form quivers, as if convulsed in my arms. What! Thou weepest?"

"Oh, I weep because I am so happy. I weep because I thought how terrible must be the suffering to give one's heart wholly away, and to receive nothing in return—nothing but death! Poor Jane!"

"Oh, what have we to do with Jane! We love each other—that's enough. Come, beloved, let me kiss away the tears from thy cheeks, let me drink this nectar, that I may become inspired and glorified as a deity! Weep no more then—no, weep not, or, if thou wilt, let it be in the excess of rapture, and because words and the human breast are too feeble to express or contain the measure of our bliss."

"Yes, yes, let us exult in our happiness, let us fade away in its delights!" she exclaimed passionately, while she flung herself with frantic violence on his breast.

They were both silent, and their hearts throbbed together in unison.

Oh, how sweet is this silence, how rapturous this mute, blissful night. How the trees outside murmur and rustle, as if they sang for the lovers a heavenly song of slumber; how curiously the pale sickle-moon peers through the windows, as if she were seeking the happy pair whose favored confidante she is.

But happiness is swiftly fled, and time flies quickly when love is its companion.

Already they must part, already take leave of each other.

"Not yet, beloved! Stay yet awhile! Look, it is still dark night—and hark, there the palace clock strikes two! No, don't go yet awhile."

"I must, Henry, I must; the hours are over when I am free to be happy!"

"Oh thou cold, proud soul! Does this head already long again for its crown, and canst thou no longer tarry for the royal purple to fall upon thy shoulders? Come, let me kiss thy shoulders, and then fancy, sweet one, that my crimson lips are royal purple."

"And a purple for which I would gladly give my crown, and even my life!" she exclaimed with enthusiasm, while she folded him in her arms.

"Dost thou then love me? Lovest thou me really?"

"Yes, I love thee."

"Canst thou swear to me that thou lovest no one else—no one but me?"

"Yes, I can swear it to thee, as truly as there is a heaven above us, the witness of my vow!"

"Then be thou blest, thou lovely—thou only—oh, how shall I name thee, whose name I dare not mention! Knowest thou, sweet one, how hard it is not to be at liberty even to utter the name of my beloved. Recall this prohibition, and grant me the painfully sweet happiness of being able at least to address thee by thy name!"

"No," she replied, with a shudder; "dost thou not know that sleep-walkers wake up from their dreams when called by their name? Now, I am a sleep-walker, who with smiling hardihood hovers about on giddy heights; only call me by my name, and I shall wake up and fall headlong and trembling into the abyss beneath. Ah, Henry, I hate my name, for it is pronounced by other lips than thine. For thee I will not be called as other persons name me. Baptise me then, Henry, give me another name—a name which is our secret, and which nobody shall know but ourselves."

"Then I shall call thee GERALDINE, and as Geraldine I will sing thy praises and extol thee before all the world, and I will repeat to thee, evermore, in despite of listeners and spies, that I love thee; and nobody, not even the king himself, shall be able to forbid me!"

"Hush!" she returned, shuddering, "speak not of him. Oh, I conjure thee, my Henry, to be cautious; remember that thou hast sworn to me ever to bear in mind the danger that threatens us both, and which beyond doubt will crush us one day if thou shouldst betray by a sound, a look, a smile, this sweet secret which binds us both together. Knowest thou what thou hast sworn to me besides?"

"I do! But it is a severe and unnatural law. What, even when I am alone with thee, shall I never dare to address thee otherwise than with the awe and reserve which are due to a queen? Even when no one can hear us shall I not be at liberty to make any, the slightest, allusion to our love?"

"No, no—don't do so, for this palace has eyes and ears everywhere—everywhere there are spies and listeners—behind the tapestry—behind the hangings—everywhere they lurk stealthily, and watch every gesture, every smile, every look, to discover if possible grounds for suspicion. No—no, Henry, swear to me by our love that thou wilt never, except here in this room, address me otherwise than as thy queen! Swear to me that in the presence of the world, thou wilt be to me nothing more than the reserved and reverential servant of thy queen, and at the same time the proud lord and earl, of whom people say that no woman had ever the power to touch his heart. Swear to me that by no look or smile, by no pressure of the hand, wilt thou ever betray what, outside of this room, would be regarded as a crime for us both. Let this chamber be the temple of our love; but when once the threshold is crossed, we will not desecrate the sweet mysteries of our happiness by suffering only a single ray to appear before profane eyes! Shall it be so, my Henry?"

"Well, yes; it shall be so!" he replied, with a sad accord, "though I must confess to thee that this terrible illusion often drives me to the verge of despair. Oh, Geraldine! when I see thee away from here, when I perceive with what a chilling and unmoved expression thine eye meets my glance, I feel as if my heart were convulsed; and I say to myself: 'This is not my beloved, not the tender impassioned woman whom I sometimes in the darkness of night fold in my arms; this is Katharine the queen, but not my beloved. A woman cannot thus dissemble; art cannot so far succeed as to be able to overcome nature itself, and to ignore the essential instincts of the human heart. Oh! there have been moments—fearful terrible moments—when it seemed to me as if all this were only an illusion, a mystification; as if some wicked demon assumed by night the form of the queen, in order to juggle me, poor frenzied enthusiast that I am, with a happiness which is unreal, and which exists only in my imagination! And then this thought excites within me a frantic rage, an overwhelming desperation, and I feel disposed, despite my oath, and even the danger which threatens thee, to rush forward to thee in the presence of all this court-rabble, and even of the king himself, and to ask thee 'Art thou really what thou appearest? Art thou Katharine Parr, the wife of King Henry—neither more nor less? Or art thou my beloved—the woman who is mine with her every thought—her every breath, who has vowed to me eternal love—unalterable fidelity, and whom, in spite of the whole world and of the king, I press to my heart as my own possession?'"

"Unhappy Henry! shouldst thou ever attempt to do so, it would be certain death to us both!"

"And so it might be! In death, at least, thou wouldst be mine, and no one should any longer dare to divide us, and those eyes would no longer look coldly and strangely upon me, as they oftentimes do at present. Oh! I entreat thee, never look at me at all, if it can only be with that cold and distant air, which petrifies my heart! Turn thine eyes away from me, and speak to me with averted countenance."

"Then people will say that I hate thee, Henry!"

"Nay, it is even more agreeable if they say that thou dost abhor me, than if they perceive that I am wholly indifferent to thee; that I am nothing to thee but the Earl of Surrey, thy Chamberlain."

"No, no, Henry, they shall perceive that thou art more to me than that! I will give thee a token of my love before the entire assembled court. Wilt thou then believe, thou dear foolish enthusiast, that I love thee, and that it is no demon that reposes here in thy arms, and swears that she loves but thee alone? Say, wilt thou then believe me?"

"I shall! But no, there needs no token—no assurances. I know it truly—I feel indeed the sweet reality, which nestles, warm, and bliss-infusing, at my side, and it is only the excess of my felicity, which makes me incredulous."

"I will inspire thee with faith, and thou shalt no longer doubt even in the intoxication of happiness. Listen then! The king, as you know, will hold a grand tournament, and a poet's banquet, which will take place in a few days.

Well then, at this festivity, I shall give thee publicly, and in the presence of the king and of the court, a rosette, which I wear on my shoulder, and in the silver fringe of which thou wilt find a letter from me. Will that satisfy thee, my Henry?"

"And dost thou still ask, my beloved? Dost thou ask if thou wilt make me proud and happy in presence of all thy courtiers?"

He pressed her firmly to his heart and kissed her. But suddenly she seemed convulsed in his arms, and started up wildly.

"Day is dawning, day is dawning!" she exclaimed. "Behold yonder a reddish streak above the horizon. The sun is about to rise, and daylight is already appearing."

He tried to hold her back still, but she tore herself away forcibly, and wrapt her head once more in her veil.

"Yes," he replied, "day is breaking and light is approaching! Let me then, at least, behold thy countenance for a moment. My soul thirsts for the sight, as the parched earth for the dew. Come; here, at the window, it is light. Let me look but a moment into thine eyes!"

But she tore herself violently away. "No, no, thou must be gone. Listen, already three o'clock. The court is already awake! Seemed it not as if some person were walking outside the door? Hasten, hasten away, if thou wouldst not have me die with fear!"

She flung his mantle around him herself, she pressed his hat over his brow, then once more she twined her arms round his neck, and imprinted a burning kiss upon his lips.

"Farewell, my beloved, farewell, Henry Howard. When we see each other again to-day, thou wilt be once more the Earl of Surrey, and I the queen—not thy beloved—nor the woman who loves thee! Happiness is over for the present, and suffering must now resume its place. Farewell!"

She opened the door herself, and forced her lover to depart. "Adieu, Geraldine, good-night, my beloved? Day is approaching, and I shall greet thee again as my queen, and once more I shall have to bear the torment of thy cold looks and the agony of thy haughty smile."

CHAPTER VI.

LOYOLA'S GENERAL.

She rushed to the window and looked after him, until he had vanished in the dim twilight, and then she uttered a deep cry of anguish, and wholly overcome by her sufferings, she sank down upon her knees, weeping and moaning, and wringing her hands despairingly to heaven.

But a few moments since so joyful and happy, she was now filled with grief and woe, and bitter sighs of lamentation trembled on her lips.

"Alas! alas!" she cried sobbingly, "what fearful agonies are these, and what desperate pain is this which rends my heart! I have lain in his arms, I have received his vows of love, I have suffered his kisses, and yet these vows are not mine, and it was not upon me that those kisses were bestowed. He kisses me and loves in me only the person whom I hate; he vows in my hands the love which he consecrates to her; his thoughts and feelings are hers and hers alone! What a terrible martyrdom is this! To be loved under her name, and under her name to accept the vows of love, which still belong of right to me—to me alone! For he loves me—me only. It was my lips that he kissed—my form that he embraced; to me are his words, his letters addressed, and it is I who answer them. He loves me, and only me, and yet believes not in me. I am for him nothing but an inanimate picture, like all other women. This he told me himself, and I did not become frantic, and I had the dreadful resolution to pretend that the tears which despair had wrung from me, were only tears of rapture.

"Oh, ignominious, horrid mockery of Fate, to be what I am not, and not to be what I am!"

And with cries of bitter lamentation she tore her hair and beat her breast, and wept and groaned aloud.

She heard nothing; she saw nothing; she felt nothing, but her own despair—her unutterable anguish.

She did not once tremble for herself. She did not even reflect for a moment that she would be lost if she were to be found here.

And yet, beyond, at the other end, a door had been opened softly and noiselessly, and a man had entered.

He shut the door behind him, and walked up to Lady Jane, who still lay upon the floor. He stood behind her. While she uttered her despairing cries—he heard every word that fell from her trembling lips; her whole agonized and woe-riven heart lay unveiled before him, and she knew it not.

He now stooped down and touched her lightly on the shoulder with his hand. She shuddered and recoiled from the touch, as if she had been stabbed with a dagger, and her sobs ceased straightway.

A fearful pause ensued. The woman lay motionless, breathless, on the floor; and tall, motionless, and cold as a brazen statue stood the man beside her.

"Lady Jane Douglas!" he said at length, in grave and solemn accents, "rise up! It becomes not the daughter of your father to lie prostrate on her knees, unless she kneels before her God. But you are not bending before God, but before an idol which you have made for yourself, and to which you have raised a temple in your heart. This idol is called '*Your personal Unhappiness.*' But it is writen, 'Ye shall have no other gods but me.' Therefore I say to you once more, Lady Jane Douglas, rise from your knees, for it is not your God before whom you are kneeling."

And as if the words had exercised a magnetic power over her, she raised herself slowly from the floor, and now stood, as cold and unmoved as a marble statue, in the presence of her father.

"Fling away from you the cares of this world which encumber you, and which hinder you from the holy work which God assigns to you," continued Lord Douglas, with his solemn and metallic voice. "It is written, 'Come to me, ye that are weary and heavy laden, and I will deliver ye,' says the Lord. But as for you, Jane, you must cast your troubles at the foot of the throne, and your burden shall become for you a crown, which shall be as a glory around your brow."

He laid his hand upon her head, but she dashed it fiercely away.

"No," she cried, with thick, stammering utterance, as if talking in a dream. "Away with the crown! I will have no crown upon which devils have pronounced their blessings. I will have no royal purple which is dyed in the blood of my beloved!"

"She is still in the delirium of her pain," murmured the earl, while he contemplated the pale, trembling woman, who had now once more sunk down on her knees, and who with wide-spread and wandering eyes stared at vacancy. But the earl's looks remained cold and unmoved, and not the slightest compassion was awakened in him for his poor, distracted, and pain-worn daughter.

"Stand up, Jane! stand up!" he resumed with stern severity. "The Church commands thee through my mouth to save her, as thou hast promised to do—that is to say, with a joyful heart, and with a God-confiding mind; with smiling lips, and a serene and cheerful look, as becomes disciples filled with the Faith, and as thou hast sworn into the hands of our lord and master, Ignatius Loyola."

"I cannot! I cannot! my father," she murmured plaintively. "I cannot show a joyful heart when this same heart is lacerated by the wild boar of despair. I cannot command my looks to be cheerful when my eyes are dimmed by the tears of agony. Oh, have mercy! have compassion! Remember that you are my father—that I am your daughter—the daughter of a woman whom you have loved, and who would find no rest in the grave if she knew how you martyr and torment me. Oh, mother, mother! if thy spirit be near me, come and protect me. Let thy mild looks fall like a shade over my head, and infuse a breath of thy love into the heart of this cruel father, who wishes to offer his child as a sacrifice upon the altar of his God."

"God has called me," said the earl; "and like Abraham, I too shall know how to obey. But I shall not adorn my victim with flowers, but with a king's crown. I shall not plunge a knife into her breast, but I will put a golden sceptre into her hand and say to her: Thou art a queen before men—but be a true and obedient servant before God. It is thine to command all. But thou art governed by the Holy Church, to whose service thou hast consecrated thyself, and which will bless thee if thou art faithful, but which will crush thee with her curse shouldst thou dare to betray her cause. No, thou art not my daughter, but the priestess consecrated to the holy service of the Church. No, I have no compassion for thy tears and pains, for I see the end of these pains, and I know that these tears will be laid as a diadem of pearls upon thy temples. Lady Jane Douglas, it is the holy Loyola who sends you his commands by my mouth. Obey, therefore, not because I am your father, but because I am the General Superior to whom you have sworn obedience and fidelity to the end of your life."

"Then kill me at once, my father!" she replied, faintly. "Let this life have an end, as it is for me but the protracted agony of martyrdom. Punish me for my disobedience by plunging a dagger into my bosom; punish me, but grant me at least the rest which the grave affords."

"Poor enthusiast," said her father, "thinkest thou we would be so foolish as to subject thee to so easy a punishment? No, no! shouldst thou dare with wicked disobedience to oppose my commands, thy atonement will be terrible, and thy punishment endless. In that case I shall not put *thee* to death, but only the man whom thou lovest,—it will be his head which shall fall, and thou wilt be his murderess. He will die upon the scaffold, and as for thee, thou wilt live in infamy."

"Oh, horror!" groaned Jane, hiding her face in her hands.

Her father continued: "Foolish, short-sighted child, that thought she could play with this sword, and did not perceive that this sword had a double edge, which might smite herself. Thou wast willing to be the servant of the Church, in order thereby to become the mistress of the world. Thou wast willing to merit a glory for thyself, but this glory, forsooth, was not to scorch thy own head with its fiery rays. Foolish child! Who plays with fire, will be consumed by fire. We, however, saw through thy purpose, and perceived the wishes of which thou wast thyself unconscious; we scanned the very depths of thy being, and as we found love there, we have used this love for our own objects, and for thy own good. Why dost thou then complain, and wherefore dost thou weep? Have we not permitted thee to love? Have we not empowered thee to yield thyself wholly up to this love? Dost thou not call thyself the Earl of Surrey's wife, and canst thou not name to me the priest who has sanctified your espousals? Lady Jane, obey, and we grant thee the happiness of thy love, but only dare to revolt against us, and disgrace and infamy shall await thee, and rejected and scorned thou shalt stand before the whole world, the paramour, the—"

"Hold, father, hold!" cried Lady Jane, springing up from the ground. "Cease your terrible words, if you do not wish that I should die with shame. No, I yield, I obey! You are right. I can no longer go back."

"Why indeed shouldst thou wish to do so? Is not thine a life of pleasure and enjoyment? Is it not a rare happiness to have one's sins proclaimed a virtue, and to be able to have one's earthly delight imputed as a heavenly merit? And why then dost thou complain that he does not love thee? Nay, he loves thee of a certainty—his vows of love still resound in thy ears, and thy heart still trembles with the happiness which thou hast tasted. What matters if Surrey sees with his inward eye, in the woman whom he holds in his arms, another person than thee? In reality he loves but thee alone; whether thou art called for the time being, by the name of Katharine Parr, or Jane Douglas, it is all the same, if thou art still his beloved."

"But a day will come when he will discover his mistake, and then he will execrate me."

"That day will not come. The Holy Church will know how to prevent that, if thou wilt only bow to her behests and obey her."

"I bow," sighed Lady Jane. "I shall obey; only promise me, my father, that no harm shall befall *him*, and that I shall not be his murderess."

"No, on the contrary, thou shalt save and deliver him. Only thou must fulfil to the letter the commands which I impose upon thee. In the first place, then tell me the result of your last interview together. He doubts not that thou art the queen?"

"No; he believes it so firmly that he would take the sacrament upon it. That is, he believes it now, because I have promised to give him a token publicly, whereby he may perceive that it is the queen who loves him."

"And this token!" asked the earl with radiant looks.

"I have promised him that the queen would present him with a rosette at the great tournament, and that in this rosette there would be a note."

"Ah the thought is worthy of all admiration!" cried Lord Douglas; "only a woman who wishes to be revenged could have invented the idea. And so by this means the queen will become her own accuser, and will herself put the proof of her guilt into our hands. The only difficulty that still remains is to lead the queen on, without rousing her suspicion, in such a way that she shall wear this rosette and give it to the Earl of Surrey."

"She will do so, if I request her, for she loves me, and I shall so represent the matter to her that she will grant it to me as a favor of love. Katharine is obliging and kindly disposed, and will not be able to refuse my request."

"And I shall apprise the king; that is to say, I shall take good care not to do so myself, for it is always dangerous to go into the cage of a hungry tiger and to take him his food, as in the eagerness of his appetite, he might easily devour one's own hand as well as the proffered meal."

"But how?" she asked, with a terrified expression, "will he content himself with punishing Katharine alone; will he not crush him, whom he must take for her paramour?"

"He will do so. But thou wilt thyself liberate and save him. Thou wilt open his prison for him, and give him freedom, for which he will love thee as the savior of his life."

"Father, father! the game which you

are playing is a hazardous one, and the result of it may be that you will yourself become the murderer of your own daughter. For hear attentively what I tell you: Should *his* head fall, I will not survive him. Should you make me his murderess, you will thereby become yourself my assassin, and I shall curse you, and shall call down imprecations upon your head from the realm of lost spirits. What care I for a royal diadem, if it be stained with the blood of Henry Howard? What matters to me honor and fame if he is not present to see my greatness, and if he cannot with his beaming looks make my crown resplendent? Protect him, therefore,—preserve his life, as the apple of your eye, if you wish that I should accept the royal crown, which you offer me, in order that the King of England may once more become a vassal of the Church!—"

"And in order that the whole of devout Christendom may praise Jane Douglas, the pious queen who succeeded in the holy work of bringing back once more the rebellious and apostate son of the Church, and conducting him penitently to the feet of the Holy Father at Rome—the sole consecrated Head of the Church on earth. Cheer up, good daughter; do not despond! A high destiny beckons to thee, and a brilliant lot awaits thee. Our Holy Mother Church will bless and extol thee, and Henry the Eighth will call thee his queen."

CHAPTER VII.

THE PRISONER.

All was yet quiet and still in the Palace of Whitehall. Nothing was moving, and no one had heard how Lady Jane Douglas had quitted her chamber and had glided along the corridor.

Nobody has heard this, no eye is awake, and no one sees what is now taking place in the queen's apartment.

She is alone—quite alone. Her attendants are all asleep in their rooms. The queen has herself bolted the doors of the ante-chamber from within, and no other door leads into her boudoir, or into her bedroom, but through the ante-chamber.

She is therefore perfectly secure from intrusion—perfectly safe.

She now proceeds to wrap herself quickly and hastily in a long dark mantle, the hood of which she draws down over her head and over her brow, and which completely covers and conceals her figure.

And now she presses a spring fixed in the frame of a picture on the wall. The picture flies back, and exposes to view an outlet, through which a person can pass quite conveniently.

Katharine steps forth. She then carefully restores the picture to its place from the outside, and for some time proceeds along a passage hollowed out in the interior of the wall, feeling her way on both sides until, at length, she finds a knob fixed in the passage. She presses this knob, and a trap-door opens at her feet—through which a feeble light penetrates, and renders visible a small narrow staircase. Katharine descends with lightning speed. Now at the foot of this flight of steps she touches another secret spring, and again a door opens, through which the queen enters a large saloon.

"Oh," she whispers, breathing more freely, "at length the garden-saloon."

She crosses the apartment swiftly, and opens another door.

"John Heywood?"

"I am here, queen."

"Quiet, quiet; go softly, that the sentinel on guard close behind the door may not hear us. Come, we have yet a considerable way to go; let us make haste."

Once more she presses a spring fixed in the wall, and once more a door opens. But before Katharine closes it she takes from the table a small lighted lamp, prepared on purpose by her faithful attendant, and which will enable them to thread their way along the dark and difficult road which they have now to travel over.

She now shuts the doors behind them, and they enter upon a long dark passage, at the end of which is another staircase, which they both descend. The number of the steps seems endless, and by degrees the air becomes denser, and the steps become damp. A deathlike silence surrounds them. Not a sound of life—not the slightest murmur is perceptible.

They are now in a subterranean passage which seems to extend before them to an interminable length.

Katharine turns round to John Heywood; the lamp lights up her countenance, which is pale, but which exhibits an expression of firmness and resolution.

"Now, John Heywood, consider this matter well! I don't ask you if you have courage, for that I know. I only wish to ascertain if you are willing to devote this courage for your queen."

"No, not for my queen, but for the noble and generous lady who has saved my son."

"Then you must be my protector on the present occasion should danger threaten us. Yet, with God's blessing, I trust we shall remain unharmed. Let us proceed."

Silently and resolutely they continue their journey along the dreary way.

At length they reach a spot where the passage widens and spreads out into a small open chamber, along the side-walls of which are fixed a few seats.

"We have now completed half our journey," said Katharine, "and we will rest here a little while!"

She placed the lamp on a small stone table in the middle of the passage, and sat down, while she beckoned to John Heywood to take a seat beside her.

"I am not the queen in this place," she continued, "and you are not the king's fool, but I am a poor feeble woman, and you are my protector. You have therefore a full right to sit beside me."

John Heywood shook his head smilingly, and sat down at her feet.

"Holy Katharine! Savior of my son, I lie down at thy feet and offer thee my prayer of thanks."

"Dost thou know this subterranean passage, John?" asked the queen.

John Heywood smiled sadly.

"Yes, queen, I know it."

"Ah! thou knowest it? I thought this secret belonged to the king alone."

"Then you will readily understand, queen, why the fool should know it. For the King of England and the fool are twin brothers. Yes, queen, I know this passage, and once before I travelled it in suffering and tears."

"What? yourself—John Heywood?"

"Yes, queen, and now I ask you if you know the history of this subterranean passage? You are silent. Well then, happy for you that you do not know it, and were I to relate to you the whole story, this night would be too short for the purpose. When this passage was built, Henry was still young, and still possessed a heart. At that time he loved not only his ladies, but even his friends and servants, especially Cromwell, the all-powerful minister. Cromwell then lived at Whitehall, and Henry occupied the royal apartments in the tower. But Henry had always a strong affection for his favorite, and so Cromwell surprised him one day with this subterranean passage, the building of which occupied one hundred men for a whole year—Ah, the king was at that time greatly touched, and thanked his great minister with tears and embraces for this surprise. Scarcely a day passed that Henry did not pay Cromwell a visit through this passage. Thus he perceived, day by day, that the palace at Whitehall was becoming more splendid and magnificent; and when he returned to the tower he found that this residence was wholly unfit for a king, and that his minister lived in far more royal state than the King of England. This, my queen, was the cause of Cromwell's fall. The king wished to have Whitehall! The wily Cromwell perceived this, and he presented him with his precious treasure—his palace, in building and adorning which he had spent ten years of his life. Henry accepted the gift, but now Cromwell's fall was inevitable. The king could not, of course, forgive Cromwell for having offered him a gift, which was so valuable, that Henry was unable or unwilling to make a return for it. He accordingly remained Cromwell's debtor, and as this piqued and annoyed him, he vowed Cromwell's destruction. When Henry repaired to Whitehall it was resolved that Cromwell should mount the scaffold. Ah! the king is a very thrifty master-builder. A palace costs him nothing more than the head of one of his subjects. With Cromwell's head he paid for Whitehall, and Wolsey died on account of Hampton Court."

"But not upon the scaffold, John?"

"Oh, no. Henry preferred breaking his heart rather than his neck. He first allowed Wolsey to present him with that palatial gem, Hampton Court, with all its treasures, and then deprived him of all his high offices and stripped him of all his dignities. At length he was travelling as a prisoner to the tower, but he died on the way thither. You are quite right! Wolsey did not die upon the scaffold, he was executed by a more tedious and cruel process."

"Did you not say, John, that you had yourself once travelled this road?"

"Yes, indeed, my queen; and it was for the purpose of taking leave of the noblest of men—the most faithful of friends, Sir Thomas More! I prayed and besought Cromwell for a long time, until at length he had compassion on my suffering and allowed me to go through this passage to Sir Thomas More, in order that I might at least receive the blessing and the parting farewell of this sainted man. Ah, queen, let us speak no more of this subject! From that day forward I became a fool, for I perceived that one was not paid for his trouble in being a serious man in this world, when such men as More were executed as malefactors. Come, queen, let us go on!"

"Yes, John, let us proceed," she replied, rising from her seat. "But are you aware whither we are going?"

"Ah, queen, do I not know you? And did I not tell you that to-morrow Maria Askew would be put to the rack if she did not recant."

"I see you have understood me," she returned, nodding to him in a friendly manner. "Yes, I am going to Maria Askew."

"But how shall you find out her dungeon without being seen and discovered?"

"Even the unfortunate have friends, John. Nay, the queen herself has a few. And so chance, or rather Providence, has ordained that Maria Askew should be confined in the little room into which this secret passage leads."

"Is she alone in this room?"

"Yes, quite alone. The sentinels stand outside before the door."

"But if they hear you, and open the door?"

"Then I am lost beyond doubt, unless God should assist me."

They proceeded in silence, both too much occupied with their own thoughts to wish to disturb each other by conversation.

But this long journey at length fatigued Katharine. She leaned against the wall quite exhausted.

"Will you grant me a favor, queen?" asked John Heywood. "Allow me to carry you—your little feet are unable to bear you any longer; allow me to be your feet, your majesty."

This offer she declined with a cordial smile.

"No, John, this is the suffering-station of a saint, and you know we are bound to perform this office upon our knees and in the sweat of our brow."

"Oh, queen, how noble and how courageous you are!" cried John Heywood. "You do good without parade, and fear no danger when a work of kindness or charity is to be accomplished."

"Indeed, John," she rejoined with an enchanting smile, "I do fear danger, and it is because I do, that I requested you to accompany me! I had a horror of this long lonely way, and of the darkness and deathlike stillness of this underground passage. Ah, John, I thought to myself that if I went this journey alone, the shades of Anne Bullen and of Katharine of Arragon would be roused from their sleep by me, who wear their crown, and that they would hover around me, and would take me by the hand and lead me to their graves, in order to show me that there was still room for me also beside them. You see then, John, that I am not courageous, but only a timid, trembling woman."

"And yet you came, queen?"

"I reckoned upon you, John. It was my duty to attempt this journey, in order, perhaps, to save the life of a poor enthusiastic maiden. For it shall not be said that Katharine abandons her friends in misfortune, or that she shrinks from danger. I am but a poor, feeble woman, who cannot defend her friends with arms, and therefore I must have recourse to other means. But look, John, the passage divides here! Alas, I only knew it from descriptions which have been given me, but I was never told that the road branched off at this point! Now, John, which way shall we take?"

"This one, queen, and here we are at the end of our journey. The other way yonder leads to the torture-chamber. That is to say, to a small grated window, through which the torture-chamber can be seen. Whenever King Henry was in a specially good humor, he repaired with his friend to that grating, in order to divert himself a little with the agonies of those who were condemned to the rack, as blasphemers. For you are well aware, queen, that the honor of the rack is only accorded to those who have blasphemed God, or in other words who have not recognized King Henry as the pope of their Church. But stay, here we are at the door; and there is the spring which opens it."

Katharine put her lamp on the ground, and touched the spring.

The door turned slowly and noiselessly on its hinges, and, softly as shadows, they both entered.

They now found themselves in a small, round chamber, which appeared to have been originally a niche wrought in the wall of the tower, rather than a room. Only through a small grated aperture in the wall a little light and air entered the dungeon, whose cold, dreary walls showed the stones of the rough masonry. Not a chair, nor a table was there in this narrow cell, but in one corner, on the ground, was a heap of straw. Upon this straw lay a pale, delicate being; her hollow and haggard cheeks as white as alabaster, her brow so pure and clear—so full of peace the whole countenance; her bare, wasted arms flung back above her head, her hands clasped above her forehead, her head turned aside in quiet, peaceful slumber, her fine delicate figure wrapped in a long dark robe, and a smile upon her lips, known to those only who are happy.

This was Maria Askew, the malefactor—the condemned. Maria Askew, who was only a blasphemer, because she did not believe in the divine attributes and lofty pretensions of the king, and because she would not subject her mind to his decrees.

"She sleeps!" whispered Katharine, deeply moved. And, quite involuntarily, approaching the couch of the sufferer, she folded her hands, and a silent prayer trembled upon her lips.

"Thus sleep the just!" said John Heywood. "The angels comfort them in slumber, and the breath of God wafts refreshment to their souls. Poor maiden, how soon, and they will strain these lovely and beautiful limbs, and torture thee for the honor of God; and this mouth, too, which now smiles so peacefully, they will distort with groans of agony!"

"No, no," returned Katharine, eagerly. "I have come to save her, and God will succor and enable me to do so. I dare no longer spare her slumbers. I must awake her."

She stooped down and imprinted a kiss upon the young maiden's brow.

"Maria, wake up, I am here! I will save thee, and will set thee free. Maria, Maria, wake up!"

She slowly opened her large brilliant eyes, and nodded a greeting to Katharine.

"Katharine Parr!" she said smiling. "I only expected a letter from you, and you have come yourself?"

"The sentinels have been dismissed, and the jailers changed, Maria, for they discovered our correspondence."

"Ah, then you will no longer write to me in future! And yet your letters were my sole comfort," sighed Maria Askew. "However, it is well, and perhaps this will only tend to lighten the road which I have to travel! The heart must be free from all earthly ties, in order that the soul may move its wings the more freely when it soars aloft to return to its home with God."

"Listen, Maria, listen!" said Katharine, softly but eagerly. "A terrible danger threatens thee. The king has directed that thou shouldst be moved to recant by means of the rack!"

"Well, and what more?" asked Maria, with a smiling countenance.

"Unhappy girl, thou knowest not what thou sayest! Little dost thou know the fearful tortures which await thee. Thou knowest not the force of pain, which is perhaps even more powerful than the spirit, and is able to subdue it."

"And if I knew all this, how far would it help me?" asked Maria Askew. "You say they intend putting me to the rack. Well then, I shall be obliged to bear it, for I have no power to change their will."

"Nay, Maria, nay; thou hast the power! Recall what thou hast said, Maria! Declare that knowledge has come to thee, and that now thou perceivest thou hadst been deceived. Say that thou wilt acknowledge the king to be the head of the Church, that thou wilt accept the six articles, and no longer believe in the Pope of Rome. Ah, Maria, God sees into thy heart, and knows thy thoughts. Thou hast no need to announce them with thy lips. He has given thee life, and thou art not at liberty to fling it away; thou must try to preserve it as long as thou canst. Retract, therefore! It is surely allowable to deceive those who wish to become our murderers. If, in their proud arrogance, they demand of thee to say what they say, why only imagine them to be men bereft of reason, who are suffered for the moment to indulge their caprice, lest they become raving madmen. After all, what matters it if thou sayest the king is the head of the Church? God looks down from his throne on high, and smiles at this petty earthly warfare, which men wage amongst themselves, and in which His honor is in no wise involved. Let learned men and theologians quarrel and dispute—that is no concern of us women. If we only believe in God, and carry His spirit within us, the form or the manner in which we do so is of little importance. Here, however, the question is not about God, but about externals, and non-essential articles of belief. What can such things matter to thee? What hast thou to do with the quarrels of priests? Retract, therefore, poor enthusiastic child, retract!"

While Katharine thus spoke with breathless eagerness, Maria Askew had raised herself up slowly from her couch, and now stood, like a slender and delicate lily, opposite the queen.

Her noble features wore an expression of deep anger. Her eyes flashed, and a disdainful smile settled on her lips.

"What! you can tender me this advice?" she asked. "Do you wish me to deny my faith and forswear my God, merely to escape earthly pain! And your tongue does not refuse to utter these words, and your heart does not recoil with shame while you offer this counsel. Look at these arms! What are they worth that I should not sacrifice them to God? Look at these feeble limbs! Are they so precious, that like a sordid miser I should save them? No, no; God is my highest good—not this feeble, tottering frame. To God I yield it up! I retract or recant?—never! Belief does not suffer itself to be hidden under this cloak or that: it must be naked and undisguised before the eyes of mankind. Such be mine! And if I am chosen to be a witness ot the true faith, which does not deny itself, but which confesses itself openly, then grant me this choice. Many are called but few are chosen. If I am one of the elect, I thank God for it, and I only bless the poor, erring mortals, who by means of the rack, have made me a chosen vessel. Ah, believe me, Katharine, I rejoice in sight of death, for this life is but a dreary, desolate, and wretched existence. Let me die, Katharine—die—that I may find immortality and bliss!"

"But poor, hapless child! This is more than death—this is the torture of earth, which threatens thee. Oh, reflect, Maria, that thou are but a feeble woman! Who knows but that the rack will yet subdue thy spirit; and that with torn and dislocated limbs, thou wilt at length, in the frenzy of pain, be brought to retract and forswear thy faith?"

"Were I capable of so doing," cried Maria Askew, with flashing eyes, "believe me, queen, that when I recovered consciousness, I would die by my own hand, in order, as a punishment for my recanting, to deliver myself up to eternal perdition! God has commanded me to be a witness for the true faith. His command shall be fulfilled!"

"Well then, be it so," said Katharine, with decision. "Do not retract, but at least save thyself from thy executioners! I, Maria, I will save thee! I cannot suffer that this graceful and fair form should fall a victim to the outrageous and contemptible prejudices of men, or that, for the honor of God, a noble image, moulded in His own likeness, should be tortured in the name of that same God! Oh, come; I will save thee! I, the queen. Give me thy hand! Follow me out of this dungeon; I know a way which will lead thee away from here, and I will conceal thee in my own apartments, until thou canst continue thy flight without danger."

"No, no, queen, it is not you that shall conceal her with you," said John Heywood. "You have favored me so far as to allow me to become your confidant. Suffer me now also to have a share in your noble work. It is not with you that Maria Askew shall find a place of refuge, but with me. Oh, come, Maria, follow your friends! It is life which summons you forth, which opens your prison doors, and which calls to you by a thousand cherished names! Hear you not all the sweet and attractive voices; see you not all those noble and smiling faces, how they greet you and beckon to you? Maria Askew, it is a noble bridegroom who calls to you. As yet you know him not, but he waits for you abroad in the world. Maria Askew, there are young children who hold out their tender arms to you. You have not yet borne them, but love holds them in its arms, and will bring them to meet you. It is the part of a wife and a mother, which the world has yet to expect from thee, Maria. Thou canst not refuse the sacred vocation which God has given thee! Come, then, and follow us; follow thy queen, who has the right of commanding her subject. Follow the friend who swears that he will watch over, and protect thee as a father!"

"Father in heaven, protect me!" cried Maria Askew, falling on her knees, and holding up her hands in an attitude of supplication.

"Father in heaven, they want to snatch thy child from Thee, and to estrange my heart from Thee! They wish to lead me into temptation, and to seduce me with their speech! Protect me, Father; make my ear deaf that I hear them not. Give me some sign that I am thine, that no one else has power over me but Thee alone;—some token, Father, that Thou callest me!"

And as if God had indeed granted her prayer, a loud knocking was now heard at the outer door, and a voice cried "Maria Askew, wake up, and prepare —the chancellor and the Bishop of Winchester are coming to take you hence."

"Alas! the rack," groaned Katharine, as she hid her face in her hands with a shudder.

"Yes, the rack," said Maria Askew with a blissful smile. "God calls me!"

John Heywood approached the queen and seized her hand with eagerness, "You see it is all in vain," he said, urgently. "Hasten then and save yourself. Haste, and quit this dungeon, ere yonder door be opened."

"No," said Katharine, firmly and decidedly—"No, I remain: she shall not surpass me in courage and greatness of soul;—she will not deny her God,—well then, I too shall be a witness for my God! I shall not cast down my eyes with shame to the ground before a young girl; like her I shall confess my belief freely and publicly—like her I shall say: God alone is the Lord of his Church. God—"

Outside, all was activity and motion—a key was heard turning in the lock.

"Queen, I beseech you," entreated John Heywood, "by all that is sacred to you—by your love, come—come away!"

"No, no!" she exclaimed with vehemence.

But now Maria Askew seized her hand, and raising her other arm to heaven, said with a loud and imperious voice: "In the name of God I command thee to leave me!"

While Katharine involuntarily gave way, John Heywood pressed her back to the secret door, through which he forced her, almost by violence, and drawing it after them both, closed it from the outside.

Scarcely was the secret door closed, when the other door opened.

"With whom were you speaking?" asked Gardiner, looking round with a searching glance.

"With the tempter, who wished to make me turn away from God," she replied, "With the tempter, who on the approach of your footsteps wished to delude me with fear, and persuade me to recant."

"Then you are firmly resolved—you will not recant?" asked Gardiner, and a ferocious joy lighted up his hard pale features.

"No; I will not recant," she replied, with a beaming and smiling countenance.

"Then I must conduct thee in God's name, and in the name of the king, into the torture-chamber!" cried the Chancellor Wriothesley, stepping forward and laying his hand heavily upon Maria's shoulder. "As thou hast refused to hear the warning and gentle voice of love, we must now endeavor by the voice of anger and of damnation to rouse thee from thy errors!"

He beckoned to his racksmen, who stood behind him at the open door, and commanded them to seize and conduct her to the torture-chamber.

Maria repelled them with a smile.

"Don't touch me, pray! that is unnecessary. The Redeemer himself went on foot, and bore his cross to the place of execution. I shall travel as he did. Show me the way, I will follow you, but let no one dare to touch me. I will show you that, not by compulsion, but freely and joyfully, I travel the path of suffering which I am to endure for the sake of my God. Rejoice my soul, sing my lips, for the bridegroom is near, and the banquet is about to begin!"

And with jubilant strains Maria Askew began to sing a spiritual song, which was not yet ended when she entered the chamber of torture.

CHAPTER VIII.

THE PRINCESS ELIZABETH.

THE king sleeps. Let him sleep on! He is old and feeble, and God has severely punished the restless tyrant—the man with the vacillating, uneasy, ne'er-contented mind—by laying fetters on his body, and making of that body a prison for his mind; by making the ambitious king, striving to attain the immeasurable, the slave of his own flesh. How high soever his thoughts may soar, the king still remains an unwieldy, powerless bondsman—a human child; however much his conscience may torment him with disquietude and anxiety, he is doomed to endure it all—he cannot fly from his conscience; God has imposed fetters on body and mind alike.

The king sleeps! But not so the queen—not so Jane Douglas—and not so even the princess Elizabeth.

She was awake, and her heart was throbbing violently. She had been walking up and down her room restlessly, and with a strange feeling of embarrassment, waiting for the hour which she had appointed for the rendezvous. And now this hour had arrived. A glowing crimson suffused the countenance of the youthful princess, and her hand trembled as she took the light and opened the secret door leading into the corridor. For a moment she lingered and stood still, and then, as if ashamed of her irresolution, she proceeded along the corridor, and up the narrow staircase which led into the tower-chamber. With a hasty movement she pushed the door open and entered the room. She had reached the goal, and Thomas Seymour was already there.

On seeing him she was seized with an involuntary fear, and now for the first time she became conscious of the venturesome step she had taken.

When Seymour, the gay and ardent man, approached her with an impassioned greeting, she drew back timidly, and recoiled from his touch.

"What! you will not allow me to kiss your hand?" he asked, and she thought she perceived on his countenance a faint smile of derision. "You make me the happiest of mortals by inviting me to this interview, and now you stand coldly and rigidly before me, and I dare not even fold you in my arms, Elizabeth?"

Elizabeth! He had addressed her by her Christian name, without her having given him permission to do so. This offended her in the midst of her confusion, this roused up within her the pride of the princess, and gave her to under-

stand how greatly she must have forgotten what was due to her own dignity, when others could so readily forget it.

This tribute, however, she wished to recover once more. She would at this moment have forfeited a year of her life, not to have taken this step—not to have invited the earl to this interview.

She wished to try and recover in his eyes the position which she had lost, and again to assume toward him the dignity and demeanor of a princess.

Her pride was still more powerful than her love. She imagined that her lover should at the same time bow before her, as her favored servant.

"My Lord Thomas Seymour," she said, gravely, "you have often requested us for a private interview, we now grant it. Speak therefore! What petition or matter have you to lay before us?"

And with a solemn and imposing air she proceeded to an arm-chair, in which she seated herself with the grave dignity of a queen, giving audience to her vassals.

Poor innocent child! who with unconscious fear wished to entrench herself behind her elevated rank as behind a shield, which should hide her anxiety and maidenly timidity.

Thomas Seymour, however, saw through all this, and his proud, cold heart revolted against it, on perceiving that this child in years attempted to set him at defiance.

He wished to humble her—to compel her to bend before him, and to sue for his love as for a favored gift.

He therefore bowed profoundly to the princess, and said, with a respectful air: "Your highness, it is true I have often begged you for an audience, but you have so long refused it to me, that at last I had not the courage to urge my request any further, and so I imposed silence on my wishes, and suffered my heart to become mute. Seek not, therefore, now, that these pains have been overcome, to call them into being once more. My lips shall be sealed—my heart dead. You have so willed it, and I have bowed submissively to your will. Farewell, therefore, princess, and may your days be more happy, more serene, than those of the unfortunate Thomas Seymour.

He then bowed profoundly once more, and proceeded slowly toward the door. He had already opened it, and was about to depart, when a hand touched him on the shoulder and drew him back into the room with violent impetuosity.

"You wish to go?" asked Elizabeth, with trembling voice, while she gasped for breath. "You wish to leave me, and with mockery on your lips, to go, perhaps, to the Duchess of Richmond, whom you love, and tell her, with derisive laughter, that the Princess Elizabeth granted you an interview, and that you treated it with scorn?"

"I do not love the Duchess of Richmond!" said the earl, gravely.

"But she will soon be your wife."

"She will never be my wife!"

"And why not?"

"Because I don't love her, princess!"

A beam of joy overspread Elizabeth's pale and troubled countenance.

"Why do you call me princess?" she asked.

"Because you have come as a princess to grant your poor servant an audience. Indeed it would be abusing your princely favor too much, were I to prolong this audience still further. I therefore retire, princess."

And once more he approached the door; but Elizabeth rushed after him, and seizing his arms with both her hands, she pushed him back wildly.

Her eyes flashed, her lips trembled, and a passionate ardor glowed visibly in her whole frame. She was now the veritable daughter of her father;—indiscreet and vehement in her anger—crushing in her fury.

"You shall not go," she murmured, with firmly compressed teeth. "I will not suffer you to go! I won't suffer you to stand before me any longer with that cold, smiling countenance. Chide me—reproach me in the severest manner for having so long attempted to defy you; execrate me if you can. Only not this smiling composure. This kills me, it stabs me like a dagger to the heart. For thou seest clearly I have no longer the power to resist thee—thou seest clearly that I love thee. Yes, I love thee with rapture and desperation, with delight and bewilderment! I love thee as my demon and my angel. I am angry with thee for having so completely subdued the pride of my spirit; I execrate thee for having made me so entirely thy slave, and, at the next moment, I fall upon my knees before God, and beseech him to forgive me these insolent and wicked thoughts to thy prejudice. I love thee, I say—not as those mild, gentle women love, with a smile upon their lips—but with rage and desperation, with jealousy and anger. I love thee as my father loved Anne Bullen, when, in the hatred of his love, and in the cruel anger of his jealousy, he caused her to mount the scaffold, because he had been told that she was unfaithful to him. Ah, had I the power, I would do as my father did. I would kill you were you to be so daring as to cease to love me. And, now, Thomas Seymour, say now, if you have the courage to wish to leave me?"

She wore a look of perfect fascination in this fiery force of her passion,—she was so young, so ardent; and Thomas Seymour was so ambitious. In his eyes Elizabeth was not only the beautiful and attractive maiden who loved him; she was more than that:—she was the daughter of Henry the Eighth; the Princess of England, and would, perhaps one day, become heiress to the throne. Her father, indeed had disinherited her, and by means of an Act of Parliament had declared her unworthy of succeeding to the crown. But Henry's vacillating mind might change, and the rejected princess might one day become queen.

This thought occupied the Earl's mind as he looked at Elizabeth, as he contemplated her, so blooming and so attractive, glowing with passion as she stood before him. This thought filled his mind as he now folded her in his arms, and imprinted an ardent kiss upon her lips.

"No, I shall not go," he whispered.

"I shall never more wander from thy side, unless it be thy wish that I should go. I am thine! Thy slave, thy vassal—to be such, and nothing more is my sole wish. Let them betray me if they will, let the king punish me as a traitor, I shall still exult with happiness, for Elizabeth loves me, and it will be for Elizabeth's sake that I shall die!"

"Thou shalt not die!" she exclaimed, clinging firmly to his side. "Thou shalt live, proud, great, and happy with me! Thou shalt be my lord and master, and should I one day be a queen—and I feel within me that I shall be a queen—then Thomas Seymour will be King of England."

"That is to say, in the quiet and privacy of thy chamber it would probably be so!" he returned with a sigh. "But in public, and before the world, I shall still be merely a subject and servant—nay, I may even be called a favorite."

"Never—never, that I swear to thee! Did I not tell thee that I loved thee?"

"But the love of women is so changeable. Who knows, when once the crown decks thy brow, how long thou wilt already have trodden the unhappy Thomas Seymour under foot?"

She looked at him with astonishment.

"Can such a thing be? Is it possible that one should forget and abandon what one has at any time loved?"

"Don't ask, Elizabeth! Has not thy father already his sixth wife?"

"True," she replied, and she bent her head sadly on her breast; "but I," she continued, after a pause, "I shall not resemble my father in this. I shall love thee eternally! And in order that thou mayest have a pledge of my fidelity, I tender myself to be thy wife."

He looked inquiringly and with astonishment into her excited and glowing countenance. He did not understand her.

She, however, continued with impassioned earnestness: "Yes thou shalt be my lord and my husband! Come, my beloved, come! I have not summoned thee in order that thou shouldst assume the ignominious part of being the secret lover of a princess. I have summoned thee that thou mayest become my spouse. I wish that a bond should unite us both—a bond so indissoluble that neither the anger nor the will of my father—but only death itself may be able to rend it asunder. I will give thee a proof of my love and resignation, and then thou wilt see how truly I love thee. Come, my beloved—that I may soon be able to greet thee as my husband!"

He looked at her as if petrified. "Whither wouldst thou lead me?"

"Into the private chapel of the palace," she replied innocently. "I have written to Cranmer to wait for me there at day-break. Let us therefore make haste!"

"Cranmer! written to Archbishop Cranmer?" cried Seymour with amazement. "What! Cranmer waiting for us in the private chapel?"

"No doubt—since I have written to him to that effect?"

"But what is he to do?—What service can he render us?"

She looked at him with surprise. "What service can he render us? Why marry us, of course!"

The earl staggered back as if stunned. "And hast thou told him that too?"

"Oh, certainly not," she replied with a charming and innocent smile. "I know very well it is dangerous to trust such secrets to paper. I have only written to him to come in his robes of office, because I have important secrets to confess to him."

"Oh, God be thanked! We are not lost," sighed the earl.

"What, I don't understand thee?" she asked. "Thou dost not give me thy hand? thou dost not hasten to conduct me to the chapel?"

"Tell me, I entreat thee, only tell me this one thing. Hast thou ever spoken to the archbishop of thy—no—of our love? Hast thou ever betrayed to him a syllable of that which moves our hearts?"

She blushed deeply beneath the keen penetrating glance which he fixed upon her. "Chide me, Seymour," she whispered. "But my heart was feeble and timorous, and however often I made the attempt to fulfil the sacred duty, and to confess all faithfully and without reserve to the archbishop, I was never once able to succeed! The words died upon my lips, and it seemed as if an invisible power paralysed my tongue."

"Then Cranmer knows nothing?"

"No, Seymour, as yet he knows nothing! But now he shall learn all; we will now go before him and tell him that we love each other, and urge him by our entreaties to bless our union and to join our hands together."

"Impossible!" cried Seymour. "That can never be done!"

"But, gracious heavens! why not?" she asked with astonishment.

"I say that Cranmer will never be so mad, so guilty as to fulfil thy wish. I say that thou canst never become my wife."

For a moment she scanned his features with looks of anxious bewilderment. "But hast thou not just told me that thou lovest me?" she asked. "Have I not sworn to thee that I love thee in return? Must we not, therefore, espouse each other in order to sanctify the union of our hearts?"

Seymour cast his eyes to the ground, and blushed with shame before her pure innocent looks. She did not understand his blushes. She interpreted his silence as a sign that he was conquered.

"Come," she said, "Cranmer awaits us!"

He raised his eyes once more, and looked at her amazed. "Then thou dost not perceive that all this is but a dream, which can never become a reality? Thou dost not perceive that this precious fantasy of thy noble and generous heart will never be realised? What? Knowest thou so little of thy father, as not to be aware that he would crush us both, did we thus dare to defy his paternal and royal authority? Thy birth would not secure thee from his rage, for thou knowest well he is inflexible and devoid of consideration in his anger; and the voice of Nature does not speak so loudly within him as not to be overpowered by the thunder of his indignation and wrath. Poor child, thou hast learned this already! Remember with what relentlessness he has already revenged upon thee the supposed guilt of thy mother—how he has carried out towards thee his vindictive feelings against her. Remember that he refused thy hand to the Dauphin of France—not for the sake of thy happiness, but because he said thou wast not worthy of such a lofty position. The illegitimate daughter of Anne Bullen could never become the Queen of France. And after such proofs of his fierce anger against thee, wilt thou venture to fling this fearful insult in his face? To compel him to recognize his subject—his servant, as his son?"

"Oh, but this servant is meanwhile the brother of a Queen of England," she returned, timidly. "My father loved Jane Seymour too tenderly not to pardon her brother."

"Alas! thou knowest not thy father! He has no feelings for the past, or if he has, it is only to punish an offence or a crime, but not to reward affection. King Henry would be quite capable of condemning to death the daughter of Anne Bullen, and of sending the brothers of Katharine Howard to the scaffold or to the rack, because both these queens once grieved him and wounded his heart; but he would not forgive in me even the slightest offence, merely because I am the brother of a queen who loved him truly and tenderly to the day of her death. But I am not now speaking of myself. I am a warrior, and both by sea and land I have looked death too often in the face to fear it now. I only speak of thee, Elizabeth! It is not thus that thou must perish. This noble head shall not be laid upon the block. It is destined to bear a royal crown. A still higher fate than that of love awaits thee—power and fame! I dare not withdraw thee from this proud future. The Princess Elizabeth, though now rejected and scorned, may still one day mount the throne of England. The Countess of Seymour—never! she disinherits herself. Pursue, therefore, your high destiny. Lord Seymour gives way before a throne."

"That is to say, you spurn me?" she asked, angrily, stamping with her foot upon the floor. "That is to say, the proud Earl of Sudley thinks the degraded daughter of Anne Bullen too mean for his lordly coronet! In other words, you do not love me!"

"No. It means that I love thee more than I do myself—more deeply, more purely than any other man can love thee; for this love is so great that it imposes silence on my selfishness and ambition, and only suffers me to think of thee and of thy future."

"Alas!" she sighed, sadly, "didst thou love me truly, thou wouldst not thus consider; thou wouldst not see danger or fear death. Thou wouldst think of nothing—know nothing—but love."

"Because I think of love, I think of thee," replied Seymour. "I think that thou shouldst go forth great, powerful, and radiant in an elevated sphere, and that to this end I am willing to lend thee my arm. I think that my queen of the future needs a general who shall win for her the victory, and that I am ready to be that general. But when this goal is attained, when thou art queen, then thou wilt have the power to make of thy subject thy husband—then will it depend upon thy will to raise me up to become the proudest, the happiest, and the most enviable of men. Then shouldst thou offer me thy hand, I shall praise and thank God that He has so favored me, and my whole existence will be spent in the endeavor to afford thee that happiness which thou art so fully justified in demanding."

"And until then?" she asked, sadly.

"Until then we will wait and love each other!" he exclaimed, folding her affectionately in his arms.

She gently repressed his ardor. "And wilt thou be true and constant to me until then?"

"True and constant until death!"

"They have told me that thou wouldst be married to the Duchess of Richmond, in order thereby at length to end the animosity between the Howards and the Seymours."

Thomas Seymour knit his brow, and his countenance grew dark. "Believe me, this hatred is invincible, and no bonds of affinity could have power to efface it. It is an inheritance of long standing between our families, and I am firmly resolved not to renounce this inheritance. I shall just as little marry the Duchess of Richmond, as Henry Howard my sister the Countess of Shrewsbury."

"Swear this, Seymour! swear to me that thou sayest the truth, and that the haughty coquette, the Duchess of Richmond, shall never be thy wife. Swear this to me now by all that is sacred to thee!"

"I swear it by my LOVE!" cried Thomas Seymour, solemnly.

"Then I shall have at least one care the less," sighed Elizabeth. "I shall have no need to be jealous. And besides, we shall see each other often—shall we not? We shall both of us faithfully and sacredly preserve the secret of this tower, and for days full of illusions and privation we shall here celebrate nights of blissful enjoyment and sweet delight. But why dost thou smile, Seymour?"

"I smile because thou art so pure and innocent, like an angel," he replied, taking her hand, which he kissed respectfully. "I smile because thou art a noble and divine child, whom one should worship on his knees, and to whom we should pray as to the chaste goddess Vesta! Yes, my charming and beloved child, we will here, as thou sayest, live many nights of blissful enjoyment, and may I become a reprobate and a castaway, should I ever be capable of betraying this sweet and innocent confidence which thou reposest in me, or of dimming the brightness of thy angelic purity!"

"Oh, we shall be very happy, Seymour," she said, smiling. "But one thing I lack—a friend of my own sex to whom I could confide my happiness, and to whom I could speak of thee. I often feel as if this love, which must be kept concealed and locked up, would at last cause my bosom to burst asunder—as if this secret must find an outlet for itself by violence, and sweep forth like a hurricane over the whole face of nature. Seymour, I want a confidante of my happiness and of my love."

"On the contrary, be most careful to avoid such a thing!" cried Seymour, with anxiety. "A secret which is known to three persons is no longer a secret, and thy confidante would one day betray us."

"Nay, I know a lady who would not be capable of so acting—a lady who loves me well enough to keep my secret as faithfully as I could myself—a lady who could be more than the confidante—who could even be the protectress of our love. Oh, believe me, if we could but win her to our side, then would our future be blest and happy, for then we might the more readily succeed in obtaining the consent of the king to our marriage."

"And who is this lady?"

"It is the queen."

"The queen!" cried Thomas Seymour, with a look of such consternation that Elizabeth trembled; "the queen thy confidante? Impossible! that would be to bring hopeless ruin upon us both. Unhappy child, take good care not to mention a word to her or even a syllable of thy relationship with me—beware of betraying to her by the slightest intimation that Thomas Seymour is not wholly indifferent to thee! Ah, her anger would crush both thee and me!"

"And why dost thou think so?" asked Elizabeth, gloomily. "Why dost thou suppose that Katharine would foam with anger because Lord Seymour loves me? Or what!—Is it she peradventure whom thou lovest, and therefore darest not confess to her that thou hast pledged thy love to me also? Ah, I now see through all—I know all! Thou lovest the queen, and her alone! For this reason thou art unwilling to go with me into the chapel; for this reason thou hast sworn that thou dost not wish to marry the Duchess of Richmond, and for this reason—ah, my forebodings did not deceive me—for this reason too that frantic ride on horseback yesterday in Epping Forest! Ah, of course the queen's courser must needs become restive, and take flight in order that the master of the horse should be able to follow his mistress and lose himself with her in the secluded thickets of the wood!—And now," she continued, with anger-flashing eyes, while she raised her hand threateningly aloft, "now I say to thee. Beware! Beware, Seymour, of betraying thy secret by a word, or even by a syllable, for this word will crush thee, Yes, I feel that I am no base-born child—but the true daughter of my father; I feel it by this anger,—this jealousy which rages within me. Beware, Seymour, for I shall go hence to accuse thee to the king, and the head of the traitor will fall upon the scaffold!"

She was beside herself. She strode with clinched hands and threatening gestures up and down the room. Tears burst from her eyes, but she dashed them away from her eyelids, and sprinkled them like pearls around her. The violent and ungovernable nature of her father strove within her, and her blood foamed furiously in her veins.

But Thomas Seymour had already regained his composure and presence of mind. He approached the princess and folded the resisting girl in his powerful arms.

"Foolish charmer!" he said, with many tender kisses. "Sweet, silly charmer, how beautiful thou art in thy anger; and how I love thee for it! Jealousy befits love, and I don't complain of it, albeit thou hast been unjust and cruel toward me. The queen has much too cold and too proud a heart for any one ever to love her. Indeed, the very thought of such a thing would be treason against her honor and virtue, and certainly she has not deserved, of either of us, that we should slander or insult her. She is the first person who was ever just toward thee, and to me she has always been only a gracious queen and mistress."

"True," murmured Elizabeth, ashamed of her suspicion, "she is to me a true friend and mother, and to her I owe my present position at this court."

Then, after a pause, she continued, with a smile, while she held out her hand to the earl: "Thou art right, it was a crime to distrust her, and I am a foolish creature. Forget it, Seymour, forget my wayward and childish anger, and I promise thee in return to betray our secret to nobody—not even to the queen!"

"Thou wilt swear that to me?"

"Yes. I swear it to thee. And I swear to thee more than that: I will never more be jealous of her."

"Then thou only dost justice to thyself and also to the queen," said the earl, smiling, while he once more embraced her.

But she gently checked his ardor. "I must now away. The day dawns, and the archbishop is waiting for me in the chapel."

"And what wilt thou say to him, beloved?"

"I shall confess to him!"

"What? betray our love to him?"

"Oh, no," she replied, with an enchanting smile, "that is a secret between God and ourselves, and it is to Him alone that we can confess it, as He alone can absolve us from what it implies. Adieu, then, my Seymour, adieu, and think of me till we meet again. But when, say when, shall we meet again?"

"When it is such a night as the one just passed, beloved,—when the moon appears not in the sky."

"Oh, then I wish we had a change of the moon every week!" she returned, with the charming innocence of a child. "Farewell, Seymour, farewell, we must part."

She clung caressingly for a moment to his tall, robust form, as the woodbine twines round the sturdy oak. And then they separated. The princess glided softly and unperceived once more back to her apartment, and thence into the private chapel; the earl again descended the winding stairs which led to the private garden door.

Unobserved and unseen he returned to his mansion; even his chamberlain, who slept in the anteroom, did not perceive how the earl crept softly along on tiptoe beside him, and retired to his bedroom.

But no sleep came to his eyes for the remainder of this night, and his soul was troubled and full of wild commotion. He was angry with himself, and accused himself of treachery and faithlessness; and then again, full of arrogant pride, he sought to excuse himself, and to bring his conscience, which sat in judgment upon him, to silence.

"I love her—her alone," he said to himself. "Katharine possesses my heart, my soul—to her I am ready to devote my whole life. Yes, I love her! I have sworn it to her to-day, and she is mine for all eternity!"

"And Elizabeth?" asked his conscience. "Hast thou not sworn love and fidelity to her also?"

"No!" he replied. "I have only accepted her vows, I did not return them; and when I promised not to wed the Duchess of Richmond, and when I swore this to her 'by my love,' I then only thought of Katharine, the proud, beautiful, and bewitching woman, whose charms are at once maidenly and voluptuous—not of the young, inexperienced, and untamed child—the unattractive little princess!"

"But this princess may one day become a queen," whispered his ambition.

"That is nevertheless very doubtful," he answered to himself. "Certain it is, however, that Katharine will one day be regent, and then, should I be her husband, I am of course the Regent of England."

This was the secret of his double-dealing and his twofold treachery. Thomas Seymour loved nothing but himself—nothing but his ambition. He would have been ready at any time to risk his life for a woman, but this woman he would have sacrificed cheerfully for the sake of power and fame.

For him there was but one goal, one object in life—to be the first man in England—high and mighty above all the magnates of the land. To reach this goal he would have spared no means—would have shrunk back from no treachery, from no sin.

With the disciples of Loyola, he said to himself by way of exculpation, "The end sanctifies the means." And therefore to him every means was just which could lead him to his end—that is to say, to dignity and splendor.

He was firmly persuaded that he loved the queen ardently, and in his better moods he really did love her. But wholly a creature of the hour, and the slave of impulse, his sensibilities and his will changed place with lightning speed, and he was evermore that which the caprice or the fancy of the moment suggested.

Accordingly, when he stood before the queen, he was not false to his nature, in protesting that he loved her passionately. He loved her so sincerely—with such seeming fervor—that to him she had become identified in a certain manner with his ambition. He worshipped her because she was the means whereby he might be able to attain his end—because she would one day hold in her hands the sceptre of England. And when this event should come to pass, he was desirous of being found her lover and her lord. As her lord she had accepted him, and he was now quite certain of enjoying his lordly prerogatives at some future period.

He therefore loved the queen; but his proud and ambitious heart could never be so wholly engrossed by a single passion as not to leave room still in it for a second—provided that this second love should offer a favorable chance for the attainment of the great object of his life.

This chance the Princess Elizabeth possessed. And if Katharine must certainly one day become the Regent of England, yet Elizabeth might perhaps at a subsequent period become its queen. Undoubtedly, up to the present moment every thing was merely contingent, but then such measures could be adopted as would make of this contingency a decided reality. Moreover, this young and passionate child loved him, and Thomas Seymour himself was too young and too susceptible that he should be able to spurn a love which offered itself to him with such alluring promises, and with splendid visions of the future.

"To live for love alone befits not a man," said he to himself, as he now pondered over the events of the past night. "He must labor to attain the summit of his hopes, the pinnacle of his wishes, and for gaining this end no means can be left unemployed. Besides, my heart is large enough to enjoy a twofold love. I love them both. Yes, I love both these beautiful women bearing a crown in their hands to anticipate my wishes. Let Fate determine to which of them both I shall eventually belong!"

CHAPTER IX.

HENRY HOWARD, EARL OF SURREY.

The court festivity, so long expected, was at length to take place to-day. The knights and the lords were preparing for the tournaments—the poets and the scholars for the encounter of wit. For the gallant and learned king wished to unite both classes on this occasion at the festivity, in order to present to the world the rare and splendid example of a king who claimed for himself all virtue and all wisdom, who was equally great as a warrior and a divine—equally famous as a poet, a philosopher, and a scholar.

The knights were to enter the list for the honor of their ladies; the poets were to recite their verses; and John Heywood was to have his merry comedy performed;—nay, even the great scholars of the day were to take part in the banquet; for the king had expressly summoned to London for the occasion his former instructor in the Greek language, the great scholar Croke, to whom belongs the merit of having been the first who made the learned world, as well in Germany as in England, acquainted with the Greek poets, and who was at that time a professor at the University of Cambridge. He wished, together with Croke, to represent before his astonished court a few scenes from Sophocles; and if indeed there were none of his audience who understood the Greek tongue, yet all must doubtless be delighted with the exquisite melody of the language, and with the wonderful learning of the king.

On every side preparations were going forward: some were decking out their minds—others their bodies.

Henry Howard, too, the Earl of Surrey, was occupied with his own part, that is to say, he had retired to his cabinet, and was busy polishing the sonnet which he intended to recite this day, and in which he celebrated the grace and beauty of his fair Geraldine.

He held the paper in his hand, as he reclined upon the velvet-covered ottoman which stood beside his writing-table.

Could Lady Jane Douglas have seen him at this moment, her heart would have been filled with a painful delight, at perceiving him with his head leaning back on the cushions, and his large blue eyes looking heavenward in dreamy contemplation; he smiled and murmured some tender words.

He was wholly plunged in sweet retrospection; he thought of those rapturous—those blissful hours which but a few days previously he had enjoyed with his Geraldine; and while he thus mused, he worshipped her in fancy, and renewed to her inwardly his vows of unchanging love and inviolable constancy.

His enthusiastic mind was wholly filled with a sweet melancholy, and he felt himself quite intoxicated by the entrancing happiness with which his Geraldine had endowed him.

She was his own—at length his own! After so many long and painful struggles—after such bitter denial and such sad resignation—Fortune had favored him at last: his pictured visions had at length become a reality. Katharine loved him—she had pledged him the most sacred vows that she would one day become his spouse—that she would become his wife in the eye of God and man.

But when would come that day on which he could present her to the world as his wife? When would she be at length freed from the burden of her royal crown; when would those golden chains at length be loosed which bound her to her tyrannical and bloodthirsty husband—the cruel, the arrogant king?

Strange! As he asked himself these questions he shuddered inwardly, and an inexplicable horror crept upon his soul.

He felt as if a voice whispered in his ear: "Thou wilt never live to see this day! The king, however old he is, will yet outlive thee! Prepare to die, for death is already at thy door!"

And it was not the first time that he had heard this voice. It had ere this often spoken to him, and always with the same words—the same warning. Often in his dreams it had seemed to him as though he felt a cutting pain at his neck, and that he had seen a scaffold, on which his own head rolled along.

Henry Howard was superstitious, for he was a poet, and to poets it is granted to imagine a secret connection between the visible and the invisible world, and to believe that supernatural agencies and unseen forms surround man, and either afford him protection or else hurl him into the abyss.

There were moments when he believed in the truth of his dreams, when he doubted not this dismal and awful fate which they announced to him.

At first he had yielded to these fancies with smiling resignation, but now since he loved Katharine, since she belonged to him, he was unwilling to die; and when life offered him its most delightful enjoyments, its most intoxicating raptures, he was loath to leave it—he now recoiled from the thought of death. He was therefore cautious and thoughtful; and knowing the king's fierce, and malignant, and jealous disposition, he had always been very careful to avoid every thing that could provoke him, or that could rouse the royal tiger from his slumber.

It seemed to him as if the king had directed his special rancor against him and his family—as if he never could forgive them that the wife he had most loved, and who had pained him the most deeply, had sprung from their race. In every look, in every word of the king, Henry Howard felt and experienced this secret animosity of his royal master, and he suspected that Henry was only watching for a favorable moment in order to seize him and send him to the scaffold.

He was therefore on his guard. For now that Geraldine loved him, his life no longer belonged to himself; she loved him; she had claims upon him—his days were therefore rendered sacred in his own eyes.

Accordingly, toward all those petty mortifications and manœuvres on the part of the king, he had maintained silence; he had even given way without a murmur, and without asking for any justification of the fact, when the king suddenly recalled him from the command of the army which was fighting against France, and had sent Lord Hertford in his place to take charge of the troops which were encamped before Boulogne and Montreuil. He had returned quietly to his mansion, without evincing animosity or pique; and as he could no longer be a general or a warrior, he became once more a scholar and a poet. His mansion now became once more the rendezvous of all the learned men of the time, and with true princely liberality he was ready to aid despised and oppressed genius, and to grant the persecuted scholar an asylum in his house. It was he who saved the learned Fox from starvation, and who received him into his palace, where Horace Junius, as his physician, and the afterward so celebrated poet, Churchyard, as his page, had already found a home.

Love, and the arts and sciences, had already healed the wounds which the king had given to his ambition, and now he no longer felt chagrined; he was almost thankful to the king. For to his recall alone he was indebted for his happiness, and Henry, who wished to mortify him, had only ministered to his good fortune and felicity.

He now smiled as he reflected that the king, who had deprived him of his staff as a general, had unknowingly given him his own queen in return, and had elevated him at the moment that he wished to humble him.

He smiled, and once more resumed his finishing touches on the poem, with which he intended this day to celebrate at the court festivity the honor and the praises of his beloved Geraldine—the beautiful, the unknown.

"These verses are harsh, he murmured, "this language is so feeble! It does not express all the fulness of worship and rapture which I feel. Petrarch was more successful. His beautiful, soft language sounds like music, and is even by itself the harmonious accompaniment of his love. Ah! Petrarch, I envy thee, and yet I should not wish to be like thee. For thy fate was a sad one and filled with bitter sweets. Laura never loved thee, and she was the mother of twelve children, of which not one was thine."

He laughed in the consciousness of his own proud and successful career as a lover, and turned to one of Petrarch's sonnets, which lay beside him on the table, in order to compare his own recent sonnet with a similar one of Petrarch's.

So completely was he engrossed by this investigation, that he never once perceived that the curtain which screened the door behind him was drawn back, and that a young woman, of striking exterior, sparkling with trinkets and resplendent with jewels, had entered his study.

She was a person of imposing beauty; her large eyes flashed and glowed, her lofty brow seemed specially formed to wear a crown, even though it was but a ducal coronet that adorned her dark hair, which fell down in long, rich clusters upon her finely-moulded shoulders. Her tall and majestic figure was clad in a robe of white satin, richly set off with ermine and pearls; two clasps with costly brilliants, fastened round her neck a short mantle of purple velvet, edged with ermine, which descended below her waist.

Thus appeared the Duchess of Richmond, the widow of King Henry's natural son, Henry, Duke of Richmond, the sister of Lord Henry Howard, Earl of Surrey, and daughter of the noble Duke of Norfolk.

Since the death of her husband, who had left her a youthful widow of twenty, she had resided with her brother, under whose protection she had placed herself, and the world called them "the affectionate brother and sister."

Ah! how little knew the world, which usually judges by appearances, of the hatred and the love which existed between the earl and his sister—how little it suspected their real sentiments toward each other!

Henry Howard had offered to his sister his mansion for her residence, because he hoped, perhaps, by his presence to impose a restraint upon her gushing and wanton disposition, and to prevent her overstepping the limits of decorum and propriety. Lady Richmond had accepted his offer, because she was obliged to do so—because the parsimonious and avaricious king only allowed the widow of his son a slender annuity, and because she had squandered her own means with lavish hand upon her numerous train of admirers.

Henry Howard had thus acted for the honor of his name and family, but he did not love his sister—on the contrary, he despised her. The Duchess of Richmond, however, hated her brother, because her proud spirit felt humbled by the gratitude which she owed him.

But this contempt and this hatred were secrets which they both studiously kept from the world, and which they scarcely ventured to acknowledge to themselves. Thus they had both concealed from each other their inmost sentiments, under the cloak of affection, and it was only at times that they each betrayed themselves to the other, by some hasty word, or by some undisguised look.

CHAPTER X.

BROTHER AND SISTER.

The duchess glided softly along toward her brother, still unobserved. The thick Turkish carpet rendered her footsteps inaudible; already she stood behind the earl, and he had not yet perceived her.

She bent forward over his shoulder, and fixed her eyes on the paper which her brother held in his hand.

And then she proceeded to read aloud the title of the piece, "A lament that Geraldine never appears to her lover, unless concealed by a veil."

"Ah," said the duchess, laughing, "I have at last discovered your secret, and you must now surrender to me, either graciously or ungraciously. Then you are really in love, and the name of the chosen one to whom you address your verses, is Geraldine? I swear to you, brother, that you shall pay me dearly for this secret."

"It is no secret, sister," said the earl, with a placid smile, while he stood up and saluted the duchess. "It is so little a secret, that I shall recite this sonnet this very evening at the court festivity. I shall, therefore, stand in no need of your secrecy, Rosabella."

"Then the beautiful Geraldine always appears to you only in a dark veil—black as night," said the duchess, with an air of thoughtfulness. "But pray tell me, brother, who is this beautiful Geraldine? I don't know at court a single lady who bears this name."

"From which you may perceive, sister, that the whole is but a fiction—a mere creation of my fancy."

"Come, come, brother, don't deceive me," she returned, smiling; "people don't write such glowing verses as these, unless they are really in love. Under the name of Geraldine you are singing the praises of some one else. That's very evident! Don't deny it, Henry, for I know very well that you have some fair object in your mind's eye. Nay, I can read it in your very looks. And now let me tell you, it is to know something of this lovely personage that I have come to see you. Really it grieves me, Henry, that you have so little confidence in me, and that you favor me with so small a share in your pains and pleasures. You really don't know how much and how tenderly I love you, my dear and noble brother."

She laid her arm affectionately on his shoulder and was about to kiss him. He bent his head back, and laying his hand upon her round dimpled chin, he looked with an inquiring smile into her eyes.

"What! you want something from me, Rosabella!" he said. "I have never had cause to rejoice in your sisterly affection, unless when you required my services."

"How distrustful you are!" she exclaimed with a charming pout, dashing his hand away from her face. "I have come, from the most disinterested sympathy, partly to warn you, Henry, and partly to learn if your love, perchance, were directed toward some lady who made my warning unnecessary."

"You see, therefore, that I was quite right, Rosabel, and that your affectionate inquiry was not without a motive. Well, then you wished to warn me? But I was really unaware to what extent I stood in need of a warning."

"Nay, brother! For surely it would be very dangerous and detrimental to you if your love, mayhap, were not in accord with the commands of the king."

A fugitive blush passed over Henry Howard's countenance, and his brow became clouded.

"With the commands of the king?" he asked, astonished. "I was not aware that Henry the Eighth had any power to govern my inclinations. At all events, I would never accord him such a right. Tell me, therefore, at once, sister, what you mean? What about the king's commands? and what matrimonial schemes have you women been again inventing? For I know very well that my mother and yourself have no rest, with the thought of seeing me still unmarried. You want to drive me into wedded bliss, and yet it seems to me that you have both of you had sufficient experience that this bliss is but imaginary, and that marriage in reality, is, to say the least, but a foretaste of hell."

"Very true," laughed the duchess; "the only happy moment of my married life was that in which my husband died. For, by that means, I am more fortunate than my mother, who has her tyrant still alive about her. Ah, how I pity my mother!"

"Don't attempt to calumniate our noble father!" cried the earl, in a somewhat threatening tone. "God alone knows how much he has suffered through our mother, and how much he still suffers. It is not he who is to blame for his unhappy marriage. But it was not in order to speak of these sad and disagreeable family matters that you came, sister! you said you wished to warn me!"

"Yes, to warn you!" replied the duchess affectionately, taking the hand of her brother and leading him to an ottoman. "Now, come and let us sit down here, Henry, and talk together, for once, with all the confidence and cordiality becoming a brother and sister. Tell me who is Geraldine?"

"A phantom, an airy vision? I've told you so already!"

"Then you really don't love any lady at this court?"

"No, not one! There is not amongst all the ladies by whom the queen surrounds herself, a single one whom I could bring myself to love."

"Ah, well in that case your heart is free, Henry, and you will be so much the more easily inclined to fulfil the wishes of the king."

"What does the king wish!"

She laid her head upon her brother's shoulder and whispered softly: "that the family of Howard and Seymour should at length become reconciled,—that by firm and sincere bonds of love they would at length allay the hatred which has divided them for centuries."

"Oh, that is what the king wishes!" cried the earl, derisively. "Well, truly, he has made a good beginning towards effecting this reconciliation. He has disgraced me in the face of all Europe by depriving me of my command, and by investing a Seymour with my rank and dignity; and now, forsooth, he wishes that in return I should love this arrogant earl who has robbed me of what was justly mine, and who, by intrigues, falsehood, and slander unceasingly beset the king's ear, until at length he succeeded in gaining his object by ousting me from my command."

"It is true the king recalled you from the army, but it was only to bestow upon you one of the highest offices at his court, by appointing you chamberlain to the queen."

Henry Howard trembled slightly, and was silent. "It is true," he murmured, after a pause, "I am indebted to the king for this office."

"And besides," continued the duchess artlessly, "besides, I don't believe that Lord Hertford is to blame for your recall. In order to satisfy you of this, he has made a proposal to the king and also to me, which must prove to you and to the whole world, how high an honor Lord Hertford esteems it to be related to the Howards, and especially to you, by the most sacred bonds."

"Ah, the noble, magnanimous lord!" cried Henry Howard, with a bitter laugh. "As he cannot advance with laurels, he tries to do so with myrtles; as he can win no battles, he wishes to try his fortune by marriage. Well, sister, let us hear what he has to propose?"

"A double marriage, Henry! He sues for my hand for his brother, Thomas Seymour, provided that you choose for your wife his sister, the Lady Margaret."

"Never!" exclaimed the earl. "Henry Howard will never give his hand to a daughter of that house—will never so far degrade himself as to elevate a Seymour to become his wife. That may be well enough for a king, but not for a Howard."

"Brother, you defame the king!"

"Be it so—then let him be defamed! He, too, has injured my fair fame, by lending himself to this unworthy scheme."

"Consider, brother, the Seymours are powerful, and stand very high in the king's favor."

"Yes, in the king's favor they do stand high! But the people know their proud, cruel, and arrogant disposition, and the people and the nobility alike despise them. The Seymours have the voice of the king on their side, but the Howards have the voice of the whole kingdom, and that is of far greater value. The king can elevate the Seymours, for they stand far beneath him! The Howards he cannot raise, for they are his equals. He cannot even degrade them. Katharine died upon the scaffold, but the king thereby only made himself a headsman, and neither our arms nor our honor were sullied by that deed!"

"Those are very proud words, Henry!"

"They become a son of the house of Norfolk, Rosabella! Ah, only imagine this petty Lord Hertford! He longs to have a ducal coronet for his sister. He wishes to give her to me for a wife; for, as soon as our poor father dies, I succeed to his title. Arrogant upstart! My coronet for his sister? your coronet for his brother's coat of arms? Never, I say, will that come to pass!"

The duchess grew pale, and her proud figure quivered. Her eyes flashed vindictively, and an angry retort already rose to her lips, but she still held it back, and constrained herself to calmness and composure.

"Consider the matter once more, Henry," she said, "don't decide too hastily. You speak of our greatness—but you forget the power which the Seymours possess. I tell you they are powerful enough, despite all our greatness and our ancient lineage, to trample us in the dust. But they are not only powerful at the present moment—but they will likewise be so in time to come; for it is well known in what views and sentiments the Prince of Wales has been educated. The king is old, feeble, and declining; death is already lurking behind his throne, and will soon seize and carry him off. Edward will then be king; with him the heresy of protestantism will be victorious; and however great and numerous our party may be, they will still be powerless and defeated—nay—we shall be oppressed and persecuted when the time comes."

"We shall then know how to struggle, and, if need be, to die!" exclaimed her brother. "It is more honorable to die upon the battle-field, than to have purchased life by humiliation."

"Yes, it is honorable to die upon the battle field, Henry, but disgraceful to fall upon the scaffold. And this, my brother, may be your fate, if you will not now curb your pride—if you refuse to grasp the hand which Lord Hertford offers you in a spirit of conciliation, and so offend him in a manner that he will never forgive. He will take a bloody revenge should he one day attain to power."

"Let him do so, if he can! My life is in the hand of God. My head belongs to the king, but my heart belongs to myself; and this I will not debase so far as to convert it into merchandise, which I could barter for a little security and royal favor."

"Brother, I entreat you, consider what you say!" exclaimed the duchess, no longer able to restrain her impassioned nature, and glowing with wild anger. "Do not venture with wanton pride to ruin *my* future prospects, at least. You may die upon the scaffold yourself, if you choose; but for my part, I wish to be happy,—I wish, at length, after so many years of anxiety and reproach, to have my share also in the joys of life. He is suitable for me, and I shall not renounce him; and you must not dare to snatch him away from me. Know, brother, that I love Thomas Seymour—my whole existence—all my hopes are bound up with him, I will not tear this love out of my heart. I will not give him up!"

"Well, if you love him, marry him by all means!" exclaimed her brother. "Become at once the wife of this Thomas Seymour. Ask the duke, our father, for his permission, and I am sure he will not refuse it, for he is prudent and thoughtful, and will be better able than I am to estimate the advantage which an union with the Seymours may procure for our family. Do this, sister, and marry your well-beloved—I don't hinder you!"

"Yes, you do hinder me—you alone!" cried his sister, trembling with anger. "You want to refuse the hand of Lady Margaret, and so mortally offend the Seymours. By this means you render my union with Thomas Seymour impossible. In the selfish pride of your arrogance you don't perceive that you are destroying my happiness, while you only think of offering insult to the Seymours. I tell you, however, that I love—nay—I worship Thomas Seymour; he is my happiness—my future—my bliss. Have, therefore, pity upon me, Henry! Grant me this happiness, for which I entreat you as for a blessing from Heaven. Prove to me that you love me, and that you are willing to make this sacrifice in my behalf. Upon my knees I beseech you, Henry! Give me the man whom I love; bend your proud head, become Margaret Seymour's husband, in order that Thomas Seymour may become mine."

She had meanwhile sunk down upon her knees, and, with her face bathed in tears, was wondrously beautiful in her impassioned emotion, while she looked up entreatingly at her brother.

The earl, however, did not raise her from her kneeling posture, but retreated a step and smiled.

"How long is it, duchess," he asked, derisively, "since you vowed that Mr. Wilford, your secretary, was the man whom you loved? Really, I believed all this; I even believed it, until one day I found you in the arms of your page. On that day I made a firm resolution never again to believe you, though you swore to me with ever so many sacred oaths that you loved a man. But stay, you do love at times, though somewhat indiscriminately;—to-day it is Thomas, to-morrow it will be John or Edward, as the case may be!"

For the first time, the earl drew aside the veil from his heart, and allowed his sister to perceive all the anger and contempt which he entertained toward her.

The duchess thus felt herself wounded to the quick by his scathing sarcasms.

She started up from her knees; her eyes flashed with anger, she gasped for breath, and every fibre in her frame seemed convulsed as she stood before her brother.

She was no longer a woman, but an infuriated tigress, ready to devour without pity the person who has dared to provoke her.

"My Lord Surrey," she said, with compressed and trembling lips, "you are a shameless slanderer! Were I a man, I would strike you to the ground, and tell you that you are a knave and a coward. But, by the everlasting God! you shall not say that you have affronted me with impunity. Once more, and for the last time, I now ask you—will you fulfil Lord Hertford's wish? Will you marry the Lady Margaret, and conduct me to the altar with Thomas Seymour?"

"No; I will not, and I never shall!" replied her brother, solemnly. "The Howards do not bow before the Seymours, and never will Henry Howard wed a woman whom he does not love!"

"Ah, you don't love her!" she said, breathless, and gnashing her teeth. "You don't love the Lady Margaret; and for this reason your sister must renounce her love, and give up the man whom she idolizes! Ah, you don't love the sister of Thomas Seymour! She is not the Geraldine that you worship, and to whom you address your sonnets! Well then, I shall discover who this Geraldine is—I shall find her out, and then woe betide her and you! You refuse me your hand, to lead me to the altar with Thomas Seymour; be it so, I shall one day offer you my hand, in order to conduct you and your Geraldine to the scaffold!"

And as she perceived how the earl shuddered and grew pale, she continued with a scornful laugh:

"Ah, you tremble, and terror steals upon you! Your conscience warns you that the strenuous champion of virtue may also stumble sometimes. You think to conceal your secret by shrouding it under the veil of night, like your Geraldine; who, as you complain in your verses, never shows herself to you without her dark nocturnal veil. Wait a little—wait! I shall kindle a flame for you, before which all your nightly veils shall be rent asunder. I shall light up your dark secrets for you, with a torch which will be large enough to ignite the scaffold which you shall one day ascend in company with your Geraldine!"

"Ah! you are now disclosing to me your true features for the first time," said Henry Howard, with a shrug. "The angelic mask drops from your countenance, and I see the Fury who was concealed behind it. You are now the true daughter of your mother, and at this moment I understand for the first time what my father has suffered, and why he did not shrink from even the disgrace of a divorce, in order to be liberated from such a Megæra."

"Oh, thank you—thank you!" she exclaimed, with a wild laugh, "you fill up the measure of your crime. It is not enough that you should drive your sister to desperation, but you must also revile your mother? You say that we are Furies; very well, we shall one day be Furies for you at least, and we will show you our Medusa's countenance, before which you shall be turned into stone. Henry Howard, Earl of Surrey, from this hour forth I am your implacable enemy! Take care of your head upon your shoulders, for my hand is raised to smite it; and in my hand is a sword! Beware of the secret which slumbers in your breast, for you have made of me a vampire which will suck your heart's blood! You have insulted my mother too, and I shall now go and inform her of it. She will believe me, for she knows well that you hate her, and that you are the true son of your father; that is to say, a pious hypocrite, a miserable wretch, who carries virtue on his lips and vice in his heart."

"Cease, I say, cease!" cried the earl, "if you would not have me forget that you are a woman and my sister!"

"Forget it at once and forever," she replied, scornfully. "I have long forgotten that you are my brother, that you are your mother's son. Farewell, Lord Surrey, I now leave you and your palace, and from this time forth I shall reside with my mother the divorced wife of the Duke of Norfolk. But mark this. We both have done with you as regards our love, but not as regards our hate! Our hatred remains with you unchangeably, and it will one day crush you to the dust! Farewell, Lord Surrey. When next we meet it will be in the king's presence!"

She rushed toward the door—Henry Howard did not restrain her. He looked after her with a smile, as she left his closet, and murmured compassionately, "Poor woman! I have perhaps disappointed her of a lover, and that she will never forgive me. Well, be it so! Let her evermore be my enemy—let her annoy me with all her petty rancor and malice, if only she be unable to injure HER. I hope, however, that I have guarded my secret carefully, and that she did not suspect the real cause of my refusal. I had no alternative but to intrench myself behind this foolish family pride, and to assume haughtiness, as a cloak for my love. Oh, Geraldine, thee I would choose wert thou the daughter of a peasant; nay I would not deem it a blot on my escutcheon, were I compelled to cross it with a bar sinister for thy sake. But hark! The clock strikes four! My service begins. Farewell, Geraldine. I must go to attend upon the queen!"

And while he retired to his dressing-room in order to prepare his toilet for the great court festivity, the Duchess of Richmond returned trembling with anger to her apartments. She passed along through the suite of rooms with eager speed, and repaired to her boudoir, where Lord Douglas awaited her.

"Well?" he asked, advancing toward her with his smooth lurking smile. "Has he consented?"

"No," she replied, gnashing her teeth. "He swears that he will never enter into any union with the Seymours."

"I knew that well," murmured the earl. "And what does your grace now purpose doing?"

"I will be revenged! He wishes to prevent my being happy—for this I shall make him unhappy!"

"In that you will do well, my lady. For he is a faithless and apostate son of the Church; he leans to the heretical sects, and has forgotten the faith of his fathers."

"I know it!" she returned, breathless.

Lord Douglas looked at her with astonishment, and continued: "But he is not only an unbeliever, but a traitor, and more than once he has defamed his king, to whom in the pride of his heart he thinks himself far superior."

"I know it!" she repeated.

"So proud is he," continued the earl—"so full of blasphemous arrogance, that he fain would stretch forth his hand to grasp the crown of England."

"I know it!" said the duchess once more. Perceiving, however, the astonished and doubting looks of the earl, she added with a malicious smile; "I know all that you wish I should know. Only accuse him—only bring some charge against him, and I shall testify to all, corroborate all that can lead to his destruction. My mother is our ally! she hates the father as heartily as I do the son. Bring forward your charges therefore, Lord Douglas, we are your witnesses."

"Oh, by no means, your grace," he returned, with his soft insinuating smile. "I know nothing at all, have heard nothing—how can I then accuse? You know all. To you he has spoken. You must be his accuser."

"Well then, conduct me to the king!"

"Will you allow me in the first place to offer you one word of advice?"

"Certainly, Lord Douglas."

"Be prudent in the choice of your means—don't exhaust them all at once, in order that if your first blow should fail, you may not afterward be wholly unarmed. It is better and much less dangerous to kill the enemy you hate by degrees, and by a slow insinuating poison, than to stab him suddenly with a dagger, which may be broken in the act, and so become useless. Do not, therefore, say all you know at once, but by degrees. Administer your poison, therefore, to the king, slowly, until you provoke his rage, and if to-day you do not succeed in bringing down your enemy, imagine that you will do so the more surely to-morrow. Don't forget, too, that we have not only to punish the heretical Henry Howard, but especially the heretical queen, whose unbelief will bring down the anger of Heaven upon this land."

"Come along to the king!" exclaimed the duchess, impatiently. "You can tell me on the way what am I to confess, and what I must withhold. I shall do exactly what you tell me! Now, Henry Howard," she murmured to herself, "get ready, the battle begins! In the pride and selfishness of your heart you have destroyed the happiness of my life—nay, my eternal felicity. I loved Thomas Seymour. I hoped to find by his side, that happiness for which I had sought so long and so vainly in the labyrinth of life. By means of this love, my soul would have been saved, and would once more have returned to the paths of virtue. My brother has otherwise decreed. He has condemned me to become, instead of an angel, a demon. I shall fulfil my destiny; I shall be to him an evil demon!"

CHAPTER XI.

THE QUEEN'S TOILET.

The festivities of the day were ended, and the brave knights and combatants, who had this day broken a lance in honor of their ladies, could now rest from their victories upon their laurels. The feats of arms were ended, and now the contests of Mind were about to commence. The knights had, accordingly, retired in order to change their armor for gold-laced and velvet trappings; the ladies, to assume their lighter evening robes; and the queen too, had withdrawn for this purpose to her dressing-room, while the ladies and gentlemen of her suite waited for her in the great ante-chamber, in order to escort her to the throne-room.

The day was already fast fading, and the twilight cast its long shadows across the saloon in which the cavaliers of the court were walking up and down with the ladies, engaged in a lively conversation, and discussing the principal incidents of the tournament which had just taken place.

Thomas Seymour—Lord Sudley, had carried off the prize of the day and vanquished his opponent, Henry Howard. The king had been delighted at this. For Thomas Seymour had for some time been his favorite—perhaps because he was the declared enemy of Howard. He had accordingly, in addition to the wreath of laurel and gold with which the queen presented the earl as his prize, bestowed upon him a diamond pin, which he commanded the queen to fasten with her own hand in the earl's collar. This office Katharine had performed with a grave expression of countenance, and with averted looks; and even Thomas Seymour had evinced but little delight at the proud honor which the queen, at her husband's command, had to confer upon him.

The strenuous Papal court party drew fresh hopes from this circumstance, and augured a revolution in the queen's sentiments, and a return to the true faith; while the Protestant, or "heretical" party looked with gloomy misgiving to the future, and feared that they were deprived of their most powerful support and their most influential protection.

No one had perceived that when the queen rose to crown the victor—Thomas Seymour—her gold-embroidered handkerchief dropped on the floor; or that the earl, after he had picked it up, and restored it to the queen, carried his hand, by an accidental and undesigned movement, for an instant to his collar, which was as white as the small folded paper which he concealed therein, and which he had found in the queen's handkerchief.

One person only had seen it. This little artifice of the queen had not escaped John Heywood, who immediately, by one of his exuberant and pungent sallies of wit, made the king laugh, and so contrived to avert the attention of the courtiers from the queen and her beloved Seymour.

He now stood in a niche near one of the windows, quite concealed behind the silken hangings; and thus, unperceived, he scanned the whole room with his eagle eye.

He saw and heard every thing, and unseen by any one, he watched and observed all.

He saw how Lord Douglas now made a sign to Bishop Gardiner, and how the latter immediately returned it.

As it were by accident, they both now quitted the groups among which they had just been laughing and talking, and approached each other, glancing round for a spot where, unobserved, and isolated from the crowd, they could converse together. All the recesses of the windows were thronged with knots of busy talkers; only one window was unoccupied—that behind the hangings of which John Heywood was concealed.

Thither Lord Douglas and the Bishop directed their steps.

"Shall we reach the goal to-day?" asked Gardiner, softly.

"With God's gracious help we shall this day annihilate all our enemies. The sword is already suspended above their heads, and soon it will descend and rid us of them," replied Lord Douglas, with grave emphasis.

"Then you are sure of it?" asked Gardiner, and an expression of ferocious joy passed over his pale, truculent features. "But tell me how comes it that Archbishop Cranmer is not here?"

"He is ill, and was therefore obliged to remain at Lambeth."

"May this illness be the precursor of his death!" murmured the bishop, clasping his hands devoutly.

"It will be so, my lord. God will destroy his enemies, and will bless us. Cranmer has been accused, and the king will judge him inexorably."

"And the queen?"

For a moment Lord Douglas was silent, and then he whispered softly: "Only wait a few hours more and she will no longer be queen. Instead of returning from the throne-room, to her apartments, we shall escort her to the Tower."

John Heywood, hidden behind the folds of the hangings, held his breath and listened.

"And are you also quite sure of our victory?" asked Gardiner. "May not some chance or accident snatch him away from us?"

"Not if the queen should present him with the rosette. For then the king will discover Geraldine's letter concealed in the folds thereof, and she is lost. All, therefore, depends upon this—that the queen should wear the rosette and not discover its contents. But see, my lord, here comes the Duchess of Richmond. There, she gives me a concerted signal. Pray for us, therefore, my lord, for now I shall go with her to the king, and she will accuse this detestable Katharine Parr! I tell you, my lord bishop, this charge will be a matter of life and death, and should Katharine escape one danger, she will perish in the other. Let your lordship wait here for me. I shall soon return and let you know the result of our scheme. Lady Jane too will soon bring you some news."

He stepped forth from the embrasure of the window, and followed the duchess, who proceeded to the other end of the saloon, and disappeared with him through the door which led into the king's apartments.

The ladies and gentlemen of the court continued their conversation and laughter.

John Heywood stood with panting heart and breathless anxiety behind the hangings, close beside Gardiner, who with his hands rigidly clasped was muttering a prayer.

While Gardiner prayed and Douglas accused and slandered—the queen—little suspecting the plots which her enemies were putting into operation against her—was in her toilet-room, attended by her ladies, who assisted in adorning their mistress for the festivities of the evening.

She looked surpassingly beautiful in her gorgeous attire. A woman at once, and a queen—simple elegance combined with splendor—with a charming smile playing around her lips, and yet commanding respect in her proud and imposing beauty.

None of Henry's former wives had so well understood how to enact the part of a queen, and retain the distinctive attributes of a woman withal.

As she now stood before the large mirror, which the Republic of Venice had sent to the king as a wedding gift, and which now reflected the form of the queen resplendent with jewels, she smiled, for she was obliged to admit to herself that she was this day very beautiful, and she thought how Thomas Seymour would behold her with a sentiment of conscious pride.

While she thus thought of him a crimson glow overspread her countenance, and then for a moment she trembled. How brave and handsome he had looked to-day at the tournament, how splendidly he had dashed into the lists, how his eyes had flashed, and how scornful his smile had sometimes been. And then the look which he cast across toward her at the moment that he had vanquished his opponent, Henry Howard, and hurled the lance from his hand. Oh! her heart could have burst with rapture and delight!

Wholly wrapt up in these blissful reveries, she sank down into her gilded armchair, and cast her eyes dreamily and smiling to the ground.

Behind her stood her women, waiting in respectful silence for the nod of their mistress. But the queen no longer bestowed a thought upon them. She believed herself to be alone, she saw nothing but the noble and manly countenance of him for whom she had prepared a place in her heart.

The door now opened, and Lady Jane Douglas entered. She, too, was in festive attire, and glittered with brilliants; she, too, was beautiful, but it was the pale, terrible beauty of a demon; and whoever had but seen her as she entered the apartment, would have trembled from a sense of undefinable fear.

She cast a rapid glance at her mistress, who was absorbed in her dream, and when she saw that the queen's toilet was finished, she beckoned to the women, who silently obeyed her, and left the room.

Still Katharine had noticed nothing. Lady Jane stood behind her, and observed her in the mirror. When she saw the queen smile, her brow darkened, and wild anger kindled in her eyes.

"Ah! she shall smile no more," said Lady Jane to herself. "My sufferings through her have been terrible. She, too, shall suffer in her turn!"

Softly and noiselessly she glided into the next room, the door of which stood open, and eagerly opened a box filled with ribbons and rosettes. She then drew forth from her velvet pocket, which hung down at her side suspended by a gold chain, a dark-red rosette, and flung it into the casket. That was all.

Lady Jane now returned to the adjoining room, and her countenance which had previously been sullen and threatening, was now elated and haughty.

With a cheerful smile she advanced toward the queen, and kneeling down at her side, kissed her hand with *empressement*.

"What is my queen musing upon?" she asked, while she laid her head upon Katharine's knees and looked up at her affectionately.

The queen started slightly, and raised her head. She perceived Lady Jane's affectionate smile and her inquiring gaze withal.

Feeling conscious of guilt, or, at least, of a guilty thought, she was upon her guard, and called to mind the warnings of John Heywood.

"She is observing me," thought Katharine to herself. "She looks very affectionate, and, therefore, she is brooding over some wily scheme."

"Ah, I am glad you have come, Jane," she said aloud. "You can help me, for, to tell you the truth, I feel quite embarrassed at the present moment. I want a rhyme, and I'm thinking in vain how I shall find it."

"Indeed, queen—then you are writing verses?"

"What, Jane, does that surprise you? Shall I, the queen, not be allowed to contend for any prize? I would freely give my most precious jewel if I could but succeed in producing a poem to which the king would have to accord the prize. But I greatly lack a musical ear—I can't find the rhyme I want, and I shall at last be obliged to give up the idea of winning laurels for myself. But how the king would rejoice at my success! For, to be candid, I believe he is rather afraid that Henry Howard will carry off the prize, and he would be very thankful to me if I could contest the palm of victory with the Earl of Surrey. You are well aware the king does not love the Howards."

"And you, queen?" asked Lady Jane, and she grew so deadly pale, that the queen herself remarked it.

"You are ill, Jane," she said, full of sympathy. "Really, Jane, you appear to be suffering. You need repose—you should rest a little."

But Jane had already recovered her calmness and composure, and she succeeded in smiling.

"Oh, by no means," she returned. "I am quite well, and am happy in being allowed to be near you. But will your majesty permit me to beg a favor of you?"

"Certainly, Jane, certainly—nay, consider it already granted; for I know that Jane will ask for nothing that her friend cannot give."

Lady Jane was silent, and cast her eyes to the ground with a thoughtful and absent air. She struggled inwardly for a firm resolution. Her proud heart revolted at the thought of being obliged to bend before this woman whom she hated, and of being compelled to approach her fawningly to ask a favor. She felt such burning hatred toward the queen, that at this moment she would willingly have given her own life could she first have seen her enemy crushed and weeping at her feet.

Henry Howard loved the queen; Katharine had therefore robbed her, Lady Jane, of the heart of the man whom she worshipped. Katharine had condemned her to the perpetual torment of abnegation—to the rack—to taste a happiness and a rapture not her own; to kindle her ardors at a fire, which, like a thief, she had stolen from the altar of another's god.

Katharine was found guilty, and condemned.

Jane had no more compassion. She resolved therefore to crush her.

"Well," inquired the queen, "you are silent? You don't tell me what I am to do for you?"

Lady Jane raised her eyes toward her

mistress, and her looks were placid and composed.

"Your majesty," she replied, "I have just met in the anteroom an unhappy man, who seems quite cast down. With you alone it rests to lift him up once more. Will you do so?"

"Will I do so!" cried Katharine with vivacity. "Oh, Jane, you know well how anxious I always am to help the unhappy, and to be useful to them. Alas, there are but too many at this court whose wounds are bleeding and torn, and the queen has so little balm to heal them wherewithal! Allow me, therefore, to have this pleasure, Jane, and all the gratitude will be on my side, not on yours. Speak, Jane, tell me at once, who it is that needs my help?"

"Not your help, queen, but your compassion—your gracious favor. Lord Sudley has this day vanquished the poor Earl of Surrey at the tournament, and you can readily understand that your chamberlain feels himself deeply mortified and humiliated."

"Can I alter that, Jane? Why does the dreamy earl—the enthusiast poet—suffer himself to enter the lists with a champion who always knows what he is about, and who always accomplishes what he has resolved. Ah, it was wonderful to see with what lightning speed Thomas Seymour lifted him out of his saddle; and the proud Earl of Surrey, that most wise and learned man, the powerful party-leady, was forced to succumb to the champion, who, like the angel Michael, had hurled him to the dust."

The queen laughed.

This laugh went like a sword through Lady Jane's heart.

"She shall atone for this!" she whispered to herself. "Your majesty is quite right," returned the maid of honor. "He deserved this humiliation; but being punished, you should now heal his wounds. Nay, don't shake your beautiful head so. Do it for your own sake, queen; do it from motives of prudence. The Earl of Surrey, with his father, is the head of a powerful party, who will return this humiliation of the Howards with increased vindictiveness toward the Seymours, and who will one day take a bloody revenge for it."

"Ah, you frighten me," said the queen, who had now become serious.

Lady Jane continued:

"I saw how the Duke of Norfolk bit his lips when his son was forced to yield to Lord Seymour; I heard persons here and there uttering bitter execrations and vows of revenge against the Seymours."

"Who did so! Who dared to do so?" exclaimed Katharine, springing up violently from her seat. "Who is there at this court audacious enough to wish to injure those whom the king loves? Name him to me, Jane; I want to know who he is, in order that I may accuse him before the king! For the king does not wish that the noble Seymours should give way to those Howards; that they, nobler, better, and more distinguished, should be compelled to bow before those ambitious, intriguing, and power-seeking papists. The king loves the noble

Seymours, and his mighty arm will protect them against all their enemies."

"And your majesty will doubtless assist him therein?" said Lady Jane smiling.

This smile made the queen once more cautious and collected.

She felt that she had gone too far, that she had betrayed too much of her secret. She must therefore make amends and cause her excitement to be forgotten.

"Certainly, Jane, I shall assist the king to be just," she replied in a calmer tone. "But I will never be unjust—not even toward those papists. If I cannot love them, at all events it shall not be said that I hate them. And besides it becomes a queen to rise above party feuds. Tell me, therefore, Jane, what can I do for poor Lord Surrey?"

"You have publicly shown the victor, at the tournament, a mark of your great favor by crowning him."

"It was the king's command!" cried Katharine with vivacity.

"Doubtless! However, he will not command you to reward the Earl of Surrey also, should he in his turn gain the victory this evening. Do it therefore of your own accord, queen. Give him publicly before your whole court a token of your favor. Princes have it in their power at all times to gladden the hearts of their subjects, and to console the afflicted, without labor or exertion. A smile, a friendly word, a pressure of the hand suffices. A mere ribbon which you wear upon your dress makes the person to whom you give it proud, even happy, and raises him for the moment high above his fellows. And consider, queen, that I am not now speaking for the Earl of Surrey—I am thinking more of your personal interest. If you have the courage publicly, and in spite of the disfavor with which King Henry threatens the Howards, to be still just toward them, and to recognize their merits like those of other persons—believe me, if you do so, the whole of this powerful party which is now hostile to you, will be overcome, and will fall down vanquished at your feet; you will at length be the all-powerful and all-beloved Queen of England, and like the heretics, the papists too will call you their protectress. Do not hesitate any longer! Let your noble and magnanimous heart prevail. Spiteful chance has flung Henry Howard in the dust; extend your hand to him, good queen, that he may be able to raise himself once more, and to stand proudly and confidently at your court, as he was wont. Henry Howard well deserves that you should be gracious toward him. Great and resplendent as a star, he shines far beyond all other men, and there is no one who can say he is more prudent or more brave, more learned or more wise, more noble or more renowned, than the noble and distinguished Surrey. All England resounds with his fame. Women repeat to themselves with delight his beautiful sonnets and love songs; scholars are proud to call him one of themselves, and warriors speak with admiration of his feats of arms. Be just, therefore, queen! Since you have so highly honored the deserts of bravery, give due honor also to the deserts of mind. In Seymour you have honored the warrior—in Howard give honor to the poet and the man!"

"I will do so," said Katharine, while she gazed with a winning smile into Jane's deeply-glowing and animated countenance. "I will do so, Jane, but upon one condition."

"And this condition is?"

Katharine threw her arm round Jane's neck and drew her close to her heart. "That you acknowledge to me that you love Henry Howard, whom you know how to defend with such glowing ardor."

For a moment Lady Jane became slightly convulsed, and leaned her head on the queen's shoulder quite overcome.

"Well," asked the latter, "do you acknowledge it? Will you confess that your proud, cold heart must at length declare itself vanquished and captive?"

"Yes, I acknowledge it," cried Lady Jane, while she flung herself at Katharine's feet with impassioned vehemence. "Yes, I love him, I worship him! I know that it is a despised and unfortunate love, but what would you have? My heart is more powerful than all else. I love him,—he is my idol, and my lord, and I worship him as I do my Redeemer. Queen, you know my whole secret now. Betray me if you will! Tell it to my father if you will, that he may curse me—tell it to Henry Howard if it should please you to learn how he scorns me. For alas, my queen, I am not loved by him!"

"Poor unhappy Jane!" cried the queen, full of commiseration.

Jane uttered a faint shriek, and raised herself up from her knees. That was too much. Her enemy pitied her. The person who was to blame for her woes expressed compassion for her!

Ah, she could have killed the queen,—she could have plunged a dagger into her heart for daring to commiserate her.

"I have fulfilled your condition, queen," said she, breathing more freely; "will you now grant my request?"

"Then you really want to intercede for this cruel, ungrateful man, who does not love you? He passes by your beauty with haughty indifference, and yet you plead for him."

"True love, queen, thinks not of itself; it gives way to its object. It asks not about the reward which it receives, but about the happiness which it has to offer. I saw by his pale, sorrowful countenance how much he suffered; was it not then my duty to try to console him? I went to him, I spoke to him; I heard his lamentations at this untoward accident, which indeed was not the fault of his skill and bravery, but, as everybody saw, was the fault of his horse, which was shy, and stumbled with its rider. And when in all the bitterness of his pain he complained, queen, that you would scorn and despise him, then I promised him, in full reliance upon your noble and generous heart, that at my request you would this very evening give him a mark of your favor in the presence of the whole court. Have I done wrong, Katharine?"

"No, Jane—no! You did right, and your promise shall be fulfilled. But how set about it? What am I to do?"

"This evening, after the king has performed in the Greek scene with Croke, the earl will read some new sonnets which he has composed. When he has done so give him some gift or token, be it what it may, so long as it is a mark of your favor."

"But how, Jane, in case his sonnets should deserve no praise, no recognition?"

"You may be sure they will deserve it, for Henry Howard is a true poet, and his verses are full of sublime thoughts and divine melody."

The queen smiled.

"Yes," she said; "you love him ardently, for you have no doubts in him. We will therefore acknowledge him as a great poet. But with what shall I reward him?"

"Give him a rose which you wear in your bosom, or a rosette fastened on your dress, and which shows your colors."

"But unfortunately, Jane, I wear neither roses nor rosettes to-day."

"Your majesty, however, may wear one if you please. A bow is wanted just here upon the shoulder. The purple mantle is too carelessly stitched, we must therefore introduce a slight decoration in the shape of a rosette or shoulder-knot."

She hastened into the adjoining room, and returned with the little box containing the queen's gold-embroidered ribands and jewelled rosettes.

Lady Jane turned them over again and again, as if unable to make choice of any. At last she took up the purple-red velvet rosette, which she had herself previously thrown into the box, and showed it to the queen.

"See, it is at once tasteful and costly, for it is held in the centre by a clasp of brilliants. Will you allow me to fasten this rosette on your shoulder, and will you give it to the Earl of Surrey?"

"Yes, Jane, I will give it to him as you wish it. But, my poor Jane, what do you gain by my doing so?"

"Well, at all events a friendly smile, queen."

"And that is enough for you? Do you then love him so very much?"

"Alas, I do!" said Lady Jane with a painful sigh, while she fastened the velvet bow on the queen's shoulder.

"And now, Jane, go and announce to the grand master of ceremonies that I am ready, as soon as the king wishes, to proceed to the gallery."

Lady Jane turned to leave the room, but she had scarcely reached the door, when she turned back once more.

"Pardon me, queen, if I venture to address to you one petition more. You have caused me this day to find in you once more the noble and faithful friend of earlier times, and therefore I urge this request with so much the more confidence."

"Well, what is it, my poor Jane?"

"I have entrusted my secret not to the

queen, but to Katharine Parr, the friend of my youth; will she preserve it, and not betray to any one my disgrace and humiliation?"

"My word upon it, Jane. No one but God and ourselves shall ever learn what has been said here."

Lady Jane kissed her hand with humility, and murmured a few words of thanks. She then left the queen's apartment, in order to repair to the grand master of ceremonies.

In passing through the queen's anteroom, she stood still for a moment and leaned against the wall, as if exhausted and quite broken down. There was no one here who could watch or observe her. She had no need to smile, no need under a calm and composed exterior, to conceal those stormy feelings of desperation which raged within her. She could give vent to her hatred and her rancor, her rage and her despair, by words and gestures, by tears and imprecations, by sobs and sighs. She could fall down on her knees and implore God for grace and mercy, and invoke satan for vengeance and destruction.

When she had done so, she rose up, and her features resumed their usual cold and placid expression. Only her cheeks were paler, and a more dismal fire glowed in her eyes, and a scornful smile played upon her thin, firmly-set lips.

She quitted the room and hastened along the corridor, and now she entered the ante-chamber of the king. On perceiving Gardiner, who stood alone, separated from the others near the window niche, she went up to him; and John Heywood, who was still concealed behind the hangings, shuddered at the terrible and scornful expression of her features.

She held out her hand to the prelate, and attempted to smile. "It is done," she murmured, in dull, leaden tones.

"What? The queen will wear the rosette on her dress?" inquired Gardiner, eagerly.

"She wears it on her shoulder, and will give it to him."

"And the note is inside it?"

"It is concealed under the jewelled clasp."

"Then she is lost," murmured Gardiner, "should the king find this paper, Katharine's death-warrant is signed."

"Hush!" said Lady Jane. "See, there comes Lord Hertford toward us. Let us go forward to meet him."

They both quitted the window-recess and walked along the saloon together.

Straightway John Heywood glided from behind the hangings, and creeping softly along by the wall, unseen by any one, left the saloon.

For a moment he stood still and reflected.

"I must probe their intrigues to the very bottom," said he to himself. "I must discover through whom, and with whom, they wish to destroy her, and, finally, I must have strong and undeniable proof at hand, in order to convict the intriguers, and to be able to accuse them successfully before the king. It is therefore necessary that I should be cautious and guarded. Let us then consider what is to be done; the simplest plan would be to beg the queen not to wear the rosette. But that would only be to destroy, for once, the web, without at the same time being able to kill the spider that wove it. She must accordingly wear the rosette, for otherwise I should never be able to learn to whom she is to give it. But the paper which is concealed inside this rosette—that I must have—it cannot be left where it is. 'Should the king find this paper then Katharine's death-warrant is signed.' Well, then, my worshipful priest of the devil, the king will not find this paper, for John Heywood won't allow it. But how shall I set to work? Shall I tell the queen what I heard! No! she would lose her composure and cheerfulness; and in the eyes of the king, her embarrassment would be the most convincing proof of her guilt. No, I must take this paper from the rosette without the queen's perceiving it. Cheer up then for the work! I must have this paper, and cheat these hypocrites. How it is to be done I don't at present exactly see; but I shall do it, and that's enough. Come, let's be off to the queen!"

With eager steps he hurried along through the saloons and corridors, while he chuckled and muttered to himself on the way; "Thank God I have the honor of being the fool; for only the king and the fool have the privilege of being able to enter every room, even that of the queen, unannounced."

Katharine was alone in her boudoir, when the little door by which the king usually visited her was opened softly.

"Ah, here comes the king!" she exclaimed, stepping forward to the door to greet her husband.

"Yes, the king is coming, for the fool is already here," said John Heywood, who entered by the private door. "Are we alone, queen—are we overheard by any one?"

"No, John Heywood, we are quite alone. What is it you bring me?"

"A letter, my queen."

"From whom?" she asked, and a deep blush suffused her cheeks.

"From whom?" repeated John Heywood, with a waggish smile—"That I don't know, queen; but, at all events, it is a begging-letter, and doubtless you would do well not to read it at all, for I would lay a wager the shameless writer of this letter requires some impossibility of you, were it only a smile, or a pressure of the hand, a lock of your hair, or, perhaps, even a kiss. Therefore your majesty had better not read this begging-letter at all."

"John," she returned, smiling and yet trembling with impatience—"John, give me the letter."

"I will sell it to you, queen. I have learned that from the king, who also bestows nothing from mere generosity, and takes more than he gives. Therefore let us make a bargain. I will give you the letter, and you shall give me the rosette which you wear on your shoulder."

"Nay, John; choose something else—the rosette I cannot indeed very well give you."

"Then by all the gods be it sworn," cried John, with comic pathos, "I won't give you the letter unless you give me the rosette."

"Why, you foolish fellow," said the queen, "I tell you I cannot! Choose something else; and now, my good John, pray do give me the letter."

"Only if you give me the rosette. I have sworn it by all the gods, and what I vow to them I perform! No, no, queen, not those black looks—not those indignant frowns. If I cannot in reality have a present made me of the rosette, why let us do like the Jesuits and the Papists, who even chaffer with their Lord God, and snap their fingers at him when the bargain is struck. My vow I must keep! I give you the letter, and you give me the rosette—but mind, you only lend it to me; and when I have had it for a moment in my hand, I shall be as magnanimous and generous as the king, and make you a present once more of your own property."

With a hasty movement the queen tore the rosette from her shoulder, and handed it to John Heywood.

"And now give me the letter, John?"

"Here it is," said John Heywood, as he took the rosette. "Take it and you will see that Thomas Seymour is my brother."

"Your brother, John?" asked Katharine, smiling, while with trembling hand she broke the seal.

"Yes, my brother, for he is a fool! Ah! I have a great many brothers. The family of the Fools is a very large one!"

The queen heard no more. She read the letter of her beloved; she had eyes only for those written words, which told her that Thomas Seymour loved her, worshipped her, and was pining away through yearning for her.

She did not perceive how John Heywood, with nimble fingers, loosed the jewelled clasp from the rosette, and took from out the folds of the velvet a small piece of paper which was hidden there.

"She is saved!" he murmured, while he thrust the fateful paper into his doublet, and once more fastened the clasp in its place. "She is saved, and for this time, at least, the king will not sign her death-warrant."

Katharine had read the letter to the end. She now concealed it in her bosom.

"Queen, you have sworn to me that you would burn every letter that I brought you from *him*; for it is a dangerous thing to preserve clandestine love-letters. One day they might gain the use of speech, and testify against you. I will not bring you another letter again, unless you burn this billet-doux at once."

"I shall burn it, John, when I have first really read it. As yet I have only read it with my feelings, and not with my eyes. Allow me, therefore, to carry it for a few hours longer next my heart."

"But swear to me that you will burn it this very evening?"

"I swear to you that I will!"

"Then for this time I shall be satisfied. Here is your rosette, and like the celebrated fox in the fable, who declared the grapes were sour because he could not reach them, I say to you, 'Take back your rosette—I don't like it!'"

He handed the rosette to the queen, and she fastened it once more, smiling, on her shoulder.

"John," she said, extending to him her hand with a bewitching smile, "John, when will you permit me to thank you otherwise than by words? When will you suffer your queen, to reward you for all your kind services, otherwise than by expressions of gratitude?"

John Heywood kissed her hand, and replied with a sad expression: "I shall demand a reward from you on the day on which my tears and entreaties shall have succeeded in persuading you to give up this sad and dangerous love. Truly on that day I should have deserved a reward, and I would accept it from you with a proud and thankful heart."

"Then, my poor John, in that case you will never receive your reward, for that day will never come!"

"Apparently then I shall receive my reward, but from the king, and it will be a reward whereby one loses his sight and hearing, and his head to boot! Well, we shall see! Until then, farewell queen; I must go to the king, for somebody might surprise me here, and might hit upon the wise thought that John Heywood is not always a fool, but is sometimes the messenger of love; I kiss the hem of your garments; farewell, queen!"

And once more he glided through the private door.

"We will now examine this paper," he murmured to himself, when he had reached the corridor, and was sure of not being seen by any one.

He drew the paper forth from his doublet and opened it. "I don't know the handwriting, but it is that of a woman."

The letter was as follows:—"Dost thou believe me now, my beloved? I swore that this day, in presence of the king, and of my whole court, I would give thee this rosette, and I have done it. For thee I gladly risk my life, for thou art my life, and it would ever more be more blissful to die with thee than to live without thee. I only live when I rest in thy arms—and those dark nights when thou art beside me—they are the light and sunshine of my days. Let us pray heaven, that speedily we may have a moonless night, for such a night brings to me my beloved, and to thee thy thrice-blest wife once more.

"GERALDINE."

"Geraldine! Who is Geraldine?" murmured John Heywood, again thrusting the paper into his doublet. "I must disentangle this web of falsehood and deceit, I must know what all this means. For this is more than an intrigue—it is a fictitious accusation! Some matter of fact is apparently involved. This letter was to be given by the queen to some man or other, and it speaks of sweet recollections and blissful nights! The person therefore who receives this letter is in the plot against Katharine, and I dare say her bitterest enemy, for he makes use of love against her. Some treachery, some trick is concealed in the background. Either the man is deceived for whom this letter is intended, and he is an unwitting tool in the hands of the papists, or else he is in league with them, and like an arrant knave, has undertaken to represent himself as the queen's paramour. But who can it be? Thomas Seymour perhaps? It were possible, for he has a cold, deceitful heart, and he would be quite capable of such treachery. If so, then I am the man who will accuse him to the king, and by Heaven his head shall fall. And now to the king!"

Just as he entered the king's anteroom, the door of the closet opened, and the Duchess of Richmond came out, accompanied by Lord Douglas.

Lady Jane and Gardiner were standing, as if by accident, in the vicinity of this door.

"Well, have we also reached our goal there?" asked Gardiner.

"We have," replied Lord Douglas. "The duchess has accused her brother of an amorous relationship with the queen. She has declared that sometimes by night he leaves his mansion, and does not return to it before morning. She has stated that four nights since she followed the footsteps of her brother, herself, and saw how he had entered the wing of the palace inhabited by the queen; and one of the women of the queen's bedchamber informed the duchess that the queen was not in her own rooms on that night."

"And the king listened to the accusation, and did not in his anger strangle you?"

"He is still in that dull state of rage when the lava is first fermenting, which will soon overflow the crater. As yet, all is quiet, but be assured there will be an eruption, and streams of seething lava will overwhelm those who have dared to provoke the god Vulcan."

"And does he know of the rosette?" asked Lady Jane.

"He knows all. And up to the critical moment he will not let his anger be suspected by any one. He says he will make the queen feel quite assured, in order thereby to be able to get into his hand the sure proof of her guilt. Now we shall certainly give him this proof, from which it follows that the queen is irrecoverably lost."

"But hark! The doors are opening, and the grand master of the ceremonies is coming to summon us to the golden gallery."

"Walk in, ladies and gentlemen—walk up!" murmured John Heywood, gliding along behind them. "I'm with you already, and I shall be the mouse to bite the net in which ye wish to catch my fine great-hearted lioness."

CHAPTER XII.

THE QUEEN'S ROSETTE.

THE golden gallery in which the poets' tournament was to be held, presented on this evening a truly enchanting and fairy-like spectacle. Mirrors of gigantic size encased in broad golden frames, decorated with carved work of the most exquisite kind, adorned the walls, and reflected in endless perspective the huge chandeliers, which with their innumerable wax tapers shed a noonday splendor throughout the immense saloon. Here and there before the mirrors were arranged groups of the choicest and rarest flowers, which emitted on all sides their overpowering yet soothing fragrance, and which in the variety and beauty of their colors outshone the Turkish carpet that covered the whole saloon, and converted the floor into one vast flower-bed. Between the different flower-groves were tables with golden vessels, filled with refreshing drinks, while at the other end of the immense gallery stood a huge buffet laid out with the rarest and most costly viands. At present the doors of the buffet—which, when it was opened, represented an entire room in itself—were still closed.

As yet the guests had not pressed forward to the material enjoyments of the evening; they were still occupied with the pleasures of the mind. The brilliant and select company which filled the saloon were yet for some time condemned to silence; they were forced to confine their laughter and their scandal, their wit and their calumny, their flattery and their hypocrisy, within themselves.

A pause had just ensued. The king, assisted by Croke, had represented to his court a scene from the "Antigone," and his audience had just begun to breathe freely after the wonderful and sublime enjoyment of having heard a language of which none of them understood a word, but which they thought very beautiful because the king admired it.

Henry the Eighth had once more flung himself back in his chair of state, and was gasping and panting, after his immense efforts; and while he rested and mused, an invisible orchestra played a piece of music composed by the king himself, which, with its grave and solemn measures, contrasted strikingly with the gay and dazzling saloon, and with the assembled company—brilliant, mirthful, and wit-abounding.

For the king had given command that his guests should laugh and be merry, that they should converse with unrestrained freedom. It was therefore but natural that they should indulge their gayety and their laughter-loving impulses, and that they did not appear to observe the exhaustion and fatigue of the king.

Au reste, the king had not for a long time been so cheerful, so youthfully active, so sparkling with wit and humor, as on this evening. His mouth brimmed over with jests, which made the gentlemen laugh, and the fair, fascinating ladies blush; more especially the young queen, who sat beside him on his splendid and costly throne, and who from time to time could only cast a stolen and yearning glance toward her beloved, for whom she would joyfully have relinquished her royal crown.

When the king saw how Katharine blushed, he turned round to her, and in his most affectionate tone begged her forgiveness for his jest, which, from its freedom, had only seemed to make his queen still more beautiful, still more charming. And then his words were so cordial and tender, his looks so full of admiration and love, that no one could doubt but that the queen was in the highest favor with her spouse, and that he loved her in the most affectionate manner.

Only the few who knew the secret of this public and unreserved show of tenderness on the part of the king, fully understood the danger which threatened the queen; for the king was never more terrible than when he flattered, and upon no one did his anger fall more crushingly than upon him whom he had just embraced and assured of his favor.

This was what Lord Douglas said to himself when he saw with what a look of cordial affection King Henry conversed with his wife.

Behind the throne of the royal pair stood John Heywood in his fantastic garb, with his noble and withal sly countenance; and one of his sarcastic and pungent repartees had just caused the king to burst out into a loud and boisterous fit of laughter.

"King Henry, your laugh does not please me to-night," said John Heywood gravely. "It smacks of gall. Don't you think so yourself, queen?"

The queen started up from her sweet reverie, and this was what John Heywood had intended. He therefore repeated his question.

"Nay," she replied, "I think the king greatly resembles the sun to-day, for, like the sun, he is bright and beaming."

"Your majesty does not mean the sun, but the pale moon," returned John Heywood, with a laugh. "But only look yonder, Henry, how cheerful Lord Archibald Douglas is gossiping with the Duchess of Richmond! I love that excellent nobleman. He always looks like a slow-worm, just on the point of biting some one in the leg; and so it is that whenever I am near his lordship I change myself into a crane. I stand upon one leg, because then I can be sure to save the other from his bite. Now, if I were you, king, I would not let those persons be put to death who have been stung by the slow-worm, but I would cause all the slow-worms to be rooted out, so that the feet of honest men may be safe from them."

The king darted a sudden and inquiring look at him, to which John Heywood replied with a smile:

"Kill the slow-worms, King Henry," he continued; "and if you should ever happen to be destroying vermin, it won't hurt if you also stamp vigorously with your foot upon the priests. It is such a long time since we burnt any of them, and they will again become wanton and wicked, as they always were and always will be. I even see the mild and pious Bishop of Winchester—the noble Gardiner—who is yonder there conversing with Lady Jane, smiling very serenely, and that's a bad sign; for Gardiner only smiles when he has once more caught a poor soul, and has prepared her as a breakfast for his master—I don't mean yourself, king, but the devil! for the devil is always ravenous after noble human souls, and whoever catches one for him, his devilship gives him absolution of his sins for an hour. And it is for this reason that Gardiner catches so many souls—for as he sins every hour, he must for every hour get absolution."

"You are very spiteful to-day, John," said the queen, with a smile, while the king cast his eyes to the ground with a thoughtful and abstracted air.

John Heywood's words had touched the sore spots in his nature, and involuntarily filled his distrustful heart with new doubts.

He suspected not only the accused but also the accuser, and if he punished the one as a delinquent, he was ready to punish the other as the denouncer.

He asked himself what object Lord Douglas and Gardiner could have had in accusing the queen, and why they had roused him up from his peace and confidence. At this moment, when he cast a glance at his beautiful wife, smiling with such calm and cheerful composure beside him, he felt his heart filled with deep resentment, not against Katharine, but against Lady Jane who had accused her.

She was so lovely and so beautiful—why did they grudge her to him—why not have left him in his sweet illusion? And perhaps, after all, she was not guilty. The eye of a guilty woman is not so clear and serene—the demeanor of one impure, not so maidenly and self-possessed.

Moreover, the king felt himself exhausted and *blasé*. Even the practice of cruelty may prove wearisome by repetition; and at this moment Henry felt quite satiated with bloodshed.

His heart—for in such moments of mental relaxation and bodily unbending even the king had a heart—was already on the point of giving way to the sentiments of mercy by which he was animated, when his eye fell upon Henry Howard, who with his father, the Duke of Norfolk, stood surrounded by a circle of noble lords, at a short distance from the royal throne.

The king felt a deadly sting in his breast, and his eyes flashed across at the group yonder.

How proud and imposing was the form of the noble earl, while his lofty stature rose high above his compeers; how noble and handsome his features, how princely his bearing and his whole appearance!

All this Henry could not but admit, and, because he was compelled to do so, he hated him.

No, there is no mercy for Katharine! If what her accusers had told him were true—if they could give him proofs of the queen's guilt, then her fate was sealed. And how could he doubt the fact? Had they not told him that in a rosette which the queen would give the Earl of Surrey, was contained a love-letter from Katharine, which he would find? Had not the Earl of Surrey communicated this fact yesterday to his sister in a confidential moment, when he wanted her to convey *billets-doux* between him and the queen? Had she not accused the queen of holding nocturnal interviews with the earl in the lone tower?

No, there must be no mercy for the queen, if Henry Howard was her lover.

Once more he glanced across at his hated enemy. There he stood as before, with his father, the Duke of Norfolk. With what activity and grace the old duke moved about, how slender his figure, and how haughty and imposing his air! The king was younger than the duke, and yet he was confined to his wheeled chair; and there he sat like an immovable Colossus upon his throne, while the duke moved about freely and easily, and only obeyed the dictates of his will—not the laws of necessity. The king could have crushed him on the spot—this proud, haughty duke, who was a free agent, while his king was nothing but a prisoner in his own flesh—the slave of his unwieldy body.

"I shall annihilate this haughty and arrogant Howard race!" murmured the king, as he turned with a friendly smile to the Earl of Surrey.

"Cousin," he said, "you have promised us some of your sonnets! Let us therefore enjoy them now—for you see how impatiently all the lovely women of our court are glancing at England's noblest and greatest poet, and how angry they would be with me, if I were any longer to debar them of this enjoyment. Even our beautiful queen longs ardently for your enthusiastic effusions, for you know well, Howard, she is a great lover of poetry, and especially of yours."

Katharine had scarcely noticed what the king had said. Her glance had encountered that of Seymour, on whom it was for an instant riveted. And then, with her eye yet filled with the image of her beloved, she cast her looks toward the ground, in order to think of him, as she dared not prolong her gaze.

But when the king pronounced her name, she started up, and looked at him inquiringly: she had not heard what he had said to her.

"Not even for an instant does she turn her eyes toward me!" said Henry Howard to himself. "Ah, she does not love me, or, at least, her understanding is stronger than her love. Oh, Katharine, Katharine, dost thou so much fear death, that thou canst on that account deny thy love?"

With a kind of desperate haste, he drew forth his portfolio. "I will compel her," thought he, "to turn her looks toward me, to think of me, and to remember her vows. Woe betide her should she not give me the rosette she promised me with such solemn protestations. If she does not, then I shall break this fearful silence and accuse her to the king, before her whole court, of treason toward her love. Then, at least, she will not be able to renounce me, for we shall mount the scaffold together."

"Will her majesty the queen permit me to commence?" he asked aloud, quite forgetting that the king had already given his commands to that effect, and that it was the king alone who could grant such permission.

Katharine looked at him with astonishment. But then her eye rested on Lady Jane Douglas, who, with an air of entreaty, gazed up at her.

The queen smiled, for she now remembered that it was Jane's beloved who had spoken to her, and that she had promised the poor young maiden to raise up once more the humbled Earl of Surrey, and to be gracious toward him.

"Jane is right," thought she, "he seems much downcast, and appears to suffer. Ah, it must be very sad to see the man suffer whom we love! I shall comply with Jane's request, for she said this would be the means of raising him up from his prostrate condition."

With a smile she bent forward toward the earl.

"I beg," she said, "your lordship will lend this festive scene its fairest embellishment, by decking it with the fragrant flowers of your muse. You see we are all glowing with the desire to hear your verses."

The king quivered with suppressed rage, and words of crushing fury trembled on his lips. But he restrained himself—he wished to have proofs beforehand—he wished to see her not only accused but condemned, and for this was required the proof of her guilt.

Henry Howard now approached the throne of the royal couple, and with beaming looks of inspiration, and with a voice tremulous with emotion, he recited his love-sonnets to the beautiful Geraldine.

A murmur of approbation rose when he had read his first sonnet; the king alone looked grave and stern, and only the queen remained cold and unmoved.

"She is a perfect actress," thought Henry Howard, in the intensity of his pain. "Not a muscle of her countenance moves, and yet this sonnet must have recalled to her mind the most blissful—the happiest moments of our love."

The queen continued cold and impassive. But if Henry Howard had looked toward Lady Jane Douglas, he would have seen how she turned pale and blushed, how she smiled with delight, and yet how her eyes were filled with tears.

Still the Earl of Surrey saw nothing but the queen, and her aspect made him tremble with anger and chagrin. His eyes flashed, his countenance glowed with passion—his whole being was filled with a kind of desperate inspiration. He would at this moment have joyfully breathed out his life at Geraldine's feet, if she would but recognize him—if she would but summon courage to call him her beloved. But her smiling composure, her cold civility drove him to desperation.

He crumpled the paper in his hand—

the characters danced before his eyes—he could read no more.

But yet he would not be mute. Like the dying swan, he would breathe forth his pain in a last melody, and give words and voice to his torment and despair. He could no longer read—he improvised.

Like a stream of seething lava, the words flowed from his lips; in fiery dithyrambs, in hymns of inspiration, he poured forth the story of his love and of his woes. The genius of poetry hovered around him, and lighted up his noble and thoughtful brow.

He became radiant with inspiration, and even the queen felt herself carried away by his words. His love-complaints, his painful yearnings, his raptures, and his gloomy phantasies found an echo in her heart.

She understood him, for she felt the same joy, the same woe, and the same rapture—only that she felt not these emotions for him.

But, as before stated, he inspired her; the stream of his passion hurried him along. She wept at his sorrows, she smiled at his hymns of exultation.

When at length Henry Howard ceased, a deep silence reigned throughout the large, resplendent saloon.

The countenances of all were deeply moved, and this universal silence was the poet's finest triumph, for it showed him that even envy and ill-will were struck dumb, and that derision itself could find no utterance.

A momentary pause ensued; it resembled that sultry and boding stillness which generally precedes the outbreak of a storm, when Nature rests for a moment to gather strength for the coming tornado.

It was a significant, a fearful pause, yet few there were who understood its meaning.

Lady Jane, breathless and overcome, was leaning against the wall. She felt that the sword was hanging over her head, and that it would destroy her, should it reach her beloved.

Lord Douglas and the Bishop of Winchester had involuntarily approached each other, and now stood hand in hand united for the deadly struggle; while John Heywood had slipped behind the king's throne, and, in his sarcastic fashion, had whispered an epigram in his ear, which made the king smile against his will.

But now the queen rose from her seat and made a sign to Henry Howard to approach.

"My lord," she said, in a tone approaching solemnity, "I thank you as a queen, and as a woman, for the noble and sublime verses which you have written in honor of a woman. And as the favor of my sovereign has raised me to be the first woman in England, it becomes me, in the name of all women, to express to you my thanks. The poet and the warrior have each their peculiar reward. The victor on the battle-field receives a laurel-crown! You have won for yourself a no less brilliant victory; for you have captivated hearts! We declare ourselves conquered; and in the name of all these noble ladies, I appoint you their champion—as a token of which, take this rosette, my lord! It entitles you to wear the queen's colors; it binds you to be the trusty knight and champion of all women!"

She loosed the rosette from her shoulder, and presented it to the earl.

He had bent on one knee before her, and was in the act of extending his hand to receive this precious and much-longed-for pledge.

But at this moment the king rose up, and with an imperious gesture, held back the queen's hand.

"Your majesty will allow me," he said, while his voice trembled with anger—"your majesty will first allow me to examine this rosette, and to satisfy myself if it be worthy to be presented to the noble lord as his sole reward! Let me see this rosette!"

Katharine looked with amazement at his features quivering with passion and rage, but she handed him the rosette without hesitation.

"We are lost!" murmured the Earl of Surrey, while Lord Douglas and Gardiner exchanged glances of triumph, and Jane Douglas, in her trembling heart, murmured prayers of anxiety and bewilderment, scarcely hearing the words of malicious joy which the Duchess of Richmond whispered in her ear.

The king held the rosette in his hand and looked at it; but his hands trembled so much that he was unable to open the clasp which held it together in the centre.

He therefore gave it to John Heywood. "These diamonds are bad," said he, in a short, dry tone. "Loose this clasp, fool, we will replace it with this pin. The gift will then acquire a double value for the earl; for it will come to him from myself and from the queen."

"How gracious you are to-day," said John Heywood, smiling. "As gracious as the cat that plays with the mouse for a while before she swallows it."

"Loose this clasp!" cried the king, in a voice of thunder, no longer able to conceal his rage.

John Heywood slowly unfastened the clasp from the ribbon. He did so with marked deliberation and circumspection; he allowed the king to see every movement and turn of his fingers; and it delighted him to keep those who had woven this plot, in fearful suspense and expectation.

While he appeared quite calm and unconcerned, his keen, penetrating glance scanned the whole assembly, and he clearly perceived the trembling impatience of Gardiner and Lord Douglas, and it did not escape him how pale Lady Jane was, and how strained with expectation were the features of the Duchess of Richmond.

"These are the authors of this plot," said John Heywood to himself; "but I shall keep silent until I can one day convict them."

"There, that's the clasp!" said he at length, aloud to the king. "It was fixed as firmly in the ribbon, as malice and hate in the hearts of priests and courtiers."

The king snatched the ribbon out of

his hand, and passed it carefully through his fingers.

"Nothing—nothing at all!" he said, gnashing his teeth; and now disappointed in his anticipations, he was no longer able to resist the fermenting torrent of anger which overflowed his heart. The tiger within him was roused once more; he had calmly awaited the moment when the promised victim should be flung to him; and now that it appeared to be withdrawn, his cruel and ferocious instincts rose up resentingly. The tiger was athirst and panted for blood, and because it was denied him he became furious with rage.

He flung the rosette on the ground with a fierce gesture, and raised his arm in a threatening attitude toward Henry Howard.

"Do not dare to touch that rosette!" he exclaimed, in a voice of thunder—"before you have justified yourself as to the guilt of which you are accused."

The Earl of Surrey looked at the king with a firm, unflinching gaze. "Then I have been accused?" he asked. "In that case I desire, in the first place, that my accusers may be brought before me face to face; and then that I may know what my crime is!"

"Ha, traitor! you dare to defy me!" exclaimed the king, stamping wildly with his foot. "Well, then, I shall be your accuser and your judge!"

"And surely, my lord and husband, you will be a just judge," said Katharine, while she bent forward entreatingly toward the king, and seized his hand. "You will not condemn the noble Earl of Surrey without having heard him; and should you find him innocent, you will punish his accusers."

But this intercession on the part of the queen made the king frantic. He dashed her hand away, and looked at her with such an anger-flashing glance, that she involuntarily trembled.

"Traitress thyself!" he cried, wildly, "speak not of innocence—you, who are yourself stained with guilt, and before you venture to defend the earl, defend yourself!"

Katharine rose up from her seat, and with a look of lofty indignation scanned the anger-inflamed countenance of the king. "King Henry, of England," she said, in solemn accents, "you have publicly, and before your whole court, accused your queen of a crime. I demand to know what it is!"

She looked supremely beautiful in her proud, defiant bearing—in her imposing and majestic calmness.

The decisive moment was at hand, and she felt conscious that her life and her future were struggling with death for the victory.

She looked across toward Thomas Seymour, and their eyes met. She saw how he laid his hand on his sword, and returned her glance with a smile of greeting.

"He will defend me, and sooner than suffer me to be hurried away to the Tower, he will himself pierce my breast with his sword," she whispered to herself, and a joyful and triumphant confidence filled her whole breast.

She saw nothing but him, the man

who had sworn that he would die with her when the decisive moment should have arrived. She looked with a smile at the sword which he had already half drawn from the scabbard, and she greeted it as a dear and long-wished-for friend.

She did not perceive that Henry Howard, too, had his hand on the hilt of his sword—that he, too, was ready to defend her—firmly resolved to kill the king himself, before his lips should have pronounced sentence of death against the queen.

But Lady Jane perceived it. She knew how to read it in the earl's countenance; she felt that he was ready to die for the object of his love, and it filled her heart at once with sorrow and delight.

She too had now firmly resolved to obey only the dictates of her heart, and the promptings of her love, and forgetting all else but this, she hastened forward and now stood beside Henry Howard.

"Be prudent, Lord Surrey," she whispered softly. "Withdraw your hand from your sword. The queen commands you by my lips."

Henry Howard looked at her with astonishment and surprise, but he suffered his hand to fall from the hilt of his sword, and looked across at the queen.

She had repeated her demand; she had once more requested the king, who, speechless and overpowered with anger, had sunk back into his chair, to name to her the crime with which she was charged.

"Well, then," he exclaimed at length, "you demand it, and you shall hear it! You wish to know the crime of which you are accused? Answer me, therefore, my lady queen? You are accused with not always remaining in your chamber at night. It is asserted that you sometimes leave it for several hours, and that none of your ladies accompany you when you go along the corridor and up the private stairs leading to the deserted tower, in which your paramour awaits you, and that he at the same time enters the tower by the little gateway from the public street."

"He knows all!" murmured Henry Howard, and again he laid his hand on his sword, and was about to draw near the queen.

Lady Jane checked him. "Wait the result!" she whispered. "There is still time enough for death!"

"He knows all," thought the queen; and now she felt within her the defiant courage to dare all, and at least not to stand convicted as a traitress in the eye of her lover.

"He shall not believe that I have been untrue to him," she thought. "I shall tell all—admit all, in order that he may know whither and for what purpose I have gone."

"Answer me, now, Lady Katharine," thundered the king. "Answer, and tell me, if you have been falsely accused. Is it true that a week since, on a Monday night, you quitted your chamber, and went secretly to the deserted tower? Is it true that you there received a man who is your paramour?"

The queen looked at him with a proud and angry glance.

"Henry! Henry! Shame upon you, that you thus dare to insult your own wife!" she exclaimed.

"Answer me. You were not in your chamber on that night?"

"No," replied Katharine, with lofty composure, "I was not there!"

The king sank back in his seat, and bellowed with intense rage. The ladies grew pale, and even the men trembled.

Katharine alone had paid it no heed; she alone had perceived nothing but the exclamation of horror which burst from Thomas Seymour, and she only saw the angry and reproachful glances which he flung across at her.

She replied to his looks with a cordial and confident smile, and pressed her hand upon her heart in returning his gaze.

"Before him at least I shall justify myself," she thought.

The king had recovered from his first shock of horror. He raised himself up once more, and his features now betrayed an inexorable and stern composure.

"Then you admit the fact?" he asked. "You were not in your chamber on that night?"

"I said so already," cried Katharine, impatiently.

The king bit his lips so violently that they bled.

"And there was a man with you?" he inquired. "A man to whom you had given a rendezvous about this hour, and whom you received in the deserted tower?"

"There was a man with me. But I did not receive him in the deserted tower, and there was no rendezvous in question."

"Who was this man?" cried the king. "Answer me. Name to me this man, if you would not have me strike you dead myself."

"I no longer fear death, King Henry," replied Katharine, with a scornful smile.

"Who was this man? Tell me his name!" exclaimed the king once more.

The queen raised herself proudly, and glanced round with an air of confidence at the entire assembly.

"The man," she replied, with measured emphasis, "who was with me on that night, is named—"

"John Heywood!" interrupted the court jester, stepping forth with a grave air from behind the king's chair. "Yes, Henry, your brother, the fool, had the proud honor on that night of accompanying your wife on her holy mission, but I assure you that he resembled the king less than the king resembles the fool just now."

A murmur of astonishment ran through the whole assembly. The king leaned back speechless in his chair.

"And now, King Henry," said Katharine calmly, "now I will tell you where I went to on that night with John Heywood!"

For a moment she was silent, and reclined in her seat. She felt that the eyes of all were fixed upon her, she heard the angry groans of the king, she perceived the reproachful glances of her beloved, she observed the derisive smiles of those high-born dames who had never forgiven her for having, from a simple baroness, become a queen. But all this only tended to give her courage and confidence.

She had reached that pinnacle of life when one must venture all to avoid sinking down into the abyss.

But Lady Jane, too, had just reached such a decisive moment of her existence. She too, said to herself, "I must now venture all or lose all." She saw Henry Howard's pale features strained with expectation. She knew that if the queen now spoke, the whole web of her own intrigues would be revealed to him.

She must, therefore, anticipate the queen. She must warn Henry Howard.

"Fear nothing!" she whispered to him. "We were prepared for this. I have put the means of escape into her hands!"

"Will you now speak at length?" cried the king, trembling with rage and impatience. "Will you tell us at last where you went to on that night?"

"I will do so!" replied Katharine, rising once more from her chair with a calm and resolute air. "But woe betide those who have driven me to it! For I tell you beforehand that the accused will become an accuser who demands justice, if not before the throne of England's king, yet before the throne of the Lord of all kings! You ask me, King Henry of England, where I went to on that night with John Heywood! I might, perhaps, as your queen and wife, expect that you would not put this question to me before so many witnesses, but rather in the silence of our chamber—but you have sought publicity, and I do not shrink from it! Well, then, hear the truth, all of you! On that night of Monday, and Tuesday morning, I was not in my chamber; because I had a serious and a sacred duty to fulfil—because a dying woman had called to me for aid and mercy. Would you know, my lord and husband, who this dying woman was? It was Maria Askew."

"Maria Askew!" cried the king, and his countenance assumed a less angry expression.

"Maria Askew!" murmured the others, and John Heywood observed how Bishop Gardiner's brow became clouded, and how Wriothesley the chancellor turned pale, and cast his eyes to the ground.

"Yes, I was with Maria Askew!" continued the queen—"with Maria Askew, whom the wise and pious lords yonder had condemned—not so much because of her belief as because they knew that I loved her. Maria Askew must die because Katharine Parr loved her? She must mount the burning pile in order that my heart, too, should be made to burn with anguish! And because such was the case, I was obliged to venture all to save her. Oh, my lord, tell me was I not bound to try every means for the purpose of saving her? For my sake it was indeed that she was doomed to suffer all these agonies. For a letter had been shamefully stolen from me, which Maria Askew in her hour of need had addressed to me; and this letter they showed you, in order to make me suspected in your eyes, and to accuse me.

But your noble heart rejected the suspicion, and then your anger fell upon Maria Askew, and she was made to suffer because I had escaped punishment. She was made to atone for having ventured to write to me. She gained from you the end she sought, of being put to the rack. But when my spouse yielded to her urgency, the nobleness of the king remained still unchanged in his nature. 'Go away,' said he, 'put her to the rack—to death, but see in the first place if she will not recant!'"

Henry looked with astonishment into her noble and resolute countenance. "You knew that?" he asked. "And yet we were alone, and there was no human being present who could betray it to you."

"When man is no longer able to help, God takes the matter in His own hands," replied Katharine, solemnly. "It was God who commanded me to go to Maria Askew, and to try if I could save her. And I went. But although the wife of a great and noble king, I am still but a feeble and timid woman. I was afraid to travel this long and dangerous way alone; I required a strong and manly arm to lean upon, and John Heywood lent me his."

"And you really were with Maria Askew?" interrupted the king, with a thoughtful air—"with that hardened sinner who despised mercy, and in the perverseness of her heart refused to accept the pardon which I had offered her?

"My lord and spouse," returned the queen, with tears in her eyes, "the woman whom you now accuse stands at this moment before the throne of the Almighty, and has received from her God the forgiveness of her sins. Be you, therefore, forgiving also; and may the flames which yesterday rose up around the noble and tender form of that young maiden, have also consumed the anger and the hatred which men kindled in your heart against her. Maria Askew has gone hence as a saint, for she forgave all her enemies and blessed her tormentors."

"Maria Askew was an abandoned sinner, who dared to oppose the commands of her lord and king!" interrupted Gardiner, with a severe and angry glance.

"And will you venture to maintain, my lord, that you have at all times accurately and punctually fulfilled, the commands of your royal master?" asked Katharine. "Did you faithfully perform them toward Maria Askew? No, I say you did not; for the king did not command you to put her to the torture—he did not direct you in blasphemous anger to lacerate a noble human form, and to disfigure this image of God by converting it into a mangled and monstrous mass, which makes one shudder to contemplate. And that, my lord, you have done! Before God and your king, I accuse you of this—I, the queen, accuse you!—For now, my lord and husband, you must know that I was present when Maria Askew was put to the rack. I witnessed her torture, and John Heywood saw it with me."

All eyes were turned inquiringly toward the king, from whom a violent outburst of choler and ferocity was now expected.

For once, however, they were disappointed. The king was so well pleased at finding his spouse blameless of the crime laid to her charge, that he willingly forgave her an offence of minor gravity. Besides, it afforded him unbounded satisfaction to find that his wife had confronted her accusers so defiantly and so loftily, and he conceived toward them no less anger and animosity than he had before entertained against the queen. He was well pleased that the knavish and unceasing persecutors of his beautiful wife were now about to be humbled before the eyes of the whole court.

He, therefore, looked with an imperceptible smile at his spouse, and said, in a more sympathetic tone, "But how did this happen, madam? By what way did you reach there?"

"That is a question which any one else but the king would be justified in asking. King Henry alone knows the way which I took," replied Katharine, with a subdued smile.

John Heywood, who still continued standing behind the king's chair, now bent forward close to Henry's ear, and spoke to him in a rapid undertone for a long time.

The king listened attentively to him, and then he murmured, loud enough to be heard by those who stood around: "By Heaven! she is a bold and a courageous woman, and we should be compelled to admit that in her favor, even though she were not our queen."

"Continue, madam," said the king aloud, turning to the queen with a look of encouragement. "Tell me, Katharine, what did you see in the torture-chamber?"

"Oh, my lord, it gives me horror only to think of it," she exclaimed, shuddering, and turning pale. "I saw, writhing in terrible agony, a poor young woman, whose rigid looks were turned to heaven with mute entreaty. She did not beg her tormentors for pity; she besought them for no mercy or compassion; she did not shriek or mourn with pain, though her joints cracked, and her limbs were torn asunder. She raised her hands to God, and her lips murmured a gentle prayer, which perhaps made the angels in heaven weep, but which had no power to touch the hearts of her torturers. You, my husband, had commanded that she should be put to the rack if she refused to recant. But she was not asked this question—the torture was applied. Still her soul was strong and courageous within her, and under the torments of the racksmen her lips remained mute. Let learned theologians decide if Maria Askew's faith was true or false, but this they will not venture to deny, that in the noble inspiration of this faith, she was a heroine who at least did not deny her God. At length, exhausted by so much useless exertion, the racksmen left off their bloody work, in order to rest from the tortures which they had prepared for Maria Askew. The lieutenant of the Tower declared the operations of the rack at an end—the highest degrees of torture had already been applied, and had been found useless. Barbarity itself had to confess that it was vanquished. But the priests of the Church demanded with eager ferocity that she should once more be stretched on the rack. Dare to deny this, my lords, ye whom I see standing yonder, with deadly-pale countenances! Yes, my king; the servants of the rack refused to obey the servants of God, for in the hearts of the racksmen there was more mercy than in the hearts of the priests. And when they refused to continue their work of blood, and when the lieutenant of the Tower, by virtue of the existing laws, declared the torture at an end, I then saw one of the first servants of the Church fling aside his sacred robe, and then the priest of God became changed into a common executioner, who, with bloodthirsty pleasure, lacerated afresh the mangled body of the young maiden, and, more barbarous than the racksmen, relentlessly broke and tore asunder the limbs which the latter had only forced into their screws. Your majesty will allow me to abstain from any further depicting this scene of horror. Trembling and sick at heart, I fled from that terrible spot, and returned to my chamber with a sad and weary spirit."

She ceased, and sank exhausted into her chair.

A breathless silence ensued. The faces of all were pale and colorless; Gardiner and Wriothesley looked gloomy and defiant, expecting that the anger of the king, breaking forth with terrible vehemence would crush and overwhelm them.

But the king scarcely bestowed a thought upon them; he thought only of his young and beautiful queen, whose daring imposed upon him, and whose innocence and purity filled him with proud and blissful joy.

He was therefore inclined to pardon those who in reality had only been culpable in having too exactly and too strictly fulfilled the commands of their master.

A long pause had once more ensued—a pause full of anxious expectation for all who were assembled in the saloon. Katharine alone seemed quite composed as she sat in her chair, and looked across with a beaming countenance toward Thomas Seymour, whose handsome features betrayed the pleasure and satisfaction which he felt at this explanation of her mysterious nocturnal wandering.

At length the king rose up, and, with a profound obeisance to the queen, he said with a loud, full-toned voice: "I have done you deep and grievous wrong, my noble spouse, and as I have publicly accused you, I will also publicly request your pardon. You are justified in being angry with me; for it was my bounden duty to believe, with implicit and unwavering confidence, in the honor and fidelity of my queen. Madam, you have procured for yourself the most brilliant justification, and it now becomes me, the king, to bow before you, and to beg that you will forgive me, and impose on me a penance by way of atonement."

"Commit to me the task, my queen, of imposing penance on this repentant sinner!" cried John Heywood, gleefully. "Your majesty is much too generous and too faint-hearted to treat my brother, King Henry, as he deserves. Leave it therefore to me to punish him; for only the fool is wise enough to punish the king according to his deserts."

Katharine nodded to him with a grateful smile. She quite understood the tenderness and the fine tact of John Heywood; she knew that he wished by means of a jest to relieve her from this delicate situation, and to bring to a conclusion this public acknowledgment of the king, which would otherwise tend to an inward reproach for herself.

"Well," she replied, smiling, "and what punishment would you then award the king?"

"That he should acknowledge the fool to be one of his own sort!"

"God is my witness that I do so!" cried the king, with an air of solemnity. "Fools we are one and all, while we lack the glory which men accord to us."

"But that's not all my sentence, brother!" continued John Heywood. "I further condemn you, King Henry, to have my poem recited in your presence, and to lend your ears, that you may hear what John Heywood, the Wise, has composed!"

"Then thou hast fulfilled my command, and written a new interlude?" cried the king, with vivacity.

"Not an interlude, king, but quite a new and merry sort of matter—a jest-and-scandal play, which will make your eyes open—not with tears I hope, but with laughter. To our most noble Earl of Surrey belongs the proud fame of having presented our happy England with the first sonnets; well, then, I too will give it something new, by presenting it with the first comedy; and as he celebrates the beauty of his 'GERALDINE,' so will I celebrate the fame of 'GAMMER GURTON'S NEEDLE!' which is the name of my new piece, and you, King Henry, shall hear it as the punishment for your sins."

"I will do so," cried the king, cheerfully, "provided that you allow it, Kate! But before I do so, I also will make another condition—a condition for you, my queen! You have scorned, Kate, to impose a penance on me, but at least you must grant me the pleasure of being allowed to fulfil some wish for your sake! Mention some request which I am to grant you!"

"Well, then, my lord and king," said Katharine with a bewitching smile, "I beg that you will no longer remember the incidents of this day, and that you will pardon those whom I have only accused because their accusation was my justification. Those who made charges against me, have at this moment had penance awarded them for their own offence. Let that suffice my king, and pardon them as I do!"

"You are always a noble and generous woman, Kate," cried the king; and while his glance was directed at Gardiner with an expression of contempt, he continued: "your request is granted! But woe to those who shall again dare to accuse you!

And have you nothing more to ask, Kate?"

"One thing more, my lord and husband!" She bent forward close to the king's ear, and whispered: "They have accused your noblest and most faithful servant, Cranmer. Do not condemn him, my lord, without having first heard him, and if I have to request a favor of you it is this—speak to Cranmer yourself. Tell him what he is charged with, and listen to his justification."

"It shall be as you wish, Kate," replied the king, "and you shall yourself be present. But let this be our secret, Kate, and we will accomplish the matter quietly.—And now, John Heywood, let us hear your comedy, and woe betide you if it does not fulfil your promise of making us laugh! For you are well aware that in that case you have fallen a hopeless victim to the scourges of our offended ladies."

"They shall flog me to death if I don't make them laugh!" cried John Heywood, gracefully, as he produced his manuscript.

Soon the hall once more resounded with loud laughter, and amid the general mirth it was not observed that Bishop Gardiner and Lord Douglas had slunk quietly out of the saloon.

For some time they continued standing outside in the anteroom, and gazed at each other with mute dismay. Their looks betokened the anger and chagrin which inwardly filled them, and they mutually understood the unspoken language expressed in each other's features.

"She must die!" said Gardiner, with sententious brevity. "She has slipped through our nets for once; but the second time we shall be careful to tie our knots more securely!"

"And I hold the threads in my hand already from which we shall weave those nets," said Lord Douglas. "To-day we had falsely accused her of amorous intrigues. When we do so again we shall have told the truth. Did you not observe the looks which Katharine exchanged with the heretical Thomas Seymour, Lord Sudley?"

"Yes, I perceived them."

"Those looks will be her death, my lord. The queen loves Thomas Seymour, and this love will seal her doom."

"Amen," responded Bishop Gardiner, solemnly, as he directed his looks piously toward heaven. "Amen! The queen has this day bitterly and grievously offended us. She has insulted and abused us before the whole court. She shall one day indemnify us for this. The torture-chamber, which she painted with such lively colors, may also open its doors for her one day—not that she may witness the agonies of others, but that she may suffer those agonies herself. We shall one day be revenged!"

BOOK IV.

THE WOMEN'S WAR.

CHAPTER I.

THE REVENGE.

MISS HOLLAND, the beautiful and much-admired mistress of the Duke of Norfolk, was alone in her richly-adorned boudoir. It was the hour when the duke usually paid his visits; she had therefore attired herself in her most attractive manner—in the loose, flowing *négligé* which the duke so much admired, as it enhanced the charms and the graceful form of his fair friend.

But on this day he had not appeared; instead of himself, his chamberlain had come, and had brought Miss Holland a note from the duke. She held this note in her hand, as, with hasty and impatient steps, she paced her boudoir backward and forward. Her cheeks glowed, and her large, haughty eyes shot forth flames of anger.

She was cast off, and had to endure the outrage of being rejected by her lordly lover.

There it stood, in the letter which she held in her hand, and which scorched her fingers like a burning coal,—there stood the announcement written, that he would see her no more—that he renounced her love, and had given her up.

Her whole form trembled as these thoughts rushed through her mind. It was not the pain of lost love that shook her frame; it was the mortified pride of her woman's nature.

He had forsaken her. No longer had her youth and beauty the power of captivating that white-haired old man with wrinkled features.

He had written her that it was not of her, but only of love, that he had grown weary; that his heart had become old and withered like his face, and that there was no longer any room left in his breast for love, but only for ambition.

Was not this a most revolting and unheard-of outrage? To forsake the most beautiful woman in England for the sake of some cold, calculating, and wretched ambition!

She opened the letter once more, and

once more perused the passage; and said, with tears in her eyes, while she gnashed her teeth—"He shall repent this! I'll be revenged for this insult!"

She thrust the letter into her bosom, and touched her silver bell.

"Let my carriage be got ready," she said, addressing the servant who entered at her summons, and who bowed in silence to her command.

"I'll be revenged," she murmured, as she wrapped herself in her shawl of Turkish fabric. "I'll be revenged; and I take Heaven to witness that it shall be a speedy and a bloody revenge! I'll show him that I, too, am ambitious, and that my pride won't bend. He said he would forget me, but I'll compel him to think of me, even though it were only to curse me."

With rapid steps she hastened through the brilliant apartments which the liberality of her admirer had so gorgeously decorated, and descended to her carriage, which already awaited her.

"To the Duchess of Norfolk's," she said, addressing the footman who approached the carriage door to receive her commands.

The servant looked at her with inquiring astonishment.

"You mean the Duke of Norfolk's, madam?"

"Certainly not. I mean the Duchess of Norfolk's," she replied, with a frown of displeasure, as she flung herself back in her seat.

After a short time the carriage stopped before the mansion of the duchess, and with a commanding air and haughty step Miss Holland entered the vestibule.

"Announce me immediately to the duchess," was her command to the servant who hastened forward at her approach.

"Your name, madam."

"Miss Arabella Holland."

The servant started back, and stared at her with visible amazement. "Miss Arabella Holland? And you wish me to announce you to her grace?"

A faint smile of contempt played for a moment around her thin lips. "I see you know me," she replied, "and you are a little surprised at seeing me here. Wonder as you will, my good friend, only conduct me at once to the duchess."

"I doubt if her grace receives visitors to-day," stammered the man, with hesitation.

"Well, go and ask her, and in order that I may know her answer without delay, I shall follow you myself."

With an air of command she directed the servant to precede her, and he had not the courage to gainsay the proud beauty.

They passed along in silence through the principal apartments, and at length stood before a door hung with curtains.

"I must beg you to remain here a moment, madam," said the servant, "while I go and announce you to the duchess, who is inside here in her boudoir."

"Never mind, pray—I'll undertake this duty myself," replied Miss Holland, forcibly pushing the man aside, as she opened the door.

The duchess was seated at her writing-table, with her back toward the door through which Arabella had entered. She did not move from her place, not having perceived the door open. She went on quietly writing.

Miss Holland walked with a firm and haughty step through the chamber until she stood close by the chair of the duchess.

"My lady duchess," she said, in a tone of calm self-possession, "I wish to speak to you."

The duchess, with a cry of surprise, looked up. "Miss Holland!" she exclaimed, suddenly rising from her seat. "What! you here beside me? in my own house? Pray what brings you here? How dare you attempt to cross my threshold?"

"I see, duchess, you still hate me, as you have always done," said Arabella, smiling. "You have not yet forgiven me that your husband, the duke, found more delight in my face, which is young and beautiful, than in yours, which is old and faded; that my lively sallies and whimsical conceits pleased him more than your cold reserve and conventional propriety."

The duchess grew pale with rage, and her eyes flashed with scorn. "Silence!" she exclaimed. "Silence! shameless woman, or I shall call my servants to rid me of your presence."

"You will not do so, for I have come to conciliate you, and to offer you peace."

"Peace with you!" returned the duchess, with derisive contempt. "Peace with an abandoned creature who robbed me of my husband—the father of my children; who exposed me to the reproach of standing before the whole world as a despised and rejected wife, that I might be compared with you, in order to decide which of us both was the most worthy of his love. Peace with you, indeed! with an insolent paramour, who with wanton prodigality dissipates my husband's fortune, and plunders my children of their lawful inheritance, with infamous effrontery!"

"True indeed, the duke is very generous," said Miss Holland, calmly. "He overwhelms me with jewels and with gold."

"For which I am forced almost to suffer want," returned the duchess, with bitter emphasis.

"Want of love, perhaps, my lady duchess, but not want of money; for you are luxuriously provided for, and it is well known that the Duchess of Norfolk is rich enough to dispense with the trifles which her husband flings at my feet. By Heaven, my lady, I would not have thought it worth while to stoop for them, if amongst these trifles I had not also seen his heart. The heart of a man is well worth the trouble of stooping for it. This you had neglected to do, and for that reason you lost your husband's heart. I picked it up—that is all. Why will you impute this to me as a crime?"

"Enough!" exclaimed the duchess. "It does not become me to dispute with you, and I only desire to know how you have had the hardihood to come to me."

"Well, my lady duchess, and do you hate me only, or do you also hate the duke your husband?"

"She asks me if I hate him!" cried the duchess, with a burst of scornful laughter. "Yes, Miss Holland, I hate him as thoroughly as I despise you. I hate him so much that I would give all I possess—nay, years of my life—if I could only punish him for the outrage which he has offered me."

"Then in that case we shall soon understand each other, for I also hate him," said Miss Holland, as she quietly took a seat on the velvet-covered ottoman and smiled at witnessing the speechless astonishment of the duchess.

"Yes, my lady, I hate him, and doubtless more intensely and more fiercely than you do yourself, for I am young and ardent, while you are old, and have always known how to keep your heart free from emotion."

The duchess quivered with suppressed rage, but she silently swallowed the drop of gall with which her malicious rival had flavored the cup of joy.

"You say you hate him, Miss Holland?" she asked, with evident satisfaction.

"Yes, I hate him, and I have come to league myself with you against him. He is a faithless man, a perjurer—a traitor, and I have resolved to be revenged for the injury which he has done me."

"Ah, then he has forsaken you too?"

"Yes, he has forsaken me too."

"Thank God!" exclaimed the duchess, and her face beamed with delight. "God is great and just, and He has punished you with the instrument of your own guilt. It was for your sake that he left me, and now he gives you up for the sake of some other woman."

"Not so, my lady duchess!" said Miss Holland, proudly. "A woman like me is not given up for the sake of another, and whoever loves me will love no one else after me. There, read his letter!"

Saying which, she handed to the duchess the letter of her husband.

"And what do you propose doing now?" asked the duchess, as she finished reading the letter.

"I'll take revenge, my lady! He says he has no longer a heart with which to love; well, then, we shall see that he has no longer a head with which to think. Will your grace consent to be my ally?"

"I will."

"And I too," said the Duchess of Richmond, who at this moment opened the door of the adjoining apartment and entered the room.

Not a word of this conversation had escaped her, and she understood quite well that the question was not one of petty revenge, but one which placed her father's head in jeopardy. She knew that Miss Holland was not one of those women who when provoked prick with a needle, but one who would seize a dagger and stab her enemy to the heart.

"Yes, I, too, will be your ally," cried the Duchess of Richmond. "We have all three been injured by the same man. Let our revenge therefore be taken in common. You both have been outraged by the father, and I by the son. Well, then, I shall help you to bring down the father, if you will lend your assistance to annihilate the son."

"Oh, I will assist you," said Arabella, smiling, "for I also hate the proud Earl of Surrey, who parades his virtue as if it were the order of the Golden Fleece, which God himself had fastened to his breast; I hate him because he has always treated me with haughty contempt, and he alone is to blame for the faithlessness of his father."

"I was present when he besought the duke our father with tears, to escape from the thraldom in which you held him, and to give up his disgraceful and dishonorable connection with you," said the young duchess.

Arabella made no reply. But she clasped her hands firmly together, and a slight pallor overspread her cheeks.

"And why are you angry with your brother?" asked the old duchess, with a thoughtful air.

"Why am I angry with him, you ask? I am not angry with him, but I detest him, and I have made a vow never to rest until I have had my revenge. My happiness, my heart, my future, lay in his hands, and he has mercilessly trodden these most precious treasures of his sister under his proud feet. It lay with him to make me the wife of the man I love, and he has not done so—although I besought him with tears and supplications on my bended knees."

"But the sacrifice which you demanded of him was a great one," said her mother. "It was nothing less than to bestow his hand on a woman he did not love, in order that you might become the wife of Thomas Seymour."

"You are defending him, mother, and yet it is he who daily accuses you—nay, it was only yesterday that he thought it quite natural and right that the duke had forsaken you."

"He thought that?" said the duchess, fiercely. "Then he has forgotten that I am his mother, and in my turn I shall forget that he is my son. I am your confederate. Revenge for our wounded feelings! Revenge on father and son!"

She held out both her hands, and the two younger women placed their hands within hers.

"Revenge on father and son!" they both repeated, and their eyes flashed, and a crimson blush suffused their cheeks.

"I am tired of living here like a recluse in my palace, banished from court through fear of meeting my husband there."

"You are not likely to meet him there again, mother," returned her daughter, laconically.

"People shall not have it in their power to laugh at and mock me; and when they know that he has left me, they shall know at the same time the revenge I took for it."

"Thomas Seymour cannot be my husband so long as Henry Howard lives, for he has mortally offended him, inasmuch as Henry Howard has rejected the hand of his sister. Perhaps I may become his wife when Henry Howard is no more," said the young duchess. "Let us therefore consider how we shall manage to take a sure aim, so as to bring them both down together."

"When three women are of one mind they may be certain of gaining their end," said Arabella, with a knowing glance. "We live, thank God, under a noble and magnanimous king, who regards the blood of his subjects with as much indifference as he does the purple of his royal robes, and who never shrinks back from signing a death-warrant."

"But on this occasion he will shrink back," said the old duchess. "He will not venture to deprive the noblest and most powerful men in his kingdom of their heads."

"It is just such an enterprise which will provoke him," replied Lady Richmond, smiling; "and the more difficult it is to remove these heads, the more impatiently will he strive to effect that object. The king hates them both, and he will thank us for converting his hatred into retributive justice."

"Then let us both lay an accusation of high-treason against him," cried Arabella. "The duke is a traitor, for I can and will prove that he has often enough called the king a bloodthirsty monster and a merciless tyrant—a man who has neither honor nor faith—although he makes pretence to be the source and stronghold of all faith."

"If he has said so, and that you heard it, you are bound to make it known to the king, unless you wish to be the accomplice of high-treason yourself," exclaimed the young duchess, with solemn emphasis.

"And have you not observed that for some time past the duke bears the same arms as the king?" asked the Duchess of Norfolk. "It does not, forsooth, suffice for his proud and ambitious mind to be the first subject in the realm, but he must needs strive to become its king and ruler."

"Tell the king so, and to-morrow morning the traitor's head falls. The king is as jealous of his kingdom as ever woman was of the man she held most dear. Only tell him that the duke bears his royal arms, and his ruin is certain."

"I shall tell him so, my daughter."

"Now we are sure of the father, but how shall we deal with the son?"

"By certain infallible means which will send him to eternity as surely as the hunter's bullet sends the proudest stag its death-wound. Henry loves the queen, and I shall convey proof thereof to the king," said the young duchess.

"Then let us go at once to the king!" cried Arabella, impatiently.

"No, not yet! That would cause suspicion, and might frustrate our whole plan," rejoined the duchess. "Let us speak to Lord Douglas first and hear his opinion. Come, every minute is precious! We owe it to our honor as women to be avenged. We ought not and will not leave unpunished those who despised our love, mortified our honor, and trampled under foot the holiest ties of nature."

CHAPTER II.

ACKNOWLEDGED.

SAD and self-contemplative sat the Princess Elizabeth in her chamber. Her eyes were red with tears, and she pressed her hand to her heart, as if to stifle the painful emotions that were struggling for utterance.

With a cheerless and wandering gaze she looked around the room, and its loneliness on the present occasion made her doubly sad, for it bore witness to her own forlorn condition, and to the disgrace which still rested upon her. Had it been otherwise, this day would have been a day of congratulations and rejoicing for the whole court.

This was Elizabeth's birthday. On this day fourteen years the daughter of Anne Bullen had been ushered into life.

Anne Bullen's daughter! That was the secret of her isolation—that was the reason why none of the lords or ladies of the court took any note of her birthday, for this would have been to call to mind Anne Bullen—Elizabeth's beautiful but unhappy mother—who had to pay the penalty of her greatness and exalted rank with her life-blood.

Besides this, too, the king had already pronounced his daughter Elizabeth a bastard, and had solemnly declared her unworthy of succeeding to the crown.

Her birthday was accordingly a day of sorrow and humiliation for Elizabeth. Reclining upon her ottoman, she bethought her of the contumely and joylessness of her past life, and of the dreary and cheerless future that lay before her.

She was a princess, and yet did not possess her birthright; she was a young maiden, and yet doomed to renounce all the pleasures and enjoyments of her youth, and to stifle the yearnings of her ardent and passionate nature in perpetual silence. For when the Infanta of Spain had sued for her hand, Henry the Eighth declared that his illegitimate daughter Elizabeth was unworthy of a princely husband. And in order to repulse any other suitors, he had declared loudly and publicly that no subject should dare be so rash as to make advances to any royal daughter of his, at the risk of being punished as a traitor.

Thus Elizabeth was condemned to remain unmarried, and yet she loved and cherished but one thought, that of becoming the wife of her beloved, and of being one day able to exchange her proud title of princess for the more lowly one of Countess of Seymour.

Ever since her love began, a new world, a new sun had dawned upon her, and, in presence of the sweet and enchanting whispers of love, the haughty and alluring voice of ambition itself was forced to be silent. She ceased to reflect that she should never be a queen, and was troubled with the sole thought that she could not be the wife of Seymour.

She had no longer a wish to rule—she only wished to be happy. But then her happiness rested in him alone—in Thomas Seymour.

These were her thoughts on the morning of her birthday, as she sat in her chamber, lonely and alone; while her eyes, red with tears, and her lips, pale and quivering, betrayed how much she had this day wept, and how much this youthful girl of fourteen had already suffered.

But she determined to think no more on this subject, and not to afford the watchful, prying, and malicious courtiers who surrounded her, the triumph of seeing the traces of tears upon her countenance, and of rejoicing in her suffering and humiliation. Hers was a proud and resolute spirit. She would rather have died than have accepted the pity of those haughty courtiers.

"I will work," she said. "Labor is the best balm for sorrow."

And she took up the elaborate embroidery which she had commenced for her poor, unhappy friend, Anne of Cleves, the rejected spouse of Henry. But the work occupied her fingers only, not her thoughts.

She flung it aside, and seized a book. It was the Sonnets of Petrarch, and his plaintive woes soothed while they moved her own love-sick spirit.

Her eyes streaming with tears, and yet smiling and filled with a sweet sadness, Elizabeth read those beautiful and pathetic strains of the great Italian poet. It seemed to her as if Petrarch had only expressed what she herself had so warmly felt. These were her own thoughts, her own sorrows. He had given utterance to them in his native language—she would now repeat them in her own. She accordingly seized a pen, and, while her hands trembled with sensibility, and wholly carried away by the glowing emotions of inspiration and delight, she began the translation of the first sonnet of Petrarch.

A loud knock interrupted her, and through the suddenly-opened door advanced the stately and graceful form of Katharine.

"The queen!" exclaimed Elizabeth, joyfully. "How kind of you to come to me so early in the morning!"

"Should I then have waited until evening to wish my Elizabeth joy on her birthday—should I first have allowed the sun to go down on this day, which has given to England so noble and lovely a princess?" asked Katharine; "or did you perchance think I had forgotten that this is your birthday, and that my Elizabeth on this day bids farewell to the years of childhood, and commences her career as a proud and hopeful maiden?"

"Hopeful?" said Elizabeth, sadly. "The daughter of Anne Bullen has no hopes, and when you speak of my birthday you remind me at the same time of the disgrace attached to my birth."

"It shall no longer be so!" exclaimed Katharine, and, putting her arm affectionately round Elizabeth's neck, she placed a small roll of parchment in her hands.

"Take this document, Elizabeth, and may it be to you the promise of a happy and brilliant future! The king, at my request, has granted this patent, and he has at the same time accorded me the pleasure of bringing it to you myself."

Elizabeth opened the parchment, and when she had read it, an expression of beaming delight overspread her countenance.

"Acknowledged! I am acknowledged!" she exclaimed. "The stigma of my birth has been removed. Elizabeth is no longer illegitimate—she is a royal princess!"

"And she may one day become a queen!" added Katharine, smiling.

"Oh," cried Elizabeth, "that is not what makes me feel so happy! But the stigma has been taken away from me, and now I can hold up my head freely, and mention the name of my mother without shame. Oh, mother, my own mother!—Thou canst now rest peacefully in thy grave, for it is no longer dishonored! Anne Bullen was no royal mistress, she was King Henry's lawful wife, and Elizabeth is her king's lawful daughter. I thank Thee, my God! I thank Thee!"

And the young, enthusiastic girl flung herself on her knees, and lifted her hands and eyes to heaven.

"Spirit of my sainted mother," she continued, in accents of solemn emotion, "I call upon thee! Oh, come to me, and overshadow me with thy smile, and bless me with thy breath! Queen Anne of England, thy daughter is no longer base-born, and no one shall henceforth dare to asperse her. Thou wast near me, mother, when I wept and suffered, and often in my disgrace and humiliation I felt as if I heard thy voice whispering comfort to me—as if I saw thine own angelic eyes shedding beams of peace and love into my heart! Oh, stay with me now, too, mother—now that the stigma is removed from me; stay with me in the day of prosperity, and watch over my heart, that it may be kept free from pride and arrogance, and may still continue humble in good fortune! Anne Bullen, they once laid thy innocent and beautiful head upon the block, but this parchment-scroll replaces the royal crown upon that head, and woe, woe to those who shall dare to insult thy memory!"

She suddenly rose from her knees, and rushed toward the wall opposite, on which hung a large oil painting, which represented herself as a little child playing with a dog.

"Oh, mother, mother!" she exclaimed, "this picture was the last earthly object on which thy looks rested, and upon the inanimate lips of thy child here painted thou didst bestow the last kiss, which thy cruel persecutors would not suffer the living child to receive.

"Oh, let me drink away this kiss from the canvas, let my lips touch the spot which thine have sanctified!"

She bent forward and kissed the picture with tenderness and rapture.

"And now come forth from thy grave, my mother," she continued, solemnly. "I have so long been obliged to hide and cover thee up. Once more thou mayst see the world and the light of day! The king has acknowledged me to be his lawful daughter, and he cannot refuse to have the picture of my own mother in my room."

So saying, she pressed a spring inserted in the gold frame of the picture, which suddenly moved and opened like a door, disclosing to view another picture concealed behind, which represented the hapless Anne Bullen in her bridal robes, in the full splendor of youth and beauty, as Holbein had painted her, at the desire of King Henry her husband.

"What a beautiful and angelic face!" said Katharine, approaching. "What pure and innocent features! And yet, unhappy queen, thy enemies succeeded in fixing suspicion upon thee, and leading thee to the scaffold. Alas, when I look at thee I shudder, and my own future rises before me like a threatening spectre. Who can be safe and free from danger, when Anne Bullen was not safe, but was doomed to suffer an ignominious death? Ah, believe me, Elizabeth, it is a melancholy fate to be Queen of England, and many a time have I asked myself in the morning if I should still be greeted as queen in the evening. We must not, however, speak of me at the present moment, but only of you, Elizabeth—of your future, and of your happiness. May this parchment prove acceptable to you, and may it be the means of realizing all the wishes that slumber in your bosom!"

"One great wish it has already fulfilled," said Elizabeth, still intently gazing on the picture—"it gives me the privilege of uncovering the portrait of my mother. That I might be able to do so one day was her last prayer, and the last wish which she charged John Heywood to convey to me. To him she committed this picture for me. He alone knew the secret of its hiding-place, which secret he has faithfully kept."

"Oh, John Heywood is a trusty and a true friend," said Katharine, earnestly, "and it was he who assisted me to incline the king's mind to our projects, and move him at a favorable moment to acknowledge you."

Elizabeth seized the hand of her friend with an expression of unspeakable delight. "To you," she said, "I owe my own honor and the honor of my mother; I shall always love you as a daughter for it, and never shall your enemies find in me a ready listener or an adherent. Let us both enter into a mutual league, offensive and defensive! Let us keep true to each other, and the enemies of the one shall be the enemies of the other, and whenever we see danger we will oppose it in common, and with the faithful eyes of sisters we shall watch over and warn each other, if any accidental gleam of light should reveal to us an enemy who may be lurking in the dark, ready to stab us unawares with his dagger."

"Be it so!" said Katharine, earnestly. "We will stand by one another faithfully and inseparably, and love each other like sisters."

And pressing an affectionate kiss on the lips of Elizabeth, she continued: "But now, princess, turn your attention once more to that parchment, of which you have as yet only read the beginning. Believe me, it is of sufficient importance for you to read it to the end; for it contains various provisions respecting your future welfare, and appoints for you an annual income and a household suitable to the rank of a royal princess."

"Oh, what care I for such things!" cried Elizabeth, gayly. "That's my steward's concern—let him look after those matters."

"But there is still another paragraph which will interest you even more," said Katharine with a sweet smile, "for there is a new and complete reparation of honor for my proud and ambitious Elizabeth. Do you remember the answer which your father gave the King of France, when the latter made suit for your hand for his son the dauphin?"

"Do I remember it?" cried Elizabeth, as her brow became suddenly clouded. "King Henry said that the daughter of Anne Bullen was not worthy to receive the hand of a royal prince."

"Well then, Elizabeth, in order that the restoration of honor in your favor shall be complete, the king, in conferring upon you your rightful title and dignity, has decreed that you should only espouse a husband of equal birth with your own, and that you cannot bestow your hand upon any other than a prince of royal blood, if you would preserve your right of succession to the throne. Indeed, there could be no more complete reparation for the former wrong done you; and for the king's having consented to do so you are indebted to the eloquent pleading of a faithful and trusty friend—I mean John Heywood."

"John Heywood!" cried Elizabeth, in an angry tone. "Oh, I thank you, queen, that it was not you who determined my father to make this decree. What! John Heywood has done so, and yet you call him my friend? You say that he is a true and devoted servant to us both? Beware of his fidelity, queen, and build not upon his devotedness, for I tell you his heart is filled with deceit, and while he appears to bow humbly before you, his eyes are only seeking for a vulnerable spot to strike a sure and deadly blow. Ah, he is a serpent—a venomous serpent—and he has just inflicted upon me an incurable and mortal wound.

"But no," she continued, with energy, "I shall not submit to this wily artifice—I will not be the slave of this untoward decree! I wish to be free to love or to hate as my heart dictates. I will not suffer myself to be chained down and compelled to renounce the man I might love, and to marry one whom I should perhaps loathe and detest."

With a look of firm and resolute decision she took the roll of parchment and handed it back to Katharine.

"Take back this parchment, queen, and return it to my father again, and tell him that I thank him for his considerate kindness, but that I renounce the brilliant destiny which this act offers me. I love liberty so well that even a royal crown cannot entice me, if I am to receive it with shackled hands and with a heart no longer free!"

"Poor child," said Katharine, with a sigh, "you little know how a royal crown always surrounds us with chains, and compels us to wear cramping-irons on our hearts. Ah, you would be free, and still be a queen! Trust me, Elizabeth, there are none who are less at liberty than crowned heads; there are none who have less right or power to dispose of their hearts than princes."

"Then in that case," cried Elizabeth, with flashing eyes, "I renounce the dreary prospect of perhaps one day becoming a queen. In that case I must reject the decree which would bind my affections and control my will. What, the daughter of King Henry of England suffer her course to be prescribed by a paltry sheet of parchment, or allow her heart and her actions to be hampered for life by a wretched brief? I am a royal princess, and therefore I am to be compelled, forsooth, to bestow my hand upon none other than a royal prince? Yes, you were right—it was not my father who laid down this law; for his own proud spirit would never brook the constraint of such miserable etiquette. He loved as his inclinations directed, and no Parliament or law had power to prevent him. I intend to be the true daughter of my father in this respect. I won't submit to this decree!"

"Poor child," returned Katharine, "you will nevertheless have to learn to submit—for one cannot be a princess with impunity. People never ask if our hearts bleed. They throw a purple robe around us, and if this should be crimsoned with our heart's blood, who is there to perceive or suspect it? You are still so very young, Elizabeth, and you still hope for so much!"

"I hope for so much because I have already suffered so much—I have already been forced to shed so many tears. Already, in my childhood, I was compelled to take my share of the sorrows and sufferings of life in advance of my age, and now I shall determine for myself my portion of life's happiness and enjoyment."

"And who has told you that you shall not have it? This law, in reality, imposes upon you no particular husband; it only gives you the proud and once-disputed right of choosing for yourself a husband from among the sons of kings."

"Oh," cried Elizabeth, and her eyes flashed, "if I were really to become a queen one day, I should feel prouder in choosing a husband whom I could raise to a throne, than one who could place a crown on my own head. You will own, Katharine, that it must be a proud and happy privilege to bestow greatness and splendor on the being that we love, and in the fulness of our love to elevate him above all other men, and humbly to lay down at his feet our own greatness and majesty, in order that he may invest himself therewith, and appropriate as his own what had been ours!"

"I vow," said Katharine, smiling, "you are as proud and ambitious as a man. The true daughter of your father! So thought Henry when he gave his hand to Anne Bullen,—so thought he, too, when he raised me to be his queen. But it becomes him to think and to act so, for he is a man."

"He thought so because he loved—not because he was a man."

"And you also, Elizabeth—you think so because, perhaps, you love?"

"Yes, I love!" cried Elizabeth, as she flung herself with violent emotion into Katharine's arms, and hid her blushing cheeks on the queen's bosom. "Yes, I love! And my love is like that of my father—not regarding my rank or birth, but only feeling that my beloved is my equal in all that constitutes true nobility of mind and spirit, and in greatness of soul; that he is superior to me in all those noble and lofty qualities which should adorn a man, and yet which are accorded to so few. Judge, therefore, queen, if this decree can make me happy. The man whom I love is not a prince—he is not the son of a king."

"My poor Elizabeth!" said Katharine, embracing the young girl tenderly in her arms.

"And why do you pity me, since it is in your power to make me happy?" asked Elizabeth, urgently. "It was you who moved the king to free me from the stigma that rested upon me. You will also have influence over him to annul this clause, which contains the sentence of doom for my heart."

Katharine shook her head with a sigh. "My power does not extend so far," she replied, sorrowfully. "Ah, Elizabeth, why had you no confidence in me? why did you not inform me sooner of this love which you cherish, and which is at variance with this decree? Why did you not acquaint your friend with this dangerous secret?"

"It is just because it is dangerous that I withheld it from you, and for this reason, too, I cannot now inform you of the name of my beloved. Through my means, at least, you shall not become liable to the guilt of high-treason toward your husband; for you are well aware that he punishes every secret not revealed to him, as a treasonable crime. No, queen, if I am culpable, you shall not be my accomplice. It is always dangerous to be the confidante of such a secret. That you may see in the case of John Heywood. He alone was my confidant, and he betrayed me. It was I myself who put the weapons into his hands, and he turned them against me."

"No, no," said Katharine, thoughtfully, "John Heywood is faithful and trustworthy, and incapable of any treachery."

"He has betrayed me," cried Elizabeth, angrily. "He alone knew that I loved, and that my lover, although of noble, is still not of princely birth. And, yet it was he who, as you tell me, moved the king to introduce this clause into the act of succession."

"Then, doubtless, he only wished to save you from an error of feeling or judgment."

"No, he feared to possess the dangerous knowledge of this secret; and, at the cost of my happiness and affections, he wished to obviate this danger. But oh, Katharine, you at least are noble, generous, and firm—you are incapable of such petty fears and base calculations; help me, therefore; be my deliverer and protectress. By virtue of the vow which we have already pledged to each other, by virtue of that alliance into which we have mutually entered, I call upon you to aid and assist me. Oh, Katharine, grant me the proud and blissful happiness of being enabled one day, perhaps, to make him whom I love great and powerful through my own will—grant me the intoxicating joy of being able to offer to his ambition, with my own hand, power and splendor, and perhaps even a crown. Oh, Katharine, on my knees I implore you, help me to overthrow this odious decree, which binds my heart and hand!"

With impassioned emotion she had flung herself on her knees before the queen, and she now lifted her hands in an attitude of supplication.

Katharine bent, smiling, over her, and raised her up in her arms. "Enthusiast!" she said—"poor young enthusiast! Who knows if you would one day thank me were I to grant your request; nay, you might curse the hour which, instead of the hoped-for happiness, should have brought you delusion and sorrow!"

"Even though it were so," cried Elizabeth, with energy, "it is better to bear self-chosen misfortune, than to be coerced into happiness. Say, Katharine, say, will you succor me? Will you urge the king to retract this hateful clause? If you will not, I swear, queen, by the spirit of my mother, that I will not obey the law, that I will solemnly and before all the world renounce the privileges offered me, and that I—"

"You are a dear, foolish child," interrupted Katharine, "a child which, in youthful self-will, would be rash enough to bring down lightning from heaven, and even to borrow thunderbolts from Jove himself. Yes, you are very young and inexperienced not to know that Fate heeds not our sighs or murmurs, and despite our struggles or gainsaying, it will only lead us the way it chooses, and not that which we prefer. You will yet have to learn that, poor child!"

"But I will not!" cried Elizabeth, stamping on the floor with all the waywardness of a child. "I will not be evermore and eternally the victim of another's caprice; and even Fate itself shall not make me its slave."

"Well, we shall see," said Katharine, smiling. "At all events we will try for this time to fight against Fate; and I shall assist you if I can."

"Then I shall love you as my mother and my sister, if you will," cried Elizabeth, as she flung herself with impassioned tenderness into Katharine's arms. "Yes, I shall love you for this, and I shall pray God to give me the opportunity of one day proving to you my gratitude, and of rewarding you for your generosity and kindness."

CHAPTER III.

INTRIGUES.

For some days past the king's sufferings from his feet had grown worse, and, much to his discomfiture and anger, had confined him a prisoner in his armchair carriage.

It was therefore very natural that the king should be sullen and morose, and that he should hurl the lightning of his anger at all those who enjoyed the melancholy preëminence of being near his person. His sufferings, so far from subduing his temper, only served to increase his natural ferocity, and ever and anon might be heard echoing through the chambers of Whitehall palace the furious bellowings of the king, and his loud invectives, which now spared no one, regardless of rank or dignity.

Lord Douglas, Gardiner, and Wriothesley understood quite well how to turn this angry mood of the king to account, and to procure for the pain-stricken monarch, at least, some compensation for his suffering, namely—the satisfaction of making others suffer also.

Never had so many scaffolds been seen in England, as in these days of the king's illness—never had the dungeons been so filled with victims—never had so much blood been shed, as King Henry now caused to flow.

But all this did not yet suffice to appease the anger and thirst for blood of the king—of his friends, counsellors, and priests.

There still remained two powerful mainstays of Protestantism, which Gardiner and Wriothesley had resolved to overthrow—these were the queen and Archbishop Cranmer.

There were still two powerful and hated enemies whom the Seymours had to vanquish, and these were the Duke of Norfolk, and his son, the Earl of Surrey.

But the different parties, who, by turns, besieged and commanded the ear of the king, were at once inflamed with the most singular hostility, and with the bitterest animosity toward each other, and mutually strove to supplant one another in the king's good graces.

To the popish party of Gardiner and Lord Douglas, it was all-important to oust the Seymours from the king's favor, and these, in their turn, wished above all things to keep in their power the young queen, who was inclined toward them, and to destroy the Duke of Norfolk, one of the most powerful chiefs of the papal side.

The one party commanded the ear of the king through the medium of the queen—the other through that of his favorite, Lord Douglas.

Never had the king been more gracious and kind to his consort—never had he stood more in need of the presence of Lord Douglas, than in those days of his illness and bodily suffering.

But there was yet a third party which held an important place in the king's favor—a power which everybody feared, and which appeared to keep itself wholly independent and free from all foreign influences. This power was John Heywood, the king's jester—the satirist dreaded by the whole court.

One person alone had influence over him. John Heywood was the friend of the queen. For the moment, therefore, it seemed as if the "heretical party," of whom the queen was regarded as the head, was the most powerful at court.

It was accordingly very natural that the papists should entertain the bitterest hatred against the queen—very natural that they should always contrive new plans and schemes to ruin her, and to hurl her from the throne.

But Katharine well knew the danger which threatened her, and she was on her guard. She kept watch over every word she uttered, and even over her looks; and Gardiner and Wriothesley could not scrutinize more searchingly, day by day, and hour by hour, the mode of life of the queen, than she did herself.

She saw the sword which daily hung over her head, and thanks to her prudence and presence of mind—thanks to the ever-active watchfulness and cunning of her friend John Heywood, she had always been able to ward off the impending sword.

Ever since the day of the eventful excursion to Epping Forest, she had not spoken to Thomas Seymour alone, for Katharine knew full well that on whatever side she turned her steps, some prying eye would follow her, and some lurking ear would penetrate, which would overhear her most softly-whispered words, and repeat them where they must be interpreted to her condemnation—to her death.

She had accordingly renounced the pleasure of speaking to her beloved, except before witnesses, or of seeing him, unless in the presence of her whole court.

But after all, what need had she of secret meetings—what did her pure and guileless heart seek, that she might not be with him alone? She was always at liberty to see him, and to imbibe fresh draughts of happiness and fortitude from the sight of his noble and handsome countenance; he was always free to be near her, and she could listen to the music of his words, and gladden her heart with the sound of his manly and sonorous voice.

Katharine, though a woman of eight-and-twenty, still possessed the enthusiasm and innocence of a young girl of sixteen. Thomas Seymour was her first love, and she loved him with that chaste and pure ardor which is peculiar to a first passion.

It, therefore, sufficed her to see him, to be near him, to know that he loved her—that he was faithful to her; that to her belonged all his thoughts, all his wishes,—as hers belonged to him.

All this she knew. For still there remained to her the sweet enjoyment of his letters—those impassioned declarations, those memorials of his love; and, though she could not tell him in words how ardently she returned his love, she yet could express her thoughts in writing.

It was John Heywood, the faithful and discreet friend, who brought those letters to her, who conveyed her answers back in return, and who, as the reward for these dangerous messages, only stipulated that both should regard him as the sole witness of their love, and that they should both destroy the letters which he brought them. He had not been able to prevent Katharine from yielding to this fatal passion, but he wished at least to preserve her from its deadly consequences. Knowing that her love required a confidant, he had assumed this character, in order that Katharine, in the ardent impetuosity of her innocent heart, should not make others the witnesses of her dangerous secret.

John Heywood accordingly watched over the safety and happiness of Katharine, as, in her turn, she watched over Thomas Seymour and her friends. He protected and defended her with the king, as she defended Cranmer, and protected him against the repeated attacks of his enemies.

That she had saved the noble and liberal-minded Archbishop of Canterbury from their toils, was what they could never forgive her. On more than one occasion, Katharine had succeeded in frustrating their wily plots, and in destroying the nets which Gardiner and Lord Douglas had so craftily and so adroitly spread for Cranmer.

If, then, they would overthrow Cranmer, they must first overthrow the queen. To this end there was a powerful means—a means of at once annihilating the queen and the detested Seymours, who stood in the way of the papists.

Could they but prove to the king that Katharine maintained culpable correspondence and relationships with Thomas Seymour, both were lost, and the power and supremacy of the papal party were secured.

But whence obtain the proofs of this dangerous secret, which the astute Lord Douglas had only read in Katharine's eyes, and for which he had no other grounds but his own impressions? By what means should the queen be moved to take some inconsiderate step, which would furnish speaking evidence of her love?

The king was growing so weary—it would be so easy to persuade him to some deed of atrocity—some speedy sentence of death!

But it was not the blood of the Seymours for which the king thirsted. This Lord Douglas well knew. He, who observed the king day and night, who probed and sounded his every sigh, his most softly-murmured words, every convulsive movement of his lips, every frown that passed over his brow,—he knew what dark and sanguinary thoughts were brooding in the king's mind, and whose the blood was for which he craved.

It was the blood of the Howards for which the royal tiger thirsted; and, that they still lived in health, and wealth, and splendor, while he, their king and master, rolled in pain and suffering upon his weary couch,—this was the worm which gnawed at the king's heart, which increased his pains, and made his sufferings more poignant.

The king was jealous—jealous of the power and greatness of the Howards. It filled him with morbid resentment to think that the Duke of Norfolk, when he rode through the streets of London, was everywhere greeted by the shouts and acclamations of the people, whilst he, their king, was a prisoner in his palace. It was to him an unceasing source of pain to know that Henry Howard, the Earl of Surrey, was regarded as the handsomest and the greatest man in

England, that he was looked upon as the most learned person and the most distinguished poet in the realm, although the king had himself written poems and learned dissertations,—nay—even had composed a devout treatise, which he had caused to be printed for the edification of his people, and which he had commanded them to read instead of the Bible.

Yes, it was the Howards who everywhere disputed his fame. The Howards supplanted him in the favor of his subjects, and usurped the love and admiration which were the king's exclusive right, and which none should dare to bestow upon any one save upon himself. There he lay upon his weary couch, and his people would doubtless have forgotten him, had he not daily put them in mind of his existence by means of the rack, the stake, and the scaffold; he lay upon his weary couch, while the duke, dazzling with magnificence and splendor, exhibited himself before the people, and excited their feelings in his favor by the lavish and princely munificence with which he scattered his gold amongst them.

Undoubtedly, the Duke of Norfolk was the king's dangerous rival. The crown was not secure upon his head so long as the Howards lived; and who could tell if the jubilant love of the people might not one day, when the king had closed his eyes, summon to the throne the Duke of Norfolk, or his noble son the Earl of Surrey, instead of the rightful heir—the boy Edward—Henry's only son?

Whenever these thoughts crossed the king's mind he felt as if his brain was on fire, he clasped his hands convulsively, he roared and bellowed aloud his threats of vengeance — vengeance against these detested Howards, who wished to snatch the crown from his son.

The youthful Edward, still in his minority, was alone the rightful and divinely appointed heir of the royal crown. It had cost his father so great a sacrifice to give his people this son and successor! In order to do so, he had sacrificed his best-beloved wife, Jane Seymour; he had suffered the mother to perish, that he might preserve the son as heir to his crown.

And the people did not once thank the husband of Jane Seymour, who had offered this sacrifice on their behalf. They shouted for the Duke of Norfolk, the uncle of that unchaste queen, whom Henry had loved so much that her infidelity had struck him to the heart like a poisoned dagger.

These were the thoughts which occupied the king as he lay upon his bed of suffering, and he revolved them in his mind with all the obstinacy and all the frenzy which a distempered fancy could suggest.

"We shall be obliged to sacrifice these Howards to him!" said Lord Douglas to Gardiner, as they had just overheard one of the angry outbursts of their royal master. "If we wish to be able eventually to succeed in overthrowing the queen, we must in the first place extirpate the Howards."

The pious bishop looked at him with inquiring astonishment.

Lord Douglas smiled.

"Your lordship is too highly elevated and too noble to understand the things of this world; your gaze, which is only fixed upon God and heavenly things, does not always perceive the minute and pitiful objects here below upon earth."

"Not exactly that," returned Gardiner, with a grim smile. "I see them, and it delights my soul when I behold how God's vengeance here on earth punishes the enemies of His Church. Prepare, therefore, without delay, the scaffold or the stake for these Howards, if their death can serve as a means for attaining our pious and godly ends. You can depend upon my aid and blessing! Only, I do not quite understand how these Howards can stand in the way of our plans, which are only directed against the queen—as they belong to the side of the queen's enemies, and are adherents of the holy and only true Church."

"The Earl of Surrey is an apostate, who has opened his heart and mind to the errors of Calvin!"

"Then let his head fall, for he is a malefactor against God, and no one dare have compassion for him! And what is the charge which we are to bring against the father?"

"The Duke of Norfolk is even more dangerous perhaps than his son, for, although a Catholic, he has not the true faith, and his heart is full of unholy pity and pernicious clemency. He commiserates those whose blood is shed for having given themselves up to the false doctrines of the priests of Baal, and calls both of us the king's bloodhounds."

"Well, then," cried Gardiner, with a sinister and ghastly smile, "we will prove to him that he has called us by our proper name—for we will rend him asunder."

"Besides this, the Howards, as we have said, stand in the way of our projects with reference to the queen," said Lord Douglas, gravely. "The king's mind is so entirely occupied with this hatred and this jealousy, that he has no room left for any other feeling. It is true he signs, often enough, those death-warrants which we lay before him, but he does it carelessly and without anger, as the lion crushes the little mouse that happens to run accidentally between his legs. But if the lion is to enter the lists and attack his equal, his anger must be roused in the first instance. And when his rage is kindled he will rend his opponent to pieces. Well, then, the Howards shall be his first booty. But we must take care that, when next he shakes his mane, his anger shall fall upon Katharine Parr and the Seymours."

"The Lord our God will be with us and will enlighten us to find the proper means of securely striking down His enemies!" cried Gardiner, raising his hands devoutly.

"I believe the proper means are already discovered," said Lord Douglas, smiling, "and that already before this day is ended, the gates of the Tower will open to let this proud and tender-hearted Duke of Norfolk and his heretical son pass through. Perhaps we may succeed in bringing down the queen and these Howards at a single blow. Look! there stands a carriage before the great gate; I see the Duchess of Norfolk and her daughter, the Duchess of Richmond, alighting. Observe, they are beckoning to us. I have promised to conduct these two noble and pious ladies to the king, and I will do so. While we are closeted, perhaps your lordship will offer a prayer that our words, like well-sped arrows, may strike home to the king's heart, and then rebound upon the queen and the Seymours."

CHAPTER IV.

THE ACCUSATION.

In vain had the king hoped to subdue his pains, or at least to forget them, while he sought for sleep. Rest had fled the king's couch; and as he now sat, weary and racked with pain, upon his rolling-chair, he reflected with brooding rancor, that the Duke of Norfolk had told him only yesterday, he had sleep at his own command, and could summon it if he wished.

This reflection made him furious with anger, and gnashing his teeth he muttered—"He can sleep, while I, his lord and king, am nothing but a poor beggar, who craves in vain of God a little sleep or a little forgetfulness of his pains. But it is this traitorous Norfolk who hinders me from sleeping. Thinking of him keeps me wakeful and restless. And yet I cannot crush this traitor with my hands. I am a king, and yet so feeble and powerless that I can find no means of accusing this delinquent, or of convicting him of his sinful and impious deeds. Oh, that I could find a true friend—a devoted servant, who would venture to understand my unuttered thoughts, and to fulfil the wishes to which I can give no name!"

As these thoughts rushed through his brain the door opened behind him, and Lord Douglas entered. His face wore an expression of exultant pride, and such wild delight shone in his eyes that even the king himself was surprised thereby.

"Oh," he said, peevishly, "you call yourself my friend, and yet you are cheerful, Douglas; whilst your king is a poor prisoner, whom the gout keeps eternally bound down in this chair."

"Your majesty is growing well, and from this captivity you will go forth like a brilliant and successful conqueror, who with the magic of his presence tramples down his enemies in the dust, and who triumphs over all those who are opposed to him, and who would betray their king!"

"Then there are traitors who would threaten their king?" asked Henry, with a dark frown.

"Yes, there are such traitors, your majesty!"

"Name them to me!" exclaimed the king, trembling with eager impatience; "name them to me, that my arm may crush them, and that my retributive justice may overtake the guilty!"

"It is superfluous to name them, for you, King Henry, the wise and all-knowing, know their names already."

And as Lord Douglas bent forward toward the king, he continued—"King Henry, I have just cause to call myself your truest and most devoted servant, for I have read your thoughts. I have understood the sublime grief that was gnawing at your heart, and which banished sleep from your eyes, and peace from your mind. You saw the enemy who was lurking in the dark. You heard the hissing of the serpent that was ready to dart its venomous sting at you. But so much were you the noble and undaunted king, that you would not yourself become the accuser, nay, would not recoil a step from the serpent which threatened you. Great and merciful like the Almighty Himself, you smiled upon him whom you knew to be your enemy. But, for my part, I have other duties toward your majesty. I am like the faithful watch-dog, who has eyes only for the safety of his master, and who attacks any one who threatens him. I have perceived the serpent which fain would sting you to death, and I will and shall bruise his head for you."

"The name of the serpent of which you speak?" asked the king, and his heart beat so violently, that he felt it trembling on his lips.

"Is Howard!" said Lord Douglas, gravely and solemnly.

The king uttered a cry, and, forgetting his pains and his gout, raised himself up from his chair.

"Howard," he said, with a grim smile,—"you say that a Howard threatens our life? Who is he? Name the traitor."

"I name them both, father and son! I name the Duke of Norfolk and the Earl of Surrey! I say that they are both arch-traitors, who threaten the life and the honor of my king, and who even dare with blasphemous arrogance to stretch forth their hands to grasp the crown!"

"Ah, I knew it—I knew it," cried the king. "And that was what made my nights sleepless, and pierced my flesh like a red-hot iron."

And as he turned his anger-flashing eyes toward Douglas, he asked, with a fierce smile, "And can you prove that these Howards are traitors? Can you prove that they are aiming at my crown?"

"I hope to be able to do so," replied Douglas. "True, there are no decided and overt acts—"

"Oh," interrupted the king, "there is no need for overt acts, only give me the slightest clew—the slenderest thread, and I'll make a rope of it which shall be strong enough to draw the father and son together up to the gallows."

"As for the son there is already proof enough," said Douglas, smiling; "and as regards the father, I shall bring before your majesty some accusers who will indeed have weight enough to send him to the scaffold. Permit me at once to introduce them to your majesty."

"Yes, bring them! bring them!" cried the king. "Every moment is precious which can send the traitors the more speedily to their doom."

Lord Douglas proceeded to the door, which he opened. Three female figures, closely veiled, entered silently, and bowed respectfully to the king.

"Ah," whispered the king with a cruel smile, as he sank back once more into his chair, "here are the three Fates who are spinning the thread of life of the Howards, and who, I trust, will now cut it short. I will give them the shears for that purpose, and if not sharp enough, why I will e'en help them to rend the thread asunder with my own royal hands."

"Sire," said Lord Douglas, while the three women, at a signal from him, unveiled themselves; "Sire, the wife, the daughter, and the mistress have come to accuse the Duke of Norfolk of high-treason; the mother and the daughter are here to denounce the Earl of Surrey for a crime equally worthy of death."

"Why, truly," cried the king, "it must be a weighty and blasphemous crime which so much provokes the loyal feelings of these noble women, as to make them disown the voice of nature!"

"Such it is," said the Duchess of Norfolk, in a solemn tone, and as she drew a few steps nearer to the king, she continued: "Sire I accuse the duke, my husband, (from whom I am separated,) of high treason and disloyalty toward his king. He has dared to assume your own royal arms, and displays upon his seal, and on his carriage, and over the portal of his mansion, the arms of the kings of England."

"It is quite true!" said the king, who now that he was sure of the downfall of the Howards, had again recovered his composure and presence of mind, and had once more resumed the air of a strict and unbiassed judge. "Yes, he bears the royal arms on his standard, but if we remember aright there is wanting in it the crown and the motto of our ancestor Edward the Third."

"He has now added both the crown and motto to his armorial bearings," said Miss Holland. "He says he is justified in doing so, for he also, like the king, is descended from Edward the Third, and therefore it is meet for him to bare the royal arms."

"If he says so he is a traitor, who presumes to consider his lord and king as his equal!" cried the king, whose countenance lighted up with ferocious joy, at the thought of having his enemy at length in his power.

"Yes, he is a traitor," continued Miss Holland. "I have often heard him say he had the same right to the crown of England as Henry the Eighth, and that a day might come when he would contest this crown with Henry's son."

"Ah!" exclaimed the king, and his eyes flashed with such angry looks, that even Lord Douglas stood aghast. "Ah! he wants to dispute the crown of England with my son. Well, that is good; for now it is my sacred duty, as a king and as a father, to crush the head of this serpent which threatens to sting me in the tenderest part; and no pity and no mercy should now restrain me any longer. And if there were no other proofs of his crime and of his guilt than these words which he has spoken to you, they will suffice, and will rise up against him as the headsmen who shall conduct him to the scaffold."

"But there are yet other proofs," said Miss Holland, laconically.

The king perforce unloosed his doublet. He felt as if his joy would overpower him.

"Name them!" he exclaimed.

"He is bold enough to deny the royal supremacy—he calls the Bishop of Rome the sole head and Holy Father of the Church."

"Indeed?" said the king, laughing. "Well we shall see whether this Holy Father will save his trusty son from the scaffold which we shall erect for him. Yes, we must give the world a fresh example of our inviolable justice, which overtakes all, however high and powerful they may be, and however near they may stand to our throne. Yet verily, it grieves our heart to fell this oak which we had planted so near our throne in order that we might lean against it for support; but justice requires the sacrifice, and we must therefore offer the victim —not with vindictiveness or anger, but that we may fulfil the sacred and painful duty of our kingship. We have greatly loved this duke, and it pains us to tear the love we bore him from our heart."

And the king with his jewelled hand wiped from his eyes the tears—that did not come.

"But how, then?" demanded the king, after a pause; "how will you have the courage to maintain your accusation before the House of Lords? Shall you, his wife, and you, too, his mistress, be willing to confirm publicly, with a sacred oath, the truth of this charge?"

"I shall be ready to do so," said the duchess, solemnly, "for he is no longer my husband—no longer the father of my children, but only the enemy of my king, whom to serve is my first and holiest duty."

"And I, too, shall be ready," said Miss Holland, with a fascinating smile, "for he is no longer my lover, but an arch-traitor and blasphemer, who has the hardihood to recognise as supreme chief of the Christian Church the Bishop of Rome, who has dared to hurl his anathemas against the head of our king. That is what has destroyed my affection for the duke, and what has caused me to hate him now as intensely as I once loved him."

The king, with a gracious smile, presented his hands to the two ladies. "You have, this day," he said, "done me a great service, for which I shall know how to reward you. To you, my lady duchess, I shall give one-half of his possessions, as if you were his lawful heir, and entitled to it as his widow; and to you, Miss Holland, I shall leave the undisputed possession of all the goods and valuables which the enamoured duke bestowed upon you."

The two ladies broke out into loud expressions of gratitude and exuberant delight toward the generous and magnanimous king, who was so gracious as to bestow upon them what they already enjoyed as their own property.

"Well, my little duchess, are you quite silent?" asked the king, after a pause, turning round to the Duchess of Richmond, who had withdrawn to the embrasure of a window.

"Sire," said the duchess, smiling. "I was only waiting for my cue."

"And pray, what is the cue?"

"Henry Howard, Earl of Surrey! Your majesty knows I am a lively but harmless creature, and I understand much better how to laugh and be merry than to talk gravely and seriously. Both of these worthy and beautiful ladies have accused the duke—my father, and they have done so in a very solemn and becoming manner; I am prepared to accuse my brother—Henry Howard, but you must be indulgent with me, sire, if my words should not be quite so grave or so solemn. They have told you that the Duke of Norfolk is a traitor, and calls the Pope of Rome Head of the Church. Now the Earl of Surrey is neither a traitor nor a papist, and he entertains no criminal designs against the crown of England, nor has he ever denied the king's supremacy. No, sire, the Earl of Surrey is not a traitor nor a papist."

The duchess was silent, and contemplated the astonished looks of those around her with a smile expressive of drollery and mischief.

The king's brow became clouded with a sinister frown, and his glance which had just been so radiant, was now directed with an angry expression toward the young duchess.

"Then, in that case, my lady, why did you come here!" he asked. "To what purpose have you come forward if you have nothing more to tell me than I know already—that the Earl of Surrey is a very loyal subject and a man wholly devoid of ambition, who neither courts popular favor, nor harbors the thought of stretching forth a traitorous hand to grasp my crown?"

The young duchess shook her head with a smile.

"I don't know if he deserves all that praise," she replied. "I have indeed heard that he has said, with bitter mockery, that you, my liege, wished to be thought the protector of religion, while you really believed in no creed or religion at all; and it was only recently that he broke forth into bitter imprecations against you, because you had robbed him of his marshal's staff and bestowed it upon the Earl of Hertford—the noble and generous Seymour. He also hinted that he should like to see if the throne of England was so firm and unassailable as not to require the aid of his hand and arm to support it. All this, indeed, I heard from him myself, but you are right, sire, it is unimportant,—not even worth being mentioned, and for that reason I do not make it the subject of accusation against him."

"Ah, you are still the same little madcap, Arabella!" cried the king, who had once more regained his cheerfulness. "You say you don't wish to accuse him, and yet you are making a plaything of his head, which you are trying to balance upon those ruby lips of yours. But, beware, my little duchess, beware, lest while you laugh, this head should be thrust away from your lips and made to roll along the ground,—for I won't undertake to keep in equilibrium the head of this Earl of Surrey, of whom you say that he is no traitor."

"But would it not be tedious and monotonous if we were to accuse both father and son of the same crime?" asked the duchess, smiling. "Let us have a little variety! Let the duke be a traitor; the son, my liege, is a criminal of a deeper dye."

"Is there then any crime more wicked or more execrable than that of being a traitor to one's lord and king, and of speaking of the Lord's anointed without reverence or love?"

"Yes, sire, there is a crime still worse—and of that I accuse the Earl of Surrey. He is an adulterer!"

"An adulterer?" repeated the king, with an expression of horror. "Yes, by God's mother, you are right; this is an odious and unnatural crime, and we shall judge it severely. For it shall not be said that honor and virtue find no protector in the king of this realm, and that he is not a crushing and avenging judge against all those who dare to violate the laws of decency and morality. Oh, the Earl of Surrey is an adulterer, is he?"

"That is to say, sire, he dares to persecute a chaste and virtuous woman with his sinful love; he dares to direct his impious glances toward a lady who is raised as far above him as the sun is beyond the earth, and who, at least, by reason of the greatness and elevated position of her spouse, should be secure against every impure wish and unchaste desire."

"Ah," exclaimed the king, uneasily, "I perceive already what you are coming to. It is always the same complaint, and now I tell you, as you said before, let us have a little variety! The accusation I have heard often enough, but the proofs were always wanting."

"Perhaps, on this occasion, sire, we may be able to furnish the proofs," said the duchess, gravely. "Would you know, my noble liege, who the Geraldine is, to whom Henry Howard addresses his amatory sonnets? Shall I tell you the real name of this lady to whom, in the presence of your sacred person and of your whole court, he offers the passionate declaration of his love, and the vows of his eternal fidelity? Well, then, this so much-worshipped and idolized Geraldine is—the queen!"

"That is false!" exclaimed the king, purple with rage, and his hands clutched with such a convulsive grasp the sides of his rolling arm-chair, that it creaked; "that is false, my lady!"

"It is true," said the duchess, proudly and fearlessly. "It is true, sire, for the Earl of Surrey has confessed the fact to me himself, that it is the queen whom he loves, and that Geraldine is only a well-sounding paraphrase of Katharine."

"What! he has confessed this to you himself?" asked the king, gasping for breath. "He dares to love the wife of his king? Woe betide him, I say, woe betide him!"

He raised his clenched hand to heaven, while his eyes flashed with a terrible expression.

"But how is this," he continued, after a pause. "Did he not lately recite before us a poem to Geraldine, in which he thanks her for her love, and declares himself for ever indebted for the kisses which she has bestowed upon him?"

"Yes, my liege, he did recite such a poem in your majesty's presence."

The king groaned, and raised himself up from his seat.

"I must have proofs," he murmured in a hoarse, dismal voice,—"proofs, or if not, I tell you your own head shall pay the forfeit for this accusation!"

"With these proofs I shall furnish your majesty!" said Lord Douglas, in a solemn accent. "You are pleased, sire, in the fulness of your pity and of your gentle disposition, to doubt the accusation of the noble duchess. Well, then, I undertake myself to supply you with infallible proofs that Henry Howard, Earl of Surrey, really loves the queen, and that he dares to extol and worship the spouse of his king, under the name of Geraldine. You shall hear with your own ear, sire, how the Earl of Surrey makes protestation of his love to the queen."

The exclamation which the king uttered at these words was so terrible, and betrayed such deep anguish, mingled with rage, that the earl became mute, while the cheeks of the ladies were blanched with fear.

"Douglas, Douglas, beware of rousing the lion!" said the king, trembling with emotion. "The lion in his fury might rend you to pieces!"

"This very night, you shall have the proofs which you demand, sire,—this very night, you shall hear how the Earl of Surrey, sitting at the feet of his Geraldine, offers to her the vows of his love."

"It is well," said the king. "This night be it then! But woe, woe to you, Douglas, unless you can redeem your promise!"

"I shall do so, sire! Only one thing is necessary, and that is, that you will graciously pledge me your royal word that you will not betray yourself by a breath or a sigh. The earl is suspicious, and the anxiety caused by an evil conscience has sharpened his ear. He would recognize you by a sigh or a whisper, and then his lips would not utter the words of avowal which you desire to overhear."

"I pledge my royal word that I will not betray my proximity by a word or a sigh!" said the king, solemnly. "Nay, I swear this by the Holy Mother of God! But enough of this now! Air, air; I cannot breathe. My brain reels! Open the windows, and let in a little air. Ah, that is a relief! This air is at least pure and unpolluted by calumny and sin."

And the king suffered himself to be wheeled toward the open window, where he inhaled in draughts the pure fresh air. He then turned with an agreeable smile to the ladies.

"My ladies," he said, "I thank you. This day you have proved yourselves to be true and devoted servants. I shall always remember this, and if ever you stand in need of a friend and protector, you may rely upon me with all confidence. We shall never forget the great service which you have this day rendered us."

Whereupon he gave them a familiar nod, and, with a majestic wave of his hand, he dismissed them, and the audience was over.

"And now, Douglas," exclaimed the king impetuously, as the ladies withdrew—"now there must be an end of this fearful torment! You tell me that I am to punish these traitors, Norfolk and Surrey, and you impose upon myself the most terrible agonies!"

"Sire, there was no other means of putting Surrey in your power. You wished to find him a criminal, and I shall prove to you that he is one."

"Then I shall at length be able to trample his accursed head under my feet!" cried the king, gnashing his teeth. "I shall no longer have to tremble before this malicious enemy, who goes about among my people with his hypocritical tongue, while I sit in the dungeon of my sick chamber tormented with pain and suffering. Yes, I thank you, Douglas, that you are about to place him within reach of my avenging arm, and my soul is filled with joy and delight at the thought. Ah, why was it necessary that you should cast a cloud over this moment of rejoicing! Why was it needful that the queen should become entangled in these dreary meshes of crime and guilt. Her cheerful smile and her beaming looks have ever been to me a source of such pure enjoyment."

"Sire, I do not by any means assert that the queen is guilty. Only there was no other means of proving to you the Earl of Surrey's guilt, than that you should yourself hear the confession of his love to the queen."

"Aye, and I will hear it!" exclaimed the king, who had now already overcome the emotions of sentiment in which he had just been indulging. "Yes, I am resolved to have the full conviction of Surrey's guilt, and woe to the queen, if I should find her also guilty! This night, therefore, Douglas! But until then silence and secrecy! We shall seize father and son at the same moment and have them arrested, for otherwise the arrest of the one might serve as a warning to the other, who might thus be able to elude our just anger. Ah, these Howards are so crafty, and their hearts are so full of malice and deceit! But now they shall no longer evade us—they are now in our power. The very thought of this does me good and makes my heart bound freely and lightly. I feel as if a new stream of life flowed through my veins and imparted fresh strength to my blood. Ah, it was those Howards who made me ill; but I shall recover my powers once more when I know they are in the Tower! Yes, my heart bounds with joy, and the present day shall be one of delight and happiness. Call hither the queen that I may rejoice once more in the sight of her rosy countenance, before I make it grow pale with terror. Yes, let the queen come in her most brilliant attire; I wish to see her once more in the full splendor of her youth and royal estate, before her brow becomes clouded. I will delight me once more in her society before I make her weep. Ah, Douglas, you know there is no pleasure at once so devilish and so divine as to see a woman who thus smiles without suspicion while she is already condemned;—who adorns her head with flowers, while the headsman is already whetting his axe; who still hopes for a future of joy and happiness, while the hours of her life are already numbered—while I have already commanded her to stand still, and to descend into the grave. Call me hither the queen, therefore, and tell her that we are merry, and would laugh and jest with her. Summon all the ladies and gentlemen of our court, and let the royal saloons be thrown open, and let them stream resplendently with light, and let us have music—loud, crashing music—for on this day at least we will have mirth and pleasure, since it appears we are about to have a dull and comfortless night. Yes, good soothe, we will have a merry and a joyous day, let what follows be as it may. The halls shall resound with laughter and glee, and nothing but shouts of mirth and exultation shall be heard in the grand saloons of the king. And invite for me, too, the Duke of Norfolk, my noble cousin, who shares with me my royal arms. Yes, invite him, that I may admire once more his noble countenance and his lofty bearing, before this exalted luminary becomes extinguished, and leaves us behind in darkness and gloom. Then, too, invite me Wriothesley, my chancellor, and let him bring with him an escort of stout and trusty soldiers of our body-guard. They shall compose the retinue of the noble duke when he leaves our festive party on his return home;—aye, home, if not to his palace, at least to the Tower and to the grave! Go, Douglas, go and see that all these arrangements are properly carried out! And send me straightway my merry jester, John Heywood. He shall help me to pass the time until the festivity begins, and shall make me laugh with his pungent drollery."

"I shall go and fulfil your commands, sire," said Douglas. "I shall make preparations for the festivity, and impart your commands to the queen and to the court. And first of all I shall send you John Heywood. But will your majesty pardon me if I venture to remind you, that you have pledged your royal word that you will not betray our secret by any allusion, or even by any symptom."

"I have given my word and I shall keep it!" said the king. "Go, now, Lord Douglas, and do as I have directed you."

Wholly exhausted by this paroxysm of grim exultation, the king sank back in his chair, and groaned aloud with agony as he rubbed his leg, the tormenting pain of which he had for a moment forgotten, but which pain, by its terrible fury, now reminded him of its presence.

"Ah, me!" sighed the king. "He boasted that he could sleep whenever he pleased. Well, this time, at least, we shall have the pleasure of lulling the haughty duke to rest; but his sleep will be one from which he shall never more awake!—"

While the king thus moaned and suffered, Lord Douglas hastened with rapid and firm steps through the long ranges of royal chambers. A proud and triumphant smile played around his lips, and a joyful expression of victory flashed from his eyes.

"Triumph! triumph! we shall conquer!" he exclaimed, as he now entered the apartment of his daughter, and presented his hand to Lady Jane. "Jane, we have at length reached the goal, and you will soon be the seventh wife of King Henry!"

For a moment Lady Jane's pale and colorless cheeks became tinged with a roseate hue, and a smile played upon her lips—a smile which, however, seemed as sad and dreary as if it had been indeed the result of an hysterical attack.

"Ah," she murmured, faintly, "I only fear that my poor head will be too weak to bear a royal diadem!"

"Courage, courage, Jane! hold up your head and be once more a brave, proud daughter."

"Only I suffer so much, my father," she sighed. "I feel as if an infernal fire were raging within me!"

"But soon, Jane, very soon, you will experience the delights of heaven! I had forbidden you to make any appointments for meeting Henry Howard, lest it might get us into danger. Well, then, to-night your tender little heart shall be satisfied. This very night you will be able to greet your beloved!"

"Alas!" she murmured, "he will again call me his Geraldine, and it will not be Jane Douglas, but the queen whom, in my person, he will embrace."

"Yes, to-night only it must be so, Jane, but I swear to you that this will be the last time that you shall so receive him!"

"The last time that I shall see him?" she inquired, with a look of terror.

"No, Jane, only the last time that Henry Howard shall, in your person, love the queen instead of yourself."

"Oh, he will never love me!" she murmured sadly.

"Yes, he will love you, Jane, for it will be you who shall save his life. Hasten, therefore, Jane, hasten, and write speedily to him one of those tender notes which you can compose with so much skill; invite him to a rendezvous for this night, at the accustomed time and hour."

"Oh, I shall at length have him beside me once more!" whispered Lady Jane, and she went to her escritoire, and began to write with trembling hand.

Suddenly, however, she ceased, and looked at her father with an air of scrutiny and suspicion.

"You swear to me, my father, that no danger threatens him if he should come?"

"I swear to you, Jane, that it will be you who shall save his life? I swear to you, too, Jane, that you shall take revenge on the queen,—revenge for all the agony, the humiliation and despair which you have suffered on her account! To-day she is still Queen of England. To-morrow she will be nothing more than a guilty creature, awaiting with sighs the hour of her execution, in the dungeons of the tower; while you will be Henry's seventh wife. Write, therefore, daughter, write, and may love inspire you with the most effectual words!"

CHAPTER V.

THE BANQUET OF DEATH.

For a long time the king had not been so cheerful as on this festive evening; for a long time he had not shown himself so much the devoted and affectionate husband, the gay companion, the sprightly man of the world.

The pains in his leg seemed to have vanished, and even the weight of his body seemed on the present occasion to be less burdensome than usual; for more than once, he raised himself from his rolling-chair and walked a few steps up and down the brilliantly lighted saloon, in which the ladies and gentlemen of his court moved backward and forward in festive attire—in which music and merry laughter resounded.

What tenderness he displayed on this evening toward his spouse, with what extraordinary favor did he greet the Duke of Norfolk—with what smiling attention did he listen to the Earl of Surrey, as the latter at the king's desire repeated some new sonnets to Geraldine!

This marked preference for the noble Howards delighted the Catholic party of the court, and filled them with new hopes and new confidence.

But there was present one person who did not suffer himself to be deceived by this mask with which Henry had for the nonnce covered his angry countenance.

John Heywood believed neither in the cheerfulness nor in the conjugal affection of the king. He understood his royal master; and he knew that those toward whom the king displayed the most cordial regard, had often the most to fear from him. He, therefore, observed him closely, and so perceived that under the guise of this friendly exterior, the king's real and angry countenance would sometimes become inflamed by a hasty and sudden glance. The pealing music and boisterous gaiety no longer deceived John Heywood. He saw death standing behind this brilliant and living throng; he scented the odors of corruption concealed amidst the fragrance of these dazzling flowers.

John Heywood ceased to laugh and ceased to chatter. He observed and kept watch.

For the first time for a long while, the king did not on the present occasion, require the inciting pleasantries and the pungent drolleries of his jester, to make him cheerful and to keep him in good humor.

The fool accordingly had ample leisure to play the part of a rational and observant being, and he took advantage of his time.

He saw the looks of mutual understanding and triumphant security, which were exchanged between Lord Douglas and Gardiner, and he felt distrustful at perceiving that those, otherwise so jealous, favorites of the king, did not appear in anyway disconcerted at the marked favor evinced toward the Howards.

Once, he heard how Gardiner, in passing near Wriothesley, asked: "And the soldiers from the Tower?" and how the latter answered, in words equally laconic—"They are standing near the carriage, waiting."

It was accordingly quite evident that some one was about to be arrested this very night. There was, therefore, amongst this crowd of laughing, jesting, and richly-arrayed courtiers, one, at least, who, when he left these brilliant saloons, radiant with splendor and filled with exuberant mirth, would have to contemplate the dreary and dismal dungeons of the Tower.

The only question was, who could the individual be for whom the brilliant comedy of this evening was to be changed into such a melancholy drama?

John Heywood felt oppressed with inexplicable anxiety, and this marked tenderness of the king toward his spouse filled him with apprehension and terror.

As the king now smiled upon Katharine,—as he caressed her cheek,—so had he smiled upon Anne Bullen within the same hour that he signed the warrant for her imprisonment; thus, too, had he stroked the cheek of Buckingham on the very day that he confirmed the sentence of death against him.

The court jester stood aghast in presence of this splendid entertainment, this crashing music, and this extravagant gaiety of the king. He recoiled from the mirthful faces and from the thoughtless witticisms which fell from the lips of the assembled guests.

Good Heavens! they laughed, and death was in the midst of them; they laughed, and already the gates of the Tower stood open, to admit one of these blithesome guests of the king into a domicile, from which in those days of Henry the Eighth, no one ever came forth, unless to go to the stake or to mount the scaffold.

Who was now the unhappy offender? For whom were the soldiers from the Tower now waiting below beside the carriage? In vain did John Heywood rack his brain to answer this question.

Nowhere was there a trace visible which could set him on the right track; nowhere a clue to lead him out of this labyrinth of terror.

"When one fears the devil, it is best to take refuge at the nearest shelter," muttered John Heywood, and he glided with a sad and trembling heart behind the state chair in which the king was seated, and crouched down beside him on the floor.

John Heywood was of such a slight and diminutive frame, and the state chair of the king was so large and broad that it entirely concealed the little squatting figure of the jester.

No one had observed that John Heywood lay concealed behind the king; no one perceived his large piercing eyes, which scanned and overlooked the entire saloon from behind the throne.

John Heywood could hear and see all that transpired in the vicinity of the king; he could observe everyone who approached the queen.

He also perceived Lady Jane, who stood beside the chair where the queen was seated. He saw how Lord Douglas approached his daughter, and how she became deadly pale as he drew near her.

John Heywood held his breath while he watched and listened.

Lord Douglas stood beside his daughter and nodded to her with a smile of peculiar significance. "Go, now, Jane," he said, "and change your attire. It is time. Just observe how impatiently and anxiously Henry Howard already looks this way, and with what languishing and amorous glances he appears to regard the queen. Go, therefore, Jane, and remember your promise."

"And will you too, my dear father, remember *your* promise?" asked Lady Jane, with trembling lips. "Will no danger threaten him?"

"I shall do so, Jane! But now hasten, good daughter, and show yourself discreet and skilful."

Lady Jane bowed, and muttered a few unintelligible words. She then approached the queen, and begged permission to leave the saloon, under plea of a sudden and violent headache.

Lady Jane's countenance was so deadly pale, that the queen could readily believe in the indisposition of her first maid of honor, and permitted her to retire.

Lady Jane left the saloon, and the queen resumed her conversation with Lord Hertford, who stood near her.

It was a very lively and earnest colloquy, and the queen accordingly gave but little heed to what was passing around her, and heard nothing of the conversation between the king and Lord Douglas.

John Heywood who was still crouching behind the king's state chair, observed all, and heard every word of this lightly whispered dialogue.

"Sire," said Lord Douglas, "it is late, and the midnight hour is fast approaching. Will it please your majesty to close the festivity? For you know we must be in the green garden-chamber, yonder, by midnight, and it is some distance thither."

"Yes, yes, by midnight," murmured the king;—"by midnight the carnival is over, and then we shall tear off the masks, and show our angry countenance to the guilty! By midnight we must be yonder in the green chamber. Yes, Douglas, we must make haste, for it would be cruel to let the affectionate Surrey wait any longer. We will also give his Geraldine leave to quit the festivity, and we must ourselves set out on our way. Ah! Douglas, the road we have to travel is a hard one, but

Nemesis and the Eumonides shall be our torch-bearers—Vengeance and the Furies our fit companions. To work, then—to work!"

The king rose from his chair and approached the queen, to whom he gave his hand, with an affectionate smile.

"It is late, my sweet lady," he said, "and we, although the king of so many subjects, are still ourself the subject of another king, that is to say, of our physician, and we must obey him. He has commanded me to seek my couch before midnight, and I obey as a loyal subject should do. We therefore wish you a good-night, Kate, and may those bright eyes of yours be as star-like to-morrow as they are this evening."

"They will be equally bright to-morrow, if my lord and spouse should be still as gracious to me as he has been to-day," said Katharine, without suspicion or constraint, as she presented her hand to the king.

Henry bestowed upon her a penetrating and distrustful look, and a peculiar and malicious expression played over his features.

"Do you believe then, Kate, that we could ever be ungracious toward you?" he asked.

"I think," she replied, smiling, "that even the sun does not always shine; and that a dark night often follows the brightest day."

The king made no reply. He looked for a moment into her face with a fixed gaze, and then his features suddenly assumed a milder expression.

Perchance he felt compassion for his young wife; perhaps he felt pity for her youth, and thought of that bewitching smile, which had so often gladdened and refreshed his heart.

Lord Douglas at least certainly feared so.

"Sire," he said, "it is late; it is near midnight already."

"Then let us go," said the king, with a sigh. "Once more, then, Kate, good-night! No, do not follow me; I wish to leave the saloon quite unobserved; and I shall be pleased if my guests will prolong this festivity until morning. All remain here; no one accompanies me but Douglas."

"And your brother, the fool," said John Heywood, who for some time had come out from his hiding-place, and now stood beside the king. "Yes, brother Henry, let us leave this banquet. It becomes not sages like us to favor the assembly of fools any longer with our presence. Come along to your couch, king, and I'll lull you to sleep with my wise proverbs, and refresh your soul with the manna of my learning."

While John Heywood was thus speaking, it did not escape him that the earl's brow became suddenly clouded, and that his features assumed a sinister expression.

"Keep your wisdom to yourself for the present, John," said the king, "for you would only be preaching to deaf ears. I am tired, and I have no wish for your learning, but for sleep. Good-night, John!"

The king left the saloon, leaning on the arm of Lord Douglas.

"So I see my Lord Douglas does not want me to accompany the king," muttered John Heywood, to himself. "He is afraid the king will tell me something about this devilish hob-goblin scene which is to take place about midnight. Well, then, I call the devil my brother, just as much as the king, and with the help of his infernal majesty, I, too, shall be in the green-room at midnight. The queen is already leaving, and there goes the Duke of Norfolk. I am rather curious to see if the duke escapes safely, or whether the soldiers who, according to Wriothesley, are standing near his carriage, will perchance be the duke's body-guards to-night."

Gliding stealthily from the saloon, John Heywood reached the anteroom before the duke, and hastened forward to the outer gate in front of which the carriages were drawn up in rank.

John Heywood leaned against one of the pillars, and watched. A few minutes and the tall, stately figure of the duke appeared in the outer hall, while his carriage was ordered by one of the servants in attendance.

The carriage advanced—the door was opened.

Two men wrapped in dark cloaks sat beside the driver; two others stood behind, while a fifth waited at the open carriage door.

The duke did not notice it until his foot had already touched the step.

"That is not my carriage! These are not my servants!" he exclaimed, drawing back. But the pretended servant pushed him forward impetuously into the carriage, and closed the door.

"Forward!" he shouted, and the vehicle rolled away.

For a moment John Heywood perceived the pale features of the duke through the open window of the carriage, and it seemed as if he stretched out his arms entreatingly for help, and then the carriage vanished in the darkness.

"Unhappy duke!" murmured John Heywood. "The gates of the Tower are heavy, and your arms will never be strong enough to open them, when they have once closed behind you. But it is useless to think of him at the present moment. The queen, too, is in danger. Away then to the queen!"

With lightning steps, John Heywood hastened back into the palace. Swiftly he glided along through corridors and passages.

He had now reached the corridor that led to the queen's apartments.

"I shall mount guard for her to-night," muttered John Heywood, as he concealed himself in a niche in the corridor. "The fool, with his prayers, will banish every devilish apparition from the door of his saints, and will protect them from the snares in which the pious Bishop Gardiner and the sly courtier, Douglas, wish to entrap them. No, my queen shall not fall a victim to their wiles. May the fool still live to protect her!"

CHAPTER VI.

THE QUEEN.

From the niche in which John Heywood had concealed himself, he had a full view of the entire corridor and of all the doors which opened upon it: he could hear all and see all, without being seen himself, for the projecting pillars of the wall securely sheltered him from observation.

Accordingly, John Heywood stood and listened. In the corridor all was still. In the distance could now and then be heard subdued sounds of music, while a confused murmur of many voices borne along from the banquet-chamber, fell upon the ear of the listener.

This was all that John Heywood could hear: beyond this there was perfect stillness.

But this stillness was of brief duration. The corridor was suddenly lighted up, and rapid footfalls were heard approaching.

It was the gold-laced footmen, bearing large silver candlesticks to light the way for the queen, who was advancing along the corridor accompanied by her ladies.

She looked extremely beautiful. The brilliancy of the wax-lights borne before her illumined her countenance, which beamed serenely. As she passed along near the pillars, behind which John Heywood stood, she spoke with unconstrained mirth and animation to both her maids of honor, and when a cheerful peal of laughter burst from her lips, she displayed to view a set of teeth of dazzling whiteness. Her eyes glowed, her cheeks were suffused with an exquisite roseate hue; the brilliants in the diadem which decked her lofty brow glistened like stars; and like liquid gold shone her rich brocaded robe, the train of which, bordered with dark ermine, was held by two youthful pages.

Having reached the door of her chamber, the queen dismissed her pages and her other male attendants: her ladies of honor alone were permitted to enter the sleeping apartment.

The pages conversed together with thoughtless gaiety, retired along the passage and down the steps. Then came the footmen who had carried the wax-lights. They too, forsook the corridor.

And now once more all was still. John Heywood continued to listen, firmly resolved to speak to the queen this very night, even though he should have to rouse her from sleep. He was only waiting a little longer until the ladies of honor should also have left the apartment.

At length the door opened and the maids of honor came out. They proceeded along the corridor in the direction in which their own chambers were situated. John Heywood heard them open their doors, and fasten the bolts when they had entered.

"Now then, only a short time, and I shall go to the queen," murmured John Heywood.

He was just upon the point of quitting his hiding place, when he heard a slight creaking sound, as if a door was being opened slowly and cautiously.

John Heywood crouched closely behind the pillars, and held his breath in order to listen.

A bright gleam of light fell athwart the corridor. The rustling of a garment was heard approaching. Astonished and amazed, John Heywood closely scanned a female form which hurried along close to the spot where he lay, but without perceiving him.

The figure was that of Lady Jane Douglas.

Lady Jane, had left the banquet-room from indisposition, in order to retire to rest. And now, when all were sleeping she was awake—when all the others had put off their festive attire, she had resumed hers. Like the queen, she wore a robe of gold brocade, bordered with ermine, and like her too, a diadem of brilliants adorned Lady Jane's brow.

She now stood before the queen's door and listened. Then a derisive and scornful smile seemed for a moment to flit over her features, which were deadly pale, and her dark eyes flashed with a fierce lustre.

"She sleeps," murmured Lady Jane. "Sleep on, queen, sleep on, till we come to rouse you up. To rouse you up! Sleep, in order that I may be able to watch in your stead!"

She raised her arm with a threatening gesture toward the door and shook her head wildly. Her long raven locks, like the snakes of Erinnys, swept around her dark brow; and pale, and colorless, and beautiful as a demon, as she was, she resembled nothing so much as the goddess of revenge, preparing with scornful triumph to trample her victim in the dust.

With a faint laugh she now glided along the corridor, but not to yonder flight of steps,—but farther on toward the end, where the large portrait of Henry the Sixth hung on the wall. She pressed a spring, the picture opened, and through a door concealed behind it, Lady Jane disappeared.

"She is going into the green saloon to keep her rendezvous with Henry Howard!" whispered John Heywood, who now stepped forth from behind the pillars. "Ah, now I understand it all—now the whole of this devilish scheme is quite clear. Lady Jane is the inamorata of the Earl of Surrey, and they will try to make the king believe that it is the queen. Doubtless this Surrey himself is in the plot, and perhaps he will even call Jane Douglas by the queen's name. The king will only be suffered to see her for a moment. She wears a robe of gold brocade, and a diadem like the queen, and by this means they hope to impose upon the king. Her figure is exactly like the queen's, and every one knows the wonderful resemblance of Lady Jane's voice to that of the queen. Ho, ho,—the trick is not bad! But with all their cunning, the victory won't be theirs. Patience, only a little patience! We, too, shall be in the green saloon, and we shall bring the real queen face to face with her would-be representative!"

With hasty steps John Heywood also quitted the corridor, which was now solitary and still, for the queen had retired to rest.

Yes, the queen slept, and yet every thing had been prepared for her reception yonder in the green chamber.

It was to be a very splendid and extraordinary reception, for the king in person had repaired to that wing of the palace, and the chief master of the ceremonies, Lord Douglas, had accompanied him.

This journey, which the king was obliged to perform on foot, had been very fatiguing to him, but this fatigue only made him all the more furious and enraged, and the least trace of mercy for his queen had now vanished from the king's breast; for it was on Katharine's account that he had been compelled to go this long distance to the green saloon, and with a grim delight Henry only thought how terrible would be the punishment of Henry Howard and also of Katharine.

Now that Lord Douglas had conducted him hither, the king no longer doubted of the queen's guilt. It was no longer an accusation; it was a proof. For never would Lord Douglas have dared to bring him, his king, to this place, unless he were certain that he could here furnish him with infallible proofs.

The king, therefore, doubted no longer. Henry Howard was at length in his power, and could no longer escape him. He was accordingly certain of being at length able to bring both his hated enemies to the scaffold, so that he should no longer feel his sleep disturbed by thinking of his two powerful rivals.

The Duke of Norfolk had already passed the gates of the Tower, and his son would shortly follow him.

This thought afforded the king such ferocious delight, that he forgot for the moment that this very sword which was to fall upon the head of Henry Howard, was also hanging over the queen.

They had already reached the green saloon, and the king, panting and groaning leaned upon the arm of Lord Douglas.

This immense saloon with its antique furniture and its faded splendor, was only dimly and scantily lighted up in the centre by the two wax tapers of the branch candlestick which Lord Douglas had brought with him,—while in the distance it seemed shrouded in darkness, and, through this darkness, appeared to the eye to extend itself to an unlimited distance.

"Yonder, through that door will come the queen," said Douglas, and he started at the loud tone of his own voice, which acquired an awful resonance in this large dreary hall. "And this, close by, is the entrance of Henry Howard. Oh! he knows the way quite well, for he has trodden it often enough in the dark already, and his foot stumbles at no obstacle."

"Perhaps, however, it will stumble on the scaffold!" muttered Henry, with a grim laugh.

"I will now allow myself to ask only one question," said Douglas, and the king little suspected how violently this question caused the earl's heart to tremble. "Will it suffice your majesty to see the earl and the queen both appear at the appointed rendezvous? Or do you also wish to hear a little of the earl's endearing protestations?"

"Not a little, but all! I will hear all," said the king. "Nay, we must let this noble swan sing his farewell song before he plunges down into the sea of blood!"

"Then, in that case," said Douglas, "we must extinguish these lights, and your majesty must be content with hearing the guilty pair, without seeing them! We will, therefore, at once, retire to the boudoir, which I have got ready for this purpose, and in which an arm-chair is prepared for your majesty. We will then place this chair near the open door, which will enable your majesty to hear every word of their tender dalliance."

"But how shall we eventually be able to gain a sight of this affectionate couple, and procure for them the dramatic surprise of our presence, if we extinguish the only lights which we have got?"

"Sire, as soon as the Earl of Surrey, has entered, twenty men of the royal body guard will take possession of the ante-room through which the earl must pass, and it will only require a summons from you to make them enter the saloon with their torches. I have also taken care that at the private door behind the palace, two coaches shall be in readiness,—the drivers of which are well acquainted with the streets which lead to the Tower."

"*Two* coaches!" said the king, laughing. "Ah, Douglas, how very cruel we are! To think of separating such a loving pair upon this journey, which indeed will be their last! Now, perhaps, we may be able to compensate them for this, by allowing these turtle-doves to travel together on their last road—the road that leads to the scaffold. No, no, we won't separate them in death. They shall both lay their heads on the block together!"

The king laughed, quite gratified with his own pleasantry, while leaning on the arm of the earl, he proceeded to the little boudoir beyond, and seated himself in the arm-chair which was placed inside the door.

"We must now put out the light, and may it please your majesty to await in silence the events which shall speedily come to pass."

The earl extinguished the light, and a profound darkness and a death-like stillness succeeded.

But this did not continue long. The sound of footsteps was heard quite distinctly; they came nearer and nearer,—and now a door was heard to open and again to shut, and it seemed as if some one were gliding gently into the saloon on tip-toe.

"Henry Howard!" whispered Douglas.

The king could scarcely restrain the cry of wild malicious joy which now rose to his lips.

The hated enemy was at present in his power; he was convicted of his crime; he was irrecoverably lost.

"Geraldine!" whispered a voice. "Geraldine!"

And as if a faint signal had already sufficed to attract the inamorata, a secret door was here opened in the immediate vicinity of the boudoir; the rustling of robes too was distinctly heard, and the sound of footsteps.

"Geraldine!" repeated the Earl of Surrey.

"Here I am, my Henry!"

With an outburst of delight, the woman rushed forward toward the sound of the beloved voice.

"The queen!" murmured Henry, and involuntarily he felt his heart seized with a bitter pang.

He saw with his inward eye how they held each other in close embrace; he could even hear the kisses which they exchanged, and the soft whispers of their mutual endearments; and all the bitterness of jealousy and anger filled his soul. But still the king succeeded in preserving silence and self-restraint, and devoured his rage inwardly. He wished to hear all—to know all.

He clasped his hands convulsively in each other, and pressed his lips firmly together, in order to check his troubled breathing. He wanted to hear.

How happy they both were! Henry Howard had quite forgotten that he had come in order to reproach her for her long silence. She, on her part, had no thought that this was to be the last time she should see the man whom she loved.

They were now together, and their hours were their own. What cared they for the whole world—why stop to inquire if afterward ruin and destruction should overtake them.

They sat down side by side on an ottoman which stood at a short distance from the boudoir. They jested and laughed in playful dalliance, and Henry Howard kissed away the tears which the rapture of the moment drew from the eyes of his Geraldine.

He vowed to her eternal, unchanging love. In blissful silence she drank in the music of his words, and then with exultant delight she returned the vows which he had pledged.

The king was now scarcely able any longer to curb his rage.

The heart of Lord Douglas bounded with satisfaction and content. "How fortunate that Jane does not suspect our presence," he thought. "She would otherwise have been more reserved and less ardent, and the ear of the king would have imbibed less poison."

Lady Jane never bestowed a thought upon her father; scarcely even did she remember that her hated rival, the queen, would this night be brought to ruin.

Henry Howard had only called her his Geraldine. Jane had quite forgotten that it was not herself to whom her lover had given this name.

But at length he reminded her of it himself.

"Do you know, Geraldine," said the Earl of Surrey, and his voice which had hitherto been so blythe and gladsome, now became sad.—"Do you know, Geraldine, that I had begun to doubt you? Oh, these were fearful, terrible hours, and in my agony of mind I at length formed the resolution of going to the king and accusing myself of this love

"THE QUEEN," MURMURED HENRY. P. 232.

which consumed me inwardly. Oh, don't be alarmed! I would not have accused you, Geraldine—nay, I would even have denied this love which you have so often avowed in words that filled me with rapture. I would have done so, in order to discover if my Geraldine could eventually gain the strength and courage to confess her love freely and openly—if her heart had the power of bursting asunder those iron shackles which the deceitful laws of the world had imposed upon it—if she would still cleave to her lover when he might be condemned to die for her sake. Yes, Geraldine, I intended to do this, in order that I might know at length whether you were swayed most by love or by pride, and whether you could even then preserve the mask of indifference, when death should flap his wings around your lover's head. Oh, Geraldine, I would have thought it a far more enviable fate to die united with thee than to be compelled any longer to bear this life of constraint and hateful etiquette."

"No, no," she replied, trembling. "We will not die! Life is filled with loveliness when you are beside me, and who knows if a happy and blissful future does not yet await us?"

"But were we to die we should be certain of this blissful future, my Geraldine! In the realms beyond the skies we shall no longer be separated or held apart; for there you will be mine, and the blood-stained form of your husband will no longer stand between us!"

"Nay, even here upon earth it shall no longer stand between us," whispered Geraldine. "Come, my Henry, let us fly, far, far hence, where we shall be unknown, and where we can fling aside all this wretched splendor, in order to live for ourselves, and for love alone!"

She threw her arms around her lover, and in the extasy of her passion she quite forgot that she could never dare to fly with him, and that he was hers only so long as he did not see her.

An inexplicable anxiety overpowered her heart, and this emotion had made her forget all—even the queen, and the vengeance which she had promised herself.

She now remembered the words of her father, and she trembled for the fate of her lover.

If her father had not told her the truth—if rather, in order to ruin the queen, he had sacrificed Henry Howard! If she were not in a position to save him, and that he, through her fault, should fall a victim on the scaffold!

But the fleeting moments were still her own, and she would fain enjoy them ere they sped.

She clung round her lover's neck, and clasped him with irresistible force to her heart, which now no longer trembled with love, but with emotions of unspeakable anxiety.

"Let us fly, let us fly!" she repeated breathless. "The present hour is still our own, let us avail ourselves of it, for who knows if the next will belong to us?"

"No, it will not belong to you!" cried

the king, springing forward from his chair like an enraged lion. "Your hours are already numbered, and the next belongs to the headsman!"

A piercing shriek burst from Geraldine's lips, and then a dull sound was heard—as of one who had fallen to the ground.

"She has swooned," murmured Douglas.

"Geraldine! Geraldine! my beloved," cried Henry Howard. "Gracious heavens, she is dying, ye have killed her! Woe betide ye!"

"Woe betide thyself!" said the king, with grave solemnity. "Forward with lights, here, my men!"

The door of the anteroom opened, and four men bearing torches immediately appeared.

"Give us lights here, and guard the door!" said the king, whose dazzled eyes were yet unable to bear the bright glare which now suddenly filled the saloon.

The soldiers obeyed his commands. A pause ensued. The king placed his hand before his eyes and struggled for breath and composure.

When at length he withdrew his hand, his features had assumed a perfectly placid and almost cheerful expression.

With a sudden glance he scanned the whole scene. He saw the queen in her gold-glistening attire; he saw how she lay upon the floor, stretched at full length with her face toward the ground, stiff and motionless.

He saw Henry Howard, who knelt beside his beloved one, and who with all the anxious pangs of a lover was bending over her. He saw how he pressed her hand to his lips, and how he laid his hand upon her head to raise it from the ground.

The king was speechless with rage; he could only raise his arm in order to beckon to the soldiers to approach, and to point to Henry Howard, who had not yet succeeded in lifting the queen from her prostrate position.

"Seize him!" cried Lord Douglas, lending utterance to the silent nod of the king. "Seize him in the king's name, and conduct him to the Tower!"

"Yes, seize him!" said the king, and advancing with youthful alacrity toward Henry Howard, and laying his hand heavily on the shoulders of the young earl, he continued with awful calmness: "Henry Howard, your wishes shall be fulfilled,—you shall mount the scaffold for which you have such an ardent longing."

The noble countenance of the earl remained placid and unmoved:—his clear, beaming eye, fearless and unflinching, met the king's anger-darting glance.

"Sire," he replied, "my life is in your hands, and I know you will not spare it! I do not therefore beg for it. Only spare this noble and beautiful lady, whose only crime is that she followed the dictates of her heart! I alone, sire, am culpable. Punish me, therefore—even with the rack, if it so please you—but be merciful to her!"

The king burst into a fit of loud laughter. "Ah, he intercedes for her," said he. "This little Earl of Surrey of ours, has the assurance to think that his sentimental woes can influence the heart of his judge! No, no, Henry Howard, you know me better! You said just now I was a cruel man, and that my crown was stained with blood. Be it so: it pleases us to set a fresh blood-ruby in our crown, and if it be our will to take it from Geraldine's heart, your poetic effusions won't hinder us, my good little earl. That is my answer for you, and I believe this will be the last time that we shall meet again in this world!"

"Then we shall again meet in the world to come, King Henry of England!" said the Earl of Surrey, solemnly. "Before a higher tribunal, Henry the Eighth will no longer be a judge, but a condemned criminal, and his bloodthirsty and accursed deeds will testify against him."

The king laughed. "You are now taking advantage of your position," he replied. "As you have nothing more to lose, and that the scaffold is your certain doom, you incur no risk in filling up the measure of your sins by blaspheming the king, whom God has sent to rule over you. But you should reflect, my lord, that before the scaffold comes the rack, and that it is very possible some crucial questions may be addressed to the noble Earl of Surrey, in answering which, his tortures may offer some impediment. And now—away! We have nothing more to say to each other upon earth."

Upon a signal from the king, the soldiers approached the earl. When they stretched out their hands to seize him, he glanced at them with such a lofty and commanding air that they involuntarily drew back.

"Follow me!" said Henry Howard, calmly, and, without deigning to cast another look at the king, he strode with proudly raised head toward the door.

Geraldine still lay on the floor with her face toward the ground. She continued motionless, and seemed to have fallen into a deep swoon. Except that when the door closed with a heavy crash behind the Earl of Surrey, a faint moaning was heard, like the sigh which bursts from the dying in their final agony.

The king heeded it not. He still continued to look with a morose and angry scowl toward the door through which the Earl of Surrey had passed.

"He is inflexible," he murmured; "even the rack has no terrors for him; and in his haughty and blasphemous pride, he went forth into the midst of the soldiers,—not like a prisoner, but like a commander. Oh, these Howards have been predestined for my martyrdom, and even their death will scarcely afford me full satisfaction!"

"Sire," said Lord Douglas, who had watched the king with a keen, penetrating eye, and who knew that the monarch had now reached that climax of his anger when he recoiled from no deed of violence or cruelty, "Sire, you have sent the Earl of Surrey to the Tower. But what is to be done with the queen, who lies there on the floor fainting?"

The king recovered from his moody

reflections, and turned his blood-shot eyes toward the motionless form of Geraldine, with such a fierce look of hatred and rage that Lord Douglas said to himself exultingly:

"The queen is lost! He will be inexorable"

"Ah, the queen?" exclaimed Henry, with a grim laugh. "Why, truly, I forgot the queen! This charming Geraldine had escaped my thoughts. But you are right, Douglas, we must think of her, and just consider for a moment what is to be done. Did you not say that a second coach was in readiness? Very well, then, we will not hinder Geraldine from following her lover. Where he is she should be. In the Tower and upon the scaffold! We will therefore rouse up this sentimental lady, and show her a final act of courtesy by conducting her to her coach!"

He was about to approach the prostrate form of the queen, when Lord Douglas restrained him.

"Sire," he said, "it is my duty as your faithful subject, who loves you, and trembles for your welfare,—it is my duty to beseech you to spare yourself, and to preserve your precious and worshipful person from the envenomed stings of care and anger. I entreat you, therefore, not to bestow upon this woman, who has so deeply offended you, another look; command me as to what shall be done with her, and permit me, first of all, to accompany you to your chamber!"

"You are right," said the king; "she is not worthy that my eye should again rest upon her; she is even unworthy of my anger. We will, therefore call the soldiers, and let them conduct this arch-traitress and adulteress to the Tower, as they have conducted her paramour."

"One formality is still wanting for that purpose, sire; the queen will not be admitted into the Tower without a written order signed and sealed by the king."

"Then I shall prepare such order."

"Sire, if it please your majesty, the necessary writing-materials will be found in this cabinet close at hand."

The king leaned in silence upon the arm of Lord Douglas, and suffered himself to be led once more into the cabinet.

The earl made all preparations with eager speed. He rolled forward the writing-table toward the king. He laid the large sheet of paper straight, and thrust the pen into the king's hand.

"What shall I write?" asked the king, who was already becoming exhausted from the efforts he had made in his nocturnal excursion, and from anger and vexation.

"An order for the imprisonment of the queen, sire."

The king wrote. Lord Douglas stood behind him with strained attention, and in breathless expectation,—his looks firmly fixed on the paper over which glided rapidly the white, plump hand of the king, glistening with costly rings.

At length he had reached the goal. If once he should hold in his hand the paper which the king was then writing, if he afterward should have induced Henry to return to his chamber before the seizure of the queen had ensued,—then the victory was his own. It would not be the woman who lay there prostrate whom he would imprison; but with the order for committal in his hand, he would go to the real queen, and conduct her to the Tower.

Once in the Tower, the queen could no longer justify herself; for the king would see her no more, and though she should protest her innocence before her judges with the most sacred oaths, yet the testimony of the king would convict her, for he himself had surprised her with her paramour.

No; there remained no further escape for the queen. She had once succeeded in clearing herself from an accusation, and proving her innocence by a well-established *alibi;* but on this occasion she was hopelessly lost, and no further *alibi* could set her free.

The king had finished his work, and stood up, while Douglas, at his command, was busily occupied in setting the royal seal to the fateful warrant.

A faint sound was now heard in the direction of the saloon, as if some one were moving about cautiously there.

Lord Douglas paid no attention to it; he was just in the act of applying the seal to the molten wax.

The king, however, heard it, and suspected it might be Geraldine who had recovered from her swoon, and who was endeavoring to rise from the ground.

He stepped forward to the door of the cabinet, and looked toward the spot where she lay; but no—she had not yet moved from her prostrate position.

"She has recovered, but she still feigns insensibility," thought the king, and he turned toward Douglas.

"Our work is finished," said he; "the warrant is ready, and sentence has already been pronounced upon the faithless queen. We renounce her from this time forth, and never more shall she behold our face, or hear the sound of our voice. Her sentence and her doom are already pronounced, and the royal favor has no further concern with such a sinner. A curse upon the adulteress—a curse upon the shameless woman, who deceived her husband, and who gave herself up to a traitorous paramour! Woe betide her, and may infamy and disgrace ever attend her name, which—"

The king suddenly broke off and listened. The sound which he had previously heard now became louder and more distinct: it came nearer and nearer.

And now the door opened, and a female form entered—a form which made the king grow pale with wonder and astonishment. She approached nearer and nearer, radiant with youthful charms. A robe of gold brocade enwrapped her figure, a diadem of brilliants gleamed upon her brow, and brighter than the jewels which she wore beamed her eyes.

No, the king was not deceived. It was the queen. She stood before him; and yet there she lay, motionless, and stiff as ever, upon the floor beyond.

The king uttered an exclamation, and recoiled with terror and amazement.

"The queen!" cried Lord Douglas, and he trembled so violently that the paper he held in his hand shook and waved as if his hand were palsied.

"Yes, the queen!" said Katharine, with a proud, triumphant smile. "It is the queen, who comes to chide her husband for being awake at so late an hour of the night, contrary to the advice of his physician."

"And the fool," said John Heywood, presenting himself with a look of comic pathos behind the queen—"the fool, who comes in order to ask Lord Douglas how be dares attempt to depose John Heywood from his office, by usurping the place of court fool to King Henry, and playing all sorts of stupid antics and masquerading pranks before his most gracious majesty?"

"Who, then," cried the king, darting at Lord Douglas a furious and scathing glance, while his voice trembled with rage—"who, then, is that woman lying upon the floor? Who has dared to impose upon the king with this accursed mummery, and to calumniate the queen?"

"Sire," said Lord Douglas, who well knew that upon the present moment depended his own and his daughter's future destiny, and to whom this consciousness speedily restored his composure and presence of mind—"sire, I entreat your majesty for a moment's private conversation, and I shall completely succeed in explaining matters to your satisfaction."

"Do not grant his request, brother Henry," said John Heywood "he is a dangerous juggler, and who knows but that in this private colloquy he might attempt to convince you that he is the king, and that you are nothing but his cringing, fawning and hypocritical servant, Lord Archibald Douglas?"

"My lord and husband, I beg of you to hear the justification of the earl," said Katharine, with a bewitching smile. "It would be cruel to condemn him unheard."

"I will hear him, but it shall be in your presence, Kate, and you shall yourself decide if his justification be satisfactory."

"No, 'pry thee, husband," said Katharine, "Let me remain quite a stranger to the intrigues of this night, so that I may feel no animosity or anger, and may not be deprived of that serenity and confidence which I so greatly need, to enable me to live happily in the midst of my enemies, and to fulfil my duties as a wife, smiling by your side."

"You are right, Kate," said the king, thoughtfully. "You have many enemies at our court, and we must take blame to ourself that we have not always succeeded in stopping our ear to their knavish whispers, and in keeping ourself untainted by the poisonous breath of their slander. Our heart is always too unsuspecting, and we can never fully comprehend what loathsome and contemptible reptiles the majority of mankind are —creatures that should be trodden under foot, but never admitted to one's bosom.—Come, Lord Douglas, I will hear you; but woe betide you if you should not be able to justify yourself!"

He retired some distance to the deep embrasure of a window. Lord Douglas followed him, and drew the heavy velvet hangings behind him.

"Sire," said he, boldly and resolutely, "The question now to be determined is, which of two heads you prefer handing over to the executioner—mine or the Earl of Surrey's. You have the choice between both! If you think that I have dared for a moment to deceive you, why send me at once to the Tower, and pardon the noble Henry Howard—that he may still continue to disturb your sleep and to poison the springs of your happiness; that he may court popular favor, and perhaps one day rob your son of the throne. Here is my head, sire; it is forfeit to the headsman's axe, and the Earl of Surrey is free!"

"No, he is not free, nor ever shall be!" said the king, gnashing his teeth.

"Then, my liege, I am justified, and instead of blaming you will thank me! It is true I played a hazardous game, but I did so in the interest of my king—I did so because I loved him, and because I had read upon his lofty but clouded brow the thoughts which obscured the mind of my sovereign and robbed his nights of sleep. You wished to have Henry Howard in your power, and this crafty and dissembling earl knew how to hide his guilt securely under the mask of virtue and noble bearing. But I knew him, and perceived behind the mask his countenance dimmed by crime and passion. I resolved to unmask him, but for that purpose it was necessary that I should first deceive him, and even deceive yourself for the moment. I knew that he cherished a criminal love for the queen, and I wished to take advantage of this infatuated passion, in order to lead him on securely and inevitably to the punishment which he so well deserved. But I was unwilling to involve the chaste and noble person of the queen in the toils which we had spread to ensnare the Earl of Surrey. I was therefore compelled to seek a substitute for her, and I did so. There is at your court a lady whose whole heart belongs, next to God, to her king, and who worships him so devotedly, that she would be ready at any hour to sacrifice for him her heart's blood—her whole existence—nay, her honor itself, if necessary;—a lady, sire, who lives by your smile, who looks up to you as to her Saviour and Redeemer,—a lady whom at your will you might make either a saint or a courtesan, and who in order to gain your favor would become an unblushing Phryne or a chaste and spotless vestal."

"Tell me her name, Douglas, tell me her name," said the king! "It is a precious and a rare happiness to be loved so devotedly, and it would be a shame not to wish to enjoy such good fortune!"

"Sire, I shall tell you her name, when you declare you have pardoned me," said Douglas, whose heart bounded with joy, and who understood quite well that the king's anger was already mitigated, and the danger almost overcome. "To this lady I said: 'You must render the king a great service—you must free him from his most powerful and most dangerous enemy! You must deliver him from Henry Howard!' 'Tell me what I must do!' she cried, with looks beaming with delight. 'Henry Howard loves the queen. You must take the queen's place for him! You must receive his letters, and reply to them in the name of the queen; you must afford him nocturnal interviews, and, favored by the darkness of the night, make him believe that it is the queen, whom he holds in his arms. You must convince him that the queen returns his passion, so that in thought and in deed he must be placed before the king as a traitor and a delinquent whose head is forfeit to the executioner's axe. Some day we shall let the king be a witness of one of the interviews which Henry Howard believes he is holding with the queen, and it will then be in his power to punish his enemy for his criminal and death-worthy passion!' And when I had thus addressed the lady, sire, she said with a sad smile: 'The task which you impose upon me is an infamous and a disgraceful one, but I accept it, since you tell me I shall thereby render the king a service. I shall dishonor myself for him, but perhaps for doing so he will deign to bestow a smile upon me, and then I shall feel that I am richly rewarded!'"

"Why, this woman is an angel!" cried the king, with ardor—"an angel before whom we should kneel down and worship. Tell me her name, Douglas!"

"As soon as you have pardoned me, sire! You know at present the full extent of my guilt, the entire measure of my culpability. For as I enjoined that noble woman—so it came to pass, and Henry Howard has gone to the Tower in the firm belief that it was the queen whom he had just held in his arms."

"But why did you also suffer me to remain in this belief, Douglas? Why did you also fill me with anger against the noble and virtuous queen?"

"Sire, I dared not reveal to you this deception until you should have condemned Surrey, for your noble and generous mind would have recoiled against punishing him for an offence which he had not committed, and in your first anger you would have blamed this devoted woman who sacrificed herself for her king."

"It is true," said the king, "I should not have known this noble woman, and instead of thanking, I would have crushed her."

"For that reason, my liege, I allowed matters to proceed quietly, even until you had drawn up the warrant against the queen. But remember, sire, that I begged you to return to your chamber before the queen should be seized. Well, I should then have revealed to you the entire secret, which I could not disclose in the presence of that woman. For she would have died with shame if she suspected that you were aware of her love; so pure and self-devoting, so silent and heroic for the king."

"She shall never learn it, Douglas. But satisfy at length my desire—tell me her name!"

"Then, sire, you have pardoned me? You are no longer angry with me for having ventured to deceive you?"

"I am no longer angry with you, Douglas, for you have done right; it was a wily and a daring scheme which you hit upon, and which you carried out with such a happy result."

"I thank you, sire, and I will now tell you her name. The lady, sire, who at my request presented herself as a sacrifice before this guilty earl, who tolerated his amatory protestations and his embraces, in order to render a service to her king,—that lady, sire, was my daughter, Lady Jane Douglas!"

"Lady Jane!" cried the king. "No, no! this is a new deception. What, this proud, chaste, and unapproachable Lady Jane—this cold and beautiful marble statue, had really a heart in her bosom, and this heart belonged to me? This Lady Jane, the modest and bashful maiden, to have made for my sake the immense sacrifice of taking the odious Surrey for her paramour, in order like a second Delilah to deliver him into my hands? No, Douglas—you are deceiving me. Lady Jane has not done this!"

"May it please your majesty to satisfy yourself by seeing the woman who now lies in a swoon beyond, and who personated the queen for Henry Howard."

The king did not reply, but drew the hangings aside, and again entered the cabinet in which the queen was waiting with John Heywood.

Henry paid her no attention; with youthful eagerness he passed through the cabinet and entered the saloon. He now stood beside the form of Geraldine, still prostrate on the floor.

She was no longer in a swoon; she had already regained her consciousness, but her heart was rent with pangs of the bitterest anguish. Henry Howard had become a victim to the headsman's axe, and it was she who had betrayed him.

But her father had sworn to her that she should save the life of her lover.

It was not therefore permitted her to die. She felt that she must live in order to set Henry Howard free.

Her poor heart was aglow with the consuming fire of remorse, but she dared not think of her own agony. She dared not think of herself, but of him whom she was bound to set free and deliver from death.

It was for him she was uttering a fervent prayer to God—for him her heart was trembling with pain and anguish, when the king now approached her, and bending down, scanned her features with a smiling expression of a peculiar and inquiring character.

"Lady Jane Douglas," said he, at length, extending to her his hand, "rise from the ground, and allow your king to thank you for your noble and generous self-sacrifice! Truly, the lot of a king is a happy one, for we have at least the power of punishing traitors and of rewarding those who serve us. The one I have already done, and the other I will not neglect. Rise, therefore, Lady Jane; it does not become you to lie on your knees at my feet!"

"Oh, let me kneel, my liege," she exclaimed in accents of passionate entreaty —"let me kneel and implore you for mercy and pardon! Have compassion, King Henry—have pity for the anguish and torment which I suffer. It is impossible that all this should be true—that this allusion should become such a terrible reality. Tell me, King Henry, I beseech you by the agonies which I endure for your sake—tell me what you purpose doing with Henry Howard? Why have you sent him to the Tower?"

"In order to punish the traitor as he deserves," said the king, glancing with a fierce and angry scowl at Douglas, who had also approached his daughter, and who now stood close beside her.

Lady Jane uttered a heart-rending shriek, and sank once more exhausted to the ground.

The king's brow became suddenly clouded. "It is possible," said he, "and I can well believe the fact, that I have this night been deceived in many ways—that my simplicity has been trifled with, in order to concoct for me a very pretty fable. In the mean time I have promised to forgive, and it shall not be said that Henry the Eighth, who calls himself the champion of God, has ever broken his royal word, or has ever punished those to whom he had promised impunity. My Lord Douglas, I shall keep my word! I pardon you!"

He presented his hand to the earl, who pressed it fervently to his lips. The king drew closer to him.

"Douglas," he whispered, "you have the wisdom of the serpent, but I now see through the plot which you so artfully concocted! You wished to ruin Surrey, but the queen was to sink with him into the abyss. While I thank you on account of Surrey, I pardon you what you have done against the queen. Beware, however, beware, lest I should once more catch you on the same path; do not dare by a word, a look, nay, even by a smile, to raise suspicion against your royal mistress. The slightest attempt would cost you your life; that I swear to you by the Holy Mother of God, and you know that I have never broken this oath! As regards Lady Jane, we will forget that she has abused the name of our illustrious and virtuous spouse, for the purpose of drawing this lustful and guilty earl into the snare which you have laid for him. She has obeyed your command, Douglas, and we will not now decide what farther motives may have urged her to this deed. That she must determine before God and her conscience: it does not become us to settle the question."

"But perhaps, my lord and husband, it becomes me to inquire by what right Lady Jane Douglas has dared to appear in this place in her present attire, and in a certain manner to present a counterfeit of her queen?" said Katharine, in a tone of firmness and decision. "I may well be allowed to ask what has caused my maid of honor, who left the banquet-room from indisposition, to become so well of a sudden, that she is able to wander about the palace by night, and in such array that it might readily be confounded with mine. I ask, sire, if perchance this disguise was a cunningly contrived artifice for the purpose of effecting a supposed identity? You are silent, my lord? Then it is true that there was a terrible plot laid here against me; and without the aid of my honest and faithful friend, John Heywood, who led me hither, I should, doubtless, at the present moment have been condemned and ruined, like the Earl of Surrey."

"Ah, John! then it was you who threw a little light upon these dark doings," said the king, with a good-humored laugh, as he laid his hand upon Heywood's shoulder. "Well, truly, what the wise and prudent were unable to discover, the fool has completely fathomed!"

"King Henry of England," said John Heywood, with solemn gravity, "many call themselves wise men, and yet are fools, and many only assume the mask of folly, because the fool alone is permitted to be a wise man!"

"Kate," said the king, "you are right—this was for you a night of evil omen; But God and the fool have saved both you and me. Let us both be thankful for it! But it is well if you do as you first intended, and inquire no further concerning the enigmas of this night. It was brave of you to come hither, and we shall not be unmindful of it. Come, my little queen, give me your arm, and conduct me to my chamber. I tell you, child, it gives me joy, to be able to lean upon your arm, and to see your charming rosy face, which shows no trace of the pallor produced by fear, or by an evil conscience. Come, Kate, you alone shall conduct me, and in you alone will I confide!"

"Sire, you are too heavy for the queen," said the fool, while he placed his neck under the other arm of the king, —"Let me share the burden of royalty with her."

"But before we go," said Katharine. "I have one favor to ask. Will you grant it?"

"I will grant every thing you ask, provided you don't request me to send you to the Tower."

"Sire, I wish to dismiss my maid of honor, Lady Jane Douglas, from her service, that is all," said the queen, while her glance was directed with a mingled expression of pity and contempt toward the form of her quondam friend, still prostrate on the floor.

"She is dismissed!" said the king. "You shall choose another maid of honor to-morrow. Come, Kate!"

And the king, supported by his spouse and by John Heywood, quitted the apartment with slow and unwieldy steps.

Lord Douglas looked after them with a sinister and vindictive scowl; and when the door closed behind them he raised his arm with a threatening gesture, and his trembling lips gave utterance to the wildest imprecations.

"Vanquished! — once more vanquished!" he murmured, gnashing his teeth. "Humbled by this woman, whom I hate, and whom I will yet bring to ruin. Yes, she has conquered this time, but we will renew the struggle, and our poisoned arrows shall eventually reach her heart!"

Suddenly he felt a hand laid heavily on his shoulder, while a pair of eyes, glowing and flame-darting, were fixed upon him.

"Father," said Lady Jane, and she raised her right hand toward heaven—"father, so truly as there is a heaven above us, I will accuse you as a traitor before the king, and betray all your execrable intrigues, if you do not aid me in liberating Henry Howard!"

With an expression of countenance almost sorrowful, her father scanned her features, which were haggard and painfully convulsed.

"I will help you," he replied. "I shall do so if you will also help me, and promote my plans."

"Oh, save Henry Howard, only save him, and I will bind myself to Satan, and seal the bond with my own life-blood!" said Lady Jane, with a ghastly smile. "Save his life, or if you cannot do that, at least procure me the happiness of being able to die with him!"

CHAPTER VII.

THE ILLUSION DISPELLED.

PARLIAMENT, which already for a long time had never dared to oppose the will of the king,—Parliament had pronounced its sentence. It had accused the Earl of Surrey of high-treason, and, upon the sole testimony of his mother and of his sister, he was found guilty of treason and *lèse-majesté*. A few casual expressions of ill-humor for having been superseded in his command—a few remarks which he had made in deprecating the executions which saturated the soil of England with blood—was all that the Duchess of Richmond had been able to bring forward against him; that he, like his father, had borne the coat-of-arms of the King of England, was the only proof of high-treason to which his mother, the Duchess of Norfolk, was able to testify.

These charges were so insignificant, that the Parliament well knew they formed no grounds, but only a pretext for his committal.

Only a pretext, by which the king said to his pliant and trembling Parliament—"This man is innocent; but I wish you to condemn him, and therefore you must consider the charges established!"

The Parliament had not had the courage to resist the will of the sovereign. Its members were little better than a flock of sheep, which, trembling before the sharp teeth of the dog, meekly follow the path which he has indicated to them.

The king wished that they should condemn the Earl of Surrey, and they condemned him accordingly

They summoned him before their tribunal, and it was in vain that he proved to them his innocence in glowing words, which seemed inspired; these guardians of the public weal would not perceive that he was innocent.

There were, indeed, a few who felt ashamed to bow their heads so unconditionally beneath the royal sceptre, which trickled with blood like an executioner's axe. There were a few to whom the evidence appeared insufficient, but they were out-voted; and in order to give his Parliament a warning example, the king caused these recalcitrant members to be committed to prison the same day, and to be accused of some crime which his fancy suggested. For the nation was at this time so enslaved by the fierce and savage barbarity of the king—the people so degenerate and so degraded in their self-consciousness, that public men could readily be found, who, in order to show their complaisance to the king, and their subservience to his bloodthirsty and hypocritical piety, lowered themselves to the grade of spies and informers, and accused of crimes those whom the angry frown of the king had indicated as offenders.

Accordingly the Parliament had condemned to death the Earl of Surrey, and the king had signed the death-warrant.

The execution was to take place early the next morning, and in the court-yard of the Tower the workmen were already busy erecting the scaffold, on which the head of the noble Surrey was soon to fall.

Henry Howard was alone in his prison. He had closed with life and with earthly things. He had set his house in order, and had made his will; he had written to his mother and to his sister, and had pardoned them their treachery and their accusations; he had written a letter to his father, in which, with noble and touching words, he exhorted him to be calm and firm, and not to weep for him—for that death was his wish, and the grave the only refuge which he sought.

He had, accordingly, as we have said, closed with life, and earthly things gave him no more concern. He was troubled by no fears and no regrets—life had left him nothing further to wish for, and he almost thanked the king for having determined to rid him so speedily of this burden of existence.

The future had nothing more to offer him—why, therefore, should he yearn for it? Why covet a life which for him could only be a gloomy and a solitary wilderness? For Geraldine was lost to him. He knew not her fate, and no information about her had penetrated the dreary walls of his dungeon. Was the queen still alive? or had the king in his fury struck her dead on that night when Henry was conducted to the Tower, and when he saw his beloved for the last time swooning, numb, and prostrate, at the feet of her husband?

What had become of the queen—of Henry Howard's beloved Geraldine? He knew nothing about her. In vain had he hoped for some sign, for some intelligence, but he had not dared to ask anybody as to her fate. Perchance the king had abstained from punishing her. Peradventure his lust for blood was appeased by slaying Henry Howard, and that Katharine had escaped the block. It might, therefore, have been ruinous to her, had he, the condemned, made inquiry respecting her. Or, if she had gone before him, he was sure of meeting her once more in a higher sphere, and of being eternally united with her in realms beyond the skies.

He believed in this future existence, and love added strength to his belief. Death had no terrors for him, for beyond the grave he should see her—his Geraldine—who was either already awaiting him in their eternal home, or would soon follow him thither.

Life had nothing more to offer him—death united him with his beloved. He greeted Death as his friend and deliverer—as the priest who should unite him forever with his Geraldine.

He heard the large clock of the prison-tower, as it announced the hours with a monotonous stroke, and he greeted each expiring hour with a throb of joyful exultation—the evening came, and night followed; the last night which was yet allotted him—the last night which separated him from Geraldine.

The jailer opened the door, in order to bring the earl a light and to attend to his commands. Heretofore the king had given special directions that he should not be allowed light in his dungeon; and he had therefore passed six long and dreary nights in his prison. This night, however, they had resolved to furnish him with light, and to grant him whatever he might still desire. Life, which in a few hours he would have to relinquish, should once more provide him with all the pleasures and all the enjoyments which he might wish to demand. Henry Howard had only to express a wish, and the prison-keeper was ready to grant his request.

But Henry Howard wished for nothing; he asked for nothing, but that he should be left alone—that light, which dazzled his sight and which opposed a stern reality to his rapturous visions, should be removed from his dungeon.

The king, who had determined to subject him to a special punishment in condemning him to darkness—the king had thus become his benefactor against his will. For with the darkness came visions and illusions—with the darkness came Geraldine.

When silence and night had enwrapped him then all became light within, and softly-murmured whispers and a sweet, seductive voice fell soothingly upon his ear. The doors of his prison flew open, and upon the wings of imagination Henry Howard took flight from his dark and lonely prison cell. Upon the wings of imagination he sought and found his Geraldine.

She was still beside him in the large silent saloon. Night once more fell around them both, and discreetly enwrapped them like a sweet veil of enchantment, concealing their embraces and mutual endearments. Solitude enabled him again to catch the rapturous music of her voice which sang for him such melodious strains of love and ecstasy.

It was necessary for Henry Howard to be alone, in order that he might be able to hear the voice of his Geraldine; it was necessary that deep darkness should surround him, in order that Geraldine should come to his side.

For the last night of his life, accordingly, he demanded nothing more than that he should be left alone and without light. The jailer extinguished the light, and left the cell, but he neither fixed the large heavy bolts of the door, nor did he turn the key in the great lock: he merely drew the door slightly to, and did not even fasten the latch.

To this, however, Henry Howard paid no heed. What did it concern him if the doors were no longer fastened—him, who had no longer a wish for liberty or for life?

Accordingly he reclined upon his seat and dreamt with open eyes. Yonder, in the court-yard, was being erected the scaffold, which Henry Howard should ascend at early dawn. The dull sounds of the hammer reached his ear, and ever and anon the torches which gave light to the workmen at their dreary task, caused a faint flicker to light up the dungeon, on the walls of which spectral forms seemed to dance.

"These," thought Henry Howard, "are the spirits of those whom King Henry has put to death; they gather round me like will-o'-the-wisps—they are dancing with me the dance of death, and in a few hours I shall be one of their own forever!"

The dull strokes of the hammer and of the axe still resounded on, and Henry Howard became plunged more deeply in contemplation and silent musing.

His thoughts, his feelings, and his will were occupied alone with Geraldine. His whole soul was filled with this single idea. He felt as though he could command his mind to see her—as though he could direct his senses to perceive her. Yes, she was there present; he felt her, he knew her. He lay once more at her feet, and leaned his head on her lap, and listened once more to those enchanting revelations of her love.

Wholly absorbed and carried away, he felt, he saw, naught else but her. The mystery of love was accomplished, and, under the veil of night, Geraldine had soared hither on airy wings to meet him.

A radiant smile played around his lips, which murmured forth words of rapturous greeting. Seized with a singular hallucination, he saw his beloved approach; he held out his arms to embrace her, and he did not awake from his reverie, even when instead of her he grasped the empty air.

"Wherefore dost thou flee from me, Geraldine?" he asked, softly. "Why dost thou withdraw thyself from the arms of thy lover, to whirl about with the will-o'-the-wisps in the dance of death? Come, Geraldine, come, my soul yearns for thee with ardent longing —my heart calls to thee with its last waning throb. Come, Geraldine, oh come!"

What was that? It seemed as if the door had opened softly, and then that the latch had faintly clicked. It seemed as if feet were floating gently along the floor—as if some human form obscured for a moment the flickering glimmer which danced along the walls.

Henry Howard did not perceive it. He saw nothing but his Geraldine, for whose presence he yearned with such ardent longing. He once more held out his arms—he called her by name with all the glowing enthusiasm of a lover.

And now he uttered a cry of rapture. His prayer of love was granted. The dream had become a reality. His arms no more embraced the empty air—they folded the woman whom he loved, and for whom he was about to die, to his heart.

He pressed his lips to hers, and returned her kisses with fervent tenderness; he threw his arms around her form, while she held him firmly to her bosom.

Was this reality? or was it delirium that had seized upon his brain and deluded him with such enthralling fantasies?

Henry Howard shuddered at the thought, and falling upon his knees, he exclaimed in a voice tremulous with anxiety and love: "Geraldine, have pity upon me! Assure me that this is no dream—that I am not raving. Tell me that thou art my own Geraldine whose knees I now embrace. Speak, oh, speak my Geraldine!"

"I am!" she whispered, softly. "I am Geraldine, I am the woman whom thou lovest, and to whom thou hast sworn eternal love and eternal fidelity! Henry Howard, my own beloved, let me now remind thee of thy vows! Thy life belongs to me—that thou hast promised—and I now come to demand possession of my treasure!"

"Yes, my life belongs to thee, Geraldine! but it is a poor, miserable possession, which thou canst call thine but for a few short hours."

She flung her arms wildly around his neck, she raised him up to her heart and kissed his lips and his brow with passionate rapture. He felt her scalding tears streaming down his face, he heard her sighs, which burst from her bosom like the throes of death.

"Thou shalt not die!" she murmured sobbing. "No, Henry, thou must live, in order that I, too, may be able to live—that I may not be driven frantic with grief and pain for thee—oh, dost thou not feel how I love thee—dost thou not know that thy life is my life, and thy death my death?"

He leaned his head on her shoulder, and, intoxicated with happiness, he scarce heard what she said. She was once more beside him. What cared he for aught else.

"Geraldine," he whispered, softly, "dost thou remember that night when we first met? How our hearts beat together in unison—with what rapturous emotion our lips .... Geraldine, my bride, my beloved, we then swore that nothing should divide us, that our love should endure beyond the grave! Dost thou still remember that, Geraldine?"

"Yes, I remember it, my Henry. But thou shalt not yet die, and not in death but in life shall thy love put mine to the test. Yes, we will live—live on! And thy life shall be my life, and where thou art, there will I also be. Henry, dost thou remember that thou hast promised me this with a solemn and sacred vow?"

"I remember it, but I cannot keep my word with thee, Geraldine! Hearest thou the hammer at work below in the court-yard? Dost thou know what that means, dearest one?"

"Yes, Henry, I know it is the scaffold which they are erecting for thee—the scaffold for thee and for me, for I too will die, Henry, if you do not live, and the axe which falls upon thy neck shall also reach mine if thou wilt not that we both should live."

"I am quite willing, dearest one, but we cannot do so."

"We can, Henry, we can! All is ready for flight! All is arranged—all prepared. The king's signet-ring has opened for me the gates of the Tower, and the might of gold has gained me the keeper of your dungeon. He will, therefore, not perceive it, if instead of one person, two should leave this cell; without let or hinderance, we shall both leave the Tower by a way which is known but to him, through secret corridors and passages, until we reach a boat which is lying in the Thames waiting for us, and which will convey us to a ship lower down the river, ready to sail the moment we have got on board, to transport us to the friendly shores of a foreign land. Come, Henry, come, lay thine arm in mine, and let us leave this prison!"

She flung her arms round his neck, and drew him forward. He pressed her closely to his heart and whispered: "Yes, come, come, my beloved! Let us fly! To thee belongs my life, to thee alone!"

He lifted her up in his arms, and hurried with her to the door. He opened it with his foot, and hastened along the corridor. But he had only reached the first turning when he staggered back with affright.

Before the door stood several soldiers with shouldered arms; there stood also the lieutenant of the Tower, and beside him were two attendants with lighted torches.

Geraldine shrieked, and, with eager speed, replaced the thick veil which she wore, and which had slipped from her face for the moment.

Henry Howard, too, uttered a cry, but not because of the soldiers and the frustration of his hopes. He stared with astonishment at the form now so closely veiled by his side. It seemed to him as if a strange countenance like that of a spectre had started up beside him—as though it were not the beloved head of the queen which was resting on his shoulder. He looked at this countenance as if it were a vision, or some strange apparition, but this he well knew—that it was not the face of his Geraldine.

The lieutenant of the Tower beckoned to his attendants, and they proceeded with their lighted torches toward the dungeon of the earl.

He then gave his hand to Henry Howard, and conducted him back in silence to his prison.

Henry Howard made no resistance; he followed him, but his hand grasped the arm of Geraldine, and he drew her along with him; his eye rested upon her with a penetrating expression, and seemed to threaten her.

They were now once more in the chamber which they had recently quitted with such blissful hopes.

The lieutenant of the Tower made a sign to the attendants to leave the apartment, and then turned with solemn gravity to the Earl of Surrey.

"My lord," he said, "it is by the king's command that I bring you these lights. His majesty knew all that has happened here this evening. He knew that a plan had been contrived for setting you free, and while the authors of this scheme thought to deceive the king, they have themselves been foiled. The king was induced under a variety of artful pretexts to lend his signet-ring to one of his courtiers. But his majesty had already been warned, and in fact he was already aware, that it was not a man, as had been pretended, but a lady, who came, not in order to take leave, but in order to liberate you from your prison.—Madam, the jailer whom you intended to bribe was a faithful servant of the king; he betrayed to me your plan, and it was I who ordered him to let you imagine that he favored your scheme. You will not be able to set the Earl of Surrey free, but, if you desire it, I will myself get you escorted to the ship which is waiting for you in the river, ready to sail. No one, madam, will hinder you from going on board. Only you must proceed alone. The Earl of Surrey cannot accompany you!—My lord, the night is already far advanced, and you know that it is to be your last. The king has commanded me to offer no impediment in case this lady should wish to spend the night with you in your chamber, but she is only at liberty to do so on condition that lights be left burning in the room. That is the express will of the king, and these are his own words: 'Tell the Earl of Surrey that I permit him to love his Geraldine, but that his eyes must be open, in order to see. In order that he may be able to see, you must give him lights, and I command him not to extinguish them so long as Geraldine shall continue with him. He might otherwise confound her with another lady; for in the dark one cannot distinguish even a counterfeit from a queen!' You have therefore to determine, my lord, if this lady is to remain with you, or if she is to go, and the light is to be put out!"

"She shall remain with me, and I shall certainly require the light as well!" said the Earl of Surrey, and his penetrating glance continued fixed upon the veiled form which trembled at his words as if seized with an ague-fit.

"Have you no other wish to express, my lord?"

"None, but that I may be left alone with this person!"

The lieutenant bowed, and left the room.

They were now once more alone, and

stood face to face in silence. The violent throbbings of their hearts were audible —while sighs, laden with anguish, burst from the lips of Geraldine.

A fearful—a terrible pause ensued. Geraldine would have gladly given her life, could she have extinguished this light, and have wrapped herself in impenetrable darkness.

But the Earl of Surrey resolved to see. He approached her with a haughty and angry glance, and as he raised his arm in a commanding attitude, Geraldine shuddered and shrank back, while she bent her head in utter prostration.

"Unveil your face!" he exclaimed, with an imperious tone.

She remained motionless. She muttered a prayer, and then she raised her clasped hands toward Henry Howard, and sighed faintly—

"Pardon! pardon!"

He stretched forth his hand and seized the veil.

"Pardon!" she repeated, in tones of deeper anguish and entreaty.

But he was inexorable. He tore the veil from her face, and stared eagerly at her for a moment; and then with a wild cry he staggered back and stood aghast, while he covered his face with his hands.

Jane Douglas, meanwhile, dared not breathe or stir. She was pale as marble; her large, ardent eyes, with an unutterable look of entreaty, were directed toward her beloved, who, overwhelmed with pain, and with his face hidden by his hands, stood at some distance away from her. She loved him more than her life—more than her hopes of eternal bliss, and yet it was she herself who had brought upon him this hour of bitter anguish.

At length the Earl of Surrey withdrew his hands from before his face, and with wild emotion dashed away the tears from his eyes.

As he looked at her, Jane Douglas sank quite involuntarily upon her knees, and raised her hands beseechingly.

"Henry Howard," she murmured, faintly, "I am—I am—your own Geraldine! It was I whom you loved, it was my letters that you read with rapture, and often have you vowed to me that you loved my mind still more than my person, and often has it filled my heart with delight, when you told me you would love me, however much my face might change with time, however much years or sickness might alter my features. Do you remember, Henry, how I once asked you whether you would cease to love me, if God were suddenly to place a mask over my face, so that my features could no longer be recognized? You answered me, 'I would nevertheless love and worship you, for it is not your fair form or your beauty which causes me such rapture, but it is yourself—your own sweet self—your innate excellence—your essential being, your mind and your heart, which never can change, which, bright and beaming, lie disclosed before me, like the pages of a sacred book!' That was your answer to me then, while you swore to love me forever. Henry Howard, I now remind you of your plighted vows! I am thy

Geraldine—it is the same mind, the same heart, only that God has placed a mask upon my features!"

The Earl of Surrey had listened to her with strained attention, and with growing amazement.

"It is she! Is it possible?" he exclaimed, when she had now ceased. "It is Geraldine!"

And completely overwhelmed and speechless with pain, he sank back upon a chair.

Geraldine flew to his side—she crouched down at his feet—she seized his hand, which hung down listlessly, and covered it with kisses; and with streaming tears, oft interrupted by sighs and sobs, she related to him the sad and dismal story of her love, and revealed to him the whole tissue of falsehood, cunning, and deceit which her father had thrown around them both. She disclosed to him the entire secrets of her heart. She spoke to him of her love, of her suffering, of her ambition, and of her remorse of conscience. She accused herself, but pleaded the excuse of her love, and, clasping his knees, she besought him with streaming eyes for mercy and forgiveness.

He thrust her aside impetuously, and stood up, while he recoiled from her touch. His noble countenance glowed with anger, his eyes flashed scornfully, his long, flowing hair shaded his lofty brow and his features as with a dark veil. He looked majestic in his anger, majestic as the archangel Michael crushing the dragon beneath his feet. And thus he bent his head forward near her, and scanned her with looks of contempt and withering scorn.

"I pardon you?" he exclaimed—"never! What! I pardon you—you who have made my whole life a ridiculous lie, and converted the tragic drama of my love into a wretched and pitiful farce? Oh, Geraldine, how great my love for you has been, and yet you have now become for me a loathsome spectre, at which my soul shudders, and which I must execrate! You have crushed my life, and even my death you have robbed of its consecrated character—for now it is no longer the martyrdom of my love, but the wild mockery of my too credulous heart.—Oh, Geraldine, how glorious it would have been to die for thee; to bid farewell to life with thy name still lingering on my lips; to bless thee, to thank thee for my happiness while the axe was already raised over my head! How delightful the thought that death did not divide us—that it was only the way that led to our eternal union—that we should only be separated here for a brief moment, in order to meet once more above, where our bliss would endure without change, without end!"

Geraldine crouched at his feet like a bruised worm, and her groans of lamentation and her stifled sobs were the heart-rending accompaniment of his melancholy words.

"But that is now all over!" exclaimed Henry Howard, and his countenance, which before was convulsed with pain and grief, now glowed once more with anger. "You have poisoned my life and my dying hour, and for this I shall curse you, and my last word will be an imprecation upon the head of Geraldine—the counterfeit—the juggler!"

"Oh! have mercy!" she groaned. "Kill me, Henry, crush my head under your feet, only let this torment cease!"

"No—no mercy!" he cried, wildly, "no mercy for an impostor, who has cheated me of my heart, and slunk into my love like a thief. Rise, and quit this chamber! Thy presence gives me horror, and when I see thee I feel that I must curse thee. Yes, Geraldine, may infamy and disgrace attend thee! Accursed be the kisses which I imprinted on thy lips—the tears of rapture which I shed upon thy bosom! When I mount the scaffold I shall curse thee, and my last word shall be: 'May woe attend the footsteps of Geraldine, for she is my murderess!'"

He stood before her with high uplifted arm, erect and haughty in his anger. She felt the scathing fire of his glance, though she dared not look up at him, but lay moaning convulsively at his feet, with her face hidden by her veil, as if she shuddered at her own image.

"And let this be my last word to thee, Geraldine," said Henry Howard, with grave emphasis: "go hence under the burden of my imprecations, and live, if thou canst!"

She unveiled her head, and raised her face toward him. A derisive smile played around her deadly pale lips. "Live?" she exclaimed. "Have we not sworn to die together? Your imprecations do not absolve me from my oath, and when you descend into your grave, Jane Douglas will stand upon the brink of it, with tears and entreaties, until you have made for her a little space beside you—until she has softened your heart, and you take her to your bosom once more in the grave as your own Geraldine. Oh, Henry, in the grave I shall no longer wear the face of Jane Douglas—this hateful face which I could tear to pieces with my nails! In the grave I shall again be Geraldine. Then I shall once more nestle near your heart, and you will again say to me, 'It is not thy face or thy outward form that I love! I love thyself, thy heart, thy mind,—for these can never change nor alter!'"

"Enough!" he exclaimed, hoarsely. "Be silent, if you do not wish to make me frantic! Fling not my own words in my face; they pollute me, for falsehood has desecrated and befouled them with its slime. No, I will not make room for you in my grave, I will not again call you Geraldine. You are merely Jane Douglas, whom I abhor, and I invoke anathemas upon your guilty head! Once for all—"

He ceased suddenly, and a slight shudder ran through his frame.

Jane Douglas uttered a piercing scream, and rose up from her kneeling posture.

Day had dawned, and from the belfry of the prison tower resounded the grave and dismal tones of the death-bell.

"Hearest thou, Jane Douglas?" said Surrey; "this knell summons me to death, and it is thou who hast poisoned this, my final hour. I was happy when I loved thee; I die in despair, for I hate and despise thee!"

"No, no, you dare not die!" she exclaimed, clinging to him with passionate anguish. "You dare not descend into the grave with these wild imprecations on your lips! I cannot be your murderess. Oh! it is impossible that they should want to kill the noble, the brave, and virtuous Earl of Surrey. Gracious Heaven! what have you done to rouse their anger? You are innocent, and they know it—they cannot put you to death, for it would be murder. You have done nothing that they could condemn you for; for it is no crime to love Jane Douglas, and me—me alone you have loved!"

"No, not you," he returned, haughtily, "I have nothing to do with Lady Jane Douglas. I loved the queen, and I believed she loved me in return. That is my crime!"

The door opened, and the lieutenant of the Tower entered in solemn silence, followed by a priest, with a few attendant choristers. At the door appeared the headsman, who, in his red, flaming attire, and with calm, unsympathizing visage, stood at the threshold.

"It is time!" said the governor, solemnly.

The priest muttered his prayers, and the choristers swung their censers. The death-bell still pealed forth its mournful dirge, and from the court-yard was heard the murmur of the populace, who, curious and bloodthirsty as ever, had thronged hither with boisterous mirth, to see this man, who was yesterday their darling, bleed on the scaffold.

The Earl of Surrey stood for a moment in silence. His features worked convulsively, and a deadly pallor overspread his countenance.

It was not the thought of death—but that of dying, which made him tremble. It seemed to him as if he already felt on his neck the cold, keen axe which that terrible man held in his hand. Oh, to die upon the battle-field, what happiness would that have been! To end one's days upon the scaffold, what ignominy was this!

"Henry Howard, my son, art thou prepared to die?" asked the priest. "Hast thou made thy peace with thy God? Dost thou repent thy sins, and dost thou acknowledge that death is thy just atonement and penalty? Dost thou pardon thy enemies, and dost thou depart hence in peace with all men?"

"I am ready to die," replied Henry Howard, with a haughty smile. "The other questions, father, I shall answer before the throne of the Almighty!"

"Dost thou admit that thou hast been a wicked traitor, and dost thou beg for pardon of thy noble, wise, and just king, for the blasphemous offences which thou hast committed against his most sacred majesty?"

The Earl of Surrey looked at him for a moment with a steadfast gaze. "Do you know of what crime am I accused?"

The priest cast down his eyes, and muttered a few unintelligible words.

Henry Howard turned aside from the priest with a haughty movement of his head, and addressed himself to the governor of the Tower:

"Do you, sir, know what my crime is?" he asked.

But the lieutenant also averted his eyes, and remained silent.

Henry Howard smiled. "Well, then, I will tell you. I have borne, as became the son of my father, the arms of our house on my shield, and over the portal of my mansion; and it has happened that the king bears the same coat-of-arms that we do. That is my crime, and the treason of which I am accused. I have also said that the king is deceived in many of his servants, and often summons his favorites to high honors, which they do not deserve. That is my offence of *lèse-majesté*; and that is the reason why I am now about to lay my head upon the block. Be not uneasy, however, I will myself increase my crimes, by adding still one more to the number, so that they may become heavy enough, in order to lighten the conscience of our just and magnanimous king. I abandoned my heart to a wretched and criminal love, and the Geraldine whose praises I sang in many an ode, and whom I even celebrated in presence of the king, was nothing more than a miserable and unchaste coquette."

Jane Douglas uttered a loud cry, and sank to the ground as if struck by lightning.

"Dost thou repent these sins, my son?" asked the priest. "Dost thou turn aside thy heart from this sinful love, in order to devote it to God?"

"I not only repent this love, but I loathe it! And now, good father, let us proceed, for you perceive his worship, the governor, is becoming impatient. He is reflecting that the king will find no rest, until these Howards have also gone to their long rest. Ah, King Henry! King Henry! Thou callest thyself the mighty king of the world, and yet thou tremblest before the coat-of-arms of thy subjects. Master governor, should you this day go to the king, greet him on the part of Henry Howard, and tell him I wish his bed may be as easy for him as the grave will be for me. And now, gentlemen, it is time; let us proceed!"

With a calm and dignified air, and with a firm step, he turned toward the door. At this moment Jane Douglas sprang suddenly from the floor, and flinging herself upon his neck, clung to him with all the force of passion and desperate grief.

"I will not leave you!" she cried, breathless and deadly pale. "You must not repulse me, for you have sworn that we would live and die together."

He flung her aside with a burst of wild anger, and drew himself up in a menacing attitude.

"I forbid you to follow me!" he exclaimed, with an imperious tone.

She tottered back against the wall, and looked at him, trembling and breathless.

He still held the mastery over her soul. She was still subject to him in love and obedience. She did not, therefore, feel within her the courage to brave his command.

She saw how he left the chamber, and how he proceeded along the corridor with his awful retinue; she heard how the sound of their footsteps gradually died away, and then how the dull rumble of the drums suddenly resounded in the court-yard below.

Jane Douglas fell upon her knees to pray, but her lips trembled so violently that she could find no words for her prayers.

At length the rumbling of the drums ceased, and only the death-bell still continued its mournful knell. She heard a voice which spoke in firm and forcible accents.

It was his voice—it was Henry Howard who spoke. And now once more came the dull roll of the drums to drown the voice.

"He is dying—he is dying, and I am not beside him!" she shrieked, with wild emotion; and springing up she rushed out of the room and flew along the corridor and down the steps with the speed of lightning.

She gained the court-yard. There, in the midst of an immense crowd of spectators, stood the scaffold—dark, awful, and hideous. Another moment, and Henry Howard knelt down. She saw the axe in the hand of the executioner. She saw him raise it to give the fatal blow.

She was no longer a woman, but a tigress. The blood forsook her cheeks. Her nostrils expanded, and her eyes darted flames.

She drew forth the dagger which she had concealed in her bosom, and cleared a path for herself through the terrified and timidly-yielding throng.

With a bound she sprang up the steps of the scaffold. And now she stood beside him—close beside the kneeling form.

A gleam flashed through the air. She heard a peculiar whizzing sound, and then a dull, heavy blow. A reeking stream of blood foamed aloft, and bathed Jane Douglas in its crimson tide.

"I come, Henry, I come!" she exclaimed, with a wild cry of exultation. "In death I shall be thine!"

And again gleamed through the air the flashing steel. It was the dagger which Jane Douglas had buried in her own heart.

The blow was well aimed! Not a sound—not a groan escaped her lips. With a triumphant smile she sank down beside the mutilated corpse of her beloved; and as her life-blood ebbed apace and mingled with that of the murdered earl, she addressed the amazed and terrified headsman, and said with her waning breath: "Let me share his grave! Henry Howard, in death, as in life, I am thine to the last!"

CHAPTER X.

NEW INTRIGUES.

Henry Howard was dead. And now one would have supposed that the king might rest contented, and that sleep would no longer forsake his eyelids, but

"I COME, HENRY, I COME!" P. 253

Henry Howard, his great rival, had closed his eyes forever; Henry Howard was no longer in the way to rob him of his crown—to fill the world with the renown of his achievements, and with his poetical fame to obscure the genius of the king.

But the king was still, as ever, discontented—still, as ever, sleep forsook his couch.

This meant, that his work as yet was but half accomplished: Henry Howard's father—the Duke of Norfolk—was still alive; this meant that the king was evermore constrained to think of his powerful rival, and these thoughts chased sleep away from his pillow; his soul was troubled because of the Howards: thus it was that his bodily pains were so grievous and terrible.

When the Duke of Norfolk should have closed his eyes in death, then would the king be able once more to close his eyes in refreshing sleep. But the tribunal of the House of Lords—which was the only one before which the duke could be tried—was so slow and so circumspect in its mode of procedure: it was by no means so prompt and so complaisant as the lower House of Parliament, which had so speedily condemned Henry Howard. Why did the old Howard possess such a privilege?—why, instead of being a duke and a peer of the realm, was he not a simple earl, like his son, in order that the obedient Commons might pass their sentence upon him without delay?

This was the gnawing pain—the canker-worm of the king, which made him frantic with rage, which irritated his temper, inflamed his blood, and thereby increased his bodily sufferings.

He raved and stormed with impatience; his wild objurgations resounded through the halls and corridors of the palace, and made everybody tremble; for no one was certain that it might not be himself who should be the next victim of the monarch's rage,—no one could feel assured that the ever-increasing thirst for blood of the king would not condemn himself at any moment.

From the seclusion of his sick-chamber the king watched, with the most jealous scrutiny, over his royal dignity, and the slightest violation thereof was sufficient to arouse his anger and his sanguinary instincts. Woe betide those who now dared to maintain that the pope was the head of the Church? Woe to those also who were bold enough to assert that God alone was the head and ruler of the Church, and who refused to honor the king as the Church's supreme and sovereign lord! Both parties alike were traitors and malefactors; and accordingly he sent Catholics as well as Protestants to the stake or to the block, however near they stood to his own person, and however cordially he was otherwise attached to them.

Whoever, therefore, could avoid it, kept far away from the dreaded person of the king, and whoever was condemned by his duties to approach the royal presence trembled for his life, and commended his soul to God.

There were still but four persons who did not fear the king, and who appeared to be secure from his crushing anger. These were the queen, who attended him with constant diligence; John Heywood, who, with unwearied zeal, supported Katharine in her onerous task, and who sometimes succeeded in winning a smile from the king; besides whom were Gardiner, Bishop of Winchester, and Lord Douglas.

Lady Jane Douglas was dead; the king had therefore pardoned her father, and had once more shown himself gracious and friendly toward the deeply-afflicted earl. Besides this, it was a source of gratification and relief to the suffering monarch to have some one near him whose troubles were still greater than his own; it consoled him to think that there could be still more terrible pains than those bodily pains of which he was himself the victim. These pains Lord Douglas was condemned to endure, and the king perceived, with a sort of malicious joy, how his hair was daily getting gray, and his features becoming more attenuated and care-worn. Douglas was a younger man than the king, and yet how old and grizzled he looked beside his blooming and rubicund master!

Could the king have glanced into the secret recesses of his heart, he would have had less compassion for the cares and anxieties of Lord Douglas.

He looked upon him only as an affectionate father who mourned the death of his only child. He little suspected that it was less the father who was painfully smitten for the fate of his daughter, than the ambitious man, the fanatical papist, the zealous disciple of Loyola—who saw with dismay the failure of all his schemes, and saw, too, the moment approaching when he should be stripped of all the power and authority which he enjoyed in the secret league of the Society of Jesus.

For him, therefore, it was less the daughter than he lamented, than *the seventh wife of the king;* and that it was Katharine, and not his daughter, Jane Douglas, who wore the crown, was the unpardonable offence for which he could never forgive the queen.

Upon the queen accordingly he wished to avenge his daughter's death; he wished to punish Katharine for his frustrated hopes, and for his plans, which she had foiled.

But Lord Douglas dared not himself renew the attempt to prejudice the mind of the king against his wife. Henry had forbidden him to do so under penalty of his anger; he had warned him in threatening words against such an enterprise, and Lord Douglas knew perfectly well that Henry was inflexible in his resolves when the question at issue was that of fulfilling a threatened punishment.

Still, what Douglas himself dared not attempt, might be attempted by Gardiner—Gardiner, who, thanks to the humors and caprices induced by the king's ailments, had again, for some days past, so unconditionally enjoyed the favor of the king, that the worthy Archbishop Cranmer had been ordered to quit the court, and to withdraw to his episcopal palace at Lambeth.

Katharine had seen him depart with anxious foreboding, for Cranmer had always been her firm supporter and friend. In the midst of this storm-lashed and passion-swayed court-life, his mild, serene countenance had ever appeared to her like a star of peace, and his gentle words and elevated sentiments had ever been like a soothing balsam to her poor, trembling heart.

She felt that by his departure she lost her most generous advocate—her most powerful succor; and that those by whom she was now surrounded were enemies and opponents.

True, she still had John Heywood, the faithful friend, the indefatigable servant; but since Gardiner had begun to exercise his sinister influence over the king's mind, John Heywood scarcely dared to approach Henry's presence. True, she still had her beloved Thomas Seymour; but she felt and knew that she was surrounded on all sides by lurking spies, and that now nothing more was wanting than an audience with Thomas Seymour—a few words of friendly greeting—nay, a look of mutual understanding and love, in order to send both him and herself to the scaffold.

She trembled—not for herself—but for her lover; this made her prudent and thoughtful; it gave her the courage always to maintain a grave and serious demeanor toward Thomas Seymour, never to meet him elsewhere than in the circle of her courtiers—never to smile upon him—never to extend to him her hand.

Still she was certain of her future. She knew that a day would come when the death of the king would liberate her from her wearisome splendor, and from the oppressiveness of her royal diadem; when she should be free—free to bestow her hand upon the man whom alone upon earth she loved, and to become his wife.

She yearned for this day, as the captive yearns for the hour of his liberation; but like him, too, she knew that a premature attempt to escape from her dungeon would only bring with it destruction and death, and not freedom.

She must, therefore, be patient, and wait; she must renounce all personal intercourse with her beloved; and even his letters she could only obtain rarely, through John Heywood, who was forced to observe the greatest caution. Often, indeed, had the faithful Heywood implored his mistress to give up this correspondence; often had he besought her, with tears in his eyes, to renounce this love, which might one day be her ruin and her death. Katharine laughed at his gloomy forebodings, to which she opposed the daring enthusiasm of her love, and the calm courage which springs from certainty of the future.

She did not wish to die—for love and happiness awaited her; this happiness and this love she was unwilling to renounce—why, otherwise, should she have been compelled to endure this life of danger, of self-denial, of enmity, and of hatred?

On the contrary, she wished to live, in order one day to be happy. This thought made her brave and resolute; it gave her the courage to confront her enemies with a serene and smiling countenance; it enabled her to sit with sparkling eyes and rosy cheeks at the side of her severe and capricious husband, and, with lively wit and inexhaustible gayety, to chase away rancor from his spirit and moroseness from his brow.

But, just because she was able to do this, she was a dangerous opponent for Douglas and for Gardiner,—exactly for this reason it must be their chief endeavor to ruin this young and beautiful woman, who dared to defy them, and to weaken their influence with the king.

It was only when they should have succeeded in effectually darkening the king's mind, when they should once more have completely filled him with fanatical zeal—then only could they hope to attain their end, which end was, to lead the king back, as a contrite and penitent son, to the only true and sanctifying Mother Church, and once more to make of this vain, haughty, and ambitious prince, a submissive and obedient son of the pope!

The king must therefore be brought to renounce this vain and blasphemous arrogance—that of wishing to be himself the head of his own Church; he must be induced to turn aside from the spirit of innovation and heresy, and to become once more a believing and devout Catholic.

But in order that this object may be attained, Katharine must needs be removed from him; he must no longer look upon her smiling and beautiful countenance, and no longer suffer himself to be entertained by her acute intellect and her lively conversation.

"We shall not be able to accomplish the queen's downfall," said Lord Douglas to Gardiner, as they both happened to be *tête-à-tête* in the king's anteroom, while the lively chatter of Katharine and the cheerful laughter of the king reached them from the adjoining room in which the royal pair were sitting. "No, no, Gardiner, she is too powerful and too cunning. The king loves her very much, and she affords him such an agreeable and refreshing *délassement!*"

"It is just for that reason that we must withdraw her from him," said Gardiner, with a sullen frown. "His heart must be diverted from this earthly love, and it will only be when we have destroyed this passion in his breast, that this fierce and haughty man will return contrite and humble to us and to God."

"But we shall not be able to destroy it, my friend; it is such an ardent, and withal such a selfish, love!"

"So much greater will be the triumph, if our pious admonitions should succeed in touching his heart, Douglas. It is true he will suffer a good deal, if compelled to give up this woman. But suffering is just what he needs, in order to become contrite and penitent. His mind must be darkened first of all, in order that we may be able to illumine it with the light of faith; he must first be rendered isolated and helpless, in order to lead him back to holy communion with the Church, and in order to make him once more accessible to the consolations which the one fold of the true faith has to offer."

"Alas!" sighed Douglas, "I fear this will be a fruitless effort. The king is so vain of his self-grounded high-priesthood!"

"But he is such a weak mortal—such a great sinner, too," said Gardiner, with a sarcastic smile. "The prospect of death and of the judgment to come makes him tremble; and the Holy Church can give him absolution for his sins, and comfort his dying hour with her holy sacraments. He is a very wicked sinner, and sometimes feels remorse of conscience. It is this which will bring him back again into the bosom of the Catholic Church."

"Ay, but when will that happen? The king is ailing, and any day may end his career. Woe betide us, should he die before he has placed the power in our hands, and made us the executors of his will! Woe betide us should the queen be appointed regent, and the king have chosen the Seymours to be her ministers! Oh, my wise and pious father, the work which you propose must be done speedily, or it will have to remain forever unaccomplished!"

"It shall be done this very day," said Gardiner, solemnly; and bending forward more closely to the earl's ear, he continued: "we have lulled the queen into confidence and self-reliance, and upon that rock she shall founder this very day. She relies so firmly upon her power over the king's mind, that she often finds the courage even to contradict him, and to oppose her own will to his. That shall, this very day, be her destruction! For, mark you well, Douglas, the king is now once more like a tiger that has fasted for a long time. He thirsts for blood! The queen has an aversion to human blood, and is horrified when she hears of executions. We must therefore take care that these opposing tendencies shall come in contact and clash."

"Oh, I understand now," whispered Douglas, "and I bow with reverence before your lordship's wisdom. They are both in a condition to let themselves be conquered with their own weapons."

"I will present a welcome prey to his blood-craving appetite, and will give her silly compassion an opportunity of struggling with the king for his booty. Don't you think, my dear lord, it will be a most amusing and delightful comedy to see the tiger and the dove engaged in single combat? And I assure you the tiger thirsts terribly for blood. Blood is the only balsam which he applies to his aching limbs, and by which alone he imagines that he can restore peace to his troubled conscience, and gain courage to face the terrors of death. Why, have we not often told him that by every fresh execution of a heretic, one of his great sins would be blotted out, and that the blood of the Calvinists would serve to wash away some of the evil deeds entered against him on the register of guilt? He is most anxious to be able to present himself pure and spotless before the judgment-seat of God, and therefore he stands in need of much heretical blood. But hark! there strikes the hour which summons me to the royal closet. The queen has now had enough of laughter and silly prate. We will now endeavor to banish smiles from her lips for all future time to come. She is a heretic and it will be a pious work, well-pleasing to the Almighty, if we hurl her headlong to destruction."

"May God be with your lordship, and in His mercy assist you to accomplish this noble work!"

"God will be with us, my son, for it is for Him that we are laboring; it is for His honor and glory that we are sending these misguided heretics to the stake, and that we cause the air to resound with the cries of agony of these racked and tortured recreants! That is a music which is well-pleasing to God, and the angels in heaven will triumph and rejoice if also this heretical and unbelieving Queen Katharine should be compelled to chant the music of these damnable apostates.—I now go forth to this work of love and divine vengeance. Pray for me, my son, that it may succeed. Remain here in the anteroom, and watch for my summons: perhaps we may require you. Pray for us and with us. Yes, we owe this heretical queen retaliation for Maria Askew. To-day we shall discharge the debt. She accused us then; to-day we shall accuse her, and on our side is God, and the host of His saints and angels!"

And the pious and Heaven-favored priest crossed himself devoutly, and with his head meekly bent, and with a gentle smile upon his thin, bloodless lips, he left the anteroom with measured step, in order to present himself in the king's apartment.

CHAPTER XI.

THE KING AND THE PRIEST.

"God bless and preserve your majesty!" said Gardiner, as he approached the king, who at this moment was engaged with the queen at a game of chess, and with knitted brows and compressed lips sat contemplating the state of the game, which was not favorable to himself, and threatened him with a speedy check-mate.

It was unwise of the queen not to allow the king to win, for his superstitious and jealous disposition saw in a chess-match gained against him a direct attack upon his own person; and whoever ventured to beat him at chess, always appeared to Henry to be a species of traitor, who threatened the kingdom, and was even daring enough to stretch forth his hand to seize the crown.

The queen knew this full well, but—Gardiner was right—she was over-confident. She believed somewhat in her power over the king; she imagined he would make an exception in her favor. And then it was so tedious always to be obliged to be the conquered party in this game,—to let the king always appear as the triumphant victor, and to lavish upon his skill praises which he did not merit! Katharine wished for once to reserve to herself the triumph of having vanquished her husband. She disputed with him piece by piece, she roused him by constantly renewed attacks, and exasperated him with the prospect of approaching danger.

The king, who at the outset had been cheerful, and had laughed when Katharine took away one of his principal pieces, now laughed no longer. It was no longer a mere game—it was a serious contest, and the king struggled with passionate zeal for the victory over his spouse.

Katharine did not once perceive the clouds which were gathering thickly upon the king's brow. Her looks were fixed upon the chess-board exclusively, and breathless with expectation, and glowing with ardor, she was considering the move which she was about to make.

But Gardiner had clearly perceived the secret anger of the king, and he saw that the conjuncture was favorable to himself.

With a light, stealthy pace he drew near to the king's chair, and, standing behind it, overlooked the game.

"In four moves more you are checkmated and conquered, my husband," said the queen, with a cheerful laugh, as she made her move.

The king's knitted brows now assumed a darker scowl, and he pressed his lips violently together.

"It is quite true, your majesty," said Gardiner, "you must soon succumb! Danger threatens you from the queen!"

Henry, with a convulsed movement, turned his face round toward Gardiner with an inquiring expression. In his irritated humor against the queen, this ambiguous expression of the crafty priest came home to him with double force.

Gardiner was a skilful hunter; already the first arrow which he had aimed had hit the mark. But even Katharine had heard the hissing of the dart. The slow, equivocal words of Gardiner had roused her up from her oblivious mood, and as she now looked at the flushed and exasperated countenance of the king, she perceived at once her imprudence.

But it was too late to make amends. The check-mate of the king was inevitable, and Henry had already observed it himself.

"It is well!" he said, with pettish vehemence. "You have won, Katharine, and, by the Holy Mother of God, you may boast of the rare luck of having conquered King Henry of England!"

"Oh! I shall not boast of it, my dear husband," she rejoined with a smile. "You have only played with me as the lion plays with a little dog, which he will not trample under foot, only because he has compassion for him, and would be sorry to hurt the poor little animal. Lion, I thank thee! Thou hast been very magnanimous to-day! Thou hast suffered me to win!"

The king's features became somewhat more serene. Gardiner perceived it, and resolved to hinder Katharine from following up her advantage any further.

"Magnanimity is a sublime, but a very dangerous virtue," said the bishop, gravely, "and kings especially should not practise it; for magnanimity pardons crime, and kings exist not to pardon, but to punish."

"How so, my lord?" said Katharine. "Surely the noblest prerogative of royalty consists in the power to pardon, and as kings are the representatives of God upon earth, they are bound to exercise pardon and mercy like God Himself."

Again the king's brow became clouded, and he fixed his eyes with a sinister expression on the chess-board.

Gardiner chuckled inwardly, but made no reply. He drew forth a roll of paper from his cassock and handed it to the king.

"Sire," he said, "I hope you do not share the views of the queen! Otherwise it would fare badly with the peace and welfare of the realm. Mankind cannot be governed by mercy—they must be ruled by fear. Your majesty holds the sword of justice in your hands, and if you are slow to let it fall upon the heads of evil-doers, they will soon wrest it from your grasp, and then you will be powerless."

"Those are very cruel words, my lord!" exclaimed Katharine, who suffered herself to be hurried away by her generous disposition, and suspected that Gardiner had come in order to urge the king to some severe and sanguinary decree.

She wished to obviate his designs—she wished to move the king to clemency. But the moment was unfavorable to her.

The king, whom she had only just now irritated by her victory over him, felt his ire increase by the contradiction which she had offered the prelate—for this contradiction was equally directed against himself. The king was by no means disposed to exercise mercy, and it was therefore a very malicious thought of the queen to praise mercy as the highest privilege of princes.

With a silent nod he took the papers from the hands of Gardiner, and opened them. "Ah," he exclaimed, turning over the pages, "you are quite right, my lord bishop; mankind do not deserve to have mercy shown them—for they are always ready to abuse it. It seems that because for some weeks past we have caused no scaffolds to be erected and no fires kindled, they imagine we are asleep, and they begin their profane and traitorous designs with redoubled violence, and raise their sinful hands in mockery against us. I see here a charge against an individual who has dared to say there is no king by the grace of God, and that the king is a miserable, sinful man, like the meanest beggar. Well, we will show this person justice; we will not be to him a king by the grace of God—but a king by God's anger! We will let him see that we are not yet quite like the lowest beggar, for we possess at least wood enough to make a fire for his use!"

And when the king had indulged in this pleasantry, he burst into a loud fit of laughter, in which Gardiner willingly joined.

"I see also a charge against two others who deny the king's supremacy," continued Henry, still glancing through the papers in his hand. "They accuse me of blasphemy, for daring to call myself the representative of God—the visible head of the holy Church; they say that God alone is head of the Church, and that Luther and Calvin are more worthy representatives of the Almighty than the king is. Verily, we should hold our kingdom and the dignity which God has bestowed upon us in slight esteem, did we not punish these transgressors, who, in our own sacred person, dare to blaspheme God Himself!"

The king had resumed the examination of the papers, when suddenly his countenance became overspread with a dark-crimson hue, and a fierce imprecation burst from his lips.

He flung the papers on the table and struck them with his clinched fist.—"What!" he exclaimed, with vehemence, "have all the devils in hell been let loose, or has the spirit of rebellion reached such a point in our kingdom that we are no longer able to suppress it? Some fanatical heretic has warned my subjects in the public streets against reading the holy book, which, like a well-meaning and careful father and teacher, I have myself written for my people, and have given them in order that they may derive edification and wisdom therefrom. And the same malefactor has shown this book to the people and said to them: 'Ye call this the king's book, and ye are right, for it is a vile and mischievous book—the work of hell—and the devil himself has been sponsor to the king!' Ah, I see we must once more show this traitorous and pitiful rabble our serious and angry countenance, in order that they may recover faith in their sovereign. The people are nothing but a contemptible and scurvy mob! They are humble and dutiful only when made to tremble and feel the lash. It is only when we trample them in the dust that they recognize us as their master; and when we send them to the rack and to the stake, then only do they respect our majesty and power. The kingdom must, therefore, be burnt into their bodies, that they may feel it as a truth. And by the God that made us, we will do so! Here, give me a pen at once, that I may sign and confirm these decrees; and let it be well dipped in the ink, my lord bishop, for there are eight sentences, and I must write my name eight times. Ah! 'tis a hard and wearisome business to be a king, and not a day passes without labor and trouble."

"Our Lord God will reward your majesty for this labor!" said Gardiner, solemnly, as he handed the pen to the king.

Henry was preparing to write, when Katharine laid her hand upon his, and restrained him.

"Oh, do not sign," she exclaimed, with tearful accents. "I entreat you, by all that you hold sacred, not to suffer yourself to be hurried away by momentary anger—let not your outraged feelings gain the sway over your princely character. Let the sun go down and rise again before you give way to vengeance, and do not decide against these unhappy persons until you are quite calm and composed. For, consider it well, my lord and husband, there are here eight death-warrants to be signed, and with a few strokes of the pen you would snatch eight human beings from life, from their families, and from the world. You would take the son from the mother, the husband from the wife, and the father from his infant children. Consider it well, Henry; the responsibility which God has placed in your hands is a heavy one, and it is presumptuous in man not to approach this duty with grave and sacred composure, and with unruffled equanimity!"

"Well, by God's Mother!" cried the king, striking the table violently, "I believe you would dare to defend these traitors and blasphemers against their king. You cannot, therefore, have heard who the accused are?"

"I have heard it," replied Katharine, with increased ardor. "I have heard it, and I still repeat, do not sign these death-warrants, my noble husband. It is true, these poor people have committed grave faults, but they erred humanly. It is not wise, my good lord, to wish to revenge so severely a slight offence against your majesty. A king should be far superior to calumny and slander; like the sun he should give light to the just and the unjust, none of whom have power to dim its rays or to obscure its splendor. Punish criminals and evil-doers, as they deserve, but be generous and magnanimous toward those who have offended against your person!"

"The king is not a person whom one may offend!" cried Gardiner. "The king is a sublime idea—a mighty, world-embracing thought. Whoever offends the king has not offended a person, but the kingdom established by God, the universal conception which holds the whole world together."

"Whoever offends the king, offends God!" exclaimed the king, "and whoever attacks our throne or slanders ourself, shall suffer the fate of the atheist and the parricide—his hand shall be cut off and his tongue be torn out from the roots!"

"Well, be it so: cut off their hands, and deprive them of the power of speech, but do not put them to death!" cried Katharine, with impassioned earnestness. "At least examine if their crime be as great as people wish to make you believe. Oh, it is now such an easy matter to be accused as a traitor or an atheist; merely an incautious word—a doubt—not as to God, but as to His priests, or as to this Church which your majesty has set up, whose proud and peculiar edifice is so new and so strange to many, that they ask themselves, doubtingly, if this be a church of God, or only a royal palace, and that they wander and lose themselves in its intricate windings, without ever being able to find the outlet!"

"If they only held the faith," said Gardiner, gravely, "they would not lose themselves; and if God were on their side, the outlet would not be blocked up against them."

"Oh, I am well aware of that—but you are always inexorable," cried Katharine, angrily. "But permit me to say that it is not you that I am begging for mercy, but the king; and I must also tell you, my lord bishop, that it would be better for you, and more worthy of a minister of Christian love, were you to join your entreaties to mine, than to attempt to urge the noble heart of the king to severity. You are a priest, and you must have discovered from your own experience that there are many ways that lead us to God, and that we are one and all liable to error in seeking for the right path."

"How so?" exclaimed the king, rising from his seat, and looking at Katharine with a searching and angry glance. "Do you mean that heretics, too, may possibly find the way that leads to God?"

"I mean," she replied, with fervent earnestness, "that Jesus Christ Himself was called a blasphemer, and was put to death. I mean that Stephen was stoned to death by Paul, and that, nevertheless, the Christian world at large now honors them both as saints, and prays to both alike. I mean that it is not because Socrates lived before Christ, and could not, therefore, be one of His followers, that he will be condemned; and that Horace and Julius Cæsar, Phidias and Plato, must be considered noble spirits, although they were only pagans. Nay, my lord and husband, I mean that lenity must be used in matters of religion, and that belief should not be forcibly thrust upon mankind as a burden, but should be granted as a favor by means of conviction."

"Then you do not consider that these eight malefactors are worthy of death?" asked Henry, with affected calmness and labored composure.

"No, my husband; I regard them as poor, erring mortals, who are seeking the right path, who would willingly walk in it, and who, therefore, inquire doubtingly on all sides, 'Is this the right way?'"

"Enough!" said the king, as he beckoned Gardiner toward him, and, leaning upon his arm, advanced a few paces toward the door. "Let us speak no more of these things; they are too serious to be decided in the presence of our young and lively queen. The hearts of women are always inclined to lenity and forgiveness. You should have thought of this, Gardiner, and not have mentioned such matters before the queen."

"Sire, it was the hour which your majesty had fixed for determining these questions."

"Oh, it was?" cried the king, with vivacity. "Then we did wrong in devoting the time to other concerns than to our serious friends; and you will excuse me, madam, if I request you to leave me alone with the bishop. Affairs of state cannot be postponed."

He presented his hand to Katharine, and conducted her with evident labor, but still with a smiling countenance, to the door. As she still continued standing, and looked at him with an inquiring and smiling gaze, while she seemed on the point of again addressing him, he waved his hand impatiently, and knit his brows.

"It is late," he said, hastily; "and we have state matters to attend to."

Katharine dared not reply—she bowed silently, and left the room. The king looked after her with an air of deep resentment and displeasure, and then turned round to Gardiner.

"Well," he inquired, "what do you think of the queen now?"

"I think," said Gardiner, slowly, and with such deliberate emphasis, that every word had time to penetrate like a dagger into the heart of the king—"I think she does not regard as criminals those who call the holy book which you have written a work of hell; and that she has a great deal of sympathy for these heretics who refuse to acknowledge your supremacy."

"Nay, by God's Mother, I believe she would hold the same language herself, and join my enemies, if she were not my wife!" cried the king, whose anger was fermenting inwardly, and ready to burst forth like lava from the volcano's mouth.

"She does so already, although she is your wife, sire! She imagines that her high position gives her impunity and shelter against your just anger, and therefore she does what no one else would dare to do, and says what in the mouth of another would be the blackest treason!"

"What does she do, and what does she say?" exclaimed the king. "Do not hesitate, my lord, to tell me. It is but right that I should know the acts and sentiments of my queen."

"Sire, she is not only the secret protectress of heretics and reformers, but is an adherent of their creed. She hearkens to their false doctrines with eager zeal, and suffers the damnable teachers of these sectaries to enter her apartments, in order that she may listen to their fanatical discourses and their hellish inspirations. She speaks of these heretics as of true believers and Christians, and calls Luther the light which God has sent into the world, to enlighten the darkness and error of the Church with the rays of truth and love—the same Luther, sire, who dared to address to you such scandalous and defamatory letters, and to deride your princely wisdom with scoffing contumely."

"In a word, she is a heretic!" cried the king.

The volcano was ripe for an eruption, and the boiling lava must needs at length find an outlet.

"Yes, she is a heretic!" repeated the king, "and we have solemnly sworn to root out these unbelievers from our kingdom."

"She knows very well that she is safe from your anger," said Gardiner, with a sly shrug. "She presumes on the ground that she is the queen, and that in the heart of her noble husband love is more powerful than faith."

"No one shall imagine that he is safe from my anger, and no one shall presume upon the safety which my love may assure him. She is a proud, insolent, and daring woman!" cried the king, whose looks were again directed toward the chess-board, and whose animosity was heightened by the remembrance of the lost game. "She is bold enough to defy us, and to have a will of her own, contrary to ours. Yes, I will show the whole world that Henry of England is ever the undaunted and incorruptible ruler. I will give heretics a proof that I in reality am the protector and defender of the faith and religion of my realm, and that no one stands on such a pinnacle that my anger may not reach him, and that the sword of justice may not fall upon his neck. She is a heretic, and we have sworn to destroy the whole brood with fire and sword. We shall keep our vow."

"And the Lord will bless you with His blessing; He will place a crown of glory on your brow! and the Church will sing your praises, as her most glorious shepherd—her most illustrious chief."

"So be it!" said the king, as with youthful activity he strode across the room, and, proceeding to his escritoire, wrote a few lines with a rapid and nimble hand.

Gardiner continued standing in the middle of the room, with folded hands, and his lips murmured a half-audible prayer, while his large, flaming eyes were fixed upon the king with a curious and searching glance.

"Here, my lord," said the king, "take this paper, and make the necessary arrangements. It is a warrant of committal, and before night sets in the queen shall be in the Tower!"

"Of a truth the Lord works mightily within you!" exclaimed Gardiner, as he took the paper; "the sacred hosts of heaven are singing hallelujahs, while they look down with rapture upon the hero who conquered his own heart in order to serve God and the Church!"

"Take it, and make haste!" returned the king, impatiently. "Within a few hours all must be done. Give this paper to my Lord Douglas, and let him go with it to the lieutenant of the Tower, in order that he may himself proceed hither, at once, with his satellites. For still this lady is a queen—and as a queen she shall be treated, though a culprit. The lieutenant himself must therefore conduct her to the Tower. Hasten, then, I say! But, hark! keep all this matter a secret, and let no one be aware of it until the decisive moment has arrived. Otherwise, her friends might assail me to entreat pardon for this frail, sinful woman, and I abhor all whining and whimpering. Keep silence, therefore, for I am tired, and require some rest and sleep! I have, as you say, just accomplished a work which is well-pleasing to God, and perhaps, as a reward, the Almighty will send me the refreshing and reviving slumbers for which I have so long sought in vain."

And the king drew aside the curtains of his couch, and, assisted by Gardiner, laid himself back on the luxurious pillows.

Gardiner closed the curtains again, and thrust the fateful paper into his pocket. Even in his hands it did not seem to him to be safe enough. But why? Might not some inquisitive eye rest upon it and guess its contents? Might not some daring and unabashed friend of the queen snatch this paper from him, and take it to her and give her warning? No, it was not safe enough in his hands, he must perforce hide it in the pocket of his gown. There no one could find it—nobody discover its purport.

There accordingly he concealed it. Within the folds of his robe it was secure; and after he had thus hidden the precious document, he left the chamber with rapid steps, in order to announce to Lord Douglas the grand result of his labors.

Not once did he look behind him. Had he done so, he would have sprung back upon his prey, like a tiger, into the room; as hawk upon the dove, he would have pounced upon that shred of paper which lay upon the floor, just on the spot where Gardiner stood when he thrust the warrant which the king had given him into his pocket.

Alas! even the robe of a priest is not always thick enough to veil a dangerous secret, and even the pocket of a bishop may sometimes have a hole in it.

Gardiner went away with the proud consciousness of having a warrant of committal in his pocket, while the fatal scroll lay upon the floor in the middle of the royal chamber.

Who, then, will come to pick it up? Who is to be the sharer of this dangerous secret—to whom will this mute document announce the fearful intelligence that the queen has fallen into disgrace, and that she is to be hurried away as a prisoner to the Tower this very day?

All is still and lonely in the royal chamber. Nothing moves—not even the heavy damask hangings around the royal couch.

The king sleeps. Even excitement and anger sometimes act like a soothing lullaby! They have so wearied and fatigued the king, that he has positively fallen asleep from sheer exhaustion.

Indeed, the king should have been grateful to his spouse; for chagrin at the lost chess-match, and anger at Katharine's heretical sentiments, have so worn him out, that he has fallen into a profound slumber.

Still the warrant lies upon the floor. And now the door opens gently and cautiously. Who is it that dares be so bold as to enter the king's chamber unsummoned and unannounced?

There are only three persons who might hazard such a step: the queen, the Princess Elizabeth, and John Heywood, the court fool. But which of these three is it?

It is the Princess Elizabeth, who comes to salute her royal father. Every forenoon about this hour she had found the king in his chamber. Where, then, was he to-day? As she glanced round the room with surprised and inquiring looks, her eye was at length arrested by the paper which lay upon the floor. She took it up, and began to examine it with girlish curiosity. What could it contain? Certainly no secret, otherwise it would not be left lying at random on the floor.

She opened and read it. Her beautiful features assumed an expression of astonishment and horror, and a slight exclamation burst from her lips. But

Elizabeth had a firm and resolute spirit, and this unlooked-for surprise did not dim her bright glance nor obscure her penetrating mind. The queen was in danger. The queen was about to be imprisoned. This was what the terrible document shouted into her ear; but she durst not suffer herself to be unnerved by the intelligence—she must act—she must warn the queen.

She hid the paper in her bosom, and vanished from the chamber with the fleetness of lightning.

With flashing eyes and her cheeks aglow from exerted speed, Elizabeth at length reached the queen. With passionate impetuosity she clasped her in her arms and kissed her tenderly.

"Katharine, my queen and my mother," she exclaimed, "we have sworn to stand by and protect one another if danger should threaten us. Fate has been favorable to me, for it has already placed in my hands the means of fulfilling my vow this very day. Take this paper and read it! It is a warrant for your committal, drawn up by the king's own hand. When you have read it, let us consider what is to be done in order to avert the danger from you."

"A warrant of committal!" cried the queen, shuddering as she perused it. "A warrant—that means a sentence of death! For to have once crossed the fatal threshold of the Tower means to abandon all hope of ever leaving it again; and when a queen is imprisoned and accused, she is already condemned. Gracious Heaven, princess, do you understand that—to be obliged to die, while the life-blood still glows with youthful ardor in our veins? To be compelled to walk forth to our doom, while the future still attracts us with a thousand hopes and wishes? My God, to be thus hurried away into a loathsome dungeon, and thence perforce to descend into the dark grave, while the world greets us with its alluring voices, and while the spring of life has scarcely wakened in our heart!"

Streams of tears burst from her eyes, and she hid her face in her trembling hands.

"Pray do not weep, my queen," said Elizabeth—herself trembling, and deathly pale. "Do not weep, but consider what is to be done! Each moment the danger increases—each moment brings the evil still nearer!"

"True," said Katharine, as she raised her head and dashed away the tears from her eyes. "Yes, very true—this is not a time for weeping and wailing. Death is stealing hither upon me—while I, on my part, am unwilling to die. As yet I have life, and while a breath remains, I will struggle against death. God will succor me—God will be my helper, and will enable me to overcome this danger also, as I have already done on many former occasions."

"But what do you propose to do? How will you set about it? You don't know who your accusers are, nor what the charge is which they lay against you."

"But I suspect it," said the queen, thoughtfully. "When I call to mind the angry countenance of the king, and the knavish smile of that malicious priest, I believe I know what the accusations are. Yes, all is quite clear to me now. Ah, it is the heretic whom they would condemn to death. Very well, my lord bishop, I am still alive, and we will see which of us both will gain the victory!"

With a resolute step and with glowing cheeks she hastened to the door. Elizabeth held her back. "Where are you going to?" she inquired, astonished.

"To the king!" she replied, with a proud smile. "He has heard the bishop, and he shall also hear me. The king's mind is fickle and easily changed about. We will now see which cunning is the stronger—that of the priest, or that of the woman! Elizabeth, pray for me; I am going to the king, and you will see me either free and happy, or you will never again behold me."

She imprinted an affectionate kiss upon the lips of Elizabeth, and left the room with hurried steps.

CHAPTER X.

THE GAME OF CHESS.

For many days the king had not been so well—for a long time he had not enjoyed such a refreshing sleep as on this day that he had signed the warrant of committal against the queen This, however, did not engage his thoughts; sleep had obliterated all remembrance of it from his memory. Like some trivial anecdote, heard for the moment with a passing smile, the whole occurrence had vanished from his mind. A transient interlude—nothing more.

The king had slept well, and nothing further troubled him. He extended and stretched himself upon his couch, and thought with delight how pleasant it would be if he could every day enjoy such sweet and refreshing repose, and if no evil dreams and no fears would scare away slumber from his eyes. He felt himself quite cheerful and composed, and to any one who had now come to beg a favor of the king he would have granted it, in the first raptures which this reviving sleep had caused him. But he was alone — no one was with him, and he must therefore suppress his gracious desires. But, no; seemed it not as if something moved and breathed behind the curtain?

The king drew aside the hangings, and a serene smile came over his features, for beside his couch sat the queen. She sat there, with her flushed cheeks and glowing eyes, and greeted him with a smile of good-humored banter and drollery.

"Ah, Kate, you there!" cried the king. "Now I understand how I came to have such a sound and refreshing sleep. You stood beside me, like my good angel, and banished away all pains and evil dreams from my pillow."

And so saying, he stretched forth his hand, and tenderly caressed her velvet cheek—never thinking for a moment that he had already, in a certain manner, devoted this lovely head to the scaffold, and that within a few hours more those dazzling eyes should dwell upon nothing but the darkness of the dungeon. Sleep, as before said, had lulled all remembrance of this matter, and as yet his malicious instincts had not again been excited. To sign a warrant of committal, or a death-warrant, was such an ordinary and every-day occurrence with the king, that it marked no epoch in his life, and neither burdened him with remorse of conscience, nor made his heart shudder or tremble.

But Katharine thought of all this, and as the king's hand caressed her cheek, she felt as if death were touching her, as though it already claimed her for its own. Meanwhile she overcame this momentary horror, and had the courage to preserve her presence of mind, and her cheerful and composed mien.

"You call me your good angel, my lord and husband," she replied, smiling; "but I am nothing more than your little household sprite, that flits and buzzes around you, and that makes you laugh sometimes with his harmless banter."

"And i'faith, a lively little sprite you are, Kate," cried the king, who continued with real pleasure to contemplate the fresh and animated countenance of his spouse.

"Then I will remain with you to-day as your sprite, and give you no more rest upon your couch," said Katharine, as she playfully attempted to lift him up. "Do you know, my husband, what I came hither for? A butterfly came fluttering to my window; only think, a butterfly in winter—that signifies, that on this occasion winter is spring, and that the clerk of the weather has converted January into March. The butterfly has summoned us forth, my king; and just look there, the sun beckons to us through the window, and tells us we should come out, as it has already dried up the walks below in the garden, and made a little grass to spring up by the wayside. Your wheeled arm-chair, too, is already at hand, and your little sprite, as you see, has already decked and garnished herself with furs against the winter, which, indeed, seems passed by."

"Well, then, come and help me, my dearest little sprite, that I may get up and obey the commands of the butterfly, of the sun, and of my lovely and charming wife!" cried the king, as he put his arm round Katharine's neck, and raised himself up from his couch.

She displayed the utmost activity and sport in attending to the king's wants; she laid her arm affectionately on his shoulder, and supported him; she adjusted the gold chain which had become displaced, over his doublet; and playfully folded and arranged the lace ruffles which he wore round his neck.

"Do you wish your attendants to come, my husband? The master of the ceremonies, who is doubtless waiting your commands in the anteroom, or my lord the bishop, who looked so scowlingly at me this morning? But, how now, my good lord, does your countenance too wear a gloomy look? or has your little sprite perchance again said something discordant to your mind?"

"By no means," said the king, gloomily; but he avoided encountering her smiling glance, and averted his gaze from her radiant and charming countenance.

The king's evil thoughts were once more awakened within him, and he now remembered the warrant which he had given to Gardiner. He remembered and repented it. For his youthful Queen was so amiable and beautiful; she so well understood how to chase away sorrow from his brow, and sadness from his heart, by her playful humor and lively wit! She was such an agreeable and entertaining companion, such a ready means of banishing weariness and *ennui*.

It was not for her sake, but for his own, that he regretted what he had done; it was his selfishness alone which made him repent having issued this warrant for the queen's incarceration. Katharine observed him, and her glance, rendered more penetrating by her inward fears, read the thoughts upon his brow, and fully understood the sigh which involuntarily escaped him. She again took courage,—she might yet succeed in smiling away the sword suspended over her head.

"Come, my lord and husband," she said, in a cheerful tone, "come, the sun is nodding at us, and the trees are shaking their heads with displeasure at our long delay."

"Yes, come, Kate," said the king, recovering himself with an effort from his thoughtful mood; "come, we will go out into the free air of Heaven. Perhaps we shall then be nearer to our Maker, who may inspire us with good thoughts and salutary resolutions. Come, along, Kate!"

The queen presented her arm, and supported by it, the king advanced a few steps. Suddenly, however, Katharine stood still, and as the king looked at her inquiringly, she blushed and averted her gaze.

"Well?" asked the king, "why do you linger?"

"Sire, I was just reflecting upon your words, and upon what you have said of the sun and of salutary resolutions; it has touched my heart and troubled my conscience. You are right, my husband, God is then abroad, and I dare not venture to look at the sun, which is the eye of God, until I have confessed and received absolution. Sire, I am a great sinner, and my conscience gives me no rest. Will you be my father-confessor and listen to me?"

The king sighed. Alas! thought he, she is herself rushing to destruction, and by her own avowal of her guilt, she will render it impossible for me to hold her innocent!

"Speak!" he replied, in a loud tone.

"In the first place," she whispered, with downcast looks, "in the first place, I must acknowledge that I have this day deceived you, my lord and king; vanity and sinful arrogance tempted me to do so, and childish petulance made me accomplish what vanity had suggested. But I repent, my king, I repent it from my inmost soul, and I protest to you, my husband, nay, I affirm by all that I hold sacred, that this is the first and only time that I ever deceived you; and never will I again attempt to do so, for it is a fearful and dismal feeling to stand before you with a conscience sensible of guilt."

"And wherein did you deceive us, Kate?" asked the king, and his voice trembled.

Katharine drew forth from her dress a small role of paper, and bending with humility, handed it to the king. "Take it and see for yourself, my husband," she replied.

The king hastily opened the paper, and then looked with complete astonishment, first at the contents, and then at the blushing countenance of the queen.

"How now?" he exclaimed. "A pawn from the chess-board? What does this mean?"

"It means," she replied, in the most contrite accents, "It means that I stole this piece from you this morning, and by such deceit, I was enabled to gain the victory. Oh, pardon me, my husband, but I could no longer bear the thought of always losing, and I was afraid you would not again grant me the favor of playing with you, if you thought what a feeble and contemptible opponent I was. This little pawn was my enemy; he stood beside my queen, and threatened to take her, while the king was held in check by your bishop. You were just about to make this move with the pawn, which must have been my destruction, when my lord, the Bishop of Winchester entered. You turned your eyes toward him for a moment, and saluted him, leaving the game unobserved. Oh, my lord and husband, the temptation was too alluring, too seductive, and I yielded to it. I took the pawn softly from the board, and let it glide into my pocket. When you turned round and resumed the game, you seemed at first astonished, but your noble and magnanimous mind did not discover my wicked fraud; and so you played on unsuspectingly, and thus I won the game. Oh, my king, will you forgive, and not be angry with me?"

The king burst into a loud fit of laughter, and looked with an expression of tenderness and affection at Katharine, who with downcast eyes stood blushing and abashed before him. This spectacle only redoubled his mirthfulness, and renewed his immoderate laughter.

"And that is your only crime, Kate?" he asked at length, drying his eyes with his handkerchief. "You have stolen a pawn from me; that is your first and only act of deceit?"

"Is it not already great enough, sire? Did I not purloin it because I was so arrogant as to wish to win a game of chess from you? Does not the entire court now know my supreme good luck, and that I have this day gained the victory, while in reality I did not deserve it, because I had so shamefully deceived you?"

"Well, truly" said the king with solemn gravity,—"happy are the husbands who are no worse deceived by their wives, than in what you have done to-day, Kate, and well for the ladies whose confession has been as pure and guiltless as yours has been. Come, raise your eyes once more, my Kate; the sin is forgiven, and it will only be attributed to you as a virtue by God and by your king."

He laid his hand upon her head, as if to bless her, and looked at her for some time in silence. And then he resumed with a laugh:

"Then according to this, Kate, I should have been the conqueror to-day and not have lost the game at chess?"

"Yes," she replied sadly, "I must have lost it had I not stolen this pawn."

Once more the king laughed.

"Believe me," continued Katharine earnestly—"believe me, my lord, that Bishop Gardiner—and he alone—should bear the blame for this unhappy occurrence. As he was present I was unwilling to lose. It roused my pride to think that this haughty and insolent priest should be a witness of my defeat. I perceived by anticipation the cold and contemptuous smile with which he would look down upon me—the vanquished; and my spirit revolted at the thought of being humbled in his presence. And this brings me to the second part of my guilt, which I will also now confess to you. Sire, I must also admit another great fault. I have this day gravely offended you, by contradicting and opposing your wise and pious words. Oh! my noble husband, it was not in order to defy you that I did so, but in order to annoy and mortify the proud priest. For I must acknowledge to you, my good lord, that I hate this Bishop of Winchester—nay more, I fear him! for my boding heart tells me that he is my enemy;' that he watches like a spy over my every look, every word, in order to convert it into a snare for my destruction. He is the evil genius who follows me stealthily about, and who would one day certainly crush me, if I were not protected by your cherishing hand and your all-powerful arm. Oh, when I see him, I should always like to take refuge in your heart, and say to you, 'Protect me, my king, and have compassion upon me. Have confidence in me and love me, for otherwise I am lost! The wicked enemy is at hand to destroy me!'"

And while she thus spoke she nestled closely by the king's side, and with her head resting on his breast, she looked up to him with an expression of tender entreaty and touching resignation.

The king bent down and kissed her fair upturned brow.

"Oh, *sancta simplicitas!*" he murmured to himself, "she knows not how near the truth she is, and how absolutely justified her evil bodings have been." He then asked aloud: "Then you believe, Kate, that Gardiner hates you?"

"I not only believe it, but I know it!" she replied. "He stabs me to the quick whenever he can; and if his wounds are but those of pins, it is only because he fears you would discover it if he were to use a dagger; whereas you will not perceive the pins with which he secretly stabs me. Indeed, what else was his visit of this morning than a new attack upon me? He well knows, and I have never made any secret of the matter, that I am an enemy to that Catholic religion whose pope has dared to hurl his anathemas against my lord and husband, and that with lively sympathy I seek to be informed as to the religious doctrines of those who are called reformers."

"They say you are a heretic," said the king, gravely.

"Yes, Gardiner says so. But if I am one, then you also are one, for your creed is mine. If I am a heretic, so is Cranmer too, for he is my spiritual guide and counsellor. But Gardiner has resolved that I am a heretic, and he wishes, moreover, that I should seem one to you. Be assured, my husband, it was on that account that he laid before you those eight death-warrants. Those were eight heretics whom you were to condemn, not a single papist was among them; and yet I know that the prisons are full of papists, who, in the fanaticism of their persecuted belief, have uttered words no less deserving of punishment than those used by the unhappy beings whom you were this day about to banish from life to death, by a stroke of the pen. Sire, I would have besought you with no less warmth, with no less entreaty, had these persons been papists, whom you were going to condemn to death; but Gardiner wished for a proof of my heretical sentiments, and so he chose eight heretics, for whose sakes he desired that I should oppose myself to your severe decree."

"It is true," said the king, "not a single papist was among them. But tell me truly, Kate, are you a heretic, and the opponent of your king?"

With a sweet smile she looked earnestly into his eyes, and crossed her arms with humility over her beautiful bosom.

"Your opponent!" she whispered; "are you not my lord and husband? Is not the woman made to be subject to the man? Man is created after the image of God, and woman after the image of man. Therefore, the woman is only the man's second self, and he must mingle compassion with his love, and bestow upon her of the fulness of his own mind, and cause her to drink from the fountains of his understanding. Your duty, therefore, is to instruct me, my husband, and mine is to learn of you: and to none, of all women in the world, is this duty rendered so easy as to myself; for God has been gracious toward me, and has given me for my husband a king, whose prudence, wisdom, and learning, are the theme and admiration of the whole world."

"What a sweet little flatterer you are, Kate," said the king, smiling; "and with what a bewitching voice you wish to conceal the truth from us. The truth is, that you yourself are a very learned little person, who does not at all require to be taught by others, but who would be quite competent to teach them."

"Oh, if that be so," exclaimed Katharine, "then I should like to teach the whole world to love my king as I do myself, and to be as submissive to him, in all humility, obedience, and fidelity, as I am."

And so saying she flung her arms round the king's neck, and leaned her head, with a languishing expression, upon his breast.

The king kissed her, and clasped her tenderly to his heart. He no longer remembered that danger was still hovering above Katharine's head; he only knew that he loved her, and that without her, life would be a very wretched and dreary wilderness.

"And now, my husband," said Katharine, releasing herself gently from his embrace, "now that I have made my confession to you, and received absolution, let us go down into the garden, that God's bright sun may shine fresh and joyful into our hearts. Come, husband, your rolling chair is at hand, and the bees and butterflies have already learned a hymn with which they are ready to greet you."

She led him along, laughing and jesting the while, into the adjoining room, where the court attendants and the rolling chair were in readiness; and the king ascended his triumphal chariot, and suffered himself to be rolled along over the carpet-laid corridors, and down the sloping passage, into which the broad marble steps had been converted, until he reached the garden.

The air, though sharp and wintry, had still somewhat of the genial warmth of spring. The grass had already begun, like an industrious weaver, to weave a carpet over the dark surface of the squares, and already here and there a modest but curious little flower began to peep forth, and seemed to smile with astonishment at the sight of its own premature existence. The sun appeared so warm and bright—the sky was so blue—and beside the king, Katharine moved along with such rosy cheeks and such brightly beaming eyes. These eyes were continually fixed upon her husband, and her lively chatter seemed to the king like the sweet melody of birds, and made his heart bound with pleasure and delight.

But hark! what was that loud bustle, which suddenly drowned the queen's merry chatter?—what was it that gleamed up at the end of the great alley in which the royal couple and their retinue happened to be promenading just at that moment?

It was the clatter of soldiery moving forward, and glittering helmets and coats of mail gleamed in the sunshine.

A troop of soldiery took up their position at the end of the alley—another troop advanced in close ranks; at their head were Gardiner and Lord Douglas, striding forward, with the lieutenant of the Tower at their side.

The king's countenance assumed a sullen and angry expression, and his cheeks became purple and scarlet. He raised himself with youthful agility from his chair-carriage, and standing erect, looked with flashing eyes at the advancing procession.

The queen seized his hand and pressed it to her breast. "Ah," she whispered, gently, "protect me, my husband, for already fear overpowers me once more.

It is my enemy—it is Gardiner that is coming, and I tremble."

"You shall tremble no longer before him, Kate," said the king. "Woe betide those who dare to make the wife of King Henry tremble! I must speak with Gardiner."

And the king, violently excited and angry, pushed along somewhat abruptly by the side of the queen, and paid no heed to the pains in his foot, while he strode forward with rapid steps toward the advancing procession.

He made a signal to halt, and called Douglas and Gardiner aside. "What do you want here, and what means all this strange parade?" he inquired, in a harsh voice.

The two courtiers stared at him with terrified looks, and dared make no reply.

"Well?" asked the king, his anger continually rising, "will ye tell me by what right ye have dared to intrude thus into our garden with an armed host, at the very moment that we happen to be enjoying a promenade with our royal spouse? Verily, there is no excuse for such a gross violation of the reverence and awe which ye owe to your sovereign, and I greatly marvel, my lord master of the ceremonies, that you did not attempt to obviate this impropriety!"

Lord Douglas muttered a few words of exculpation, which the king did not, or would not, understand.

"The duty of a chief master of the ceremonies is to protect his king against every injury and intrusion, whereas, you, my Lord Douglas, bring insult yourself home to my very face. Perhaps you thus wish to prove to me that you are weary of the office. Very well, my lord, I release you from such duties; and in order that your presence may not again remind me of the disagreeable incidents of this morning, you shall quit the court and leave London at once! Farewell, my lord."

Lord Douglas, pale and trembling, retreated a few steps, and looked at the king with blank astonishment and dismay. He wished to speak, but the king waved his hand imperiously, and commanded him to be silent.

"And now, to you, my lord bishop!" said the king, and his eyes turned upon Gardiner with such an expression of anger and contempt, that the latter grew pale and cast his looks to the ground. "What means this strange retinue with which the priest of God this day approaches his royal master, and from what motive of Christian love do you purpose to-day holding a wild-beast hunt in the garden of your king?"

"Sire," said Gardiner, beside himself "your majesty well knows what I come for; it is by your majesty's command that I have come, together with Lord Douglas and the lieutenant of the Tower, in order—"

"Silence! not another word!" cried the king, who felt enraged that Gardiner did not understand him, and would not perceive the king's altered disposition. "How dare you parade my commands, when full of just astonishment I ask you the cause of your appearance? This means, sir, that you wish to give your lord and king the lie—you wish to excuse yourself, by accusing me. Ah! my worthy lord bishop, you have made shipwreck of your schemes this time, and I disown both you and your foolish enterprise. No, there is no one here whom you wish to arrest, and by God's mother if your eyes were not blind you would have seen that here, where the king is enjoying the air with his queen, no one could abide whom these myrmidons had to seek! The vicinity of royal majesty is like the vicinity of God himself; it sheds peace and happiness around it, and whoever comes within the precincts of its halo, receives thereby sacredness and pardon."

"But, your majesty," cried Gardiner, whom anger and disappointed hopes had caused to forget all discretion and reserve, "you wished that the queen should be arrested. You gave me the command to do so yourself, and now, when I come to execute your wishes, you now disown me!"

The king uttered an exclamation of rage, and with uplifted arm advanced a few paces toward Gardiner.

But suddenly he felt his arm restrained. It was Katharine, who had hastened forward to the king. "Oh, my husband," she whispered, gently, "whatever he may have done, spare him! He is still a priest of the Lord, and so let his sacred garb protect him, even though, perhaps, his deeds should condemn him."

"Ah, you intercede for him?" cried the king. "Verily, my poor wife, you do not suspect what little ground you have to pity him, and to beg me to pardon him. But you are right, we will respect his priestly robe, and no longer reflect what an arrogant and intriguing man that robe covers. But beware, priest, beware of again reminding me of this; for my anger would inevitably fall upon you, and I would show you as little mercy as you say I am bound to exhibit toward other evil-doers. And as you are a priest, suffer yourself to be impressed with the gravity becoming your office, and the sacredness of your calling. Your episcopal seat is at Winchester, and I believe your duties summon you thither. We require your services here no longer, for the wise and discreet Archbishop of Canterbury returns back to us, and will have to fulfil the duties of his office beside the queen. Farewell!"

He turned his back upon Gardiner, and leaning upon Katharine's arm returned to his carriage chair.

"Kate," he said, "just now there was a dark cloud hanging over your sky, but thanks to your smile and to your innocent countenance, it has passed away without harm. It would seem to us that we are specially bound to thank you for this matter, and it would afford us a great pleasure to be able to testify this to you by some token of love. Is there nothing, Kate, that would give you special satisfaction?"

"Oh, certainly," she replied, with delight. "There are two great wishes which I ardently cherish."

"Then name them, Kate, and by God's mother, if it be in the power of a king to accomplish them, it shall be done!"

Katharine siezed his hand and pressed it to her heart. "Sire," said she, "you were this day requested to sign eight death-warrants. Oh, my good lord, make these eight culprits, eight happy and grateful subjects, teach them to love their king whom they have calumniated—teach their children, their wives and mothers to pray for you, by restoring freedom to their sons, husbands and fathers, and by granting them pardon with that greatness and clemency most like the divine attributes."

"It shall be done!" cried the king, cheerfully. "Our hand shall this day have no other labor than to rest in yours, and we will spare it the trouble of these eight signatures. As for the eight malefactors they are pardoned, and they shall be free this very day!"

With an outburst of delight, Katharine pressed Henry's hand to her lips, and her countenance became radiant with pure joy.

"And your second wish?" inquired the king.

"My second wish," she replied, smiling, "also begs for freedom for a poor prisoner—for freedom for a human heart, sire!"

The king laughed. "A human heart? What! does it then run about the streets in such a way, that it can be caught and made a prisoner of?"

"Sire, you sought it out and imprisoned it in the bosom of your daughter. You wish to keep Elizabeth's heart in fetters, and by an unnatural law you want to compel her to renounce the freedom of her own choice. Oh, sire, it is not the princess, but myself, whom this law has painfully touched. Only imagine: to attempt to command a woman's heart, to inquire first after pedigrees and coats-of-arms, before any regard should be had to the individual who might be the object of her choice!"

"Oh, women, women, what foolish children ye are!" exclaimed the king, laughing. "A throne is at stake, and you are thinking of your hearts. But come, Kate, you shall explain that matter to me at a greater length, and we will not recall our word, for we have pledged it to you from a free and a joyful heart."

He took the queen's arm, and leaning upon it, walked with her slowly along the avenue. In silence and at a respectful distance, followed the ladies and gentlemen of the court, and no one suspected that the royal lady who moved along before them with such a proud and stately air, had but just then escaped from a deadly danger which threatened her—or that this man, who with such yielding tenderness now hung upon her arm, had but a few brief hours before, doomed her to destruction.

And while they both thus wandered along the walks and alleys in confidential discourse, two other individuals with bowed heads and pallid features, quitted the royal palace, which henceforth should be for them a lost paradise. Their hearts were filled with gloomy rancor and fierce hatred, but they were compelled to bear it in silence; they must smile and look happy, in order that they might not prepare a malicious joy for the court. They felt the spiteful glances of all these courtiers; although they passed them by with downcast looks; they though they heard their jeering whispers, and their mocking laughter, and it pierced them to the heart like a dagger.

At length they had passed this ordeal—at length the palace lay behind them, and they were now at least free to give utterance in words to the torment which consumed them—free to break forth into bitter complaints and curses and imprecations, at their recent discomfiture.

"Lost! all is lost!" said Lord Douglas, in accents of dull despair. "I have made shipwreck of all my plans. I have sacrificed to the Church my life, my property—nay my own daughter—and all to no purpose! I am now left alone and comfortless like a beggar in the streets; and the Holy Mother Church will no longer regard the son who loved her, and who sacrificed himself for her sake, for he was unsuccessful, and his sacrifice has been unfruitful."

"Do not despond," said Gardiner, with a solemn air. "The clouds are now gathering overhead, but they will again become scattered; for after the storm comes the sunshine. "Our day will come, my friend. We are now going hence, our hearts bowed down and our heads bestrewed with ashes; but, believe me, a time will come when we shall return with radiant countenance and exultant hearts; and the flaming sword of divine vengeance will gleam in our hands, and we shall wear a purple robe dyed in the blood of heretics, whom we will offer to the Lord our God as a well-pleasing sacrifice. The Almighty is reserving us for a better time, and trust me, my friend, our banishment is but a place of refuge which the Lord has provided for us for the evil times which are at hand."

"You speak of evil times, and yet you hope, my lord?" asked Douglas, gloomily.

"And yet I hope!" replied Gardiner, with a strange and ghastly smile, and stooping forward toward Douglas, he whispered: "The king has but a few more days to live. He does not suspect how near he is to death, and no one has the courage to tell him so, but his physician has told me the fact in confidence. His vital powers are exhausted, and death now stands at his door ready to strangle him."

"And when he is gone," said Lord Douglas, with a shrug, "his son Edward will be king, and those heretical Seymours will guide the helm of state! Does your lordship consider that a hopeful symptom?"

"I do."

"Then you are not aware that Edward,—albeit so young—is a fanatical adherent of the heretical doctrines, and likewise a furious opponent of our Holy Church?"

"Yes, I am aware of all that, but I am also aware that Edward is a delicate boy; and a holy prophesy is current in our Church, which declares that his reign will be of brief duration. God only knows how his death will come about, but the Church has already often seen her enemies die suddenly; and death has often been the most powerful ally of our Holy Mother. Believe, therefore, my son, and hope; for I tell you Edward's reign will be a short one! And after him, *she* will ascend the throne—the noble and pious Mary, the strict and fervent Catholic, who hates the heretics as much as Edward loves them. Oh, my friend, when Mary ascends the throne, then shall we go forth from our humiliation, and power will once more be in our own hands. Then will all England become one vast temple, and on its altars will be kindled the fires in which we shall consume the heretics, and their moans and lamentations will be the sacred hymns which shall be sung to the honor of God and of His Holy Church. Look forward with hope to this time, for I tell you it will speedily arrive!"

"If you say so, then it will come to pass, my lord," said Douglas, significantly. "I shall therefore hope and wait. Anticipating the evil days I shall retire to Scotland, and look forward to the better days to come."

"And I shall withdraw, as this king by God's anger has commanded, to my episcopal seat. God's vengeance will soon summon Henry from hence. May his dying hour be one of torment, and may the anathema of the holy father cling to him, and be fulfilled in this life and in the next! Farewell, we are departing with the olive branch of peace thrust upon us, but we shall return with the flaming sword, and the blood of the heretics shall trickle down from our hands!"

Once more they exchanged greetings before parting, and ere sunset they had both quitted London.

A short time after this eventful promenade in the garden of Whitehall, the queen entered the apartments of the Princess Elizabeth, who with joyful impatience hastened forward to meet her, and folded her impetuously in her arms.

"Saved!" she whispered. "The danger is surmounted, and you are once more the powerful queen—the adored wife!"

"And it is you I thank for it all, princess. Without this warrant of committal which you brought me I must have been lost. But oh, Elizabeth, what a trying ordeal, what a martyrdom have I not undergone! To smile and jest while my heart was trembling with anxiety and terror; to seem easy and composed when I felt as if I already saw the axe gleeming in the air, ready to fall upon my neck. I have suffered the torments and the agony of a whole life in this one hour; my soul within me is worried to death, and my strength is quite exhausted. I fain would weep—weep unceasingly over this wretched and deceitful world, in which it is not enough to wish what is right and to do what is good—in which one must practice falsehood and flattery, deceit and dissimulation, to avoid becoming a victim of unkindness and malice. But ah, Elizabeth, even my tears I dared only weep inwardly, for a queen has not the right to be sad, she must always be cheerful, always contented and happy, and only God and the still silent night know her sighs and tears."

"And I, too, might be a witness of them," said Elizabeth, earnestly, "for you well know that you may trust me, and depend upon me."

Katharine kissed her tenderly.

"You have this day done me a great service, and I have not come merely to thank you with sounding words, but with deeds; Elizabeth, your wish will be granted. The king will revoke the decree which would compel you to give your hand only to a husband of equal birth with yourself."

"Oh," cried Elizabeth, with radiant looks, "then I shall perhaps one day be able to make the man I love a king!"

Katharine smiled.

"You have a proud and ambitious heart," she said. "God has endowed you with extraordinary abilities; be careful of them, and increase them, for my boding heart tells me that you are destined one day to become Queen of England. But who knows if you will then still wish to raise the man whom you now love to be your husband. A queen such as you will be, sees with other eyes than those of the young and inexperienced maiden. Perhaps I have not done right in urging the king to make this alteration in the law, for I don't know the man whom you love, and who knows if he be worthy that you should bestow upon him your pure and guileless heart."

Elizabeth twined her arms with caressing tenderness round Katharine's neck.

"Oh," she exclaimed, "he would even be worthy of your own love, Katharine, for he is the handsomest and noblest cavalier in the whole world; and though he is no king, yet he is a king's brother-in-law, and will one day be the uncle of a king."

Katharine felt as if her heart was convulsed, and a slight shudder ran through her whole frame.

"And am I to know his name?" she inquired.

"Yes, you shall know it now, for there is no longer any danger in knowing it. The man whom I love, queen, is Thomas Seymour!"

Katharine uttered a loud cry, and thrust Elizabeth violently away from her.

"Thomas Seymour!" she exclaimed, in threatening tones! "what! you dare to love Thomas Seymour?"

"And why should I not dare to do so!" asked the young maiden, astonished. "Why should I not give him my heart, since, thanks to your intervention on my behalf, I am no longer constrained to choose a husband of royal birth? Is not Thomas Seymour one of the first noblemen in this kingdom? Does not all England look upon him with pride and affection? does not every woman feel honored by his mere notice? and does not the king himself smile and look pleased when Thomas Seymour, the gay, the brave and courageous warrior, stands by his side?"

"You are right," said Katharine, to whose heart every one of these words of ecstasy penetrated like a dagger. "Yes, you are right, he is worthy of being loved by you, and you could hit upon no better choice. It was merely momentary surprise which caused me to see matters in a different light. Thomas Seymour is the brother of a king, and why, therefore, should he not be the husband of a royal princess?"

Elizabeth, with a modest blush, hid her face on Katharine's bosom. She did not perceive with what an expression of agony and horror the queen regarded her—how her lips were pressed together convulsively, and how her cheeks assumed a death-like paleness.

"And he?" she asked softly. "Does Thomas Seymour love you?"

Elizabeth raised her head and looked at her interrogator with surprise.

"What! is it then possible that one could love without being loved in return?"

"You are right," sighed Katharine, "one must be very weak and lowly-minded to do so."

"Good heavens, how pale you are, queen!" exclaimed Elizabeth, who now for the first time observed the pallid countenance of Katharine. "Your features are quite altered, and your lips tremble. Tell me, I entreat you, what does this mean?"

"Oh, it is nothing," replied Katharine, with a painful smile. "The excitement and terror of this day have exhausted my strength. That is all. Besides this, a new suffering threatens us, of which you are at present quite unaware. The king is dangerously ill. He was seized with a sudden giddiness, which caused him to sink down almost lifeless beside me. I came to you to bring you the king's message, and now my duty recalls me to the sick chamber of my husband. Good bye, Elizabeth!"

She waved her hand in farewell greeting, and left the room with hurried steps. She summoned up courage and resolution to repress her feelings, and to hide the anguish of her heart, in order that she might be able to maintain her proud and lofty bearing, while passing through the saloons; for to the courtiers who bowed before her, she wished to preserve the composure befitting a queen, lest any one should suspect the agony which she endured, and which preyed upon her inwardly like a consuming fire.

But at length, having reached her boudoir, and being secure from observation, she was no longer a queen, but only a sensitive woman, overwhelmed with acute pain and suffering.

She fell upon her knees, and exclaimed in accents of heart-rending agony, "Oh, God,—my God, suffer me to become delirious, that I may no longer be conscious that he has forsaken me!"

CHAPTER XI.

THE DENOUEMENT.

After days of secret anguish and hidden tears, after nights of painful sobbing and distressing grief, Katharine had at length found relief; she had at length formed a firm and decisive resolution.

The king was ill beyond recovery, and however much she had suffered and endured through his means, yet he was still her husband, and she was unwilling to stand beside his dying bed as a forsworn deceiver. She was unwilling to be obliged to cast her eyes to the ground before the waning glance of the dying king. She wished to renounce her love—this love which had been as pure and chaste as the prayer of a virgin, which had stood above her as unapproachably distant, and yet as great and all-illuming as the morning sun, and which had shed upon the dark path of her life the rays of a heavenly light.

She wished to make a sacrifice the most difficult—to relinquish her lover in favor of another woman. Elizabeth loved him. Katharine sought not to fathom or discover if Thomas Seymour loved her in return, or if the vows which he had plighted to herself the queen, had been in reality nothing more than a phantasy—a falsehood. No. She did not believe it. She would not believe that Thomas Seymour was capable of treachery and double-dealing. But Elizabeth loved him, and she was young and beautiful, and a splendid future lay before her. Katharine loved Thomas Seymour sufficiently to be unwilling to withdraw him from this future, but to offer herself joyfully as a sacrifice to the happiness of her beloved. What was she—a woman matured by pain and sorrow, compared with the youthful Elizabeth in the bloom of early life? What had she to offer to her beloved beyond a life of retirement, of love, and of secluded happiness? When once the king was dead, and she herself set free, Edward the Sixth would ascend the throne, and then Katharine would be nothing more than the displaced and forgotten widow of a king; while Elizabeth—a king's sister, would perhaps be able to bring the man she loved, a crown, as her dowry and offering.

Thomas Seymour was ambitious, and this Katharine well knew. A day might come when he would repent having chosen the widow of a king, rather than the heiress of a throne.

Katharine wished to anticipate this day; she resolved to relinquish her lover of her own free will, to the princess Elizabeth. She had violently struggled with her heart to achieve this sacrifice. She had repressed its groans, and smothered its cries of lamentation.

She went to Elizabeth, and said to her with a smile: "To-day, princess, I shall bring your beloved to see you. The king has fulfilled his promise; he has, this day, with his last fainting strength, signed the decree which gives you the liberty not only of choosing your husband from amongst the ranks of princes, but of following in your choice the dictates of your own heart. This act I shall convey to your beloved, and shall assure him of my own aid and coöperation. The king is to-day in a most critical state, and his consciousness is fast fading. Be assured, however, that if he should be in a condition to hear me, I shall exert all my powers of persuasion to incline him to your wishes, and to induce him to give his consent to your marriage with Lord Sudley. I am now going to receive the earl. Wait, therefore, in your chamber, princess, for Seymour will soon come to bring you the decree."

While she thus spoke, she felt as if her heart were being pierced with red-hot daggers—as if a two-edged sword were penetrating her breast. But Katharine had a firm and resolute spirit, and she had made a vow to bear all this agony to the end, and she bore it. Not a quiver of her lip—not a sigh—not an exclamation betrayed the pain which she suffered; and even though her cheeks were colorless, and her eyes dim, it was because she had spent long and dreary nights of wakefulness and watching beside her husband's sick-bed, and because she mourned for the dying king.

She had the heroism to embrace affectionately this young maiden, to whom she was about to yield up her love as a sacrifice, and to listen with a smile to the earnest words of gratitude, of rapture, and of expectant happiness, which Elizabeth addressed to her.

With tearless eyes, and with a firm step, she returned to her apartments, and her voice trembled not, as she commanded the gentlemen-in-wating to summon to her the master of the horse—the Earl of Sudley. Only, she had a feeling as if her heart were broken and crushed, and she murmured gently and with complete resignation: "I shall die when he is gone! But while he is present I will live, and he shall never suspect what I suffer!"

And while Katharine suffered thus fearfully, Elizabeth was exulting with rapture and delight, for now at length she had reached the goal of her wishes, and this very day would see her the affianced bride of her beloved. Oh, how slowly and tediously the minutes crept along! What ages she had still to wait until he should come—her lover—and soon to be her husband!

Was he still with the queen? Should she yet wait for him? She stood at the window like an exile, and looked across toward the court-yard.—Through yonder great gateway he must come—through yonder door he must pass, in order to reach the apartments of the queen.

She uttered an exclamation, and a lively glow suffused her countenance—there, there he was! There his carriage had stopped, and his gold-laced footman opened the door. and he alighted. How handsome he was, and how noble his bearing! How proud and lofty his form—how regular his features—how blooming his youthful countenance! How fearless was his haughty smile, and how his eyes flashed and blazed with excess of youthful wantonness and ardor! For a moment his looks were directed toward Elizabeth's window. He saluted her, and then entered the door which led to the wing of the palace in which the queen's apartments were situated. Elizabeth's heart throbbed so violently that she felt as if deprived of breath. He must by this time have reached the grand staircase—now he had gained the top—now he had entered the queen's apartments—he had passed through the first, second, and third saloons. In the fourth, Katharine was awaiting him.

Alas! Elizabeth would willingly have given a year of her life to hear what Katharine would say to him, and what he would reply on learning this surprising intelligence—a year of her life to be able to witness his delight, his astonishment, and his joy.

He was so handsome when he smiled—so captivating when his eyes flashed with love and pleasure.

Elizabeth was a young, impetuous child. She felt as if she must choke with the agony of delay; her heart was on her lips, and she could scarcely breathe. She was so impatient to be happy!

"Oh, if he does not come soon, I shall die," she murmured. "If I could only see him, or at least hear him—" She suddenly ceased, her eyes glistened, and a smile of inward satisfaction played upon her features. "Yes," she continued, "I will see him and hear him too. I can and will do so! I have the key which the queen gave me, and which opens the door that divides my room from hers. With this key I shall reach her bedchamber, and adjoining the bedchamber is her boudoir, in which she will doubtless receive the earl. I shall enter quite softly, and concealing myself behind the *portière* which separates the bedroom from the boudoir, I shall be able to see him and to hear all he says."

She laughed aloud with the merriment of a child, and rushed across the room for the key, which lay upon her writing-table. She seized it, and swinging it above her head like a trophy, she exclaimed, "I shall see him!"

And then with a light step, and with a joyful and beaming countenance, she left the room.

She had judged rightly. Katharine received the earl in her boudoir. She was seated on an ottoman facing the door which led into the great reception-saloon. This door stood open, and Katharine could therefore command a view of the whole of this large room. She could see the earl as he passed through. She could, once more, with painfully sweet emotion, delight herself in contemplating his noble and lofty bearing, and suffer her looks to dwell upon him with love and worship.

At length, however, he had entered the boudoir; and now her happiness and her sweet visions were over—her rapture and her hopes were at an end.

She was now nothing more than the queen—the wife of a dying king. No longer the beloved of the Earl of Sudley—no longer his future bride—his happiness.

She summoned resolution to greet him with a smile, and her voice betrayed no emotion as she commanded him to shut the door leading into the saloon, and to let the hangings fall.

He did so, while he looked at her in utter astonishment. He did not understand how she could venture to grant him this interview; for the king was still alive, and even with his faltering tongue he could yet crush them both.

Why did she not wait till the next morning? By that time the king might be dead, and then they could see each other without constraint and without danger. Then she would be his own, and nothing could any longer intervene between them and happiness. Now, when the king was at the point of death, he loved her only—he loved Katharine alone. His ambition had decided against his inclinations, and death had become the umpire between Seymour's waning love, and his divided affections; and with Henry's death faded also the star of the Princess Elizabeth.

Katharine was the widow of a king, and doubtless this affectionate husband had appointed his young and cherished wife as regent during the minority of the Prince of Wales. Katharine would accordingly enjoy five years of rule, authority, and power. Were Katharine his wife, then he, Thomas Seymour, would share this power with her, and the purple robes of royalty which rested upon her shoulders would also cover him, and he would help her to bear this crown, which doubtless would press heavy on her brow from time to time. He would be regent in reality, and Katharine would be so in name only—she the Queen of England, and he the king of this queen. What a proud, intoxicating thought was this, and what plans, what hopes were associated therewith! Five years of uncontrolled sway—was not this period long enough to undermine the throne of this royal youth, and to subvert his authority? Who could guess whether the people, once accustomed to the regency of the queen, would not prefer remaining under her sceptre, rather than confide themselves to a feeble boy? The people must be induced so to think, and to make of Katharine, the wife of Thomas Seymour, their ruler and queen.

The king was at the point of death, and beyond doubt Katharine was regent—perhaps one day would become the reigning sovereign:

The Princess Elizabeth was only a poor princess, virtually excluded from all prospect of the throne, for before her came Katharine and Edward, and finally Mary, Elizabeth's elder sister. Elizabeth had therefore no hope of the crown, while Katharine, who stood next to it, had the best hopes conceivable.

These considerations occupied the mind of Thomas Seymour as he proceeded through the apartments of the queen, and when he entered her boudoir he had quite convinced himself that he loved the queen alone, and that it was she alone whom he had always loved.

Elizabeth was forgotten and despised. She had no prospect of the throne. Why, therefore, should he love her?

The queen, as already stated, commanded him to shut the door of the boudoir which led into the reception-room, and to draw the hangings. At the same moment that he did so, the *portière* which conducted from the boudoir into the queen's bedroom, also moved—perhaps it was caused by the current of air from the door just closed.

Neither the queen nor Thomas Seymour, however, paid any attention to the incident. They were both too much occupied with themselves; they did not perceive how the curtain waved and moved gently again and again; they did not notice that a slight opening was cautiously made in the middle; neither did they observe the flashing eyes that glanced forth suddenly through the opening in the curtain, nor suspect that it was the Princess Elizabeth who had concealed herself behind the *portière*, the better that she might be able to see and hear what took place in the boudoir.

The queen had risen from her seat and advanced a few steps toward the earl. As she now stood confronting him, and as their eyes met, she felt her courage sink, and her heart ready to break.

She cast her looks on the ground, in order that he might not perceive the tears which involuntarily rose to her eyes. With a subdued greeting she presented her hand to him. Thomas Seymour pressed it violently to his lips, and fixed his eyes upon her countenance with a glance of impassioned tenderness. She was obliged to collect all her strength, in order that her heart might not betray itself. With a sudden movement she withdrew her hand from his, and took from a table the roll of parchment which contained the new act of succession lately signed by the king.

"My lord," she said, "I have summoned you hither that I may have the pleasure of conveying to you a certain commission. I beg of you, therefore, to be good enough to take this parchment and carry it to the Princess Elizabeth. But before you do so, I will make you acquainted with its contents. This document contains a new act, sanctioned by the king, regarding the succession. By virtue of this law, the royal princesses are no longer compelled to ally themselves to a sovereign prince as their husband, if they wish to preserve undiminished their hereditary claims to the throne. The king grants the princesses the right of following their own inclinations, and their claims to the crown are in no wise to suffer, even though the husband whom they may choose should neither be a prince nor a king. That, my lord, is the purport of this document, which you are to convey to the princess, and doubtless you will thank me for having selected you as the herald of this grateful intelligence."

"And why?" he asked, with astonishment. "Why does your majesty believe that this intelligence should afford me special satisfaction?"

She collected all her energies—she besought her own heart for firmness and self-control.

"Because the princess has made me the confidante of her love, and because I therefore know the tender bond which binds you to her!" she replied, gently, and she felt that the blood had fled from her cheeks.

The earl looked at her for a moment with mute astonishment, and then glanced round the room with an inquiring and scrutinizing gaze.

"Then we are watched?" he asked, softly. "We are not alone?"

"We are alone!" replied Katharine, aloud. "No one can hear us, and God alone is the witness of our conversation."

Elizabeth, who stood behind the curtain, felt her cheeks burning with shame, and she began to repent what she had done. It was certainly mean and unworthy of a princess to listen, but she was at this moment but a young maiden who loved, and who merely wished to observe her lover. She remained accordingly. She laid her hand upon her anxiously-throbbing heart, and murmured to herself: "What will he say? What means this anxiety which has come upon me?"

"Well, then," said Thomas Seymour, in quite an altered tone, "if we are alone, I may let fall the mask which hides my features, and let the coat-of-mail which confines my heart be rent asunder. And now, Katharine, my day-star, my hope, receive my greetings! No one, you say, hears us but God alone, and God knows our love, and He knows with what ardent longing, and with what rapture, I have looked forward to the present hour. Oh, Katharine! it seems an eternity since I saw you; my heart is athirst for you like one that is famished. But blessings attend thee, my beloved Katharine, that thou hast at length summoned me hither!"

He held out his arms to embrace her, but she recoiled, and repelled his advances with energy.

"You mistake the name, my lord," she replied, sarcastically, "you say Katharine, and you mean Elizabeth! It is the princess whom you love. Elizabeth is the idol of your affections, and she has consecrated her heart to you. Oh, my lord! I shall be quite prepared to favor this love, and be assured I shall not cease my prayers and entreaties until I have inclined the king to your wishes, and obtained his consent to your marriage with the Princess Elizabeth."

Thomas Seymour laughed.

"Come, Katharine, this is really a masquerade, and you still continue to wear a mask over that beautiful and charming face of yours. Away with this mask, then! I wish to see you as you are. I wish once more to see your own amiable self. I wish to see the woman who belongs to me, who has sworn to be mine, and who has vowed with a thousand sacred promises to love me, to be constant to me, and devote her life to me as her lord and husband! Or, how, Katharine, could you have forgotten your vows—could you have become unfaithful to your own heart? Do you wish to cast me off, and like a plaything of which you have yourself become weary, to fling me aside to another?"

"For my part," she replied, quite unconsciously,—"for my part, I can never forget and never become faithless!"

"Well, then, my Katharine, thou bride and wife of my future days, why do you speak to me of Elizabeth—of this little princess, who yearns for love as the rosebud yearns for the sun, and who mistakes the first person she meets on her way, for the sun itself, for which she sighs? Why trouble ourselves with Elizabeth, my Katharine, and what have we to do with this child at this longed-wished-for hour of meeting?"

"Oh, he calls me a child!" murmured Elizabeth. "I am nothing but a child to him!" and she pressed her hands firmly on her lips, in order to check the cry of pain and anger which struggled for utterance.

Thomas Seymour folded Katharine in his arms with irresistible force. "Withdraw thyself from me no longer," he cried, with tender entreaty; "the hour has at length arrived which must decide upon our whole existence. The king is dying, and my Katharine will at length be free—free to follow the impulse of her heart. Call to mind at this hour the vows which thou hast plighted! Dost thou still remember that day on which thou didst indicate to me this present hour—when thou didst engage to be my wife, and didst accept me for thy future lord? Oh, my beloved, the crown which then weighed so heavily on thy brow is, at length, about to be removed. I now once more stand before thee as thy subject, but in a few hours it will be thy lord and husband who will stand before thee, and he will ask thee: 'Katharine, my bride, hast thou been constant and faithful to me, as thou hast sworn to be? Hast thou been true to thy vows and to thy love? Hast thou preserved from every stain my honor, which is also thy own honor, and canst thou look me in the face with the eyes of innocence?'"

For a moment he gazed at her with haughty and flashing eyes, and before his commanding glance her strength and her pride melted away like ice before the noontide sun. He was once more the master of her heart, and she once more the meek and submissive woman, whose sweetest happiness it is to yield and bend to the will of her beloved.

"I can freely meet your gaze," she murmured, "and no guilt oppresses my conscience. I have loved but thee alone, and besides thee none reigned in my heart but God."

In an ecstasy of happiness, and quite overpowered with emotion, she leaned her head on his shoulder, and, as he folded her in his arms, and covered her no longer resisting lips with kisses, then, indeed, she felt how unspeakably she loved him; and that her future happiness was indissolubly bound up with his.

It was a sweet dream—a moment of blissful rapture. But it was only a moment. A hand was laid impetuously upon her shoulder; a hoarse and angry voice called her by name; and as Katharine looked up, she encountered the fierce looks of Elizabeth, who, with cheeks of deadly paleness, with trembling lips, and with distended nostrils, stood before her, and from whose eyes shot forth flames of animosity and rage.

"This then is the service of affection which you promised to render me?" she exclaimed, gnashing her teeth. "You creep stealthily into my confidence, and with mocking laughter upon your lips you spy out the secrets of my heart, and then go away to betray them to your paramour, and in his arms to heap ridicule upon a hapless maiden, who in an unguarded moment suffered her heart to betray her, and mistook a guilty malefactor for an honorable man. Woe, woe betide you, Katharine, for I tell you I shall have no pity for an adulteress who has mocked me, and deceived the king, my father!"

She raved—she was beside herself with rage; she dashed away the hand which Katharine laid upon her shoulder, and, like an infuriated tigress, she recoiled from the touch of her adversary.

The blood of her father boiled and foamed in her veins, and, like a true daughter of Henry the Eighth, she harbored in her breast naught but bloodthirsty and revengeful thoughts.

She cast at Thomas Seymour a look of direful anger, and a smile of contempt played around her lips.

"My lord," she said, "you called me a child, who suffers herself to be easily deceived because she so ardently longs for the sun and for happiness. You are right; I was a child, for I was foolish enough to take a pitiful liar for a nobleman, whom I deemed worthy of the proud fortune of being loved by the daughter of a king! Yes, you are right, that was a childish dream. Thanks to you, I have now woke up from this wretched delusion, and you have matured the child into the woman, who laughs at her youthful folly, and to-day despises what she yesterday worshipped. With you, however, I have nothing more to do; you are too mean and contemptible for my anger. But I tell you that you have played a dangerous game, and that you will lose it. You wooed a queen and a princess at the same time, but you will not secure them both,—the latter, because she despises you, and the former, because she will speedily mount the scaffold!"

With a wild burst of laughter she rushed toward the door, but Katharine restrained her with a firm hand, and compelled her to remain.

"What are you going to do?" she asked, quite calm and composed.

"What am I going to do?" echoed Elizabeth, and her eyes flashed with wild rage. "You ask me what I am going to do. I am going to my father, the king, to tell him what I have here witnessed! He will listen to me, and his tongue will have strength enough left to pronounce for you a sentence of death! Ah! my mother died upon the scaffold, and yet she was innocent. We shall now see if you will escape the same fate—you who are guilty!"

"Be it so—go to your father," said Katharine; "go and accuse me. But before you do so you shall hear me. I was willing to renounce this man, whom I loved, in order to give him to you. By the avowal of your love you had destroyed my happiness and my future hopes; but I was not angry with you; I understood your affection, for Thomas Seymour is worthy of being loved. But you are right—for the wife of a king it was sinful to cherish this love, however innocent and pure it might be. I was therefore willing to renounce it in your favor, and I resolved, upon your first avowal, to sacrifice myself in silence. You have now rendered that impossible. Go, therefore, and accuse us to your father, and do not fear that I shall disown my affection. Now that the decisive moment has come, it shall find me prepared, and even upon the scaffold I shall still rejoice, for Thomas Seymour loves me!"

"Yes, he loves you! Katharine," he exclaimed, quite overpowered and enraptured by her noble and majestic demeanor. "He loves you so fervently and devotedly, that death with you seems to him an enviable fate, which he would exchange for no crown—no throne upon earth."

And while he thus spoke he put his arms round Katharine's neck, and pressed her ardently to his heart.

Elizabeth uttered a wild shriek, and sprang toward the door. But what sound of uproar was that which was suddenly heard approaching, and which moved along like a tumultuous wave, and filled the anteroom and the saloons? What meant those screams and shouts of terror-stricken voices, calling for the queen, the physician, and the priest?

Elizabeth stopped in her course, and listened. Thomas Seymour and Katharine, locked in each other's arms, stood beside her; they scarcely heard what was going on; they gazed at each other, and smiled and dreamed of love and death, and of the eternity of their happiness.

The door flew open; there was the pale face of John Heywood, there were the ladies of honor, and the court officials, all shouting and lamenting:

"The king is dying; he has had a sudden attack! The king is expiring!"

"The king calls you! the king wishes to die in the arms of his wife!" said John Heywood, and while he pushed Elizabeth, who was pressing forward eagerly aside from the door, he added, —"the king will see no one else but his wife and the priest, and he has commanded me to call the queen."

He opened the door, and through the ranks of the weeping and lamenting courtiers and servants Katharine rushed along to the dying bed of her royal husband.

CHAPTER XII.

LE ROI EST MORT, VIVE LA REINE.

King Henry was expiring. This life of sin, of bloodshed and crime, of treachery and deceit, of hypocrisy and cruelty, of fanaticism and ferocity, was at length drawing to a close; the hand which had signed so many death-warrants, was now clinched in the throes of death—benumbed at the very moment that the king was about to sign the death-warrant of the Duke of Norfolk. And the king died with the gnawing consciousness that he was unable to destroy this enemy, whom he hated; the once mighty king was now but a feeble and dying old man, who was no longer able to hold the pen to sign this decree

—his last, his most cherished wish. God, in His wisdom, had imposed upon him the severest and the most terrible punishment—he had paralyzed not his mind, but his body; and this rigid, unwieldy, and torpid mass, which lay there upon the purple-and-gold-bedecked couch, was—the king—a king whom remorse of conscience would not suffer to die, and who now trembled and shuddered at death, to which he had dispatched so many of his subjects with such relentless cruelty.

Katharine and the Archbishop of Canterbury, the noble Cranmer, stood by his bedside; and while he held Katharine's hand with a grasp of convulsive agony, he listened to the devout supplications which Cranmer pronounced in his behalf.

Once he asked with faltering tongue: "What manner of world is this, my lord, where those who sentence others to death are themselves condemned to die?" And when the pious Cranmer—touched by the agony, and by the remorse which he read in the king's looks, and filled with compassion for the dying tyrant, sought to comfort him, and spoke to him of the mercies of God—the king replied with a groan: "No, no! there is no mercy for him who himself showed no mercy."

At length this fearful struggle of death with life was over, and death had gained the victory. The king had closed his eyes upon earth, in order to open them once more, as a guilt-laden sinner before the throne of the Eternal.

For three days his death was kept secret, in order that every thing might be arranged, and that the gap which his death had caused might first be filled up. These measures were adopted with a view that when the people should be informed of the death of the deceased monarch, they might at the same time look upon the living king; and as it was well known that the people would not weep for the dead, so they might at least hail the living sovereign with joyful acclamations. Though no psalms of lamentation would be chanted, yet hymns of rejoicing might be sung.

On the third day the gates of Whitehall were opened, and a gloomy mourning-procession moved along through the streets of London. Silent and sullen stood the populace to gaze upon the coffin of the king as it passed by; that king before whom they had once trembled, but for whom no word of sorrow or regret now escaped them; not a tear did they shed for the dead monarch who for thirty-seven years had been their king.

The coffin was conducted to Westminster Abbey to be laid in the costly tomb which Wolsey had caused to be erected there for his royal master. But the way was long, and the mourning-clad horses attached to the hearse were forced from time to time to rest on their journey to fetch breath. And, suddenly, as the vehicle pulled up in one of the public thoroughfares, blood was seen to issue from the coffin of the king. It flowed forth in purple rills, and trickled down upon the stones in the streets. The spectators crowding around shuddered as they saw the blood of the king streaming forth; and they remarked how much blood he had caused to be shed on the same spot—for the coffin stopped at the very place formerly set apart for executions, and where fires had been kindled, and scaffolds had been erected, for hundreds of hapless victims.

As the people stood and beheld the blood that flowed from the coffin of the king, two dogs sprang forth from among the crowd, and with panting tongues licked the blood of King Henry the Eighth. The spectators, however, horror-stricken and dismayed, turned from the revolting spectacle, and recounted to each other the fate of the unhappy priest who only a few weeks before was executed upon this very spot, for having refused to acknowledge the king as the head of his Church, and the vicegerent of the Almighty; they related how this ill-fated man cursed the king, and said upon the scaffold: "May the dogs one day lap the blood of this king who has shed so much innocent blood himself!"—and now the curse of the dying man was fulfilled, and the dogs had licked the blood of the king.

When the gloomy mourning train had left the palace of Whitehall, and as the dead body of the king no longer infested the saloons with the pestiferous odors of corruption, and the court was preparing to do homage to the boy Edward, as the new king, Thomas Seymour, Earl of Sudley, entered the apartment of the royal and youthful widow; he came in solemn mourning attire, and his elder brother, Edward Seymour, and Cranmer, the Archbishop of Canterbury, accompanied him.

Katharine, blushing, greeted them with a sweet smile.

"I come, this day, your majesty," said Thomas Seymour, solemnly, "to remind you of your vows! Do not, I pray you, blush—nor cast down your eyes for shame. The worthy archbishop knows your heart, and he knows that it is as pure as the heart of a virgin, and that no unchaste thought has ever stained your soul; and, moreover, my brother would not be here if he had not entire faith in and respect for a love, which through storm and danger has been so intrepidly preserved. I have chosen these two noble friends to be the witnesses of my espousal, and in their presence I will ask you—Queen Katharine, the king is dead, and no fetters any longer bind your heart; will you now bestow it upon me to be mine? Will you accept me as your husband, and sacrifice to me your royal title and your elevated rank?"

With a bewitching smile she presented to him her hand. "You know well," she whispered, "that I sacrifice nothing to you, but that I receive every thing that I hope for of love and happiness."

"Then in the presence of both these friends you will accept me as your future husband, and pledge to me the vows of your faithfulness and love?"

Katharine trembled and cast her eyes to the ground with the bashfulness of a young maiden. "Alas!" she sighed, "do I not still wear the weeds of mourning? Is it, then, becoming in me to think of happiness when the funeral bells have scarcely ceased to toll?"

"Queen Katharine," said Archbishop Cranmer, "let the dead bury their dead! Life, too, has its rights, and man should not give up his claim to happiness, for it is a sacred possession. You have borne and suffered much, queen, but your heart remained pure and blameless, and for this reason you should greet happiness at the present moment with a serene conscience. Linger not, therefore. In the name of God, I am come to bless your love and to consecrate your happiness."

"And I," said Edward Seymour, "have requested my brother that I might have the honor to accompany him, in order to assure your majesty that I am fully sensitive of the high honor which you manifest toward our family, and that as your brother-in-law I shall always be mindful that you were once my honored queen, and I your devoted subject."

"And I, for my part," cried Thomas Seymour, "would not delay coming to you, in order to testify to you that love alone conducted me, and that no other consideration had any influence in guiding my decision. As yet the king's last will has not been opened, and I am innocent of its contents. But in what way soever its provisions may affect us all, it will neither be able to increase nor diminish my happiness in the possession of so great a treasure. Whatever may be your position, you shall always be for me an adored wife—a fondly-loved spouse; and it is only to confirm to you the assurance of this, that I have already presented myself this day."

With a smile of winning sweetness Katharine presented her hand. "I have never doubted you, my Seymour," she whispered, "and never did I love you more than at the moment when I was about to renounce you."

She bent her head on the shoulder of her lover, and tears of pure joy bedewed her cheeks. The Archbishop of Canterbury united their hands together and confirmed their betrothal; and the elder Seymour, the Earl of Hertford, greeted them as an affianced pair.

On the same day the will of the king was opened; in the large gilded saloon, in which had so often resounded the mirthful laughter and the thundering voice of King Henry, were now read his last commands. The whole court was here assembled as in former times, amidst gay banquets and festive scenes, and Katharine sat once more upon the royal throne; but no longer by her side was the dreaded tyrant, the bloodthirsty King Henry the Eighth, but only the poor, pale boy Edward, who had inherited neither his father's mind nor his energy, but only his sanguinary propensities and his arts of pietistic dissimulation. Near him stood his sisters, the Princesses Mary and Elizabeth—both with pale and sorrowful countenance: but it was not their father whom they lamented.

Mary, the bigoted Catholic, saw with terror and bitter pain the day of affliction dawning upon her religion; for Edward was a fanatical adversary of the old faith, and she knew that he would shed the blood of the papists with unrelenting cruelty: for this it was that she mourned.

But as for Elizabeth—the youthful maiden with the glowing heart—she thought neither of her father, nor of the calamities which threatened the Church;—she thought only of her love; she only felt that she had been robbed of a hope—of an illusion; that she had been roused from a sweet and delightful dream to vain but stern realities. She had given up her first love, but her heart bled, and the wound still pained her.

The will was read. Elizabeth looked across at Thomas Seymour during this solemn and significant recital. She wished to read upon his brow the impression which those grave and momentous words made upon him; she wished to penetrate into the depths of his soul, and to probe the secret thoughts of his heart. She saw how he grew pale, when, *not* Katharine, but his own brother, the Earl of Hertford, was named regent during Edward's minority. She saw the gloomy and almost angry look which he cast at the queen, and with a malicious smile she murmured: "I am revenged! He loves her no longer!"

John Heywood, too, who stood near the queen's throne, had perceived this look of Thomas Seymour, not as Elizabeth had, with an exultant, but with a grieving heart, and he hung his head and murmured: "Poor Katharine! He will hate her, and she will be very unhappy."

But as yet she was happy. Her eyes beamed with delight when she learned that her beloved, by virtue of the royal will, was appointed High-Admiral of England, and guardian of the young king. She thought not of herself but of her beloved, and it filled her with the proudest satisfaction to see him invested with such high honors and dignities.

Hapless Katharine! Her eye perceived not the murky cloud which hung over the brow of her beloved. She was so happy, so unsuspecting, and so unambitious! For her there was but one happiness—that of being the wife of Thomas Seymour.

And this happiness was to be hers. Thirty days after the death of the king, she became the wife of Thomas Seymour, Earl of Sudley, the High-Admiral of England. Archbishop Cranmer blessed their nuptials in the chapel of Whitehall, and the lord protector, now Duke of Somerset, brother of Thomas Seymour, and formerly Earl of Hertford, was the witness of their union, which was still treated as a secret, and of which there were no other witnesses. Meanwhile, as the party entered the chapel, the Princess Elizabeth advanced toward the queen and offered her hand.

It was the first time that they had met since that fearful day on which they stood opposed to each other as rivals and enemies; it was the first time that they had seen each other face to face.

Elizabeth had struggled with her heart for this sacrifice; her proud spirit revolted at the thought that Thomas Seymour might suppose she still regretted him—that she still loved him. She wished to show him that her heart had quite recovered from this first dream of her youth, and that she no longer felt pain or regret.

She greeted him with a cold and haughty smile, and presented her hand to Katharine.

"Queen," she said, "you have so long been to me a faithful and kind mother, that I may once more venture to claim the right of being your daughter. Allow me, therefore, as your daughter, to be present at the solemn ceremony which is about to take place, and permit me to stand at your side and to pray for you, while the archbishop performs the sacred ceremony which shall make the queen a Countess of Sudley. May God bless you, Katharine, and bestow upon you all the happiness that you deserve!"

And the Princess Elizabeth knelt at Katharine's side as the archbishop consecrated her marriage vows; and while she prayed, her eye glanced across to Thomas Seymour, who stood beyond, at the side of his young wife. Katharine's countenance beamed with beauty and happiness, but upon Thomas Seymour's brow still rested the cloud which had settled upon it on the day on which the king's will was read—this will which, contrary to his expectations, did *not* make Katharine regent, and thereby destroyed the proud and ambitious designs of Thomas Seymour.

And this cloud still hung over his brow. It descended still lower and lower; it soon overshadowed Katharine's wedded life, and woke her from her brief dream of bliss.

What she suffered—what secret anguish and silent woe she endured, who can tell—who can discover? Katharine had a proud and reserved spirit; she veiled her pains and her sorrows modestly from the world, as she had once concealed her love. Nobody suspected what she suffered, or how she struggled with her crushed affections.

She never complained. She saw the blossoms of her life wither and decay—she saw the smile vanish from the lips of her husband—she heard his once tender and affectionate voice growing harsh by degrees—she felt his heart growing colder and colder, and his love changing to indifference, perhaps into positive dislike.

To her love she had devoted her whole heart, but she felt, day by day and hour by hour, that the heart of her husband grew colder. She felt it with terrible, with heart-rending certainty. She was his with all her love; but he was no longer hers.

And she tormented her heart in order to discover why he no longer loved her; wherein she had offended, that he had turned aside from her. Seymour had not the delicacy nor the magnanimity to disclose to her his mind; and at length she understood why he had turned away.

He had hoped that Katharine would be the Regent of England, and that he would accordingly be the husband of the regent. Because she had not become so, his love had vanished.

Katharine felt this, and it caused her death.

But not suddenly—death did not at once release her from her pains and her anguish. For six months she suffered and endured her woes. At the end of six months she died.

Dismal rumors were spread about respecting her death, and never did John Heywood pass by Lord Sudley without looking at him with a stern, angry glance, and saying:

"You have murdered the beautiful queen! Deny it if you can."

Thomas Seymour laughed, and did not consider it worth the trouble to defend himself against the accusations of the court fool. He laughed, although he had not laid aside his mourning attire for Katharine.

And still in this garb he had the hardihood to present himself before the Princess Elizabeth, and to make to her protestations of ardent love, and sue for her hand.

But Elizabeth rejected him with proud contempt and cold disdain, and, like John Heywood, the stern princess replied:

"You have murdered Katharine; I will not be the wife of a murderer!"

And soon the justice of God punished the murderer of the noble and innocent Katharine, for scarce three months after the death of his wife, the high-admiral was compelled to mount the scaffold, and was executed as a traitor.

By Katharine's wish, her books and papers were given to her faithful friend, John Heywood, who applied himself with the most devoted diligence to the examination of them. Among those papers he found many pages written with her own hand—many verses and poems, which breathed the weariness and the sadness of her spirit. With her own hand Katharine had collected these fugitive pieces, and with her own hand she had written upon this book the title, "*The Sighings of a Sinner*."

Katharine had wept much while penning these "Sighings," for in many places the manuscript was illegible—her tears had effaced the characters.

John Heywood kissed those spots where the traces of her tears had remained, and murmured:

"The sinner by her sorrows has proclaimed herself a saint, and these poems are the cross and memento which she herself prepared for her own grave. I will set up this cross, that the good may derive consolation, and that the wicked may flee when they see it."

And he did so. He caused the "Sighings of a Sinner" to be printed, and this book was Katharine's worthiest memento.

THE END.

www.ingramcontent.com/pod-product-compliance
Lightning Source LLC
Chambersburg PA
CBHW031404270326
41929CB00010BA/1326
* 9 7 8 3 7 4 3 3 1 0 0 3 2 *